FLAWED VICTORY

FLAWED VICTORY

Jutland, 1916

Keith Yates

VICTORY

CHATHAM PUBLISHING

LONDON

First published in 2000 by the Naval Institute Press, Annapolis, Maryland

First published in Great Britain in 2000 by Chatham Publishing,
61 Frith Street, London W1V 5TA

Chatham Publishing is an imprint of Gerald Duckworth & Co Ltd

British Library Cataloguing in Publication Data
A catalogue for this book is available from the
British Library

ISBN 1 86176 148 1

Printed in the United States of America on acid-free paper

To June

Ah! What avails the classic bent,
And what the cultured word,
Against the undoctored incident
That actually occurred.

—Rudyard Kipling

Contents

Preface

It has now been about fifty years since I first read anything about the Battle of Jutland. At the time I was an impressionable teenager, and I never forgot the stirring accounts of courageous sailors and the ships—from mighty battleships to frail destroyers—in which they served and often died. My interest in things nautical was reawakened during my brief and utterly undistinguished service as a seaman in the Royal Navy. Although this was in peacetime, I thought I had gained some appreciation of what it must have been like for the men on board these ships. As an Englishman, I was naturally disappointed at the outcome of the battle. Thinking about the might-have-beens continued to pique my interest, although for many years I was not in a position to pursue the subject other than superficially.

Jutland was probably the most fascinating, and certainly the most analyzed, naval battle in history. Other great battles, such as Trafalgar, Tsushima, and Midway, left no doubt as to who had won, and why, but not Jutland. The post-Jutland debate and controversy that raged for more than a decade after the Great War was almost as interesting as the battle itself.

Now that more than eighty years have passed since 31 May 1916, it is perhaps an appropriate moment to take a fresh view—distanced in time and completely detached from the events and personalities involved on that momentous day. I approached the subject of Jutland with no preconceived notions or partisan feelings and have tried at all times to keep an open mind and to be fair to all those engaged in the battle, British or German. If I have not entirely succeeded in this, which would not be surprising, human nature being what it is, I am sure there will be those who will point out where I have failed. I did not set out to write a deliberately revisionist history of Jutland, or the naval actions preceding it, and have tried strenuously to avoid this currently popular approach. But I have reached some conclusions which are at variance with widely accepted views of the battle and its major figures.

I have also done my best to avoid taking too much advantage of the dazzling clarity of perfect hindsight and the distinct benefits of a leisurely examination of the track charts, maps, and battle reports that are available to the critic but not to the admirals at the time they had to make crucial decisions, often swiftly and in the heat of battle.

The book is aimed intentionally at the general reader with an interest in naval history, like myself. For this reason I have not included any footnotes in the text, because these tend to distract the average reader from the flow of the narrative. Nonetheless, I hope the book will be regarded as a worthwhile reassessment of this intriguing battle and its equally fascinating aftermath.

In researching this book, I found such a wealth of published material that I had to be selective if I was going to keep it to a digestible length. It is not directed at academic historians, and it would have been presumptuous of me to attempt such a work. However, I have striven for factual accuracy. I have invented nothing and done my best to stay clear of the "faction" approach to the narration of historical events. Any errors are solely my responsibility.

As the bibliography will show, the book is based almost entirely on secondary sources, and I make no apology for this. It was never intended to be a piece of original scholarly research. There are surely no relevant facts or important details that have not been revealed after all this time in the many accounts and analyses written on the subject of Jutland. I believe I have not omitted or distorted any significant facts concerning the battle, or the North Sea actions preceding it.

In reading the works listed in the bibliography, I have been most impressed by the balanced and dispassionate accounts and interpretations, to say nothing of the staggering thoroughness and professionalism, of two writers in particular—Sir Julian Corbett and Professor Arthur Marder. This is not to deny the great benefit and enjoyment I have derived from reading the briefer but equally balanced accounts of the battle by other authors, such as John Irving, Donald Macintyre, Stephen Roskill, and John Winton. Three less-comprehensive accounts of Jutland and the naval actions preceding it, which are remarkable for their readability, are contained in James Goldrick's *The King's Ships were at Sea,* Geoffrey Bennett's *Naval Battles of the First World War,* and Richard Hough's *Great War at Sea,* and I have made extensive use of these excellent sources.

From the German side, although much less has been published on the subject, the six-volume series *Der Krieg zur See* (editor in chief, Admiral E. von Mantey) proved indispensable. Also invaluable were

V. E. Tarrant's recent book giving the German perspective on the battle, and Holger Herwig's writings on the Imperial German Navy.

In addition, I have found the results of the meticulous and exhaustive research contained in N. J. M. Campbell's and Jon Sumida's books extremely useful in assessing the gunnery of both sides. Finally, the annotations contained in Eugene Rasor's comprehensive bibliography of Jutland were very helpful in a cautionary sense. For general background on pre-1914 Europe and the Great War, the books of Liddell Hart, Cyril Falls, Martin Gilbert, James Morris, and Frederic Morton were especially useful. For technical details of warships, I have relied on the nonpareil *Jane's Fighting Ships* in its various editions, and the authoritative four-volume Conway series, *All the World's Fighting Ships*. There are occasional differences between these two sources, but none of great import.

As far as direct quotes are concerned, in most cases the practice of previous authors has been to give abridged versions, presumably for reasons of space. I have generally followed this practice, since the abridgments did not significantly affect the sense or context. But in a few cases I have given the complete quotation, to convey the full flavor.

I have attempted to describe the battle, and the events leading up to it, in the form of a chronological narrative, including all important movements and engagements but not giving the mass of factual detail contained in Corbett's *Official History of the War: Naval Operations* or the *Krieg zur See* series, or with as much accompanying commentary as in Marder's series. Analyses and judgments for the most part have been left to the concluding sections of the book.

I have tried my best to remember at all times what the commanders actually knew at the time (from what they could see), or believed (from what they had been told), and to judge their actions on this basis. But I have also kept in mind what any capable and experienced senior officer should have known, or might reasonably have been expected to do in the circumstances, based on established tactical practice. At the same time it is essential to bear in mind constantly each commander's personal situation at the time of decision, subjected to the noise of guns and bursting shells, the danger from flying shrapnel, and the swirling clouds of smoke and mist lying over the battle scene.

It is important to remember at all times that the senior officers at Jutland were in just as much physical danger as the men they commanded that day, unlike the generals in Flanders, who could plot their moves and make their decisions in headquarters that were miles outside of enemy artillery range. Jellicoe, and especially Beatty, could easily have been killed in an awful conflagration if a lucky shell had found one of the magazines in the *Iron Duke* or the *Lion*—just as Admiral Hood was killed when his flagship blew up. Equally, Scheer or Hipper could have been the victim of a shell that penetrated the lightly armored bridge of the *Friedrich der Grosse* or the *Lützow.*

The book is in three sections. The first deals with the background to the naval arms race leading up to the Great War and describes the North Sea actions and other important naval engagements preceding Jutland. The experience of modern sea warfare gained by the two navies during these encounters is vital to a full understanding of how and why the battle came to be fought. The second section consists of a narrative of the battle itself, and the concluding section describes its aftermath and the postwar controversy.

Acknowledgments

To the librarians at the Universities of Toronto and Victoria I would like to express my appreciation for their help in tracking down source material, and offer particular thanks to Warren Holder, Head of Circulation at the Robarts' Library, and to Evelyn Kurtz of the McPherson Library, for their liberal interpretation of the borrowing regulations. I also found useful material in the museum and library of HMCS Naden in Esquimalt, and I thank the staff for granting me access and offering assistance.

I greatly appreciate the comments and suggestions of those who read the manuscript in draft form, in particular Don Hutchinson. I would also like to thank my friends and colleagues Professors Bill Nelson and Bill Callahan of the University of Toronto for encouraging me to venture into their territory—history—which, after working in a totally disparate field for so long, I did with some trepidation. I am grateful to Beverley Slopen, Ian Montagnes, and Ian Marshall for their kindness and encouragement in the past.

Special thanks are due my daughter Nicola Fillier for leading me through the intricacies of WordPerfect. I also thank Deidre and Adam Reid for their excellent drawings of maps, and Deidre Reid and Bill Hayward for their help with the illustrations.

Last but far from least I thank my wife June for her constant support and patience.

Abbreviations

AP	Armor-piercing (shells)
BC	Battle cruiser
BCS	Battle cruiser squadron (usually three to four ships)
BS	Battle squadron (usually six to eight battleships)
C-in-C	Commander in chief
CID	Committee of Imperial Defence
DF	Destroyer flotilla (usually sixteen ships plus a flotilla leader)
GFBOs	Grand Fleet Battle Orders
GMT	Greenwich Mean Time (the German time zone was one hour ahead of GMT)
HMCS	His/Her Majesty's Canadian Ship
HMS	His/Her Majesty's Ship
LCS	Light cruiser squadron (usually four ships)
RN	Royal Navy
RNVR	Royal Naval Volunteer Reserve
SG	Scouting group (squadron of battle cruisers or light cruisers)
SMS	*Seine Majestäts Schiff*
TBF	Torpedo boat flotilla (usually eleven boats including a flotilla leader)
USS	United States Ship
W/T	Wireless telegraphy

Prologue

Two hours before dawn on 31 May 1916, the German High Seas Fleet began to put to sea from its base at Wilhelmshaven. The sleek gray battle cruisers of the 1st Scouting Group led the way out of the anchorage in the Jade roadstead, escorted by their protective screen of light cruisers and torpedo boats. Ninety minutes later, the lumbering battleships of the 1st, 2d, and 3d Battle Squadrons followed them into the choppy waters of the North Sea, also attended by their coterie of smaller warships. As they moved slowly into the safe channels that had been swept through the minefields, all they could make out was the dark shape and dim stern light of the next ship ahead. As it reached open waters, the fleet increased speed.

Once at sea, the ships stayed well to the west of the Horns Reef, out of sight of the Danish coast, as they headed north toward the mouth of the Skagerrak. Next morning, the Germans meant to show their leading ships off the southern tip of Norway in broad daylight and attack any British merchant ships and escorts they found in the area. They knew the Norwegians would be sure to report their presence to the British. The battle squadrons stayed sixty miles astern of the battle cruisers, where they could not be seen by observers on shore. The hope was that once the battle cruisers' feint had been reported, it would draw a numerically inferior enemy force out of its bases on the east coast of Scotland, to be led into a trap by the battle cruisers then fallen on by the full might of the German battle fleet. If the German battleships were able to inflict severe losses, the enemy would lose its superiority in numbers and the balance of power might swing in the Germans' favor.

The plan was flawed from the start. There was no British shipping in the area—sailings had been postponed. Unknown to the Germans, the British Admiralty had intercepted and decoded their signals and had known for two weeks that some major operation was being planned. The signal to begin the operation on 31 May had also been intercepted by British naval intelligence the previous day. The commander in chief of the British Grand Fleet had already ordered his ships to weigh anchor and leave their bases at Scapa Flow, Rosyth, and Cromarty on the evening of 30 May, four hours before the first German ship set sail. By the time the High Seas Fleet had cleared the sandbars at the mouth of the Jade River, the two main divisions of the Grand Fleet—the Battle Fleet and the Battle Cruiser Force—were a hundred miles out to sea, on their way to a rendezvous off the coast of Denmark. After they joined forces, they would try to cut the Germans off from their home base. With its superior numbers the Royal Navy hoped to inflict a second Trafalgar on the Kaiserliche Marine.

But neither side could be sure where, or indeed if, it would encounter the enemy. To many of the crews, especially the British, it seemed more likely that it would turn out to be another futile and boring sweep into the North Sea, of the kind they had experienced time after time during the past two years. The Germans certainly had no idea they might be up against the whole of the Grand Fleet, and due to a faulty intelligence report, the British believed that the main German battle fleet was still in harbor several hours after it had left the Jade.

Because of the courses set by the two commanders in chief, their paths were almost bound to cross at some point, but it was only due to a freak encounter with a harmless Danish merchant ship that the two spearheads made contact when and where they did, off Jutland Bank at 2:30 P.M. on 31 May. This fortuitous skirmish led to a full-scale fleet action that raged on and off for twelve hours—in both daylight and darkness. Fortunes swung first to one side then to the other. The battle took place over a wide area, and the action was often confused by swirling patches of mist, clouds of smoke belching from hundreds of guns and funnels, and finally by total darkness after the sun had set on the battle scene. No one on either side, including the fleet commanders, really knew what was going on during most of the action, except for brief periods of clear visibility. There was no radar or effective aerial reconnaissance to help them. By the time the northern sun rose in the early hours of 1 June, it was all over. Both sides went on to claim victory, but when the results were fully disclosed, neither could be satisfied with the outcome. Jutland was certainly no Trafalgar, but it was, and still is, the greatest naval battle that ever took place entirely on the surface of the sea.

FLAWED VICTORY

PART 1

THE ROAD TO JUTLAND

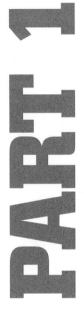

The End of the Pax Britannica

CHAPTER 1

In the coming century, the German people
will become the hammer or the anvil.

—Bernhard von Bülow

The road to Jutland began before the turn of the century. To understand why and how the battle was fought, it is worth tracing its origins and the background of the personalities involved.

On the afternoon of 22 June 1893, the ships of the Royal Navy's Mediterranean Fleet were returning to port after a day's exercises off the coast of Lebanon. It was a clear sunny day, and visibility was unlimited. As they approached Tripoli, where they were due to anchor for the night, the commander in chief, Vice-Adm. Sir George Tryon, decided to have them carry out one more maneuver before arriving at the anchorage. The ships were steaming in two parallel lines, about twelve hundred yards apart—one line of five battleships and a cruiser led by the flagship, HMS *Victoria,* and to port a second line of three battleships and two cruisers led by Tryon's second in command, Rear-Adm. Sir Albert Markham, in HMS *Camperdown.*

Tryon gave the order for the ships in each line to turn in succession through 180 degrees toward the other line, to form two new parallel lines. When they saw the signal flags being raised on the *Victoria,* it was hard for the ships' captains to see how the maneuver could possibly be carried out in the sea room available. The minimum turning circle of each ship was more than four cables, so that at least two thousand yards would be needed to perform such an exercise safely. No one was overly concerned—Tryon was an excellent seaman, with a reputation for performing intricate and seemingly dangerous maneuvers quite successfully. He had amazed his captains once already that day by having the ships in his division steam in line abreast through the two-hundred-yard gaps in Markham's division. This was a risky procedure, but Tryon had pulled it off without mishap.

None of the ships' captains dared question Tryon's latest order, although Markham had the temerity to raise the *Camperdown*'s "signal-repeat" flags to half mast to indicate that the order had been received but not understood. He was convinced that the maneuver was impossible. He also semaphored: "Do you wish the evolution to be performed as indicated by the signal?" Tryon left him in no doubt as to what he intended and semaphored back with the sharp response: "What are you waiting for?" The only person on the bridge of the *Victoria* who had the nerve to express doubts about the safety of the maneuver was Tryon's own staff captain, but the admiral angrily told him to hold his tongue. The captain of one of the other battleships remarked at the time, without any sense of irony, "Now we shall see something interesting."

When the *Victoria*'s signal flags were lowered, making the order executive, Markham gave the command for his helmsman to put the *Camperdown*'s helm hard over to starboard to begin her inward turn toward the other line. At the same time, the *Victoria* swung hard aport. It soon became evident that the two leading ships would come very close to each other long before they had completed their turning circles. The officers on the *Camperdown*'s bridge began to think that perhaps Tryon intended them to pass by the flagship on its starboard side, so that they would lead their ships safely to the far side of the other column. But when it became obvious that the *Camperdown* and *Victoria* were unquestionably on a collision course, orders were belatedly given to close all watertight doors.

In the end, when a collision seemed unavoidable, the two captains prevailed upon Tryon and Markham to put their engines full astern, but it was too late. The bow of the eleven-thousand-ton *Camperdown*, with its sharp underwater ram, sliced into the hull of the *Victoria* with a terrible sound of rending metal, punching a hole nine feet deep in the side of the flagship, just ahead of the bridge. The gash stretched twelve feet below the waterline. The *Camperdown* still had way on, and as her momentum dragged her free of the *Victoria*, she tore an even larger opening in the side of the stricken flagship and thousands of gallons of seawater streamed in.

Within eight minutes the *Victoria* had taken on two thousand tons of water, despite frantic efforts to stem the flow with collision mats. The ship began to list heavily to starboard, but nobody left his post because no order had been given—not even to the engine- and boiler-room staff, who were in the most perilous position below decks. The *Victoria* began to list more heavily, until it was nearly impossible to stand on her deck without holding on to something. Finally the order was given for the hands to fall in on deck, but tragically, amid the confusion the message was not passed down to the engine room.

At the moment of collision, a young commander lay in bed in his cabin with a severe bout of dysentery. He had been running a temperature of 103 degrees and was still in a weakened condition. Throwing on some clothes, he made his way to his post on the after bridge, but it was obvious the ship was doomed. As she began her final roll, about ten minutes after the collision, he and a friend walked down the ship's side into the water and began swimming away as hard as they could to avoid being sucked down when the ship sank. With the help of a cadet, the exhausted young man reached one of the *Camperdown*'s hastily lowered boats and was hauled on board. The officer's name was John Rushworth Jellicoe. By 1914 he would rise to the rank of admiral. As commander in chief (C-in-C) of the Grand Fleet, he would lead it into battle against the High Seas Fleet at Jutland in 1916.

Jellicoe was luckier than the 358 officers and men who went down with the flagship, especially the engine-room staff, most of whom were trapped below decks. Even those few who managed to get free were mangled by the *Victoria*'s still spinning propellers. In all, less than half her crew were rescued. Admiral Tryon was not among the survivors.

As was customary after a collision, the entire crews of the ships involved were court-martialed, although the trial centered on the senior officers. It was not clear whether Tryon had mistaken turning radius for circle or had suffered a mental aberration of some kind, but in any event he hadn't been about to pay attention to the concerns of his subordinates. All of the officers, including Tryon's second in command, Admiral Markham, were acquitted on all charges, although naturally their reputations were not enhanced by their performance. But they had after all only been following Tryon's orders, and in the Victorian navy orders were meant to be rigidly obeyed, no matter what the circumstances.

Sadly, the inquiry revealed that neither of the captains had closed the watertight doors, ports, and hatches on his own initiative. They had not even asked their admirals to take such obvious emergency measures, but had waited until the admirals had ordered them to do so. An Admiralty board was of the opinion that had the captain of the *Victoria* acted sooner, "the ship would have been saved, notwithstanding the crushing blow which she received from the *Camperdown*."

The conduct of the senior officers of the two ships may seem reprehensible, but their values were fairly typical of those prevalent among the officers of the Victorian navy. They had been brought up to believe that the only things that mattered were obedience, seamanship, and paintwork. Prized above all was the ability to handle a ship skilfully through a series of "quadrille-like movements carried out at equal speed in accordance with geometrical designs in the signal book," even though such complicated maneuvers would be of no practical use in wartime. The emphasis on appearances went so far that some captains spent their own money to decorate the ship with extra brasswork and gilded fittings. This outlook was also reflected in the colors used to paint British warships, even as late as the Spithead review in 1897. Other navies were changing to gray of various shades, to make their ships less conspicuous targets, but the Royal Navy still painted its ships' hulls red and black, with white upperworks and buff-colored funnels and masts.

At the time of Queen Victoria's Diamond Jubilee in 1897, her navy had suffered no serious challenge to its supremacy since Nelson and Collingwood had smashed the French and Spanish fleets at Trafalgar in 1805. For most of the nineteenth century the world was free of major conflicts, and this long period of relative peace became known as the Pax Britannica. Britain's growing industrial strength and her mastery of the oceans allowed her to impose her colonial style of overseas trade on the nineteenth century. The Royal Navy gradually assumed the role of world policeman. As one officer wrote, "We considered that our job was to safeguard law and order throughout the world—safeguard civilization, put out fires on shore, and act as philosopher, guide and friend to merchant ships of all nations."

As decade after decade of peace rolled by, the navy gradually changed from a tough, efficient fighting service into a complacent, near-moribund organization. It had lost its sense of purpose, although not its ineffable sense of its own superiority. Its wardrooms were dominated by members of the gentry and nobility, and in many ways it had become an exclusive aristocratic yacht club. Naval officers scorned any knowledge of steam engines, or the other technological developments that were taking place, especially in gunnery, which had evolved from smoothbore muzzle-loading cannons to rifled breech-loading weapons. Officers knew that promotion depended on seamanship, paintwork, and instant obedience to superior officers. Any use or expression of personal initiative, unless asked for, amounted to insubordination.

The wardroom's attitude toward the lower deck was one of lofty paternalism, enforced by rigid, petty, and often harsh discipline. Officers showed little or no concern for the poor pay and cramped living conditions of their men. A seaman might be paid as little as six pence a day, while his admiral received five pounds, or two hundred times as much. Ratings had to eat their food—miserable and monotonous as it was— using their fingers. Spoons were permitted for eating soup. The Admiralty considered the use of knives and forks to be unmanly and not conducive to sound discipline. That "fraternity between officers and the lower deck, which was the strength of Nelson's navy" had been lost.

The officers' personal lives were comfortably insulated from the real world, and they were content to focus on social and athletic events, with no thought for such "intellectual" pursuits as the study of tactics or strategy. The appearance and handling of the ship was everything. For an officer to be called "clever" was a pejorative expression. Their ships were scattered over the oceans of the world, often based on foreign stations set up long ago to counter traditional enemies and threats which no longer existed. Increasingly, they lived a pleasant, aimless existence, steaming from port to port to show the flag and enjoying themselves ashore, attending balls or playing polo. One gunboat captain used to greet his officers in the morning with, "Well boys, where shall we go today?"

Gunnery, the heart of a warship's purpose, was scandalously neglected. Gunnery practice was held every three months, but no further instructions were given than to go to sea, use up a quarter of the ship's outfit of shells, and return to port. Naturally gunnery practice was haphazard, and rather than fire the guns and dirty the paintwork, there was nothing in the orders to prevent officers from throwing their quarterly allowance of shells overboard instead, which some of them did.

This was the state of the navy's preparedness for war at the time of the Spithead review in 1897, held to mark the monarch's Diamond Jubilee. Nonetheless, Queen Victoria and her subjects were naturally proud of their magnificent fleet of 330 ships, manned by ninety-two thousand men. Even though only half of them were present at the review—no ships had been withdrawn from foreign stations to swell the numbers—it was still the greatest assemblage of warships the world had ever seen. Ship after ship, anchored in five perfectly straight lines, they stretched for seven miles toward the open sea, a spectacularly impressive sight with their bright paintwork and profusion of gaily flying flags and pennants. Over 30 of them were majestic battleships, bristling with huge 10- and 12-inch guns. British observers were bursting with pride, and the invited foreign naval officers and dignitaries were suitably overawed by this superb fleet, as they were meant to be. It left them in no doubt that Britannia ruled the waves.

Other, lesser navies had paid her navy the ultimate compliment of copying its uniforms and ranks, and a dozen foreign navies were dependent on

British armorers, shipyards, and naval architects for their guns and ships. Compared with the Royal Navy's 330 ships, the French had the second largest fleet with only 95 ships, and the Russians were third with 86. The Italian and Austrian navies were even smaller, and although the Germans had some 68 ships in service, their navy was in reality a coastal defense force. Even those future naval giants, the United States and Japan, had less than a quarter of the ships that the Royal Navy could muster. The Two Power Standard was clearly being maintained. This policy had been formulated by Castlereagh at the beginning of the century and had passed into law in the Navy Bill of 1889. It stated the that Britain must at all times have a fleet that was at least equal in numbers and strength to that of any other two naval powers combined. Ironically, the policy had originally been directed at France and Russia, who were to become Britain's staunch Allies in 1914.

It is hard to exaggerate the position of high regard and trust that the navy occupied in the eyes of the British people. It was their bulwark against any threats to its trade or coastline. As Sir Walter Raleigh had said three centuries earlier, "There are two ways in which England may be afflicted. The one by invasion, . . . the other by impeachment of our Trades." The navy was there to see that such afflictions did not occur. As to a possible invasion of the British isles, nothing had changed since St. Vincent had tersely informed the Admiralty a hundred years ago, "I do not say they cannot come, my Lords. I only say they cannot come by sea."

The British public looked on the Royal Navy not only with feelings of confidence and pride, but with great affection. It was common for young girls to wear lockets containing the pictures of famous seamen, and for young boys to be dressed in sailor suits, proudly wearing the cap ribbons of the latest battleships, much as young people today wear the t-shirts and caps of popular sports teams. Outwardly, all was well with the Queen's Navee that Gilbert and Sullivan had gently satirized in *HMS Pinafore.*

Internally it was a different story. The Royal Navy was a deeply conservative body, reluctantly accepting the great changes in naval technology that had taken place in the ninety-two years since Trafalgar. Nelson's wooden walls had given way to ironclads, then to hulls made entirely of iron. Sail had been replaced by steam, although for a long time it was not trusted as the sole means of propulsion. There were still some ships in commission carrying that unlovely combination of smoke-belching funnels and full-rigged masts and yards. Nelson's inboard mounted guns had slowly been replaced by rotating barbettes, then by armored gun turrets. The Royal Navy had been the last major navy to switch from muzzle-loaders to breech-loading weapons in the 1880s, but even at Spithead in 1897 there were some ships still armed with muzzle-loading guns.

To understand the actions and attitudes of the admirals at Jutland, it is worth remembering that most if not all of the senior officers commanding squadrons of battleships or battle cruisers (BCs) in 1914 had been trained under sail in ships carrying muzzle-loading guns. Many of them had achieved their first command in such ships. It was also true that few of them had ever heard a shot fired in anger. Even those officers who had fired their guns against a real enemy had only done so in close-range bombardments of forts or other stationary targets on shore. Moreover, the upper echelons of the service had no strategic ideas about how to employ a modern fleet in time of war. There was no such thing as a naval staff, or even a staff college to train officers in tactics or strategy.

More profound technical advances and challenges were on the way—long-range guns, mines, submarines, torpedoes, and aircraft—but there would not be decade after decade of peacetime in which to adapt to these newfangled weapons. The training of naval officers to meet the new challenges was almost totally neglected. A contemporary of Jellicoe (possibly Jellicoe himself), writing in 1878 under the pseudonym "A Naval Nobody," had severely criticized the education he had received at the Royal Naval College, Greenwich. Complaining about the lack of training in gunnery, torpedoes, navigation, and steam engines, to say nothing of general subjects, he wrote, "I call the whole system of our naval education utterly faulty; not only that education which does not bear directly on our profession, but to that which does do so. I say that we, our nation's youth, are in some professional matters most deplorably ignorant, and the day will come when we and England will wake up to the fact with a start."

That day was not far off, because of events taking place across the North Sea in the kaiser's Germany. Rapid and dramatic changes would be forced on the Royal Navy, although old attitudes and practices would persist into the twentieth century—most seriously the rigid adherence to orders and the lack of exercise of personal initiative or individual judgment.

The unification of Germany began when Prussia forcibly annexed eighteen other German kingdoms, principalities, duchies, and free cities in 1867. It was cemented as a result of victory in the Franco-Prussian War. The humiliating surrender of the French army at Sedan in 1870, followed by the siege of Paris and its eventual capitulation in 1871, led to the coronation of the king of Prussia in the Palace of Versailles. He became

Kaiser Wilhelm I, emperor of the first German Reich. The well-trained and equipped Prussian army under Moltke had humbled the Austrians in 1866 and the French in 1870, and established itself as the dominant military force in continental Europe. It also occupied a commanding position in the new state of Germany. The army was its first shield, with the navy in very much a secondary role, the reverse of the situation in Britain. The navy was in reality a coastal defense force, whose function was to guard the army's flank by preventing military landings and protect the Baltic ports against naval bombardment. As late as 1888 it was still commanded by army generals.

The chancellor, Prince Otto von Bismarck, had been the architect of unification and wanted to maintain the primacy of the army. His main interest was in consolidation of the gains in Europe, not expansion. He believed that the navy should become no stronger than was necessary to protect seaborne trade and the territories of the empire. He had no wish to offend Britain by a large increase in naval strength which might appear to threaten Britain's supremacy at sea, and lead to armed conflict.

All this was to change when the emperor died in 1888 and his grandson succeeded him as Kaiser Wilhelm II. In the words of Holger Herwig, the leading historian of the Imperial Navy, Wilhelm II was "ruthless, clever, domineering, patriotic, indefatigable, aggressive." But he was also vain, erratic, lacking in judgment, impulsive and unrealistic, and, in the view of his ministers, not altogether sane. When it came to the naval matters he was full of romantic notions and inclined to fantasize about the fleet and his future role as the self-styled "Admiral of the Atlantic." Since childhood, he had been obsessed with ships and navies, and he grew up both admiring the Royal Navy and envying his grandmother, Queen Victoria, for having such a splendid fleet. When he became emperor, his driving ambition was that Germany too would become a major naval power—perhaps not the equal of the British navy, but strong enough to challenge its complete mastery of the seas. After declaring himself supreme war lord, in command of both the army and navy, he needed an instrument to achieve his goal of making the navy as powerful and important as the army. That instrument was Rear Adm. Alfred von Tirpitz. In 1897 Wilhelm appointed him state secretary of the Reichsmarineamt, the Imperial Navy Office.

Tirpitz was an ideal choice. He was an experienced sea officer, just returned from command of the East Asiatic Squadron based at Tsingtao. He was also a specialist in the new underwater weapons, torpedoes and mines, although not yet convinced of the value of the submarine. Tirpitz was a giant of a man, with a fierce countenance and forked white beard, but a surprisingly high-pitched and somewhat squeaky voice. To go with his formidable appearance, he had a determined and forceful personality, and because of his important post and his privileged relationship with the "All-Highest," he soon became the dominant figure in the German navy.

Unlike his master, Tirpitz was patient, effective, and skillful at manipulating both the public and the legislators in the Reichstag, at the same time being secretive about the true extent of his plans. As he said, the ultimate size and purpose of the German navy "revolved around thoughts . . . which one can certainly think, at times must . . . but which really cannot be written down." He created what was in effect a propaganda department within the Reichsmarineamt to popularize the idea of a strong navy with the press and the masses and persuade the deputies of the Reichstag to vote the necessary funds for a great expansion of the naval shipbuilding program. Supported by political pressure groups such as the Pan German Society and the Colonial League, mass rallies were organized to promote naval construction. Naturally these groups received the full support of industrialists such as Alfred Krupp, who founded the Deutscher Flottenverein, or Navy League, to arouse "enthusiasm for this *one* great national issue." It would be Krupp's arms factory and his Germania shipyard which would supply many of the guns and ships that Tirpitz wanted.

The time was ripe for Tirpitz, because of Germany's rapid industrial expansion and its equally rapid increase in population. In addition, between 1871 and 1898, it had annexed territories in Africa and the Pacific and acquired a colonial empire of a million square miles with a population of thirteen million.

The kaiser was developing interests in *Weltpolitik,* which required an aggressive foreign policy. The foreign secretary, Bernhard von Bülow, remarked prophetically, "In the coming century, the German people will become the hammer or the anvil." Bismarck was an obstacle to such ideas, so the "wise old pilot" was unceremoniously dropped in 1890. Germany had already established itself as a *Grossmacht* (great power) through its victories over the Austrians and the French, but now Wilhelm wanted it to become a *Weltmacht* (world power). A large empire obviously needed a powerful navy to protect its overseas territories, but that pretext was not uppermost in the minds of either Wilhelm or Tirpitz. They wanted a fleet that was so strong that Britain would hesitate before interfering with German plans for expansion at home or abroad. They thought that it might even coerce Britain into a tacit agreement to share in dominating the world's trade. At the center of their naval plans lay the *Risikogedanke,* or "risk theory." As stated by Tirpitz, "Germany must have a fleet of such strength that even for the mightiest naval power, a war with her would involve such high risks as to jeopardize its own supremacy."

The Imperial Navy was to become a *Riskflotte*—a fleet that was not the equal of the Royal Navy but if challenged in a major sea battle, even though it might be defeated itself, could inflict such losses on the British that they would lose their numerical superiority over other potential enemies. Tirpitz believed that Britain would not run such a risk, and thus Germany might achieve her goals from a position of naval inferiority.

The kaiser wholeheartedly supported these ideas—he was determined that Germany would have her "place in the sun." He pledged, "As my grandfather did for the army, so I will for my navy . . . so that it may also stand on an equality with my armed forces on land, and so that through it, the German Empire may also be in a position abroad to attain that place which it has not yet reached."

Both men were greatly influenced by the writings of an obscure captain in the U.S. Navy, Alfred Thayer Mahan. Mahan was the foremost naval thinker of his time, and his famous book, *The Influence of Sea-Power upon History,* had a dramatic impact on both sides of the North Sea. Mahan's main thesis was that sea power was of paramount importance to a state's ability to accumulate wealth and power. By sea power he meant the possession an ocean-going fleet, strong enough and ready if necessary to engage any enemy that stood in its way in a decisive battle—or *Entscheidungsschlacht.*

The kaiser devoured Mahan's ideas and became an ardent "navalist," or believer in the predominance of naval interests. To him the corollary to Mahan's thesis was obvious. Without sea power, Germany would never be a world power. Tirpitz had Mahan's book translated and copies distributed to all ships in the Imperial Navy. It became the German naval officer's Bible.

When the Reichstag passed the Navy Laws of 1898 and 1900, Tirpitz obtained the funds to begin an ambitious shipbuilding program. From a paltry five battleships in 1895, the navy would have nineteen battleships and twelve big armored cruisers by 1902, and from 1900 onward it planned to launch three battleships a year. The naval race was under way. Later *Novellen,* or supplementary bills, authorized the construction of even more battleships and armored cruisers and allowed for the regular replacement of older ships. Tirpitz referred to these plans as the "patient laying of brick upon brick." The supplementary bills also made further large sums available to be spent on enlarging harbors and docks to accommodate these big ships. The Kiel Canal had already been completed in 1895, effectively doubling Germany's strategic capability by allowing rapid deployment of the fleet between the North Sea and the Baltic.

By the time of the naval review at Kiel in 1904, Germany was able to display a fleet that included no less than twenty-three battleships before the apprehensive eyes of British visitors. These included King Edward VII and the earl of Selborne, First Lord of the Admiralty. As he watched from the reviewing yacht, the king "exchanged many meaningful looks and words with Selborne, which impressed me unpleasantly," said Tirpitz. He had objected to this parading of virtually the whole of Germany's naval strength for the world to see. He was not yet ready to begin an open naval race with Britain, and would have preferred to keep the size of the fleet a secret for as long as possible, but the kaiser was too proud of his fleet to listen.

This was not the end of Tirpitz's plans for the fleet. He aimed to have forty-one battleships and twenty armored cruisers by 1917, so that the *Riskflotte* would present a real and dangerous threat to the Royal Navy. He hoped to attain near parity with Britain by 1920. But the Germans were confident that even with a numerically smaller fleet, their superior and more rapid ship construction, the higher quality of their guns and shells, and the better training of their officers and men would carry them to victory on *Der Tag,* as the Germans referred to the day of the eventual *Entscheidungsschlacht* against the Royal Navy.

The passing and implementation of the two Navy bills meant that Tirpitz and Wilhelm had taken the first steps on the road to Jutland. There would be no turning back.

Fisher and the *Dreadnought*

CHAPTER 2

The only thing in the world that England has to fear is Germany.

—Adm. Sir John Arbuthnot Fisher

The British public didn't take the rise of German sea power too seriously at first, in spite of the impressive public display laid on at the Kiel review. News of fresh battleship launchings at Wilhelmshaven and Kiel tended to cause annoyance rather than alarm. After all, Britain had by far the largest number of battleships afloat, and her navy had a long tradition of naval supremacy. The British did not believe that a continental land power like Germany was capable of building a navy, more or less from scratch, that would be a real challenge to the Royal Navy. But as the evidence mounted that the Germans were bent on acquiring a major fleet by laying down ever larger numbers of battleships, the British press and magazine writers, as well as the novelist Erskine Childers with his book *The Riddle of the Sands,* did their best to alert the public to the dangers inherent in the German naval buildup, especially the threat of invasion.

There was a public clamor for more battleships—the most visible and potent yardstick of naval power. As their role was to smash an enemy fleet and so eliminate any threat to Britain's security, the more battleships the better. There was widespread obsession with sheer numbers. Such matters as exactly how these ships would be employed—their gunnery and tactics were secondary.

But even as far back as the 1880s the British government had been concerned that Britain might be in danger of falling behind other major naval powers. This had led to passage of the Naval

Defence Act of 1889, which launched a new program of warship construction. It was planned to have twenty-nine up-to-date, or so-called first-class, battleships by 1898, with twelve more building. The passage of the German Navy Laws only increased the government's anxiety. The second law in particular, with its preamble about the concept of a *Risk-flotte,* was seen as a direct challenge to the Two Power Standard. If Britain's shipbuilding program did not keep pace, such a fleet might in time become strong enough to wrest control of the seas from the Royal Navy.

It was manifest that Germany meant to rival Britain as a naval power, and there could only be one reason. The Germans certainly didn't need more and more battleships to defend their coastline or colonies. The new fleet of the Kaiserliche Marine was being built first and foremost to challenge Britain at home, in the North Sea, and only later to rival her abroad in the quest for trade and territory. As the First Lord of the Admiralty, the earl of Selborne, had stated to Balfour's cabinet in 1901, "The naval policy of Germany is definite and persistent. The Emperor seems determined that the power of Germany shall be used all the world over to push German commerce, possessions and interests. . . . The more the composition of the German fleet is examined the clearer it becomes that it is designed for a possible conflict with the British fleet."

But public concern still did not develop into serious alarm. Even with the evidence of the Kiel review before it, Britain could still count three times as many first-class battleships as Germany. The British believed that their shipbuilders were the best and fastest in the world, and if Parliament voted the necessary funds, there would be no problem in maintaining traditional superiority in both numbers and quality of warships. Between 1903 and 1906 Britain completed eighteen new battleships— better than four a year, while German shipyards could only manage eleven, less than the planned three a year. At this rate Britain would easily maintain its large numerical edge. But the Two Power Standard was revised in 1904 to include a 10 percent safety margin.

The Germans on the other hand were convinced they would eventually outstrip British shipbuilders in both numbers and quality of battleships. Besides the Imperial Navy yards at Kiel and Wilhelmshaven, the main shipbuilding firms Vulkan, Germania, Blohm and Voss, and Schichau were gearing up for increased production and hoped to equal Britain's shipbuilding capacity by 1909. Krupp had also been stockpiling naval guns in its armaments factory. This was always a limiting factor in the rate of production of warships. Germany had already surpassed Britain in steel production, especially high-grade armor plate—a vital commodity in a battleship race. But with Britain's huge established lead,

Germany had a long way to go before she could hope to catch up. The Germans knew they would not be able to match the British fleet ship for ship, nor did they need to because of their more limited overseas responsibilities.

The large expenditures made on these costly weapons in both countries came at the expense of badly needed social reforms such as old age pensions and social insurance. There were arguments in Parliament and the Reichstag between the navalists and the economists. In Germany the main opposition to naval expansion came from deputies of the Social Democratic and Catholic Center parties, who demanded cuts in the shipbuilding program, but Tirpitz was too adroit for them in manipulating public opinion, particularly that of the middle class, who would provide most of tax money needed. In Britain the official Opposition was the Liberal party, "those cheese-paring Cobdenites" as the conservative press called them. Ironically, the Liberals were to carry on with the Conservatives' naval building program when they came to power in 1906, at least in the beginning. There was also widespread and often vitriolic debate in the national press. The *Daily Mail* thundered, "Is Britain going to surrender her maritime supremacy to provide old age pensions?"

There was great popular interest at the time in the design of new warships, especially battleships. The public in both countries was deluged with a stream of newspaper and magazine articles, books and pamphlets, giving all the details of the latest battleships—their tonnage, speed, number of guns, weight of broadside, and so on. All of this naturally stirred up feelings of national pride and intense rivalry between Britain and Germany. There was as keen an interest in naval affairs then as there is nowadays in the performance of national football teams during a World Cup year.

There was a resurgence of jingoistic sentiment in Britain. Originally aimed at the Russians, it was now directed at the Germans. In the words of a Victorian music-hall song:

> *We don't want to fight;*
> *But by Jingo, if we do,*
> *We've got the ships, we've got the men,*
> *We've got the money too.*

The naval buildup in Germany brought a deepening distrust of German motives and a growing animosity toward the German people. The British responded to news of fresh German launchings with cries of "Two keels to one." This was matched by increasing Anglophobia in Germany, originally inspired by Britain's unpopular actions in the Boer War and fanned by the kaiser's inflammatory telegram of support to President Kruger. Wilhelm II was fond of referring publicly to "perfidious Albion" and was disdainful of the British as a "hateful, mendacious, unscrupulous race of shopkeepers."

Mutual suspicion of each other's motives, and the stirring up of nationalistic emotions by the popular press, doomed any real attempts to halt the naval buildup. Among the many causes of the Great War, there is no doubt that the battleship race and the deep hostility it generated was the salient factor as far as Germany and Britain were concerned.

The Germans planned to concentrate the bulk of their naval forces—and certainly all of their precious battleships—in the North Sea. They believed that the Royal Navy would find it difficult to match them there because of its need to station many ships overseas. The Mediterranean had traditionally required a strong naval presence since Napoleonic times. Squadrons were also stationed in the Far East as a possible check to Russian expansion. It was believed that the czar had his eye on India, the jewel in the imperial crown. There were other demands of empire— in the South Atlantic, Indian Ocean, and Australasian and North American waters.

It was obvious that Britain could not be strong enough everywhere to protect its trade and colonies, and still maintain the supremacy in home waters that was vital to its very survival. It was of paramount importance to guard against an invasion of the British Isles, just as it had been in Nelson's day.

The government knew that the empire was becoming increasingly vulnerable in the face of the German threat, and was reluctantly obliged to seek allies. This marked the end of traditional freedom from continental entanglements—Canning's long-established policy of "splendid isolation." First a treaty was signed with Japan in 1902. Its intent was to curb possible Russian expansion in the Far East (which the Japanese navy was to do at Tsushima in 1905). Next came the Entente Cordiale with France in 1904, forged with the aid of the francophile King Edward VII. The role of the French fleet based at Toulon was to secure the Mediterranean against the small but powerful Austrian navy, and so permit the Royal Navy to withdraw some of its battleships to home waters. This was ironic since the French had been the reason for having a strong Mediterranean fleet in the first place. The Entente Cordiale was expanded in 1907 to form the Triple Entente, with Russia as the third partner, to counter the Triple Alliance of Germany, Austria-Hungary, and Italy, which had been formed in 1882 and renewed yearly until 1913, when Italy withdrew.

These continental alliances were a severe blow to Tirpitz's plans. Instead of Britain being isolated and threatened by several European enemies, as he had hoped, it was now Germany that was encircled by formidable foes. Italy and Austria were of little account as military allies in comparison with France and Russia. A Reichstag deputy lamented at the time, "Germanism has three enemies in the world—Latins, Slavs and Anglo-Saxons—and now they are united against us."

Britain also had one great strategic advantage that Germany could do nothing about: its geographical position. As Marder wrote, the British Isles lay "like a breakwater across the exits from the North Sea." Mahan had stressed the importance of this factor and the ability it gave her navy to deny Germany access to the world's oceans. As he put it, "She cannot help commanding the approaches to Germany by the mere possession of the very means essential to her own existence as a state of the first order." He had already emphasized the value of the weapon of blockade, both for its economic impact on an enemy, and as a means of neutralizing its military threat, just as it had been in Nelson's day when "those far-distant storm-beaten ships upon which the Grand Army never looked" had put a stop to Napoleon's ambitions for world domination.

German warships would have to fight their way past the Royal Navy to get to the Atlantic, or else stay locked up in the Heligoland Bight and the Baltic. Tirpitz had acknowledged this when he stated, "Our fleet must be so constructed that it can unfold its greatest military potential between Heligoland and the Thames." Germany would also be subject to the traditional British weapon of economic blockade. With its merchant fleet denied access to the world's sea lanes it would be unable to carry on any overseas trade. Some Germans believed that if a war against Britain and her Allies could not be won quickly, the blockade would bring Germany to ruin within a year.

Although the British position at the time seemed impregnable, the government knew that its vaunted naval strength was not as sound as it looked on paper. The quality of Royal Navy squadrons around the world varied considerably. Many of the stations were manned by old, slow, obsolescent ships. Reform of the navy was long overdue, and the government recognized this. According to Marder, even though the navy "was numerically a very imposing force, it was in certain respects a drowsy, inefficient, motheaten organism."

A small group of younger officers was well aware of its state of decay and the need for drastic reforms. They were under no illusions about Germany's aims and capabilities. Leading them was one of the most remarkable figures in the history of the Royal Navy, Adm. Sir John

Arbuthnot Fisher, who wrote, "The only thing in the world that England has to fear is Germany." He was to be Britain's answer to Tirpitz.

Fisher, universally known as "Jacky," had reached flag rank at the early age of forty-nine, after holding several important seagoing commands. He was short of stature, with close cropped hair and a prominent cowlick. His face had a somewhat oriental appearance, with yellowish skin, slightly slanted brown eyes, and high cheekbones. Born in Ceylon, the son of a coffee planter, his appearance gave rise to persistent but unfounded rumors (fostered and circulated by his enemies, of whom there were many) that he was half Sinhalese, possibly the product of his father's liaison with a Sinhalese princess. This led to various nicknames— "the Old Malay," "the Half-Caste," "the Mulatto," or "that unscrupulous half-Asiatic"—the choice depending on the speaker's degree of animosity toward Fisher and his reforms. He provoked either loyal support or bitter enmity among those he dealt with in the navy— there were no neutrals. He had one powerful friend and loyal admirer in King Edward VII.

Fisher was a fascinating character, gifted with great energy and enthusiasm, talented, determined, devious, aggressive yet persuasive. "A mixture of Machiavelli and child" was how one associate described him. He could be a staunch and affectionate ally, or an implacable, vindictive foe. He often signed letters to his friends with "Yours till Hell freezes." He was forceful in argument and explanation, even with his friends. The king once complained to him, "Fisher, I do wish you would leave off shaking your fist in my face."

He had a flamboyant, colorful writing style, being fond of epigrams, underlining, capital letters, and exclamation marks. As second sea lord in 1902, he wrote, "I see my way clear *to a very great reduction* WITH INCREASED EFFICIENCY! But the reform will require the three 'R's: _R_uthless, _R_elentless, _R_emorseless."

He had begun to make reforms even before this, while he was commander in chief of the Mediterranean Fleet. He improved the fleet's efficiency and instituted realistic fleet maneuvers in place of "quadrille-like movements." He made his ships carry out gunnery practice repeatedly and had them steam at fifteen knots and fire at moving targets from a range of six thousand yards, instead of the previous practice of near-point-blank firing at moored targets from two thousand yards. Fisher also encouraged the study of tactics and strategy among his officers, an unusual step for a fleet admiral to take.

When he became second sea lord, "his energy and drive were already legend in the service," according to Winston Churchill, who was to become Fisher's longtime associate, friend, and confidant. Two years later, at the age of sixty-four, Fisher was appointed First Sea Lord, the pinnacle of a naval officer's career. He was now in full control of the Royal Navy, subject only to its civilian head, the First Lord of the Admiralty. He served with four different First Lords, who either allowed him free rein or gave him their full and enthusiastic support.

Fisher was like a whirlwind blowing through the Admiralty. He brooked no opposition to his ideas for change. As he said, "Those who get in my way had better look out. I'll ruin anyone who tries to stop me." During his reform period, as Churchill wrote, "he made the Admiralty quiver like one of his great ships at full speed. . . . But the Navy was not a pleasant place while this was going on." Fisher, truly the savior the service badly needed, didn't care that he "left many foes foaming in his wake." He knew that had the Royal Navy entered the Great War in the state it had been in at time of the 1897 Spithead review, the consequences for Britain and its Allies would have been catastrophic.

Fisher realized the growing threat from the rise in German sea power and suggested, half-seriously, that the Royal Navy "Copenhagen" the German fleet in Kiel and Wilhelmshaven before it became too strong— as Nelson had done to the Danes in 1801. He expressed this idea at the peace conference at the Hague in 1907, with predictable results. The conference achieved nothing. His comments became widely known and were taken seriously in Germany. When he made this suggestion to his friend King Edward VII, the royal response was, "Fisher, you must be mad!"

But in Churchill's words, Fisher "hoisted the storm signal and beat all hands to quarters." By the time he had finished he had transformed the navy from a "drowsy, inefficient, motheaten organism" into a tough, efficient fighting service. Some flaws would remain, of course, but these were cobwebs gathered during a century of peacetime inactivity, and not easily swept away, especially ingrained ideas and attitudes in the senior ranks.

Once in power, Fisher wasted no time in forcing through a crash program of major reforms. His proposals and solutions had already been laid out in the Selborne Memorandum of 1902, and he presented them to the First Lord of the Admiralty on the day he formally took office as First Sea Lord, 21 October 1904, the ninety-ninth anniversary of Trafalgar— "a good fighting day to begin work," in his words. (His appointment was actually effective as of the twentieth, but Trafalgar Day sounded better to Fisher.)

First, he drastically reorganized and modernized the training of all future officers at the naval colleges of Osborne and Dartmouth, beginning as cadets at age twelve and a half. The syllabus was changed radically.

The subjects taught were to be common for all entrants and included engineering and other specialized technical branches, not just seamanship and navigation. He raised the status of the maligned engineering branch, known to the executive officer class as "greasers," resulting in opposition from the traditionalists, who grumbled that Fisher was "making greasers of us all."

The lot of the lower deck was improved with better pay and food. Fisher introduced bakeries on all ships to provide freshly baked bread instead of ship's biscuit. In future, sailors would get to eat their meals with knives and forks instead of spoons and fingers. Some of the more severe punishments, such as death for striking an officer, were abolished. During Fisher's time the harsh and often petty discipline was eased, and the number of court-martials in the lower ranks dropped by more than threefold.

Next there was a wholesale scrapping of obsolescent ships— "a miser's hoard of useless junk," in Fisher's opinion. No less than 154 ships of all types—gunboats, old cruisers, even battleships—were decommissioned. This was as many warships as had been present at Spithead in 1897. Fisher claimed that most of these elderly vessels could "neither fight nor run away," and a fast armored cruiser "would lap them up like an armadillo let loose on an anthill." They were sent to the breakers yard or sold to minor navies. The great savings achieved by removing so many ships from the active list, and releasing their crews for other duties, enabled greater efficiency and much lower maintenance costs. This meant more funds available to build newer and better ships. A favorite Fisher maxim was "Build First, Build Fast, Each one Better than the Last."

Fisher also reorganized the fleets based on modern strategic needs, not outworn romantic notions of where ships should be stationed. He especially strengthened the Home Fleet, which was renamed the Channel Fleet and later became the Grand Fleet. It was to have three quarters of the navy's battleship strength. The North Sea became the focal point of British sea power, not the Mediterranean. The former Channel Fleet became the Atlantic Fleet, based on Gibraltar, where it could be redeployed if necessary to reinforce the Channel or Mediterranean stations.

Fisher set up a new Reserve Fleet, with permanent nucleus crews, including specialists from all branches. Its ships could be recommissioned at very short notice, ready to reinforce the Home Fleet or be sent wherever they were needed, unlike the former fleet reserve, which had consisted of old ships, unmanned and neglected, that "cluttered the creeks and backwaters of Portsmouth and Devonport."

He also promoted the development of submarines and torpedo boats—later to be called destroyers—although he neglected the development of mines. These new weapons were not held in favor by many senior officers. As late as 1902 one British admiral had called the new underwater weapons "underhand, unfair, and damned unEnglish." Fisher related that a former First Sea Lord had confided to him, "There were no torpedoes when I came to sea," and that he "didn't see why there should be any of the beastly things now." There were also protests and fierce opposition from the traditionalists, who did not hold with other technological advances taking place. They firmly believed that in battle it was the character of their men, not their matériel, that counted. Fisher paid them no attention. He dismissed the critics as "prehistoric fossils" or "the syndicate of discontent." Like Tirpitz, he was skillful at public relations, and he shamelessly courted and exploited both newspapermen and parliamentarians to gain popular support for his reforms.

While these sweeping changes were taking place, Fisher was planning an even bolder move, one which would revolutionize the nature of the battleship. The armament of existing battleships consisted of a profusion of different weapons. The main armament was at most four big guns, usually 11- or 12-inch, with a secondary armament of twenty or thirty guns of lesser calibers. In battle, the big guns were for aiming at the enemy's hull, and the rest were to concentrate on the gun turrets, masts, and superstructure. The idea was to smother the enemy with a "hail of fire." This was all very well for close-range engagements, but as gunnery ranges increased, the smaller-caliber weapons were not effective. There were also logistical problems with the stocking and supply of several different caliber shells and charges to the various gun turrets. With so many independent gunnery officers, firing was disorganized, and the gunlayers had great difficulty in spotting their own fall of shot amid a forest of different splashes in order to correct their aim. The "hail of fire" idea had long outlived its usefulness.

Technological advances in guns had led to much longer range gunnery, mainly to counter the threat of attack by torpedo boats and submarines. The trend was toward big guns and armor-piercing (AP) shells packed with high explosive and triggered by time-delayed fuses. The heavier shells were also more accurate, especially at long range, because of their flatter trajectory and better ballistics. Uniform armament also allowed salvo firing. When all the shells had the same time of flight, it resulted in a tighter group of splashes, which made it much easier to spot the misses and alter the guns' elevation and deflection until the target was straddled, with at least some of the salvo hitting the target.

Fisher and others clearly recognized that the prime function of the battleship was to destroy enemy battleships. To do this, what was needed were armor-cracking guns, which could penetrate an opponent's vitals, not smaller-caliber weapons that could only damage its superstructure. To be most effective you needed the biggest guns possible, and as many as possible. All-big-gun ships were being planned in the United States, where the *Michigan* and the *South Carolina* had been authorized by Congress in 1904 (they were not to be completed until 1910). Japan had also drawn up plans to build two all-big-gun ships, the *Settsu* and the *Kawachi*, although they were not laid down until 1909. The well-known Italian naval architect Vittorio Cuniberti had published an article with a design for an all-big-gun battleship in the 1903 edition of *Jane's Fighting Ships* with the title "An Ideal Battleship for the British Fleet."

Fisher took the plunge. It was clearly an idea whose time had come, and in his view, if Britain didn't take the lead with it, some other nation soon would. He was determined to get the jump on the rest of world, particularly Germany. Fisher was appalled by the prospect that Germany might build such ships before Britain did. He convinced the First Lord to set up a high-powered committee, with himself as chairman, which consisted of leading naval architects, scientists (among them Lord Kelvin), and several of the brightest young naval officers, including Capt. John Jellicoe, then director of Naval Ordnance. Its task was to consider possible designs for an all-big-gun ship, carrying as many of the largest-caliber weapons as feasible. Another Fisher maxim, borrowed from Napoleon, was "Hit first, hit hard, and keep hitting."

The design finally agreed upon by the committee also incorporated the new steam turbines, which the inventor Charles Parsons had impudently but effectively demonstrated by gate-crashing the 1897 Spithead review with the thirty-four-knot steam yacht *Turbinia*. The onlookers had never seen anything afloat that could move so fast. The Parsons turbines had great advantages over reciprocating engines, being much more reliable, easier to maintain, more compact, and lighter in weight. But they had never been used before in a large warship. At the time, turbines were only just being installed in a few of the latest transatlantic liners, but they had not yet reached the sea-trial stage. Fisher's decision to use them in a battleship was a real gamble. It paid off handsomely. The engines generated twenty-three thousand horsepower, which gave the ship a speed of twenty-one knots, three knots faster than most existing battleships. Fisher's credo was that speed allows you to fight "*When* you like, *Where* you like, and *How* you like."

The turbines' smaller engine and boiler rooms also allowed greater compartmentalization, making the ship less sinkable. (Although the Germans were to carry this idea much further than the British.) The ship's design incorporated recent advances in armor plate, and the decks were armored, as well as the sides and turrets, to counter longer-range, plunging fire. This was not the case in older battleships, in which only the ship's central citadel was given significant armor protection. Fisher gave the new ship the working name "Untakeable."

When she was launched by King Edward VII at Portsmouth on 10 February 1906, she bore the name HMS *Dreadnought,* the ninth of that name to serve in the Royal Navy. As the *Times* put it, "There are few acts more poetical than that of launching a great ship, few spectacles more moving." The king, dressed as an admiral of the fleet, with a jubilant Fisher at his side, smashed the ceremonial bottle of wine against her bow. Accompanied by a band playing "Rule Britannia" and flying a huge white ensign, the 526-foot hull began to slide slowly and majestically down the greased slipway. Once afloat, the great vessel came to a stop surrounded by a swarm of tugboats, within sight of Nelson's *Victory.*

When the hull was fully equipped it would carry no less than twelve 12-inch guns—no other battleship had more than four. These were mounted so as to give it a broadside of eight. The only other guns she had were 12-pounders, for use in beating off torpedo boat attacks. The big guns could fire a broadside of at least twice the weight of shell as those of any other battleship afloat, neglecting their ineffective secondary batteries of smaller guns. She could also outfire them by three to one ahead, as in pursuit of a fleeing enemy, which appealed to Fisher's aggressive nature.

The *Dreadnought* was heavily protected, with up to twelve inches of armor plate over her vitals and up to four inches of deck armor. The extra armor and gun turrets gave her a displacement of more than twenty thousand tons when fully loaded. This made her three thousand tons bigger than typical battleships of the day, yet she could still outsteam them by several knots. The ship was built with amazing speed and secrecy. From the time she was laid down, it took only four months to launching and twelve months to sea trials, a record that has never been surpassed. This was in an era when it normally required around three years to build a battleship. The ship's sudden appearance caught the rest of world, particularly Germany, completely by surprise. Fisher had created a new type of warship which made all other battleships obsolete overnight, including those hurriedly being built in German shipyards.

Naming the ship *Dreadnought* was typical of Fisher, who, when he later became a baron, chose "Fear God and Dread Nought" as the motto for his coat of arms. The name became the generic name of a new class of warship. In future all capital ships were rated as to whether they were dreadnoughts or the now outclassed predreadnoughts.

The launching of the *Dreadnought* nullified Tirpitz's building program in one stroke. But at the same time it had wiped out Britain's great numerical superiority in modern battleships. Fisher's critics—and there were many—were quick to point this out. The famous naval architect Sir William White claimed that Fisher was putting all his "naval eggs in one or two vast, costly, majestic, but vulnerable baskets." It had been a risky step to take, certainly, but in Fisher's opinion, if he hadn't gone ahead with it, some other navy would have developed such ships before Britain did, with the same result. This way Britain got off to a head start.

The Germans halted construction on their *Nassau* class battleships for eighteen months while their naval architects labored to redraw the designs to convert them into dreadnoughts. Meanwhile, Britain continued to lay down more of these powerful ships, and by May 1910 it had ten of them in service before the first true German dreadnoughts—the modified SMS *Nassau* and *Westfalen*—had completed their sea trials. Ironically, the ship whose launching had contributed so much toward the inevitable North Sea confrontation between Germany and Britain was not destined to be present at Jutland. HMS *Dreadnought* was on patrol in the Channel when the battle was fought.

Another type of dreadnought, even closer to Fisher's heart than *Dreadnought* itself, was a fast, heavily gunned armored cruiser to which he gave the working name "Unapproachable." He recognized that in order to sink an enemy battle fleet, first you have to find it, then break through its protective screen and maintain contact until your own battle fleet comes up. Cruisers traditionally fulfilled this role, but existing cruisers were too slow and too vulnerable. Even armored cruisers could be easily brushed aside or driven off. Fisher saw the need for a new type of armored cruiser—almost as heavily armed as a battleship, with eight 12-inch guns, but much faster. The first ship in this class was completed in 1907, less than a year after the *Dreadnought*. She was named with typical Fisher panache: HMS *Invincible*. Two more *Invincible*-class cruisers quickly followed.

HMS *Invincible* was much bigger than existing armored cruisers, but she could steam at twenty-seven knots—an incredible speed for a seventeen-thousand-ton warship. But something had to be sacrificed to attain such speed—armor protection. She had only four to six inches of armor belt over her vitals and even less on her deck. The deck armor, an inch or even less, would be like cardboard against the plunging fire of heavy shells. Fisher dismissed such criticisms with "Speed is armour." He was to be proved wrong.

Fisher misled the Germans into believing that this new type of cruiser would carry nothing bigger than 9.2-inch guns—hence their first response was the unfortunate *Blücher,* which was not really a dreadnought at all. This was to have tragic consequences for her crew. The Germans' first real answer to this new type of cruiser was the *Von der Tann,* completed in 1910, by which time the Royal Navy had three *Invincibles* in service and five newer versions under construction. But German shipbuilders soon began to catch up, producing improved versions of the *Von der Tann.*

The main advantages of this type of ship, which became known as battle cruisers, were their speed and heavy armament. To Fisher, they were his "New Testament" ships, because they fulfilled the promise of the "Old Testament" dreadnoughts. The British battle cruisers were not badly designed ships, but they did have one hidden flaw, which was to show up with catastrophic results in a few cases.

The main problem with the battle cruisers was not their design but their intended purpose and the way admirals actually used them. They were meant to destroy enemy surface raiders or, more important, to play a scouting role with the battle fleet. Their primary function was to serve as the eyes of the fleet, just as Nelson's frigates had done. Their job was to locate the enemy fleet, and try to maintain contact under long-range fire, reporting its position, course, and speed to their fleet commander until he could bring up his battle squadrons (BSs) and engage the enemy in a Trafalgar-like fleet action. Finally, they were to mop up any crippled enemy battleships after the battle fleet had done its work.

Such lightly armored ships were never meant to stand in the line of battle and slug it out with modern battleships, but it was inevitable that admirals would not be able to resist using them in this way because of their battleship-sized guns—even the name "battle cruiser" suggested that use. They took a terrible battering when they did.

The Germans didn't go as far with Fisher's assertion that "speed is armour." They gave the *Derfflinger* and *Lützow* heavier armor, resulting in less speed, and only 11-inch guns. These were better constructed ships, with greater compartmentalization and extra bulkheads which made them nearly unsinkable. Tirpitz's dictum was, "The supreme quality of a ship is that it should stay afloat . . . so long as a ship is afloat it retains a certain fighting value and afterwards can easily be repaired."

The fact that the Germans concentrated more on the defensive aspects of their ships was not surprising for the weaker naval power. They clung to the idea of a "fleet-in-being," which would remain a constant threat to a superior fleet and tie it down. This was somewhat contradictory in view of their original designation of their fleet as a *Riskflotte*. Events would show that the Germans were unwilling to risk action unless it was against a clearly inferior force.

The launching of the *Dreadnought* and *Invincible* gave a fresh impetus to the Anglo-German naval competition. From 1906 onward it became a dreadnought race. The newly elected Liberal government planned to continue laying down four new dreadnoughts per year, in accord with the policy of their Conservative predecessors as set out in the Cawdor Memorandum of 1905. But by 1909 the Admiralty and the Opposition felt that the naval situation demanded six. The Liberals agreed to build the four, with a contingency plan for four more, if it could be shown to be necessary. An alarmed British public was stirred by an Opposition member's cry: "We want eight; we won't wait." The *Observer* newspaper chimed in with "The eight, the whole eight, and nothing but the eight." In the end, public fears and reconsideration of German dreadnought launchings led the government to decide that the contingency plan *was* necessary. Churchill, who was then home secretary, later remarked drily, "The Admiralty had demanded six ships; the economists offered four; and we finally compromised on eight."

Fortunately, with the head start Fisher had given it, Britain was able to stay in front despite the best efforts of German shipyards, which never did manage to outstrip British shipbuilders. By 1912 she had seventeen dreadnought battleships and battle cruisers to Germany's eleven and was able to maintain and even increase her lead for the next two years. At the end of 1914 Britain would have thirty-six dreadnoughts in service to Germany's twenty-one, and by the time Jutland was fought, Britain's shipbuiding industry had increased this lead.

The introduction of the dreadnoughts meant that the Germans were forced to widen and deepen the Kiel Canal to take these larger ships. This was expensive, which meant less money available for naval construction. It was also time-consuming: the project took eight years to complete. But until it was finished the canal couldn't take such big ships to and from the Baltic, which seriously limited the capability of the German fleet.

But the British had problems of their own. New harbors with dockyard facilities capable of repairing dreadnoughts were badly needed. The major fleet bases of Devonport and Portsmouth were both well equipped, but they had been established for cross-Channel enemies such as France and Spain and were too far away from the North Sea area. The other first-class naval base at Chatham was in the North Sea, but it was too far south to serve as the main fleet base. But it was harder to get Parliament or the Admiralty to spend money on such mundane facilities as dry docks than it was on the more glamorous dreadnoughts. New bases at Rosyth and Cromarty were under construction, but by the time war broke out, they were still not properly equipped to repair capital ships. The main North Sea fleet base at Scapa Flow had no dockyard facilities at all, and at the start of hostilities this vast anchorage didn't even have defenses against submarine or torpedo boat attack.

Fisher made one other significant but unofficial move while he was in power. It was to have far-reaching consequences, especially for the way the Battle of Jutland was fought. He gathered around himself a team of bright, young, progressive officers who collectively became known as the "Fishpond." The two key figures in this group were the gunnery expert, Capt. Percy Scott, and Capt. John Jellicoe, who was in charge of ship design and ordnance.

In 1903, Scott was appointed to the command of HMS Excellent, the navy's gunnery school at Portsmouth, where he had to fight against long-established ideas and practices. He introduced simple but effective mechanical devices for training gunlayers, but his major improvement in gunnery, supported by Jellicoe, came after Scott retired in 1909. This was based on the idea of central control and the installation of the director firing system. In the new system, all the guns on the ship could be trained to exactly the same range and deflection by one man, the director, who was situated high above the deck in the fighting top, where he had a clearer view of the target and was less subject to interference from spray and smoke from the funnels and guns than the gunlayers at deck level. He used a master sight connected electrically to each of the gunsights and, when ready, could fire all the guns simultaneously by depressing a key.

There was also a single spotting officer in the fighting top. He made continuous aim corrections by observing the near misses and transmitted these to the director. This system replaced individual turret firing, whereby each gunnery officer was solely responsible for establishing the range and deflection of the guns in his turret, and for spotting his own fall of shot from a position at deck level. The new system ran into fierce but understandable opposition from gunnery officers because it minimized their expertise and responsibilities.

Finally, a test was arranged in 1912 between HMS *Thunderer* and her sister ship, the *Orion*, both using the same target and range but with a director controlling the gunnery of the *Thunderer* and individual gunlaying on the *Orion*. Despite the fact that the *Orion* was then the top gunnery ship in the navy, it was no contest. The *Thunderer* scored six times as many hits as her sister ship. In spite of this conclusive demonstration, opposition continued, and by 1914 only eight battleships had been fitted with Scott's director system. By the time Jutland was fought, however, all but two of the British capital ships had the new system.

Scott, who was denigrated as "a notorious self-publicist," was an abrasive character who didn't suffer fools gladly, and he became extremely unpopular within the navy because of his reforms and the way he forced them through. But as Fisher said, "I don't care if he drinks, gambles and womanises; *he hits the target.*"

Fisher had also picked Jellicoe out as early as 1898 as the man to lead the fleet in war. He wrote, "By far the best officer in my opinion and that of the Captain of the *Excellent* is Lieutenant J. R. Jellicoe." He made sure that Jellicoe was given a series of appointments that would bring him the necessary knowledge and experience to be a fleet commander. With Fisher's constant support and encouragement, and no less because of his own undoubted ability and talent for leadership, Jellicoe rose to become an admiral and, eventually, commander in chief of the newly named Grand Fleet.

When Fisher became First Sea Lord, he took Jellicoe with him as his director of Naval Ordnance because he was "profoundly knowledgeable on gunnery and shells." Like Fisher, he believed in the "supreme importance of big guns." But he was completely different from his mentor in other ways.

Short of stature and unimpressive in personal appearance, Jellicoe was anything but flamboyant or pugnacious. He had a "tight mouth, watchful, calm brown eyes . . . [that] steadily looked out beyond a prominent nose." Unlike Fisher, he was "cool, controlled, always polite, profoundly self-confident." Jellicoe was also a highly intelligent, even brilliant individual, whose "well-ordered mind" had an amazing capacity for storing and analyzing a vast amount of technical data. In all, he was a consummate professional.

During his tenure as director of Naval Ordnance, he became dissatisfied with the protection offered by British armor plate compared with that of German warships, and more particularly the effectiveness of British shells and the totally inadequate method used to test them. Unfortunately he was moved to the Admiralty as third sea lord before he could make changes, and his successors did nothing to correct the serious faults he had detected. At Jutland the deficiencies in British shells were to have a critical effect on the results of the battle.

Jellicoe was a realist who had no illusions about the quality of the opponents the Royal Navy would have to face. Shortly before the war, he wrote, "Assuming equality in design it is highly dangerous to consider that our ships as a whole are superior or even equal fighting machines."

In contrast to Fisher, Tirpitz, who was the dominant figure in the Kaiserliche Marine, had surrounded himself with second-rate people. The chief of his Naval Staff—the Admiralstab—was Adm. Hugo von Pohl, clever enough but "a compliant nonentity." The head of the Marinekabinett, Adm. Georg von Müller, was dismissed by Tuchman as a "pederast and sycophant." The commander in chief of the navy was Adm. Friedrich von Ingenohl, who was defensive-minded, timid, and indecisive. He has been described as being "as much a courtier as a naval officer," and he was afraid of offending the "All-Highest" by taking risks.

There was also an unhealthy rivalry among the Imperial Navy Office, the Admiralty, and the Naval Cabinet, which was not helpful in formulating cohesive war plans. Superimposed on these pressure groups was the overall negative influence of the kaiser, who was obsessed with the fleet-in-being idea and couldn't bear the thought of losing any of his precious battleships—unlike Tirpitz, who wanted the fleet he had built to go out and fight. Wilhelm, increasingly, hoped to preserve his fleet intact as a bargaining chip in postwar peace negotiations.

The problem with the self-styled "Admiral of the Atlantic" was that he had assumed command of the navy, and the right to make decisions of every kind, "down to the last petty detail." But Wilhelm simply did not have the ability or professional experience to live up to the role he had assigned himself. When faced with the task of planning the winter fleet maneuvers, for example, which he had decided was his prerogative, he was incapable of making actual decisions, and in the end burst out with, "I am tired of these discussions. I simply command and that is that. . . . I am finally tired of this. To hell with it, I am the Supreme War Lord, I do not decide, I command."

As time went by Tirpitz simply bypassed Wilhelm's power to make important decisions by working out meticulous plans with his aides and advisers then submitting them to the kaiser in great detail, backed up by cogent arguments. Whereupon Wilhelm, unable to argue effectively against Tirpitz's proposals, simply accepted them. In effect, Tirpitz presented Wilhelm with a series of faits accompli. But by 1914 Tirpitz's influence on the future conduct of the naval war had waned. He had requested that he be appointed commander in chief of German naval forces, but the kaiser had refused. Tirpitz remained secretary of the navy, but this was a purely administrative post, and it wasn't until later in the war that Germany acquired the vigorous leadership of Reinhard Scheer and Franz von Hipper, who commanded the German forces at Jutland.

Fisher too was gone from a position of influence before the war began. He was the victim of his enemies—principally Adm. Lord Charles Beresford, C-in-C of the Channel Fleet—and of his own arrogant and increasingly autocratic rule. The Admiralty set up a committee of enquiry as result of the feud between these two major figures, which had become a public scandal that threatened the unity, effectiveness, and morale of the navy. The open and bitter dissension between the First Sea Lord and the C-in-C of his most important fleet was very dangerous at a time when war seemed possible, if not very likely, in the near future. Fisher got rid of Beresford by rearranging the fleets to eliminate his position. Despite the fact that Beresford had constantly been insubordinate and clearly failed to back up his accusations against Fisher, the committee's report was wishy-washy and did not vindicate Fisher to his satisfaction. The First Sea Lord was deeply hurt, after all his many and important contributions to the navy, and he felt obliged to resign in 1910—although he would be back at the Admiralty with a vengeance at the end of 1914. During his years in the wilderness Fisher corresponded frequently with Churchill, who became First Sea Lord in 1912, to offer suggestions, advice, and support.

When the fleet paraded before King George V at Spithead in 1911 to mark his recent coronation, it was completely different in both appearance and reality from the one which had been reviewed there in 1897. Gone were the brightly painted and flag-bedecked obsolescent ships of Queen Victoria's navy, many of them still sporting fully rigged masts and yards as well as funnels. Now there was row upon row of stark gray shapes, lying low in the water, stripped down to two funnels and a tripod mast. There was nothing romantic about their appearance—they looked businesslike and menacing. It was now a modern battle fleet in every sense of the word. Fisher deserved full credit for dragging and bullying the Royal Navy into the twentieth century and strengthening its fleet so that it was once again the mightiest in the world.

In the years following Fisher's resignation, the naval arms race continued unchecked, and Europe remained in a state of uneasy peace. By the summer of 1914, almost everyone in Britain and Germany took it for granted that a war between the two countries was inevitable, but few realized how near it was. Fisher had predicted years ago that Armageddon would come in the autumn of 1914. He was not far off the mark.

In the early summer the Royal Navy was engaged in planning a test mobilization, which was to precede the annual Royal Review at Spithead. This was to be followed by fleet exercises in the Channel. The

Kaiserliche Marine was similarly occupied, getting ready for Kiel Week, which was due to begin on 23 June. This year it was to be a special occasion to mark the official reopening of the newly widened Kiel Canal. As an overtly friendly gesture, the kaiser invited a British squadron to attend and take part in the festivities. The Royal Navy sent four of its most powerful dreadnoughts and three modern cruisers, under the command of Vice-Adm. Sir George Warrender. They were able to observe and be impressed by the strength of their rivals, while the kaiser reviewed his fleet from the deck of the imperial yacht *Hohenzollern*.

The festive mood was shattered by a telegram from Vienna on 28 June. The heir to the Austro-Hungarian throne, Archduke Franz Ferdinand, and his wife, Duchess Sophie of Hohenberg, had been assassinated in Sarajevo during a state visit to the recently annexed province of Bosnia. The assassin was an eighteen-year-old Bosnian nationalist named Gavrilo Princip. The Austrians discovered that the assassination had been planned while he was in Belgrade, and that Princip and his co-conspirators had been aided and financed by a Serbian secret society called the Black Hand, which was dedicated to the unification of the southern Slavs.

The news from Sarajevo caused all remaining official functions at Kiel to be canceled as the German court went into mourning. When the British squadron set off for home by way of the Kiel Canal—as they had been invited to do in another friendly German gesture—the visit had been so congenial that Admiral Warrender was actually moved to hoist a signal to the German fleet: "Friends in the past, friends for ever."

The Eve of War

If there is ever another war in Europe, it will come
out of some damned foolish thing in the Balkans.

—Prince Otto von Bismarck

The news from Sarajevo did not immediately lead to a crisis in Anglo-German relations, although the political situation in Europe became tense and uncertain. Until it became clear how Austria-Hungary was going to react, no one could foresee what the aftermath of the assassination might bring. A period of deceptive calm settled over Europe while the Austrians pondered their response but took no overt action against the Serbs for three weeks. The initial Serbian reaction to the news was conciliatory, if insincere. They sent a telegram of condolence to Vienna, declaring that Serbia would "certainly, most loyally do everything to prove that it would not tolerate within its borders the fostering of any agitation . . . calculated to disturb our already delicate relations with Austria-Hungary." But the Serbs had known all along of the activities of Colonel Dimitrejević and his Black Hand society and had done little to deter him.

The Austrians knew that Serbia was somehow implicated in the assassination plot, and their foreign minister, Count Leopold von Berchtold, and the head of the Army General Staff, Gen. Franz von Hötzendorf, were determined to use Sarajevo as a pretext to "crush the Serbian skull." They hoped that war on Serbia would stem the rising tide of nationalism in the Balkans and put an end to pan-Slavic movements which threatened the fragile unity of their elegant but rickety empire. But first they needed to assure themselves of German support, as taking any military action against Serbia would inevitably bring the Russians to the defense of their Slavic cousins. Berchtold also had to work hard to convince Franz Josef that war against Serbia was the only acceptable response to the assassination of his great-nephew. This took some time, because the eighty-three-year-old emperor was not really interested in fresh military adventures or territorial expansion.

Over the next few days, diplomatic exchanges between Vienna and Berlin yielded the result the Austrians wanted—what became known as the "blank check." On 5 July the kaiser instructed his chancellor to inform Vienna that the Germans would stand by them, no matter what the Austrians decided to do. With German support now assured, the Austrians planned to send an ultimatum to Belgrade which was so strong that Serbia could never accept it and remain independent. Berchtold postponed sending it until he had obtained his emperor's approval. On 20 July he showed the final polished draft to Franz Josef. Although couched in suave diplomatic French, it provoked this exchange:

"This note is pretty sharp."
"It has to be, Your Majesty."
"It has to be indeed. You will join us for lunch."

General Hötzendorf and his staff went ahead with their plans for war on Serbia.

Meanwhile, in Britain, naval affairs in the post-Fisher era were being dominated by another forceful and vigorous character—Winston Churchill. The committee of inquiry whose report had led to Fisher's downfall in 1910 had been very disturbed by the lack of a naval war staff at the Admiralty. Fisher had always opposed the idea of a "thinking department" as he called it, because he saw it as a threat to his increasingly autonomous rule. He had once derided the idea of a naval staff as "a very excellent organization for cutting out and organizing foreign newspaper cuttings." Fisher's attitude was not at all uncommon in naval circles. Reacting to the suggestions of staff officers, one leading admiral said, "My motto is: Damn the Staff." Another equally prominent flag officer once remarked, "They pay me to be an admiral. They don't pay me to think."

The Army General Staff was frustrated by its inability to make joint plans with the Admiralty for the movement of an expeditionary force to France. The Admiralty was uncooperative and gave the impression that the navy could win the war all by itself—the army was merely necessary for making landings on the Baltic coast or the Friesian Islands. As

Fisher had once disdainfully told a group of army staff officers, "The Army is a projectile to be fired by the Navy."

At the time of the Agadir crisis in 1911, when war with Germany seemed imminent, Lord Haldane, the secretary of state for war, was so upset by the lack of ideas as to how this vast and costly fleet was going to be employed that he threatened to resign if changes were not made in the Admiralty, starting at the top. He demanded that the Admiralty introduce a naval war staff and begin to cooperate more closely with the War Office in planning joint operations.

Finally, in October 1911, Prime Minister Asquith decided that matters called for more determined and effective naval leadership, and he replaced McKenna as First Lord of the Admiralty with the dynamic, brash, thirty-seven-year-old Churchill. Churchill threw himself totally into his new job. He involved himself in every aspect of naval affairs, from the broadest strategic to the most detailed and technical. This did not make him popular with the admirals, who resented his interference with what they saw as matters best left to the professionals. Although he was completely inexperienced in naval affairs, Churchill had great intelligence and intuition. His consuming interest in the navy led him to read so widely and voraciously that he soon became remarkably well informed.

Churchill's first important move was to establish the Naval War Staff. He got rid of Wilson—known as "Old 'Ard 'Art"—as his First Sea Lord, then tried Adm. Sir Francis Bridgman, but couldn't get along with him. He finally settled on Adm. Prince Louis of Battenberg. This was a sound choice. Battenberg had behind him a long and distinguished career as a seagoing officer and was known as a skilled strategist and tactician. Just as important, he was tactful and able to get on well with the ebullient and impatient Churchill and appreciated the First Lord's burning desire to get things done. He was also highly respected within the service, and this allowed him to smooth over the often stormy relations between Churchill and the admirals. Battenberg and his staff began to draw up detailed plans as to how the Grand Fleet should be employed in wartime. There wasn't enough time to develop a truly effective naval staff before war broke out, but the step Churchill had taken certainly came better late than never.

Even though Fisher no longer had any official position or real power, he kept in constant communication with Churchill with a stream of correspondence offering ideas and advice. His influence on the First Lord was probably greater than Battenberg's, who frequently proved to be too compliant when faced with the forceful arguments and proposals of the dynamic First Lord. Battenberg so frequently wrote "Quite concur" on Churchill's memos that he became known in Whitehall circles by this nickname.

Churchill made other important and far-reaching changes during his brief tenure at the Admiralty before war broke out. He began the conversion of the fleet from coal to oil. Oil-fired ships were capable of greater speed and longer range than coal-burners. In adddition, the slow, tedious business of coaling ensured that a sizable proportion of the Grand Fleet's ships might be in harbor for refueling at a time when they were urgently needed for action. Refueling with oil was much quicker, but the problem was that Britain had a plentiful supply of anthracite but no assured source of oil. Churchill solved this by having the government purchase controlling shares in the Anglo-Persian oil companies.

He also pushed the development of superdreadnoughts. These ships were armed with 13.5-inch guns, instead of the dreadnoughts' typical 12-inch, giving them greater range, accuracy, and firepower. Churchill went the next logical step with the 15-inch *Queen Elizabeth* class, laid down as part of the 1912 program and launched between 1913 and 1915, in time for Jutland. The five *Queen Elizabeth*s were oil-fired and fast, capable of twenty-four knots or better. War College studies had concluded that a fast battleship wing would be more effective in a fleet action than a squadron of battle cruisers. The performance of these superb ships at Jutland was to confirm this.

Churchill made two other crucial decisions that were to have a profound influence on the outcome of the war at sea: his choices of the men to lead the Grand Fleet against the Germans. Fisher had long ago selected Jellicoe to be his "Admiralissimo when Armageddon comes," and Churchill was in full accord with this choice. Adm. Sir George Callaghan, whose appointment as commander in chief had been extended, was not due to step down until the end of 1914. Churchill appointed the fifty-five-year-old Jellicoe to act as Callaghan's second in command until that time, but he soon became convinced that the able and popular Callaghan was not in good enough health and was, at sixty-two, too old to stand the enormous strain of commanding the fleet in what might well be a long war. With Battenberg's concurrence, he decided that if war seemed imminent before the end of 1914, Jellicoe would take over command of the Grand Fleet before the expiry of Callaghan's term.

Churchill's second crucial decision concerned the man to lead the battle cruiser squadrons (BCSs). Vice-Adm. Sir David Beatty was twelve years younger than Jellicoe and had made extraordinary progress through the ranks ever since he was a lieutenant in command of a gunboat on the Nile in 1896. He had shown skill and courage during the attack on the forts at Omdurman, for which he had received the Distinguished

Service Cross. Like Jellicoe, he had also distinguished himself in China during the Boxer Rebellion, where both men had been wounded and mentioned in dispatches. Promotions came so rapidly for Beatty that he had reached the rank of captain at twenty-nine, at a time when the average age of captains was forty-three. After being in command of several cruisers, and finally the battleship *Queen*, he reached the top of the Captains List without the six years of sea service necessary for promotion to flag rank. Fisher got Beatty over this hurdle in 1910 by means of a special order-in-council, and he was made a rear admiral shortly before his thirty-ninth birthday—even younger than Nelson had been when he first hoisted his flag.

Beatty was offered the post of second in command of the Atlantic Fleet but turned down this coveted appointment because he wanted a more independent command. The Board of Admiralty were not pleased and put Beatty on half pay until his next appointment. He could well afford this financially, because his American wife was the only daughter of the owner of the Marshall Field store chain, but he could not afford it when the Admiralty decided not to offer him further employment, because it meant that in three years time he would be forced to retire. Before this period expired, he arranged for an apppointment to see the First Lord.

Churchill and Beatty hit it off right from the start of their meeting. Churchill began by remarking that Beatty looked very young to be an admiral, to which Beatty shot back that Churchill looked very young to be First Lord. He invited Beatty to become his naval secretary, which was a powerful and influential position in the Admiralty. The longer they worked together, the more Churchill became convinced that Beatty was just the man to lead the battle cruisers in action. It is worth quoting at length Churchill's somewhat unusual reasons for making this decision:

> He viewed naval strategy and tactics in a different light from the average naval officer. He did not think of *matériel* as an end in itself but only as a means. He thought of war problems in their unity by land, sea and air. His mind had been rendered quick and supple by the situations of polo and the hunting field and enriched by varied experiences against the enemy. I had no doubts whatever, when the command of the Battlecruiser Squadron fell vacant in the spring of 1913, in appointing him over the heads of all to this incomparable command.

At first Beatty was only given command of the 1st Battle Cruiser Squadron, but subsequently he took command of all three squadrons, which became known as the Battle Cruiser Force, and eventually the Battle

Cruiser Fleet. This was the second most important and prestigious command in the navy, after C-in-C, Grand Fleet.

Churchill's decision was not a popular one with many naval officers. They had long resented Beatty's rapid promotions, and no less his decision to turn down the plum the Admiralty had first offered him, which they would have been overjoyed to accept. Indeed, few of them could have financially afforded to turn it down. It was also hard for senior flag officers to accept that an admiral who had so little sea time, and had never commanded a squadron of anything, let alone a fleet, had the experience needed for such an important command.

Beatty and Jellicoe were a study in opposites. Beatty, the tall, handsome, dashing young fellow who played polo and rode to hounds, had what is nowadays called charisma. With his cap worn at a jaunty angle above a jutting jaw and his nonregulation six-button jacket, he became as recognizable to the public as Montgomery was to become twenty-five years later. He was soon the darling of the press. Although he did not, like Fisher, manipulate the press, he was not averse to the publicity. By contrast, Jellicoe was short, unprepossessing in appearance and lacking in color. Quiet and thoughtful, always calm and polite, he was nonetheless highly regarded in the service and popular with officers and men alike because of his obvious ability, fairness, and unruffled air of always being in control of the situation. Jellicoe had no time for newspapermen and believed that giving too much information to naval correspondents was a threat to security, an attitude that did not endear him to the members of the Fifth Estate.

Fortunately, the two admirals got on very well together. They respected, and indeed admired, each other, and even though he was Beatty's superior, Jellicoe had the good sense to keep him on a fairly loose rein. Beatty was to play a pivotal role in all major actions in the North Sea, especially Jutland.

As the threat of war loomed ever closer, the Royal Navy's staff situation was less than ideal, and at the top there was an insufficient willingness to delegate. But the staff's line of command through Churchill, Battenberg, and Jellicoe was clearer and much better organized than that of its opponent. The German command structure lacked coherence, due to the erratic nature of Wilhelm II as supreme war lord, the power-seeking intrigues of Tirpitz as secretary of the Imperial Navy Office, and the unhealthy rivalry between Tirpitz and the heads of the Naval Staff and the Naval Cabinet. In spite of his preeminent position among senior flag officers as *Grossadmiral*, Tirpitz had no authority to make operational decisions. This was nominally vested in Admiral von Pohl as head of the Admiralstab, and Admiral von Ingenohl as C-in-C of the High Seas

Fleet, but neither could make any important decision without the approval of the kaiser. This fragmented and unsound command structure made it impossible to develop any unified strategic policy or dependable war plans.

Tirpitz recognized the problem, since he had helped create it, but like Fisher he had always been more concerned with the buildup of matériel rather than precisely how it was going to be used in wartime. At the eleventh hour he proposed that a naval high command be organized, with himself as its head, to direct all operations. Neither Wilhelm nor his senior flag officers had any enthusiasm for this idea, and Tirpitz's proposal was bluntly rejected by the kaiser. Naval operations were left in the timid and indecisive hands of Pohl and Ingenohl, who were subject to the whims and interference of the kaiser, and ever worried lest they incur the imperial wrath if anything should go wrong. Unfortunately, Wilhelm's ideas and judgments tended to be influenced by the last person he had talked to, and there were all too many senior officers with the right of direct personal access to the kaiser—the *Immediatstellung.*

The war plans of the two navies in July 1914 were quite different, but even at this late date neither side had worked out a detailed and well-developed strategy or tactics for fighting the war at sea. The Admiralty had only recently changed its mind and decided in favor of a distant blockade rather than a close blockade of German seaports. This was intended to pen the Germans inside the North Sea. The decision was to come as a surprise to the Germans, who had assumed all along that the enemy would adopt the traditional British weapon of close blockade, which Nelson and Collingwood had used so effectively against the French and Spanish fleets. But times had changed since Nelson's day. The enemies and the geography were not the same, and the ships and their weapons were totally different. Nelson's ships-of-the-line and even his frigates could stay at sea for months, far from their home ports, but whether coal- or oil-fired, battleships could only stay at sea for a week or so, and cruisers and destroyers for merely a few days, before having to return to port for refueling.

Also unlike the situation in Nelson's time, there were the twin underwater perils of mines and torpedoes to consider. A close blockade would be extremely hazardous, because the enemy would inevitably sow minefields outside its harbors and send submarines, undetected, to attack the ships on blockade duty with their torpedoes. Admiral Togo had lost a third of his battleship strength to Russian mines while blockading Port Arthur in 1904, and this had impressed itself deeply on the psyche of admirals everywhere. There were no defenses against mines in 1914—effective minesweeping with paravanes was not developed until later in the war. Neither was there any satisfactory counter against submarine attack. There was no sonar to detect them or depth charges to sink them in 1914. Only the chance sighting of a periscope or torpedo track would allow a captain to take any action at all. Even then there was nothing to be done but head for the submarine and try to ram it or force it to submerge, and comb any observed torpedo tracks to avoid being hit. Fortunately, submarines were slow and torpedoes had only a short range in 1914, and the fear of underwater attacks proved to be overly exaggerated.

Moreover, the main German estuaries of the Ems, Jade, and Elbe were heavily fortified, as was the island fortress of Heligoland, which would make a close blockade very hazardous. While in power, Fisher had come up with various harebrained schemes, such as landing troops on the Pomeranian coast less than a hundred miles from Berlin, to threaten the German right flank, or occupying one or more of the Friesian Islands to put closer pressure on the High Seas Fleet bases. These proposals were rejected out of hand by the cabinet and the Army General Staff as both impractical and dangerous. As far as the government was concerned, the navy's prime responsibilities were to ensure the safe passage of troopships to France and protect the British coast against attack or invasion.

In addition to these defensive tasks, which would be left to the weaker Second Fleet, the Admiralty envisioned a more offensive strategy for the Grand Fleet. Its role was to entice the High Seas Fleet out of its bases into the North Sea and engage it in a decisive fleet action. They were confident that the Grand Fleet would prevail—in Trafalgar style. But they were less clear as to how such a fleet action could actually be brought about. It did not seem to occur to them to ask why the Germans, with the weaker battle fleet, should oblige them by conforming to their idea of how the war in the North Sea should be fought.

The Germans on the other hand adopted a more defensive strategy, which was reasonable for the weaker opponent. They realized the difficulty of their fleet breaking out into the North Atlantic to attack shipping. The northern routes were out of the question because the Grand Fleet would come out of its Scottish bases and stop them. Even if the Germans were successful in brushing aside or even overwhelming the weaker Channel Fleet, which was mainly manned by predreadnoughts and armored cruisers, they would be cut off from their bases by the Grand Fleet long before they could steam several hundred miles back to safety.

U-boats were not yet in favor for attacking shipping, for both technical and diplomatic reasons, particularly because of the effect on neutrals such as the United States. As Tirpitz put it in his memoirs, "The question as to how far our submarines were capable of rendering material assistance in the war had not been settled in July 1914." Their main role was to act as advance forces for the High Seas Fleet. They were to be sent out to torpedo enemy battleships before a fleet action began, cutting down the British advantage in numbers, and later to pick off enemy ships that had been slowed down or crippled by battle damage.

The main German strategy was for its battle fleet to stay in port most of the time and to make occasional sallies with its 1st Scouting Group of battle cruisers to bombard towns on the east coast of Britain. The idea was to lure part of the enemy fleet out of its harbors in response. The scouting group would then draw inferior British units into a trap between itself and the battle squadrons, which would come out of the Jade at the right time to close the trap and destroy its weaker opponent. In this way, the Germans hoped by gradual attrition to reach near parity with the Grand Fleet, and only then, on *Der Tag*, would the High Seas Fleet come out in full force to meet the Royal Navy in an *Entscheidungsschlacht*.

These two views of naval strategy were incompatible—and liable to lead to stalemate unless one side or other was prepared to take risks. The Germans were not likely to with the kaiser at the helm, and with the cautious, uninspired leadership of Ingenohl. The British didn't need to take risks, except to fulfil the expectations of the public (and those of the Royal Navy, which was eager to come to grips with its rivals). The years of public sacrifice required to build this expensive fleet demanded another Trafalgar. But even if a decisive battle could not be forced on the Germans, the overall strategic situation was definitely to Britain's advantage. The Royal Navy would remain in control of the North Sea.

One important factor was that the problems of communications and control of large battle fleets were not fully realized by either side. There was an almost complete lack of experience of major fleet actions in the modern era. There was only Tsushima to go by, and the technological improvements that had taken place since 1905 meant that many of the lessons learned during the Russo-Japanese conflict were no longer relevant in 1914. The ships were faster, and the distances between different units of the fleet were likely to be greater. Signaling by means of flags or semaphore lamps would be uncertain at these distances, and although wireless telegraphy (W/T) was available on all ships, there was a reluctance to rely on it for both technical and security reasons. Although Jellicoe was to issue clear instructions that all important visual signals must be repeated by W/T, this practice was not always followed by officers steeped in traditional methods of signaling.

The fear of torpedoes and the advent of newer and bigger weapons had driven expected gunnery ranges up from the five thousand yards or less that was involved during most of the action at Tsushima to fifteen thousand yards or more. Such a distance between the fleets would keep the battleships well outside of the limited range of enemy torpedoes, unless their torpedo boats could break through the battle fleet's protective screen of destroyers and cruisers and get close enough to launch a mass attack.

The problems created by the new long-range guns were exceedingly complex and difficult to solve. An enemy ship's range, speed, and bearing might be changing continuously, and even the rate of change of these quantities might also be varying in a manner hard to predict. It was no easy task to fire a salvo from a rolling, pitching, yawing gun platform at a target eight miles away and have the salvo land in the area the enemy ship would have got to during the time of flight of the shells, which could be twenty seconds or more. It was an extremely difficult mathematical problem whose solution called for complex and continuous calculations. Even if the enemy's initial range, speed, and course were known exactly— which they usually weren't—the problem of obtaining accurate firing solutions, to set the guns for the next salvo, was really beyond the technology of the day.

Nonetheless, the Royal Navy had made great advances in long-range gunnery. Apart from Scott's improved methods for the training of gun-layers, and his institution of director firing, several inventors had come up with ingenious devices to help solve the gunnery control problem. A young lieutenant named Dumaresq had invented a type of trigonometric slide rule to calculate changes in range and bearing. The values from the "dumaresq" were transmitted to a so-called range clock which made continuous calculations of changes of rate of range and deflection that were used to plot the enemy's expected course. Such "clocks" were forerunners of the modern computer.

The most adequate of these was the Argo clock, invented by the civilian Arthur Pollen. In essence the first practical analogue computer, it was automatic and plotted the enemy course with a variable speed mechanical drive. At about the same time Capt. Frederic Dreyer, who later became chief gunnery officer on Jellicoe's flagship *Iron Duke,* had developed a mechanical device for carrying out the same type of calculations. Known as the Dreyer Fire Control Table, Mark I, it was decidedly inferior to Pollen's invention. It was manually operated and plotted the enemy range and deflection separately, before firing solutions could be worked out. It was too slow to cope with the rapid changes of rate and deflection expected under battle conditions. Although Dreyer made improvements which shamelessly incorporated Pollen's ideas, his later Fire Control Tables (Mark II to IV) remained inferior to Pollen's system. Despite this, the Admiralty rejected Pollen's invention and adopted the Dreyer system in most of its battleships. The few ships that had been equipped with the Argo clock showed consistently good gunnery performance. The Admiralty's reasons for rejecting Pollen's device and adopting a clearly inferior system were based largely on the fact that Dreyer's device was cheaper and had been developed in-house by a professional gunnery officer who was Jellicoe's protégé, rather than by a civilian inventor. Pollen's difficult personality also played a part in the decision.

The Germans had developed similar methods of gunnery control, but their system was less technically advanced than that of the British. They had an equivalent device to the "dumaresq" to obtain range and bearing values and a mechanical range clock to allow for the rate of change of these values. Corrected elevation and training was passed by mechanical telegraph to each gunlayer, who set an indicator on his gunsight to conform to the corrected values. The German system was simpler and better able to cope with rapid changes than the Dreyer Mark I Table. But the gunlayers required months of training, and too much reliance was placed on the skill and concentration of individual operators, whose performance was likely to fall off under real battle conditions. Also, there was no central director firing, as in most ships of the Royal Navy.

But the Germans had one technical advantage over their opponents: much better range finders—at least at the start of the war. The Royal Navy ships were equipped with one or more Barr and Stroud range finders, which operated on the principle whereby the images obtained from each end of the range finder were shown on a split screen and brought into coincidence by the operator to obtain a trigonometric estimate of the distance to the object. As with any range finder, the longer the base, the more accurate the estimated range. The early Barr and Stroud models had only a four-foot six-inch base and were not accurate above five thousand yards. By the time of Jutland these had been replaced by nine-foot models, and the 15-inch-gunned superdreadnoughts had fifteen-foot models that were accurate above fifteen thousand yards.

The German ships on the other hand were equipped with up to seven three-meter Zeiss stereoscopic range finders that were positioned at different points in the ship. The values obtained were then averaged mechanically. The stereoscopic devices gave more accurate values, especially for blurred images of the enemy ship, as might be the case under battle conditions due to interference from smoke or mist. As with the gunlayers, the problem was again that the German system placed too great a reliance on the skill and training of individual operators. They had to have perfect vision in both eyes and needed long periods of training. They were even ordered to abstain from beer and sex while preparing to go to sea. Their performance required intense concentration and was likely to suffer under real battle conditions from the noise of their own guns and the impact of enemy shells.

The Germans had one other advantage. They spent more time and effort on gunnery practice, which was carried out in the relative seclusion of the Baltic, under realistic battle conditions, often in poor weather, with the ships moving at high speed and making sharp turns to test the range-takers and gunlayers. Despite their more advanced technology, British practice shoots before the war had shown appalling results. Jellicoe was determined to raise gunnery standards in the Grand Fleet as quickly as possible, which he did using the excellent facilities for gunnery practice at Scapa Flow.

Overall though, by the time of Jutland, the quality of the gunnery of both navies was about even. Each side had advantages and disadvantages which tended to balance out. But at Jutland there were to be some conspicuous exceptions to this, involving examples of both excellent and atrocious gunnery.

In mid-July, while the post-Sarajevo situation was quietly simmering away, the High Seas Fleet was on exercises in the Skagerrak prior to a planned cruise to Norwegian waters in the latter part of July. The Admiralstab had timidly opposed the Norwegian cruise because they felt it might be regarded by the British as a provocation, but the kaiser overruled them. The Royal Navy was in the middle of a test mobilization prior to the annual Spithead review on 20 July. This was to be followed by fleet exercises in the Channel. The two most powerful fleets the world had ever seen were steadily gearing themselves up for a possible showdown in the North Sea.

On 23 July the Austrian Foreign Office informed Germany of the stiff ultimatum they had prepared for the Serbs before sending it to Belgrade. They gave Serbia just forty-eight hours to reply. This set off a chain of events that led inexorably to the start of the Great War.

The next day, Britain learned of the terms of the ultimatum. Churchill received a copy from the Foreign Office, and later wrote, "This note was clearly an ultimatum; but it was an ultimatum such as had never been penned in modern times. As the reading proceeded, it seemed absolutely impossible that any State in the world could accept it, or that any acceptance, however abject, would satisfy the aggressor." This was exactly what Berchtold and Hötzendorf had intended.

On 25 July the kaiser was on board his yacht *Hohenzollern* in Sogne Fjord, where he had gone to accompany the High Seas Fleet during its exercises. On hearing of the ultimatum, he ordered Ingenohl to take the fleet into the Baltic and prepare to strike the first blow against Russia. The admiral knew that France, and then Britain, would inevitably be dragged into the war on the Russians' side. He managed to convince the kaiser to let him send part of the fleet back to its main North Sea base in the Jade. By this time, the Grand Fleet had also returned to its home ports in the Channel after completing its maneuvers.

On 26 July Churchill left London for Cromer to be with his wife, who was ill. This left Battenberg to keep an eye on developments. The increasing tension between Austria and Russia caused the situation to deteriorate, and before Churchill could return to the Admiralty, Battenberg decided on his own initiative to send Callaghan an order: "No ships of First Fleet or Flotillas are to leave Portland until further orders." Summer leave was canceled, and the fleet remained practically on a war footing instead of being stood down after exercises as planned. The Royal Navy quietly continued its mobilization for war.

The Admiralty wired Callaghan again: "The First Fleet is to leave Portland tomorrow, Wednesday, for Scapa Flow. Destination is to be kept secret." That night, an eighteen-mile-long procession of ships moved stealthily out of Weymouth Bay and steamed at high speed under cover of darkness toward its northern base.

The Serbian reply to the Austrian ultimatum was conciliatory, almost abject. The two "All-Highest" began to have second thoughts. When Franz Josef noted that "the rupture of relations needn't necessarily mean war," a nervous Wilhelm commented, "More than one could have expected! A great moral success for Vienna! All reason for war is gone!" But it was too late for second thoughts. Events and personalities had conspired to thwart any hope of halting the momentum toward a European conflagration.

Austria declared war on Serbia on 28 July, one month to the day after Sarajevo. From now on, each day would bring Europe closer to the brink. The next day, the Admiralty canceled all leave and issued the Warning Telegram. This message meant that the navy was to take all measures and precautions short of actual hostilities.

On 31 July Russia ordered general mobilization. The next day Germany issued a clumsy ultimatum to St. Petersburg, demanding demobilization within twelve hours, and that Russia make a "distinct declaration to that effect." The Russians ignored it, and so on 1 August, Germany declared war on Russia.

General mobilization of both the Grand Fleet and the High Seas Fleet was ordered that day. The two fleets were soon at full battle readiness, poised and waiting for the order to open hostilities. It was hard to predict what would happen if they did—would it be Fisher's Armageddon or a stalemate?

The Germans enquired what France's position would be in a German-Russian conflict. When France agreed to honor its treaty with Russia and stated that it would come to Russia's aid if she were attacked by Germany, the kaiser declared war on France on 3 August.

Britain's position was less clear. It was not legally bound by its treaties with Russia and France to enter the war, but it did have a formal treaty with Belgium. War with Germany now seemed inevitable, because Britain knew that a German attack on France would almost certainly go through the Low Countries as it had in 1870, to repeat the successful Schlieffen Plan.

On 2 August Churchill decided to go ahead with the replacement of Callaghan as C-in-C, Grand Fleet. This was a bold step to take on the very eve of war, but Churchill felt the present crisis demanded it. Jellicoe was ordered to go to Scapa Flow as second in command and hoist his flag in the battleship *Centurion.* He carried with him a sealed envelope containing the order to take over as C-in-C. He would be instructed to open the envelope as soon as war was inevitable. Jellicoe knew very well what the envelope contained, but as his train sped north, he began to have serious misgivings about the advisability of such a changeover at the eleventh hour. He was principally worried about its effect on the morale of the fleet, and naturally concerned about how little time there would be for him to familiarize himself with the fleet before leading it into action.

He wired London explaining his concerns. He warned Churchill, "The step you contemplate is fraught with gravest danger at this juncture." He repeated his concerns after he reached Scapa Flow, but Churchill responded, "I can give you 48 hours after joining Fleet. You must be ready then." During the next two days, Jellicoe sent several more telegrams, but Churchill had made up his mind and wired back: "I am telegraphing to the Commander-in-Chief directing him to transfer command to you at the earliest moment suitable to the interests of the service."

It came as a great shock to Callaghan to be told, "You are to strike your flag forthwith, . . . reporting yourself at the Admiralty thereafter at your earliest convenience." Callaghan knew of course that Jellicoe was scheduled to replace him eventually, but not so brusquely and without any warning. It was personally painful for Jellicoe as well, since he and Callaghan were old friends. But to their great credit, the two managed the changeover smoothly and without acrimony.

Once the news was out, there were strong objections from senior flag officers, including Beatty, who felt the dismissal was unfair. There was also general indignation in the fleet that their well-liked and admired leader had been shunted aside in such a cavalier fashion. Nonetheless, the two admirals had behaved so impeccably that these feelings of indignation soon died away, and in a short while, Jellicoe had won the respect and confidence of the fleet. It gradually came to be accepted that Churchill had been right, and that the "grand old man" was near the end of his active career and probably could not have stood the strain of command for long.

The same day as Jellicoe took over the government sent an ultimatum to Berlin demanding that Belgian neutrality be respected. The deadline for response was 11:00 P.M. Greenwich Mean Time (GMT) on 4 August. The Germans made no reply before time ran out, and the Admiralty immediately signaled all ships and shore establishments: "Commence hostilities against Germany."

In the end, it had turned out just as Bismarck had once predicted: "If there is ever another war in Europe, it will come out of some damned foolish thing in the Balkans."

Action in the North Sea

CHAPTER 4

*Jellicoe was the only man on either side who by his actions
could lose the war in an afternoon.*

—Winston Churchill

As the two mighty fleets confronted each other across the five hundred miles of North Sea separating Scapa Flow and the Jade estuary, there wasn't any doubt which was the stronger—at least in terms
of numbers. The Germans had lost the battleship race by a wide
margin, and they knew it. The Grand Fleet had twenty-one dreadnought battleships at Scapa Flow to the High Seas Fleet's fourteen
at Wilhelmshaven. Jellicoe also had eight battle cruisers under the
command of Vice-Admiral Beatty at Rosyth, to match Ingenohl's
five under Rear Admiral Hipper.

The British margin of superiority in dreadnoughts would be even
greater by the time of Jutland, because they had more ships under construction than the Germans. There were also three superdreadnoughts
nearing completion in British dockyards. These had been ordered by
the Chilean and Turkish navies, but the Admiralty commandeered
them for the Royal Navy. Churchill was taking no chances on any of
these foreign purchases falling into the hands of a potential enemy.

The Grand Fleet's protective screen of light cruisers barely outnumbered that of the High Seas Fleet, by twenty-three to twenty,
but this margin would also be much greater by the time Jutland was
fought. In August 1914, however, Jellicoe's destroyer screen had only
two flotillas consisting of about forty ships, compared with Ingenohl's
ninety torpedo boats. Even though the British destroyers were bigger
and more heavily gunned than German torpedo boats, the Grand

Fleet was seriously under strength in terms of these valuable little ships. Neither side had many modern seagoing submarines at the start of the war. There were none stationed at Scapa Flow, while the Germans had nineteen U-boats attached to the High Seas Fleet to act as an unseen and deadly spearhead.

The Royal Navy's traditional emphasis on the offensive spirit was reflected in its warship design. British battleships and battle cruisers carried bigger guns, which fired much heavier projectiles, than their opposite numbers. They had 12-, 13.5-, or 15-inch main armaments compared with the German 11- and 12-inch batteries, and their ships were several knots faster than their counterparts. It will be recalled that Fisher's view had always been "Speed is armour."

By contrast, German designers had made protection paramount. They had given their ships thicker armor and much greater subdivision into watertight compartments to help keep the ship afloat should the hull be seriously holed by enemy shells or torpedoes. They had designed their ships to be as nearly unsinkable as possible, in accord with the Tirpitz dictum stated earlier. The Germans' emphasis on defensive aspects was natural—they had the smaller fleet and could afford less than the British to lose major units.

There was also the kaiser factor; Wilhelm II looked on the fleet as his own personal collection of warships and couldn't bear the thought of losing any of his precious dreadnoughts. He expected that his army would sweep victoriously through Belgium and France as swiftly as it had done in 1870, and that this would soon force Britain to the peace table, where an intact High Seas Fleet would be a valuable bargaining chip.

Not surprisingly, then, the German naval stance was primarily defensive, whereas the Royal Navy had historically stressed offense and scorned any undue emphasis on protection and defense. Some of the British ships were to display a surprising frailty toward the new underwater weapons, especially mines. Ship for ship there is no doubt that the German warships were more sturdy, but because they were heavily outgunned, they needed to be. Their battle cruisers in particular were well designed and capable of standing up to all but the most modern superdreadnoughts.

Comparing personnel, the Royal Navy was better off in terms of admirals—at least at the outset. Although Churchill was to complain of a "frightful dearth of first class men in the Vice Admirals and Rear Admirals lists," there were some notable exceptions, besides Beatty. Bayly, Hood, Sturdee, and Evan-Thomas were all highly capable squadron commanders; although they were not without faults, they were certainly better than Ingenohl and Pohl. The only outstanding German fleet commander was Hipper, who commanded their scouting groups (SGs) of cruisers and battle cruisers. The able and aggressive Scheer was not to play a major role until 1916, the year of Jutland.

As Churchill complained later, at the start of the war, "We had more captains of ships than captains of war." He meant that they were highly competent ship commanders, but they were insufficiently aware of strategy and tactics. This may have been true in general, but there were some excellent younger officers, among them rising stars such as Chatfield, Pound, Brock, and Kelly. The Germans were to show that they had captains of similar caliber in Hartog, Levetzow, Zenker, and Egidy.

The real strength of the Royal Navy lay in its petty officers and men. They were well trained, knowledgeable, experienced professionals. Most of the men were long-service ratings who had volunteered for an initial twelve-year term, usually followed by a further ten years' service. The German sailors were no less well trained, and they soon proved their discipline and courage under fire in a way that often amazed the British. Steadiness under fire was taken for granted in the Royal Navy. But the German sailors did not have the same seagoing experience as the men of the Royal Navy. They were mainly three-year conscripts who spent most of their time ashore in barracks and only went aboard ship before exercises or actual operations. This was true of their officers as well, who in many cases lived ashore with their families.

German warships had not been constructed to accommodate their crews over long stretches, and despite the imposing name of their fleet, they were not designed to ply the high seas. The North Sea was their "High Sea." As members of a "barracks navy," the crews were less familiar with their ships and less attached to them. The British had responsibilities that took them all over world, and the qualities of their men and ships reflected this.

The officers and men of the Royal Navy had one priceless advantage— an ingrained feeling of confidence and superiority. Victory was assured; defeat was unthinkable. This feeling was born of an experience of the sea going back hundreds of years, which the Germans lacked. Theirs was a young navy, completely untried at sea, and there is no doubt that they felt a deep sense of inferiority toward their rivals in the Royal Navy. In spite of their frequent toasts to *Der Tag*, they were not really so anxious for that day to come. Scheer wrote that they were up against a fleet that "had the advantage of looking back over a hundred years of proud tradition which must have given every man a sense of superiority based on the proud deeds of the past."

It must be emphasized though, that in the beginning neither side had any firsthand experience of a modern sea battle. They were equally ignorant of the awful effects of the new weapons—long-range guns, submarines, torpedoes, and mines—and the complexities they would impose on a twentieth-century fleet action. The two sides entered the war with feelings of uncertainty about how they and their ships would perform in this new era of naval warfare.

The problems facing the two commanders in chief were quite different. Jellicoe had to determine how to entice the High Seas Fleet to come out of its well-defended bases and fight without jeopardizing his complete command of the sea. There was no absolute need for a decisive naval victory, even though the country fully expected one. Jellicoe knew that a second Trafalgar would not necessarily win the war, but a major defeat might very well lose it. Churchill's famous remark that Jellicoe was "the only man on either side who . . . could lose the war in an afternoon" may have been a bit of an exaggeration, but the consequences of a major defeat would be calamitous. If the Germans were able to seize control of the world's sea lanes, it would not be long before they brought Britain and her Allies to their knees.

Ingenohl's problem was how to whittle down Jellicoe's strength without incurring heavy losses, which would be devastating for his smaller fleet. A defeat at sea is potentially much more serious than a defeat on land. A beaten army can always fall back and regroup, taking advantage of what the terrain offers while it waits for reinforcements to arrive. It is relatively easy to call up more men to replace its losses. But in a sea battle there are no defensive positions to fall back on, and if a fleet suffers a heavy loss of ships, it takes years to replace them.

Despite its clear superiority in numbers and overall command of the sea, the first months of the war were not a happy time for the Royal Navy, at home or abroad. A series of setbacks shook the confidence and morale of its senior officers. The feelings of despondency reached as far as the normally ebullient Winston Churchill. But amid the gloom there were one or two bright spots, especially when the British battle cruisers played the role they were really designed for.

The first night of the war, the steamer *Königin Luise,* which had been converted into a minelayer, penetrated the British defensive patrols and laid mines indiscriminately between the Thames and the Dutch coast. The mines were a danger to all merchant ships, Allied or neutral, and without giving any warning to shipping, the German action was contrary to international law. It was the first indication of the ruthless way they intended to conduct the war at sea. Destroyers from Harwich spotted the *Königin Luise* the next morning and sank her after a short chase. Her first victim was not a merchant ship, but the flotilla leader HMS *Amphion.* On

6 August the brand-new light cruiser hit one of the *Königin Luise*'s mines off the Suffolk coast. Shortly afterward another mine shattered her hull, and she sank almost immediately, with heavy loss of life.

A few days later a far more serious setback took place in the Mediterranean. This had been set in motion even before the formal declaration of war and was to have a far-reaching and grave impact on the entire Allied war effort. Some of the lapses that led to this incident would be repeated at Jutland.

At the beginning of August, the new battle cruiser *Goeben* was cruising in the Mediterranean, in company with the light cruiser *Breslau*. This compact but far from insignicant squadron was commanded by the wily Adm. Wilhelm Souchon. His intentions were unknown to the British: Would he concentrate on attacking French troop convoys from North Africa or would he try to join up with the Austrian fleet in the Adriatic? In fact, he had received tentative instructions from the Admiralstab to head for Constantinople. As a counter to Souchon's squadron, the Royal Navy had stationed three of its older battle cruisers in the Mediterranean, under the command of Adm. Sir Berkeley Milne in HMS *Inflexible*. Milne also had four armored cruisers, led by his second in command, Rear-Adm. Ernest Troubridge, in HMS *Defence*. This was an overwhelming force compared with Souchon's two ships.

On the morning of 4 August one of Milne's battle cruisers, the *Indomitable,* sighted the *Goeben* and *Breslau* off the Tunisian coast. In spite of the fact that the Germans had just finished bombarding French ports in Algeria, there was nothing the British commander could do but shadow the German ships. France was already at war, but the British ultimatum did not expire until 11:00 P.M. that night. Throughout the day the Germans' superior speed allowed them to pull farther and farther ahead, until they vanished into the darkness long before the Admiralty signal to "commence hostilities" came into effect.

During the next few days the *Goeben*'s eastward trail was picked up by the light cruisers *Gloucester* and *Dublin* off the coast of Greece. By the evening of 6 August Troubridge was south of Corfu with his armored cruisers and learned that if he kept on, he would be in a position to intercept Souchon at daylight next morning. But Troubridge had been ordered by the Admiralty that he was not to "get seriously engaged with a superior force." Confusingly, he had also been told by Milne to prevent the Germans from entering the Adriatic to join up with the Austrian fleet. On the advice of his flag captain, Fawcet Wray, who told him that an attack on the *Goeben* would be suicidal, Troubridge decided that a battle cruiser was indeed a superior force to four armored cruisers. Troubridge broke off the chase and headed for the mouth of the Adriatic.

It proved to be the worst decision of his life, and it involved much more than the escape of two enemy warships.

On 10 August the *Goeben* and *Breslau* entered the Dardanelles, and although the battle cruiser struck three Turkish mines on the way, the two ships reached Constantinople safely the following day. Souchon's action set off a chain of events that brought Turkey into the war on the German side. The Germans "sold" the *Goeben* and *Breslau* to the Turkish navy as a replacement for the two dreadnoughts commandeered by the Admiralty—an action which had naturally angered the Turks and made them even less sympathetic to the Allied cause.

The Court of Inquiry laid most of the blame for the fiasco at Troubridge's door. They declared his conduct "deplorable and contrary to the tradition of the British Navy" and found that he "had a very fair chance of at least delaying the *Goeben* by materially damaging her." He was court-martialed. Because a charge of cowardice was rejected as too difficult to prove, the charge read that he did, "through negligence or through other default, forbear to pursue the chase of His Imperial Majesty's Ship *Goeben,* being an enemy then flying." He was honorably acquitted, however, because of the confusion between the Admiralty instruction "not to get seriously engaged with superior force" and Milne's order to guard the entrance to the Adriatic.

In spite of Troubridge's timidity, and his poor judgment in being so easily swayed by his flag captain, it was a just verdict. He was only one culprit, and the most junior at that. The others were Milne, for his inept handling of the forces at his disposal, and the Admiralty—including Churchill—for issuing ambiguous and confusing orders by W/T from thousands of miles away instead of leaving decisions to their men on the spot. This would not be the last time they were guilty of this practice.

Nonetheless, Troubridge's career was wrecked. He was never given another sea command. Milne was denied the appointment as C-in-C of the Nore that he had fully expected, and Fawcet Wray was ostracized throughout the fleet. The Admiralty staff came through unscathed, apart from the criticism implicit in the acquittal verdict. They refused to accept any responsibility for mistakes that had been made, as they were to do again after Jutland.

Within the navy, the reaction to the debacle was predictable. Beatty wrote to his wife, "To think that it was the Navy that provided the first instance of failure. God it makes me sick." Fisher was even more furious: "Personally I should have shot Sir Berkeley Milne."

The end of August brought better tidings. The war was nearly a month old, and the Royal Navy had yet to come to grips with the enemy. The

Germans were beginning to crow that the British were afraid to come out of their harbors. Tyrwhitt and Keyes were becoming increasingly frustrated by the lack of action, particularly Keyes. He submitted a bold proposal to the Admiralty to harass the Germans on their own doorstep by raiding German destroyer patrols off the island fortress of Heligoland, barely thirty miles from the mouth of the Jade River, where Ingenohl's dreadnoughts were anchored. The British knew that the Germans made daily patrols to deter enemy mine-laying or submarine operations in the Heligoland Bight.

Keyes proposed that Tyrwhitt's two light cruisers, the *Arethusa* and *Fearless,* and thirty-five destroyers make a high-speed dash from Harwich during the night to intercept the German patrols at dawn. The Germans would be sure to send out bigger ships in support of their destroyers, and Tyrwhitt would lead them into into a trap set by Keyes with eight of his submarines, lying in wait to the north of Heligoland. Tyrwhitt was enthusiastic about Keyes's plan, and on 24 August, Battenberg and Churchill approved it. To the First Lord it was a welcome demonstration of the offensive spirit. The raid was scheduled for the morning of the twenty-eighth.

When Jellicoe heard about it, he wanted to send the whole of the Grand Fleet in support, in case the German battle fleet came out and overwhelmed the British light forces, but the Admiralty said no; he could send some of his battle cruisers "if convenient," but that was all. Beatty urged his C-in-C to let him go, and Jellicoe ordered him to take the 1st and 2d Battle Cruiser Squadrons—five ships altogether. Beatty also took Goodenough's 1st Light Cruiser Squadron (LCS) as an advanced screen.

The plan was flawed from the start. Jellicoe didn't inform the Admiralty of his decision to send Beatty until the twenty-seventh, by which time the battle cruisers were already at sea, on their way to Heligoland. This information arrived at the Admiralty at the last minute, and the news never reached Tyrwhitt or Keyes. There was still plenty of time for the Admiralty to let them know that Beatty and Goodenough were going to take part in the operation, but the signal arrived at Harwich after Keyes and Tyrwhitt had put to sea. There was a crucial staff error. Instead of the message being forwarded to the two commodores by W/T, it lay in somebody's in tray until they returned to base after the operation was over. Equally seriously, the Admiralty did not see fit to inform Beatty that Keyes's submarines were taking part in the raid. There was a real danger that the various British units might attack each other in the belief that they were the enemy, especially if there was poor visibility, a not unlikely state of affairs in the typically misty North Sea.

Not surprisingly, the poor communications and lack of coordination gave rise to a thoroughly confused engagement on the morning of 28 August. The commanders were often uncertain who was firing at them, friend or enemy. By chance, Tyrwhitt's forces sighted Goodenough's squadron north of Heligoland just after dawn. Luckily, they recognized each other in time, so that one danger was averted. At 7:00 A.M., in misty conditions, Tyrwhitt spotted two German torpedo boats chasing after one of Keyes's submarines and opened fire. The German ships headed for safety in the haze. As Tyrwhitt pursued them, it brought his flagship, HMS *Arethusa*, within range of the German flotilla leaders *Stettin* and *Frauenlob*, which had come up in support and headed toward the sound of the guns. The two German light cruisers engaged the *Arethusa* and *Fearless* with accurate fire, and in a running battle they scored ten hits on the *Arethusa*, one of them in the engine room. Fortunately, one of her 6-inch guns made a direct hit on the bridge of the *Frauenlob*, and another shell knocked out the *Stettin*'s wireless. The Germans broke off the action and retired behind the shelter of the fortress to make repairs.

Tyrwhitt, who by now was getting too close to Heligoland for comfort, continued his eastward sweep with his destroyer flotillas (DFs) to search for other German patrols. He didn't know that the Germans had responded to the first reports of the raid by sending out every available light cruiser, and that the *Cöln, Strassburg, Ariadne, Danzig, Stralsund,* and *Kolberg* were all heading toward him. Instead of leading the Germans into a trap, Tyrwhitt was about to run into a "hornets' nest" himself.

At 11:00 A.M. the *Strassburg* appeared and opened fire on the *Arethusa*. Ten minutes later she was joined by the *Cöln*, flagship of Rear Adm. Leberecht Maass. In less than half an hour Tyrwhitt's flagship was nearly crippled. One by one her guns were put out of action, until she had only a single 6-inch gun still firing. Three of his destroyers were also battered. The *Fearless* and her destroyers managed to drive off some of the attackers, but Tyrwhitt's whole force was in a perilous position.

At this point, Beatty was marking time forty miles to the northwest of Heligoland. Although he hadn't received any clear reports of the action, he sensed that things were not going according to plan, and he ordered Goodenough to take his light cruisers to support Tyrwhitt. This was a timely decision, but there was a series of dangerous mixups resulting from the naval staff's poor communications. One of Keyes's submarines had already launched a torpedo attack on Beatty's battle cruisers. The torpedoes happily missed their target, and Keyes was then informed of Beatty's presence by W/T. But he still didn't know that Goodenough's light cruisers were also part of Beatty's force. When Keyes's flagship, the destroyer *Lurcher*, sighted Goodenough's cruisers, he reported them

to Tyrwhitt as enemy ships. As the *Lowestoft* and *Nottingham* approached
to give him support, Tyrwhitt, who by now knew that the 1st Light Cruiser
Squadron was taking part in the raid, signaled Goodenough to chase off
the newcomers—in effect asking his ships to chase themselves. Fortunately, Keyes identified Goodenough's flagship, the *Southampton,* but
only after one of his submarines had launched an unsuccessful attack
on her. Before any real damage was done an exchange of signals had
cleared up the confusion.

Meanwhile, three more German cruisers had showed up to threaten
Tyrwhitt's heavily engaged force, which had now been in more or less
continuous action for four hours. The newcomers were the *Stralsund,
Danzig,* and *Ariadne.* They were joined by the freshly repaired *Stettin.* Tyrwhitt was now in an extremely critical situation. His flagship was practically crippled, and if help did not arrive very soon his whole force was
likely to be overwhelmed and, probably, annihilated. An hour earlier he
had sent out several distress signals by W/T explaining his predicament.
Beatty heard these cries for help—the first clear news he had received
of the progress of the battle—and in his words, "At 11.30 I decided that
the only course possible was to take the BCS at full speed to the eastwards.
To be of any value the support must be overwhelming, and I did not
deem the 1st LCS to be strong enough. I had not lost sight of the danger to my squadron from U-boats, mines, our own submarines, and the
possible sortie of a large enemy force."

Before reaching this decision, Beatty had asked Ernle Chatfield, his
flag captain, "Am I justified in going into that hornets' nest with these
great ships? If I lose one it will be a great blow to the country." Chatfield's advice was quite unlike that which Fawcet Wray had given
Troubridge a few weeks earlier. He replied, "Surely we must go." That
was enough for Beatty.

It was a bold move. Beatty's strike would take him to within thirty
miles of a heavily armed German fortress, and a not much greater distance from the main German fleet base. If the High Seas Fleet came out
quickly, he would, even apart from mines and torpedoes, be in grave
danger. It was a calculated risk, and Beatty courageously took it.

As the five British battle cruisers, led by Beatty in the *Lion,* were racing to Tyrwhitt's rescue at twenty-eight knots, three of Goodenough's ships
were pursuing yet another German cruiser. She was the *Mainz.* Goodenough soon overtook her, and when the fourth member of his squadron
showed up with six destroyers, she was cut off and surrounded. Each of
the British cruisers was more heavily armed than the unfortunate *Mainz,*
and after she had been hit several times, her fate was sealed when her rudder jammed and her port engine stopped. All she could do was circle

helplessly as she was hit time after time by 6-inch shells. Inside of half an hour, they had silenced most of her guns and killed or wounded their crews, but the Germans refused to surrender. A British officer wrote, "The *Mainz* was immensely gallant. The last I saw of her she was absolutely wrecked, her whole midships a fuming inferno. She had one gun forward and one aft still spitting fury and defiance, like a cat mad with wounds."

Then the *Mainz* was hit by a torpedo from the destroyer *Lydiard,* and her captain gave the order: "Abandon ship." Goodenough signaled his ships to cease firing and sent the destroyer *Lurcher* over to pick up survivors. She went alongside the sinking cruiser and managed to save more than three hundred of the crew, who were taken prisoner. The *Lurcher* hailed two young officers who were standing stiffly to attention on the deck of the sinking ship and asked them to leap across to the British destroyer. "Thank you. No," one of them replied. Shortly afterward, the *Mainz* rolled over and sank.

During the final agony of the *Mainz,* Beatty's battle cruisers arrived on the scene just in time to save Tyrwhitt's embattled force. One of his destroyer officers wrote, "There straight ahead of us in lovely procession, like elephants walking through a herd of 'pi-dogs,' came our battlecruisers. How solid they looked, how utterly earth-quaking! . . . They passed down the field of battle . . . and a little later we heard the thunder of their guns."

Their first victim was the *Cöln.* The German admiral's flagship and the *Strassburg* had been engaging the *Fearless,* but as soon as they saw Beatty's battle cruisers, they broke off action and quickly headed for the protection of the mist. The *Strassburg* made it to safety, but the *Cöln* was doomed. The *Lion* rapidly overhauled the light cruiser, and with a few salvos from her 13.5-inch guns, reduced the German ship to a blazing wreck. The *Cöln* enjoyed a brief respite and managed to limp away when another victim, the little *Ariadne,* stumbled onto the scene. Launched in 1901, the old cruiser was far too slow to escape her nemesis. Although she zigzagged desperately to alter the range, the *Lion* needed only ten minutes to reduce the *Ariadne* to a "a mass of flames." She was listing heavily and obviously in a sinking condition, so Beatty left her to her fate. Amazingly, she stayed afloat for another three hours.

Beatty decided that his work was done. He had saved Tyrwhitt's force from destruction and scattered the German ships. It didn't seem worth running any further risks to chase after their cruisers in the mist. For all he knew, major German units might be on their way from Wilhelmshaven. His forces were deep inside enemy waters, with at least eight hours steaming ahead of them before they reached the safety of the British coast. Beatty therefore gave the general signal: "Retire."

As he turned back, he made for the spot where he had left the crippled *Cöln*. When she came in view through the mist, she was limping along very slowly. Her colors were still flying, and Beatty had no choice but to finish her off. After she was hit by two salvos, she suddenly capsized and sank. Beatty sent four destroyers to search for survivors, but all they could find was one stoker. Admiral Maass and 380 of his men had gone down with his flagship.

The British forces reached their bases without mishap. The battle-scarred *Arethusa* was towed into Chatham for repairs. Tyrwhitt commented, "We had a great reception all the way from the Nore to Chatham. Every ship and everybody cheered like mad. Winston met us at Sheerness and came up to Chatham with us and fairly slobbered over me."

The Royal Navy had clearly won the Battle of Heligoland Bight. Tyrwhitt and Beatty were hailed as heroes—especially Beatty. His difficult decision and bold intervention had turned what might have been a catastrophe into a decisive victory.

German losses had been serious—three light cruisers and a destroyer sunk, and three more cruisers damaged. Their crews had sustained heavy casualties, with nearly twelve hundred killed, wounded, or taken prisoner. Among the dead were the cruiser admiral and the destroyer commodore; one of those fished out of the water and taken prisoner was Wolf Tirpitz, son of the *Grossadmiral*. As soon as Churchill learned this, he wired Tirpitz to assure him of his son's safety.

By contrast, the Royal Navy had lost no ships, and even though a cruiser and three destroyers had been badly damaged, they were soon repaired. British casualties were remarkably light: thirty killed and about forty-five wounded, most of them aboard the *Arethusa*.

Because of the complete lack of coordination between the four British squadrons, and the poor Admiralty communication with its forces, the whole plan had been a recipe for disaster. But due to a combination of good luck, Jellicoe's foresight, Tyrwhitt's dogged courage, and Beatty's boldness it had been turned into a minor triumph. The popular press loved it. "We've gone to Heligoland and back. Please God, We'll go again!" brayed the *Daily Express*. The *New Statesman* took a more sober view: the battle was of "immense moral, if slight material, importance in its effect upon the two fleets." The kaiser and his navy were shocked by the daring penetration of their home waters. The raid put an end to their jibes and reinforced their feelings of inferiority toward the men of the Royal Navy.

The German performance in the battle was no better. They had sent out their cruisers one after the other with no clear plan in mind except to repel any raiders they came across. They also failed to send out any big ships in time to help their light forces or to cut Beatty off and harass his retirement. Ingenohl learned of the raid soon after it began, and as early as 8:00 A.M. he ordered the battle cruisers to get steam up. But they were not ready to sail until noon because Hipper's flagship *Seydlitz* had engine-room problems. By this time the tide was too low to let his ships pass over the sandbars at the mouth of the Jade. They finally arrived at the battle area at about 3:00 P.M., long after Beatty had left. All they could do was help to search for survivors from the ships that had been sunk. Fortunately, the two young lieutenants who had refused to abandon the *Mainz* were both rescued.

Some valuable lessons had been learned on both sides. Jellicoe analyzed the battle reports and made recommendations about the need to issue clearer orders, to report speed and course as well as position, and to repeat all important flag signals by W/T. Whether all these lessons had sunk in was not to be fully revealed until Jutland. The Germans learned one important lesson. It concerned the poor quality of British shells. Many of them were observed to break up on impact instead of penetrating to do vital damage. More of their ships might easily have been sunk if the shells had done what they were supposed to do. The Germans naturally kept this knowledge to themselves.

Tirpitz called the defeat "fateful in its after-effects" because Wilhelm ordered his fleet "to hold itself back and avoid actions which can lead to greater losses." His admirals were told not to go beyond the Bight or the Skaggerak, or to engage an enemy unless they were in clearly superior force. The fatal consequence of this kind of order has already been seen in the *Goeben* fiasco, described earlier. In future, the operations of the High Seas Fleet were to be limited to occasional sorties by Hipper's battle cruisers. The kaiser's restrictive influence explains why so much time was to pass before the Battle of Jutland took place.

The Grand Fleet was also being restricted at this time, for a different reason. There was increasing evidence that German submarines were now able to operate as far from their bases as the northern area of the North Sea. One U-boat had been rammed and sunk by a British cruiser. When a periscope was spotted inside the fleet anchorage on 1 September, it led to what became known as the "First Battle of Scapa Flow." The sighting occurred just before dusk. It had been a misty day and visibility was poor. When a cruiser near the entrance opened fire on the intruder, Jellicoe immediately ordered the fleet to raise steam and put to sea. Then there were other "sightings," and several more ships opened fire on the presumed submarine. After a lot of confused signaling and dashing about by escort vessels, Jellicoe took his twelve battleships safely out to sea and remained there until dawn.

It turned out that the periscope had most likely been a seal. The frequent false sightings of submarines around this time grew to an epidemic of what some cynic dubbed "periscopeitis." A great deal of fuel and effort was wasted chasing imaginary U-boats. As the noted historian Richard Hough commented wryly after describing these incidents, "That seal had a lot to answer for!"

But it was not long before near-farce changed into tragedy. During the night of 21–22 September the armored cruisers *Hogue, Aboukir,* and *Cressy* were patrolling the "Broad Fourteens" off the Dutch coast. These old cruisers, vintage 1900, were known in the fleet as "the live bait" squadron because of their vulnerability. On this particular run, their destroyer escorts had been left behind because of rough seas. At 6:30 A.M. on the twenty-second, the *Aboukir* was struck by a torpedo. There was a violent explosion and the stricken ship began to list heavily. The order was given to abandon ship, but all her boats but one had been smashed by the explosion. The captain of the *Hogue* lowered his boats to help the *Aboukir*'s crew, and in spite of the danger chivalrously stood by to offer assistance. The *Aboukir* capsized and sank, twenty-five minutes after she had been hit. While the captain of the *Hogue* waited for his boats to return with survivors from the *Aboukir,* his own ship was hit by two torpedoes inside of five minutes. Very soon the *Hogue*'s decks were awash, and she too had to be abandoned.

Meanwhile the *Cressy* had also launched her boats and was standing by to pick up survivors. Her lookouts spotted two torpedo tracks, but before they could get under way one of the torpedoes struck the ship. Shortly afterward, another torpedo came from the opposite direction and struck the cruiser amidships. She rolled over and floated upside down for about fifteen minutes before she sank. This was the saddest case of the three. When she was hit, all her lifeboats were away helping her consorts, and the loss of life on board the *Cressy* was particularly heavy. In all, 837 officers and men were saved from the three cruisers, as other ships arrived in response to distress calls, but nearly 1,400 drowned. As the distinguished historian Sir Julian Corbett put it, "One more tragedy was added to the tale of those useless sacrifices which never cease to darken naval memory."

At first the British refused to believe that a single U-boat could have fired all six torpedoes and sunk three twelve-thousand-ton cruisers in less than an hour, but it was true. Korvetten-Kapitän Otto Weddigen of the U-9 had acted alone. He returned to a hero's welcome in Berlin and was awarded the Iron Cross, First Class. His hour of glory was brief. Weddigen was to lose his life in March 1915, when the submarine U-12 was rammed and sunk by HMS *Dreadnought*.

The disaster increased the navy's fears of U-boat attack. It also illustrated starkly how much naval warfare had changed as a result of the new underwater weapons. The loss of the three armored cruisers was not very important because they were obsolete ships, but the loss of the men was something "to be lamented, the more since so much magnificent material perished helplessly by such insignificant means," in Corbett's words.

Jellicoe was gravely concerned about the lack of submarine defenses at Scapa Flow, and on 7 October he decided to move the Grand Fleet temporarily to Loch Ewe on the west coast of Scotland while antisubmarine booms and nets were being installed at Scapa. When a submarine was sighted in Loch Ewe, however, he moved the fleet again, this time to Lough Swilly on the northwest coast of Ireland. At this time, Beatty's battle cruisers were in a temporary anchorage at the island of Mull. These moves left the whole of the British east coast in a dangerously vulnerable position and weakened the northern blockade. The Germans didn't realize that their U-boats had driven the Grand Fleet into the Atlantic. If they had known, Hipper's battle cruisers would have been able to strike anywhere they pleased in the North Sea with complete impunity.

One result of Jellicoe's move to Lough Swilly was that the fast North German liner *Berlin* was able to slip through the weakened blockade, and after passing round the north of Scotland, she sowed mines off the north of Ireland on 22 October. The minefield was aimed at shipping going to and from Liverpool. Through ill luck, the *Berlin*'s first victim was much more valuable than any merchant ship.

When they mined the area, the Germans had no idea that Jellicoe's fleet was at Lough Swilly. On the morning of 27 October, he sent the 2d Battle Squadron out of the lough for gunnery practice. They were steaming in line ahead, about thirty miles off the coast, when the brand new superdreadnought *Audacious* struck one of the mines. There was a dull explosion underneath her keel, and she began to sink by the stern.

Captain Dampier headed slowly for the nearby shore, in the hope that his ship could be beached and later salvaged. The White Star liner *Olympic* arrived on the scene four hours later and offered to tow the crippled battleship to safety. Her crew were taken off by the liner, but the tow line parted. Other ships came up and made repeated efforts to tow the *Audacious,* but by now she had taken on so much water that she became unmanageable. Twelve hours after she struck the mine, and half way to safety, the *Audacious* suddenly blew up and sank. The sinking of the *Audacious* stands in stark contrast to the ability of the *Goeben* to make it to Constantinople under her own steam after striking three mines. The loss of the *Audacious* was serious, and the Admiralty tried to con-

ceal it from the Germans. But because of the tourist box cameras click-
ing away on board the *Olympic,* this proved futile.

A few days after the *Audacious* was mined, Jellicoe wrote to the Admiralty
expressing his concern about the deadly new undersea weapons. He outlined the way he expected the Germans to use them tactically when the
two fleets met: "They rely to a great extent on submarines, mines and torpedoes, and they will endeavour to make the fullest use of these. However, they can not rely on having their full complement of submarines and
minelayers in a fleet action unless the battle is fought in the southern
North Sea. My object will therefore be to fight the fleet action in the northern portion of the North Sea."
He thought the Germans would try to lure him into a trap:

> If the enemy turned away from us, I should assume the intention was
> to lead us over mines and submarines, and decline to be drawn. This
> might result in failure to bring an enemy into action as soon as is expected
> and hoped, but with new and untried methods of warfare, new tactics
> must be devised. These, if not understood, might bring odium upon me,
> but it is quite possible that half our battle fleet might be disabled by
> underwater attack before the guns open fire at all. The safeguard will
> consist in moving to a flank before the action commences. This will
> take us off the ground on which the enemy desires to fight, and may
> result in a refusal to follow me; but if the battle fleets remain in sight
> of one another, I should feel that after an interval of high speed maneu-
> vering, I could safely close.

Jellicoe's cautious approach was approved by the Admiralty Board,
including the offensive-minded Churchill. They assured him of "their
full confidence in your contemplated conduct of the fleet in action." Jellicoe kept firmly in mind at all times that a decisive fleet action was not
to be sought at any cost. The consequences of a defeat were too grave.
He was not going to risk his firm command of the sea, and the blockade
it maintained, simply to seek the glory of a second Trafalgar.
Jellicoe's reluctance to fight anywhere except in the northern part of
the North Sea, coupled with the kaiser's unwillingness to let his battleships go very far beyond Heligoland, meant that the likelihood of an imminent clash between the Grand Fleet and the High Seas Fleet was virtually
non-existent. It would take an unusual combination of circumstances to
alter this situation.

At home, feelings of disillusion with the Royal Navy had set in, stretching from the man in the street all the way up to King George V. Prime

Minister Asquith had informed the king that the cabinet considered the list of setbacks suffered so far was not "creditable to the officers of the Navy." Even the normally buoyant Churchill was in low spirits. Public expectations of a quick and decisive victory over the German fleet had not been realized, and the people were deeply disappointed by the lack of achievement of a navy which had always filled them with pride and confidence. The disillusion was all the greater because they had paid for its expensive fleet at such great cost to their social benefits. They compared its minor successes with the heroic achievements of the British Expeditionary Force during the bloody battles in northern France, this "contemptible little army" that had put an end to German dreams of a quick victory on land.

The press wanted to know: What was navy doing? Not much apparently, except for dealing with enemy light forces in the Heligoland Bight. It had sunk a few small ships but had not managed to engage any major German forces, not even the *Goeben* when it had the chance. Yet it was continually losing men and ships to mines and torpedoes. The effect of the relentless and silent pressure of the blockade on the German war machine was not the stuff of which newspaper headlines are made, alas.

The news from overseas was no better. The raider *Emden* was loose in the Indian Ocean, paralyzing merchant shipping and holding up troop convoys. The navy had also lost track of Vice Adm. Graf von Spee's dangerous East Asiatic Squadron somewhere in the vastness of the Pacific. Worse news was to come. The Admiralty had sent out an ill-assorted collection of mainly older warships under the command of Rear-Adm. Sir Christopher Cradock to search for Graf Spee. Cradock had been assigned the task of preventing Spee's squadron from threatening the vital South American trade routes. Cradock's ships may have looked adequate for the job on paper, at least to Churchill and his staff far away in the War Room, but Cradock was under no illusions about his chances against the crack German squadron. When Graf Spee and Cradock met off the Chilean port of Coronel on 1 November, the brave but headstrong Cradock did not hesitate to engage the enemy with his outgunned squadron.

It was no contest. With their opening salvos, the accurate gunners of Spee's armored cruisers crippled Cradock's flagship, HMS *Good Hope,* and his other armored cruiser, the *Monmouth.* Both of them were finished off in less than two hours and went down with all hands—sixteen hundred officers and men altogether, including Cradock. The other two cruisers of Cradock's ill-fated squadron were forced to flee for their lives. Their humiliation was intense. An officer on one of these ships wrote, "We hardly spoke to one another for the first twenty-four hours. We felt so

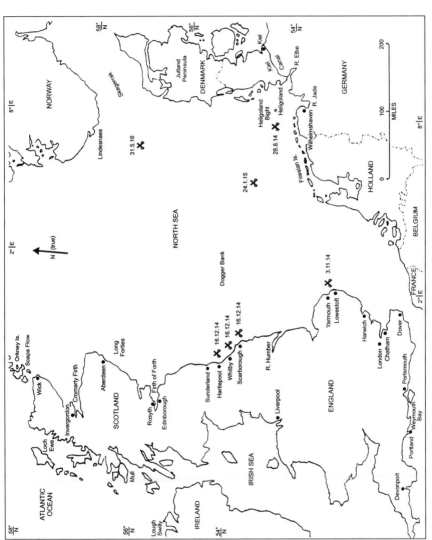

North Sea naval actions, 1914–18

bitterly ashamed of ourselves for we had let down the King. We had let down the Admiralty, we had let down England."

Coronel came as a devastating shock to the navy. This was its first defeat at sea in over a century, and as the elated Germans put it, Coronel had "shattered the myth of British naval invincibility once and for all."

One outcome of Coronel was that it brought Fisher back to the Admiralty. Battenberg had been hounded out of office by the gutter press because of his German ancestry and family connections. With scant justice, they held him to be largely responsible for the navy's poor performance to date, and on the verge of a nervous breakdown, he resigned. Churchill secured Fisher's reappointment as First Sea Lord, over the objections of both King George V and the cabinet, by threatening to resign. Back in office, Fisher wasted no time in sending Vice-Adm. Sir Doveton Sturdee to the South Atlantic with two battle cruisers to track down Spee's squadron.

Two days after the tragic news from Coronel, the Germans made their first attack on the British coast—the so-called Gorleston raid. Several German torpedo boats had recently been sunk while on a mine-laying mission off the Dutch coast, and Ingenohl begged the kaiser to be allowed to retaliate. Given the imperial approval, he sent Hipper with five battle cruisers and four other cruisers on a lightning dash across the North Sea under cover of darkness. At dawn on 3 November, the battle cruisers opened fire on the undefended seaside towns of Gorleston and Yarmouth. Most of the the shells landed on the beach. After an hour's bombardment, the Germans turned for home. The raid caused little damage and no casualties. It had been intended as a diversion to cover mine-laying operations by Hipper's light cruisers.

On news of the raid, Tyrwhitt brought out his destroyer flotillas, hoping to harass the Germans' retirement, and Beatty came thundering down from Cromarty with his battle cruisers to try to intercept Hipper before he reached Heligoland, but they were both too late.

In December 1914 the Admiralty obtained an invaluable asset—the ability to decipher the coded wireless messages the Germans sent to their ships. One of the most significant but little known events of the war had occurred at the end of August, when the German cruiser *Magdeburg* ran aground on an island in the Gulf of Finland. Helpless, she was destroyed by gunfire from the Russian cruisers *Pallada* and *Bogatyr*. Among the wreckage the Russians discovered an intact copy of the German naval code book. The Russian admiralty sent its ally "these sea-stained priceless documents," as Churchill described them, but they didn't reach London until the end of October. Another amazing stroke of luck provided the Admiralty with the secret operational grid of the North Sea that was used by the Germans to identify the position of its own as well as enemy warships. This chart had been thrown overboard by the crew of a sinking German destroyer and was discovered in the net of a British trawler.

The Admiralty established a secret unit to capitalize on this intelligence bonanza. It was located in an out-of-the-way section of the old building of the Admiralty, and to the few who knew anything of its existence or function, the organization was referred to as Room 40 OB, or simply Room 40. It was headed by Sir Alfred Ewing, an electronics expert and former director of naval education. Ewing's men set to work to decipher German wireless messages. The Germans made unrestricted use of W/T, and Room 40 was soon able to pass valuable information about German plans and ship movements to the Operations Division, and hence to the C-in-C, Grand Fleet. Security was extremely tight. To avoid raising questions about their origin, all messages intercepted and decoded by Room 40 were referred to as "Japanese telegrams."

The head of Naval Intelligence, Capt. William "Blinker" Hall, cooperated closely with Ewing. He set up a chain of direction-finding stations on the east coast of Britain to monitor the extensive German radio traffic. These stations took multiple bearings of any ship sending wireless signals, which enabled them to pinpoint its location with great accuracy. Such data, combined with information from the German operational grid and the decoded signals, enabled the British to obtain advance warning of enemy activities in the North Sea throughout the war.

It soon became evident to the Germans that the Royal Navy was somehow acquiring foreknowledge of their movements. They were eventually forced to accept the unpalatable conclusion that their naval codes must have been compromised. They tried to counter this by frequently changing the ciphers and keys to their code books, but the brilliant cryptographers of Room 40 were able to overcome these problems. In frustration, the Germans were obliged to introduce a whole new signal book, but by this time Room 40 had gained so much experience at analyzing wavelengths, signal duration, and sender's location that it slowly built up a new signal book of its own. This was not perfect, but Room 40 was able to decipher German signals sufficiently well to send a steady flow of vital intelligence to the Operations Division. Two more windfalls, one from a sunken U-boat and the other from a downed Zeppelin, later provided the cryptographers with new signal books, so that they continued to forewarn the Admiralty of every naval operation being planned by the Germans.

The work of Room 40 has been described as Britain's "principal war-winning weapon," but it was occasionally blunted by the poor rapport between the mostly civilian staff of Ewing's department and the naval staff of the Operations Department. The staff officers firmly believed that the role of the "boffins" in Room 40 was simply to decode the messages, and theirs was to interpret and evaluate them. Consequently, the intelligence provided by Room 40 was not always fully exploited by the Admiralty. There were to be some critical breakdowns in its communication with the fleet. At Jutland, the Admiralty failed to inform Jellicoe of vital clues to the Germans' probable movements.

In the meantime, Sturdee had reached the Falkand Islands with his battle cruisers, along with five other cruisers that had joined his forces on the long voyage south. He stopped to coal at Port Stanley on 9 December, planning to go on and search for Graf Spee in the Pacific. Before the search had even begun, chance intervened.

The following morning, when Sturdee's ships were in the midst of coaling, the German squadron arrived off the islands. Spee had rounded the Horn, intending to head home to Germany. He had stopped off at the Falklands to destroy the Port Stanley coaling base and sink any ships he found there. He had been assured by German intelligence in Punta Arenas that he would find nothing more than merchant ships and possibly a few cruisers. As they approached the harbor entrance, the Germans were appalled to see the tripod masts of battle cruisers. Spee immediately gave the order to turn away and head south, not realizing how vulnerable the enemy was with his ships tied up alongside their colliers.

By the time Sturdee's ships had steam up, the Germans had a twenty-mile head start. But they knew it was only a matter of a few hours before the speedy battle cruisers caught up with them. The weather was clear, and Sturdee had plenty of time before nightfall to get the enemy in the sights of his 12-inch guns. The chase continued throughout the afternoon, with the stokers on both sides working like trojans to squeeze every extra knot out of their engines. The Germans prayed for the foggy conditions typical of the area, but it stayed clear. The end was inevitable. After a gallant rearguard action by Spee with his 8.2-inch guns, the battle cruisers sank his flagship *Scharnhorst* with all hands, then his second armored cruiser, the *Gneisenau,* had to be scuttled. The Germans had refused to strike their colors, even though their position was hopeless. In separate actions, the other British cruisers caught and sank the *Leipzig* and the *Nürnberg.* Altogether, the Germans lost more than two thousand men, among them Graf Spee and his two lieutenant sons, Otto and Heinrich. The fast cruiser *Dresden* was the sole member of Spee's squadron to escape, only to be caught by British cruisers in the Pacific a few months later, after she had run out of coal. Facing certain destruction, her captain scuttled her.

The victory at the Falkands was a tremendous and timely tonic for the Royal Navy. The annihilation of Graf Spee's famous squadron had avenged Cradock and restored British naval prestige. Morale was high; Churchill was jubilant and Fisher was absolutely elated—his beloved battle cruisers had been vindicated once again.

A few days after the good news from the South Atlantic, the work of Room 40 began to pay off. On the evening of 14 December it informed the Naval Intelligence Division that the Germans were planning a sortie with their battle cruisers. They had learned that Hipper had been ordered to leave the Jade on the morning of the fifteenth with his five big ships, accompanied by light cruisers and destroyers, and that he was to return to base on the evening of the sixteenth. This information was invaluable, but like many intelligence reports, it was incomplete. The intercepted signals had given no clue as to where the Germans intended to attack, or whether Ingenohl's battle squadrons would be supporting the operation. Naval Intelligence deduced that the Germans were planning another hit-and-run raid somewhere on the east coast on 16 December, probably timed for dawn, like the one on 3 November.

The Admiralty staff immediately set up plans for a counterattack. Because the precise location of the raid was unknown, they couldn't prevent it from taking place, but they hoped to cut off the Germans' return to base, wherever they attacked. They ordered Jellicoe to send Beatty out with four battle cruisers, and Vice-Adm. Sir George Warrender with the 2d Battle Squadron of six superdreadnoughts, to set a trap for Hipper. This force was more than sufficient to deal with five German battle cruisers, but Jellicoe also ordered out Rear-Adm. Sir William Pakenham's 3d Cruiser Squadron and Goodenough's 1st Light Cruiser Squadron in support. In addition, Tyrwhitt was to told to stand by with the Harwich light forces and Keyes was ordered to lie in wait off the Dutch coast near Terschelling with eight submarines, ready to pick off any German ships that went south to evade the trap.

As senior vice-admiral, Warrender was in command of all the seagoing forces, but Jellicoe remained in overall command of the operation. Once again he wanted to bring out the whole of the Grand Fleet, to support Warrender in case the German battle fleet came out, but once more the Admiralty said no. They did not believe Ingenohl would leave the Jade. Jellicoe ordered Beatty and Warrender to rendezvous with the other forces off the southwest corner of the Dogger Bank on the morning of the sixteenth. The location he chose was ideal for them to be in position to intercept Hipper, wherever he attacked. As soon as reports of the raid came in, they would head toward the unsuspecting Hipper's route back to Wilhemshaven and cut him off.

But Ingenohl was laying a trap of his own. He planned to take advantage of the known absence of three of Beatty's battle cruisers in the South Atlantic and Caribbean. Unknown to Room 40, he was going to put to sea with the whole of his battle fleet and stay well astern of Hipper's squadron. He knew that the attack on the British coast would provoke an immediate response from the Royal Navy, and he judged, correctly, that they would only send out part of their battle fleet— enough to deal with Hipper's battle cruisers but not to take on the full might of the High Seas Fleet. His plan was for the fleeing Hipper to lure this inferior enemy force into the jaws of his battle squadrons before it realized the danger. If Ingenohl could smash the squadrons led by Beatty and Warrender, he would at one stroke realize Germany's dream of achieving parity with the Grand Fleet.

In the early morning of the sixteenth, the two British admirals had joined forces and were steaming toward the rendezvous, which they were supposed to reach by 7:30 A.M. But well before dawn, Warrender's destroyer screen sighted several German torpedo boats south of the Dogger Bank and opened fire on them. Shortly afterward, several German light cruisers showed up, and soon the British flotillas were heavily engaged in a confused close-range action. In fact, Warrender had run into the advanced screen of the High Seas Fleet. Fortunately for Warrender, Ingenohl turned away when he heard reports of the skirmish. It was still over two hours to daybreak, and he was mortally afraid of a massed destroyer attack in the dark. He was also worried that the presence of the destroyer flotillas might mean that the Grand Fleet was out. He had brought his battle fleet farther than he should have without the approval of the High Command, and he was fearful of incurring the kaiser's wrath if he were to suffer serious losses from enemy torpedoes. Ingenohl decided to turn tail and head for home at full speed. He signaled Hipper to go ahead with the raid, but didn't bother to inform him that he was now on his own.

When Beatty heard about the destroyer action, he made for Warrender's position at full speed. The two admirals followed the retiring German cruisers and destroyers, unaware that they were chasing after the whole of the enemy battle fleet. If Ingenohl had realized this, all he had to do was reverse course and within a quarter of an hour he would have had four British battle cruisers and six superdreadnoughts at the mercy of his twenty-two battleships. The loss of these valuable ships would have altered the course of the war.

Luckily for Beatty and Warrender, they received wireless reports shortly after daylight that Hipper's battle cruisers were shelling the Yorkshire coast. When these reports were confirmed by the Admiralty, they broke off their dangerous pursuit and headed westward to intercept the raiders.

At about 8:00 A.M., the *Derfflinger* and *Von der Tann* had begun shelling the undefended seaside resort of Scarborough. During a thirty-minute bombardment, they damaged many buildings in the town and caused forty-five civilian casualties. Then they headed north to attack the equally defenseless fishing port of Whitby. After a ten-minute bombardment which resulted in little damage and only two casualties, they continued northward to join up with Hipper. The other three battle cruisers, Hipper's flagship *Seydlitz* and the *Moltke* and *Blücher*, had been shelling the port of Hartlepool since 8:15 A.M. The bombardment caused tremendous damage in both the port area and the town itself. The port's only defenses were three 6-inch guns, scarcely an answer to Hipper's 11-inch weapons. Civilian casualties in the town were heavy—86 men, women, and children killed and 424 wounded.

Shortly before 9:00 A.M., Hipper ceased firing and turned eastward to link up with his other two ships. He gave the order to head back to base. He had three possible lines of retreat through the extensive German minefields off the mouths of the Tyne and Humber. The British knew this and were moving to seal them off. Warrender was covering the southern escape route with his six battleships. Jellicoe had sent the 3d Battle Squadron down from Rosyth, under the command of Vice-Adm. Sir Edward Bradford, and he was guarding the northern route. This left Beatty and his battle cruisers to block the central gap between the minefields. This was the path Hipper chose, because it was his most direct route to Wilhelmshaven. He had no reason to suspect he was in any danger, because Ingenohl had not informed him that he had been in action with British advanced forces off the Dogger Bank more than four hours earlier.

The Admiralty were confident that Hipper was trapped whichever route he took. Churchill and his staff in the Admiralty were on tenterhooks as they waited impatiently for fresh news. As he wrote, "Subject to moderate visibility we hoped that a collision would take place about noon. To have this tremendous prize—the German battlecruiser squadron whose loss would fatally mutilate the whole German Navy and could never be repaired—actually within our claws." At about this time, the two battle cruiser squadrons were about fifty miles apart, and a clash seemed inevitable.

Around 11:30 A.M., the weather began to change for the worse, with mist and rain squalls that limited visibility to a few miles. Goodenough's flagship HMS *Southampton,* which was on the port wing of Beatty's screen, sighted a German light cruiser and several destroyers coming out of the mist. He immediately opened fire and signaled his other three cruisers to close him. In a few minutes, the *Southampton* and the *Birmingham* were heavily engaging the German ships and driving them southward. The *Nottingham* and *Lowestoft* were speeding south to join him.

At this point, Beatty's staff made a disastrous signaling error. Believing that Hipper's squadron was immediately ahead of him, Beatty flashed a message to the *Nottingham* and *Lowestoft* to rejoin his screen. He thought the *Southampton* and *Birmingham* were sufficient to deal with a German light cruiser and several destroyers. But the signal read "Light cruisers—resume your position for lookout. Take station five miles ahead."

As the names of the cruisers were not mentioned, the captain of the *Nottingham* quite correctly repeated the message to his commodore, who was out of visual contact with Beatty's flagship. Goodenough had little choice but to obey the order. He reluctantly broke off contact with the enemy, and all four cruisers returned to their station at the head of Beatty's advanced screen.

Added to the signaling error, the contact with Goodenough's light cruisers had warned Hipper that an enemy formation lay somewhere ahead of him. He turned his squadron to a southeasterly course, unwittingly avoiding a head-on meeting with Beatty's battle cruisers. Just as one stroke of luck had saved Warrender and Beatty from doom at the hands of Ingenohl's battle squadrons, another had seemingly saved Hipper from a similar fate.

By now the weather had deteriorated further, so that visibility was down to four thousand yards at best. In spite of the missed opportunity, all was not lost for the British forces. As Hipper headed southeast, his advanced screen ran into part of Warrender's squadron. One of his light cruisers was spotted by the battleship *Orion* through a break in the rain squalls. The *Orion* was flying the flag of Warrender's second in command, Rear-Adm. Sir Robert Arbuthnot. His flag captain, the gunnery expert, Frederic Dreyer, trained his guns on the enemy ship and asked Arbuthnot for permission to open fire. His response was, "No, not until the Vice-Admiral signals open fire."

The captain of the German cruiser naturally warned Hipper that British battleships were in the vicinity, and before Warrender got within range, Hipper turned northeast and disappeared into the mist. By now Hipper was fully alert to the danger in the route he had taken and made a wide sweep around the northern side of the Dogger Bank. Because of Arbuthnot's rigid adherence to standing orders another golden opportunity to intercept Hipper had been wasted.

There was one last slim chance to inflict some damage on the raiders. This time the British were thwarted by the weather alone. Several hours previously the Admiralty had signaled Keyes to leave the Terschelling area and take his submarines into the Bight to wait for the returning German fleet. But due to the rough seas, only the E11 could get close to the German ships as they headed toward the Jade. She fired a torpedo at the battleship *Posen* from four hundred yards away—nearly point-blank range. But the E11 was rolling and pitching so badly at periscope depth that her torpedo ran too deep and passed harmlessly under the battleship's keel.

The failure to intercept the raiders brought bitter recrimination. Beatty was furious with Goodenough and held him entirely responsible for breaking off action with Hipper's advanced forces and losing contact. He asked Jellicoe to replace him as commodore of the LCS. "I do not understand," Beatty complained, "how the Commodore could have thought that the signals made to *Nottingham* and *Falmouth* applied to him." But Goodenough was not in visual range of the flagship at the time, and for all he knew Beatty might have had some compelling reason for the recall, such as the sight of enemy battle cruisers dead ahead. Therefore he obeyed the signal. To have questioned his admiral's direct order about such an obvious possibility might have brought a sharp rebuke. If Goodenough could be blamed for anything, it was for not keeping his commander fully informed of the enemy strength and direction. He had sighted several more enemy cruisers as he returned to his station but had not reported them.

Those mainly responsible for the failure to intercept Hipper were Beatty himself and his flag lieutenant, Lt.-Cdr. Ralph Seymour. When Beatty decided to recall part of his screening force it was because he guessed that he was about to run into Hipper's battle cruisers. In fact Hipper was fifty miles to the west of him at the time and on a parallel course to the south. The forces engaged by Goodenough were part of a far-advanced screen. Had Beatty waited a little while until he got further reports from the *Southampton* and *Birmingham,* he would probably have headed in their direction instead of ordering them to join him.

But the real culprit was Seymour. Beatty was undoubtedly busily engaged in directing his squadron and gave Seymour the recall order in plain English. The flag lieutenant's job was to interpret his admiral's intentions and choose the appropriate message from the signal book. This he did not do. He even got the *Nottingham*'s call sign wrong. It is often stated in explanation that Seymour was not a trained signal officer. If so, what was he doing in such an important post? This was only the first of four critical signaling errors he made during the war; he would make another at the Dogger Bank action, and two more at Jutland.

It was Seymour who should have been replaced, not Goodenough. Yet Beatty retained his services for the rest of the war, to his great cost. Beatty was well known for his loyalty to subordinates, and his concern for the effect on morale if he dismissed any of them, but his reasons for not getting rid of Seymour are incomprehensible. In the end, Goodenough was not replaced either. Jellicoe was at first inclined to agree with Beatty about the commodore's performance, but after reading all the reports, and listening to Churchill, he ignored Beatty's request. This was a sound decision. Goodenough was acutely aware of his shortcomings on 16 December, and he learned his lesson. At Jutland his scouting activities and reports were outstanding.

Corbett summed up the failure: "In all the war there is perhaps no action which gives deeper cause for reflection on the conduct of operations at sea. . . . Two of the most efficient and powerful British squadrons . . . knowing approximately what to expect, and operating in an area strictly limited by the possibilities of the situation, had failed to bring to action an enemy . . . with whose screen contact had been established."

Fisher's summary was more trenchant: "All concerned made a hash of it."

The Germans had little reason to be satisfied with their performance, either. The raid had only been successful as a cover for further mine-laying operations by Hipper's light cruisers. Their battle cruisers had achieved nothing of military significance, and the battle fleet had missed a glorious opportunity to strike a telling blow against British naval supremacy. Tirpitz wrote, "On December 16, Ingenohl had the fate of Germany in his hand. I boil with inward emotion whenever I think about it."

The captain of the *Moltke,* Magnus von Levetzow, was more scathing. Ingenohl had run away from "eleven British destroyers which could easily have been eliminated. . . . Under the present leadership we will achieve nothing."

A major aim of the Yorkshire raid had been to induce Jellicoe to spread his forces more thinly in an attempt to protect the whole of the east coast against such raids. This didn't work either. Jellicoe remained steadfast in concentrating his forces in his northern bases. The only result of the raid was that he moved Beatty's battle cruisers and Goodenough's cruiser squadron from Cromarty to Rosyth, thus placing Beatty a hundred miles nearer to the German bases and giving him a better chance of intercepting future raids.

The Yorkshire raid produced a great public outcry. An enemy force had actually killed people on English soil—the first time this had happened since a Dutch fleet under de Ruyter had sailed up the Medway in 1667.

At the Scarborough inquest the coroner asked, "Where was the Navy?" This cry was taken up by the popular press in headlines and editorials. There was also a flood of letters to the newspapers expressing both anger and disappointment that the Germans had been able to launch an attack on the British coast and get away with it. Public confidence in the Royal Navy reached a new low. There were also feelings of outrage directed at the Germans for their inhumane shelling of undefended towns. This was contrary to the terms of the Hague Convention, to which Germany had been a signatory. Hipper's men were branded variously as "butchers," "bandits," "murderers," "assassins," or, in Churchill's words, "the baby-killers of Scarborough."

The popular press demanded to know, "What was the navy doing to stop these baby-killers?" The more responsible newspapers recognized the navy's problem in trying to prevent such raids. As the *Observer* soberly concluded, "The best police force may firmly preserve general order, but cannot prevent some cases of murder, arson and burglary."

In spite of the missed opportunities on 16 December, the decisive victories at Heligoland Bight and the Falklands had given a much needed double fillip to the navy's confidence and morale, especially that of its officers. The year ended on a positive note for the navy. It had been taught some valuable lessons, but whether it would profit from its mistakes remained to be seen.

The German coastal raids may have been mere pinpricks in a military sense, but they had been a great embarrassment to the Royal Navy. Beatty wrote that the missed opportunities had "left a mark which nothing can eradicate except total destruction of the enemy. We were within an ace of accomplishing this. Our advanced ships had sighted them! I can't bear to write about it."

The Germans had sent their ships into the British navy's back yard and shelled defenseless British towns. Each time they had got away scot free. Beatty was determined to catch the "baby-killers" the next time they tried it.

First Clash of the Dreadnoughts

CHAPTER 5

The disappointment of that day is more than I can bear to think of.
Everybody thinks it was a great success, when in reality
it was a terrible failure. I had made up my mind
that we were going to get four, the lot,
and four we should have got.

—Vice-Adm. Sir David Beatty

Beatty did not have to wait very long for another crack at Hipper's battle cruisers. Around noon on 23 January 1915, Admiral Oliver, the chief of staff, and Admiral of the Fleet Sir Arthur Wilson came to Churchill's room at the Admiralty to tell him, "First Lord, those fellows are coming out again." "When?" asked Churchill. "Tonight," replied Wilson. "We have just got time to get Beatty there." At 12:35 P.M. (although one source claims it was later than this) the Admiralty made a signal to Beatty at Rosyth: "Get ready to sail at once with all battlecruisers and light cruisers and seagoing destroyers. Further orders follow."

For several weeks the German Naval Staff had been planning a reconnaissance of the Dogger Bank area, but it had been postponed due to bad weather. The reason for the sortie was their realization that the British must be obtaining advanced knowledge of their fleet movements. It seemed too much of a coincidence that during the 16 December raid, the enemy had arrived on the scene at exactly the right time and place to intercept Hipper on his way back from Scarborough. At this point, the staff of the High Seas Fleet were still unwilling to accept the unpleasant idea that their naval code might have been compromised and chose to believe instead that spies were passing information to the enemy about their ship movements. Some of these spies were supposedly operating from inside German dockyards, but Ingenohl and Hipper preferred the notion that it was British trawlers in the Dogger Bank who were the real culprits. Every time German warships entered the area, they invariably sighted large numbers of trawlers. This was hardly surprising because the Dogger Bank was the best fishing ground in the North Sea. These little boats were flying neutral flags—usually Dutch—but the Germans concluded that among them were British spy ships that were sending wireless signals to the Admiralty. They were determined to clear the Dogger Bank of all fishing boats, and attack any enemy patrols they found there. The raid might also serve to avenge the humiliating defeat at the Heligoland Bight in August.

The weather cleared on 22 January, and the forecast for the next few days was good. At 10:00 A.M. the next day, Ingenohl sent Hipper the following wireless signal—naturally in code: "To *Seydlitz,* for Senior Officer Scouting Vessels. First and Second Scouting Groups, Senior Officer of torpedo boats and two flotillas chosen by Senior Officer of Scouting Vessels to reconnoitre the Dogger Bank. Proceed to sea this evening after dark, and return after dark on the following evening."

Across the North Sea, "Blinker" Hall's wireless stations were listening in, and they passed the intercept on to Room 40 for deciphering. It wasn't clear from the decoded message exactly what the Germans had in mind. Perhaps they were planning another raid on the east coast. Later intercepts indicated that Hipper's main force was probably made up of four battle cruisers and six light cruisers. In fact, the big ships were the *Seydlitz, Moltke, Derfflinger,* and *Blücher.* The sixteen-thousand-ton *Blücher* was not a true battle cruiser, with only 8.2-inch guns and a top speed of twenty-three knots, but Hipper was reluctantly obliged to take her with him because the *Von der Tann* was in dock after a collision with a light cruiser. The *Blücher's* presence would slow his squadron down and make it difficult to escape if he were intercepted by Beatty's twenty-seven-knot vessels.

While Beatty's ships were in the Firth of Forth getting up steam, the Naval War Staff were busy putting a prearranged plan into motion, to lay a trap for Hipper that he would not be able to escape. They ordered Beatty's five battle cruisers and Goodenough's four light cruisers to rendezvous near the northeast edge of the Dogger Bank, just after dawn on the twenty-fourth. This was roughly midway between Rosyth and Wilhelmshaven. Tyrwhitt was to meet them there with his three light cruisers and thirty-five destroyers. From the estimated steaming times from Rosyth and Wilhelmshaven to the point chosen for the rendezvous, the staff calculated that by daylight, the British ships would be in position about ten miles to the east of Hipper's squadron. With Beatty's forces spread out between the German raiders and their base, Hipper would be trapped.

Bradford's 3d Battle Squadron and Pakenham's 3d Cruiser Squadron were ordered to rendezvous fifty miles north of the Dogger Bank and "be prepared to intercept the enemy if they are headed off by our battlecruisers and attempt to escape north." The Admiralty concluded, just as they had on 16 December, that it was unlikely the High Seas Fleet would come out in support of Hipper's sortie. In case it did, they told Jellicoe to patrol 130 miles north of the Dogger Bank with three of his battle squadrons. To the south, Keyes was ordered to station his submarines between the Borkum Riff and Heligoland, ready to attack any ships going in or out of the Jade.

The only possible avenue of escape from the trap was to the southeast, if Hipper could manage to skirt around Beatty's intercepting force. Even if he succeeded, it was assumed that the faster British ships would soon catch up with him. By now the Admiralty had learned about the presence of the *Blücher*, which would limit Hipper's squadron to a speed several knots slower than that of Beatty's battle cruisers.

Tyrwhitt was the first to set sail. He steamed out of Harwich at 5:30 P.M. on the twenty-third, a quarter of an hour before Hipper's ships left the Jade. In another fifteen minutes Beatty's battle cruisers were on their way out of the Firth of Forth. Jellicoe's battle squadrons were the last to leave harbor, their orders to raise steam having been delayed by the Admiralty. By 9:00 P.M., all the British forces were far out to sea, well on their way to their assigned positions. As they steamed through the night, their crews realized from all the activity that something was definitely in the wind. They were naturally kept ignorant of Room 40's intelligence reports, for security reasons, but they were convinced that this was not going to be yet another boring sweep across the North Sea that didn't lead to anything. As one of them wrote, "We were confident . . . in a way we had never been before, that we should meet the enemy on the morrow. No one had any doubts about it and there was an air of suppressed excitement which was very exhilarating."

Hipper had no reason to suppose that he was in any particular danger as he steamed toward the Dogger Bank. Even if he were spotted by trawlers at daybreak and reported to the British, there wouldn't be enough time for them to send out their big ships before he had finished his sortie and turned for home. His biographer was to write, "No one on board had any idea that the plan was known to the enemy and that every movement and disposition was followed . . . as accurately as if the British themselves were directing them."

Hipper was worried about the *Blücher*, though. He knew she would be a serious liability if he encountered major enemy units; not just because of her slowness but also her vulnerability. The Falkands had already shown what happened to armored cruisers when they came up against battle cruisers. He was also concerned that Ingenohl had not seen fit to bring out his battle squadrons to back him up in case he ran into trouble.

In the last hour before dawn on the twenty-fourth, Beatty was heading south toward the rendezvous, with Goodenough's light cruisers ahead of him on his port wing. Tyrwhitt's forces, led by the *Arethusa* and *Aurora,* were coming up to meet him from the south. When the sun rose above the horizon, it promised to be a fine day. The sea was calm, and there was no sign of the mist that had helped the Germans to escape the trap on 16 December.

At 7:05 A.M., the *Aurora* sighted a German light cruiser and four torpedo boats four miles to the east and opened fire. She signaled Beatty: "Am in action with German Fleet." This sweeping overstatement was received with amusement on the bridge of the flagship. As a scouting report, it was unhelpful in the extreme, because it gave no inkling of the enemy strength, position, or course. The amusement was soon tempered by the realization that they had probably reached the rendezvous area a bit too early to place themselves between the Germans and their base.

The *Aurora* was in fact engaging the *Kolberg,* which was on the far left of Hipper's advanced screen. After each ship had scored several direct hits on the other, the *Kolberg* turned away and headed east toward Hipper's position, pursued by Tyrwhitt's cruisers and destroyers, which were determined to maintain contact. The *Kolberg* warned Hipper that she was in action with British light forces. As soon as Beatty saw the gun flashes on the dawn horizon, he changed course to southeast and increased speed from eighteen to twenty-three knots. This was below the battle cruisers' top speed, but there was no great urgency until the nature of the enemy force became clear. At this point, although they weren't yet aware of it, Beatty and Hipper were on a collision course.

By 7:30 the *Southampton* sighted two more German cruisers to the southeast, and Goodenough reported this to Beatty. They were the *Stralsund* and *Graudenz,* which were on Hipper's starboard wing. Shortly afterward, the *Aurora* sighted huge palls of black smoke in the distance— a sure sign of enemy battle cruisers. When the news was signaled to the flagship, it produced feelings of euphoria on the bridge. They were finally about to confront the enemy under ideal weather conditions. Visibility was excellent—at least twelve miles—and there was a gentle breeze blowing from the northeast, which gave them the weather gauge. The Germans' view would be hampered by the wind blowing the smoke from their own guns and funnels toward the enemy. The lee position of Beatty's ships meant his gunners would be free of smoke interference.

The *Stralsund* signaled Hipper that she had sighted eight big ships to the northwest. The German admiral was puzzled, because he knew from intelligence reports that Beatty had only five battle cruisers available at the time. Could the others be forerunners of Jellicoe's battle squadrons? The Zeppelin L4 was in the area at the time, but surprisingly, Hipper made no use of her to check whether Beatty was being backed up by battleships. It didn't really matter whether the *Stralsund's* numbers were correct or not, because Hipper realized that every minute he continued steaming northwest would place him in even greater danger than he was in already. He ordered his ships to reverse course and head southeast toward Wilhelmshaven. The planned reconnaissance was over.

He wirelessed Ingenohl to let him know what was happening and to ask for support. But the commander in chief felt confident that with a clear path to Wilhelmshaven, Hipper could outrun the enemy. There seemed to him to be no great urgency in the situation. He did order his battle fleet to begin raising steam, but it was going to take at least four hours before they cleared the Jade. Once again Hipper was on his own.

Meanwhile, Beatty was still unaware of the exact nature of the enemy force and the course it was taking, so he kept on to the southeast until he could see their ships more clearly. Finally, at 7:50, he sighted the heavy smoke clouds coming from the German battle cruisers at an estimated range of twenty-five thousand yards. He gave the order to increase speed to twenty-five knots. Ahead of him on his port bow, Goodenough had a better view of the enemy, and by 8:23 he was able to signal both Beatty and Jellicoe: "Position Latitude 55° 02'N. Longitude 4° 04'E. Enemy in sight consisting of four battlecruisers, steaming between east and south-east."

This was a model scouting report, because it gave his superiors the information they needed most—the enemy strength, position, and course. Goodenough had learned his lesson on 16 December, and he was one of the few subordinate commanders who would remember to keep his admiral fully informed at Jutland, when his scouting reports to Jellicoe throughout the battle were impeccable.

Beatty now gave orders for his battle cruisers to work up to twenty-six knots, then a few minutes later signaled for twenty-seven knots. His flagship *Lion* was in the van, followed by his other two 13.5-inch gunned ships, *Tiger* and *Princess Royal*. Admiral Moore was bringing up the rear with the older 12-inch-gunned vessels *New Zealand* and *Indomitable*. Beatty arranged his line in echelon to port, intending to engage the enemy ships on their starboard quarter once he drew within range. By now Hipper's squadron was strung out in a ragged line, led by the flagship *Seydlitz*, followed by the *Moltke* and *Derfflinger*, with the vulnerable *Blücher* in the rear, nearest to the enemy.

A grim chase unfolded, with Beatty's ships slowly but steadily gaining ground on the fleeing Germans. He ordered another increase in speed, this time to twenty-eight knots. Such speed was impossible for the *New Zealand* and *Indomitable*, whose best speed during trials had been around twenty-five knots. Gaps began to open up between the three leading ships, the so-called "splendid" cats, and Moore's division. The *Indomitable* was vainly struggling to keep up but was even falling behind the *New Zealand*, in spite of the amazing response of her engine- and boiler-room staff. One of her officers wrote:

> Anyone brought up in the oil fuel age can have no idea of the effort required of the stokers of a coal-fired ship steaming at high speed. With the fans supplying air to the boilers whirring at full speed the furnaces devoured coal just about as fast as a man could feed them. Black, begrimed and sweating men working in the bunkers in the ship's side dug the coal out and loaded it onto skids which were then dragged along the steel deck and emptied onto the floorplates in front of each bunker in turn. . . . If the ship rolled or pitched there was always the danger that a loaded skid might take charge with resultant danger to life and limb. Looking down from the iron catwalk above, the scene had all the appearance of one from Dante's *Inferno*. . . . Watching the pressure gauges for any fall in the steam pressure, the Chief Stoker walked to and fro encouraging his men. Now and then the telegraph from the engine room would clang and the finger on the dial move round to the section marked "MORE STEAM." "What do the bastards think we're doing," he would exclaim. "Come on boys, shake it up, get going," and the sweating men would redouble their efforts, throw open the furnace doors and shovel more coal into the blazing inferno.

Conditions must have been just as hellish in the boiler rooms of the fleeing German ships, especially in the *Blücher*. Her crew knew very well they were in mortal danger at the end of the line, and that their lives depended on the efforts of their stokers.

Shortly before 9:00 A.M. the gunnery officer of the *Lion* reported to Captain Chatfield that the range was down to twenty-two thousand yards. This was the supposed maximum range of the 13.5-inch gun, but the battle cruisers had never practiced firing at greater than sixteen thousand yards. Furthermore, British range finders were not accurate at this distance, and Chatfield knew that salvo firing would be a waste of ammunition. With Beatty's approval, he ordered a sighting shot at the *Seydlitz* from a single gun of the *Lion's* midships Q turret, firing at maximum elevation. This was the first shot of the war to be fired by one dreadnought at another. Not surprisingly, it fell far short of the target.

Impatient to close the range, Beatty now ordered the battle cruisers to work up to twenty-nine knots. He knew perfectly well they could never attain this unheard of turn of speed, but he wanted to spur them on to the absolute limit of their engines. Throughout the action it is probable that few of them actually exceeded twenty-seven knots. But before long they had gained enough distance on the Germans that the *Lion's* slow and deliberate ranging shots were creeping closer and closer to the unfortunate *Blücher*. Just after 9:00 A.M., when the range had fallen to less than twenty thousand yards, Beatty signaled his captains: "Open fire and engage the enemy."

The leading British ships began firing full salvos. The *Lion* shifted her target up the line to the *Derfflinger*, and the *Tiger* and *Princess Royal* began aiming at the *Blücher*. The *New Zealand* and *Indomitable* were still too far astern to obey Beatty's order. Hipper's ships were unable to fire back for a quarter of an hour, because the range was still too great for their smaller-caliber guns, and the gunners were hampered by their own funnel smoke.

During this first part of the battle, things looked very promising for the British. They had gained so much on the fleeing enemy that Beatty ordered speed temporarily reduced to twenty-four knots to allow his rearmost ships to close up and get into action. He also signaled his destroyers to move up and repel a possible attack by Hipper's torpedo boats, some of which were busy laying smoke between the the two fleets. (This was the first time a smoke screen had been used in a naval battle.) Beatty then made a slight turn to starboard to clear the view and allow all his ships to bring their after turrets to bear on the enemy battle cruisers and start firing regular salvos.

At first the British shooting was better than that of the Germans, who were now being hampered by their own gun smoke as well as that from their funnels. Beatty's gunners were straddling the German ships and scored five direct hits, one on the *Blücher* and two each on the *Derfflinger* and *Seydlitz*. In return, the *Lion* was the only British ship to suffer, being hit twice. None of these early hits caused any serious damage.

Filson Young, a journalist who had been given a temporary appointment as an RNVR lieutenant, was attached to Beatty's flagship as an observer, and he wrote, "There was no mistaking the difference between the bright, sharp stab of white flame that marked the firing of the enemy's guns and this dull, glowing and fading glare which signified the bursting of one of our own shells."

Up to this point, firing had been irregular on both sides, with each ship aiming at the most visible target. By 9:35 the range had dropped to about seventeen thousand yards, and Beatty signaled: "Engage the corresponding ships in the enemy line." Since he had five ships to the enemy's four, the signal was open to misinterpretation. Chatfield knew that the *Indomitable* was so far behind that she had not yet opened fire—her older 12-inch shells had a maximum range of only sixteen thousand yards—so it was really four ships to four at this stage. He suggested to Beatty that the *Lion* engage the *Seydlitz,* the *Tiger* the *Moltke,* the *Princess Royal* the *Derfflinger,* and the *New Zealand* the *Blücher.* Beatty agreed, but his signal didn't make this clear, and Captain Pelly of the *Tiger* misunderstood the admiral's intentions.

Apparently unaware that the *Indomitable* was not yet in action, he thought the extra ship should join the flagship in concentrating on the enemy van, according to standard practice, and began firing at the *Seydlitz.* To make things worse, the green crew of the *Tiger,* who had never fired their guns at a moving target, initially took the *Lion's* fall of shot for their own, although their shells were actually landing three thousand yards beyond the German flagship. Their aim was corrected by a signal from Goodenough, but the *Tiger* continued firing at the *Seydlitz.*

Pelly's error unfortunately left the *Moltke* unfired upon, completely free to carry out undisturbed target practice. It was a cardinal rule of naval tactics that if possible, no enemy ship should be left unengaged. Hipper was quick to take advantage of the error. He ordered the *Moltke* to join the *Seydlitz* in concentrating her fire on the *Lion.* The *Moltke's* gunners made the most of their opportunity, and it was not long before the *Lion* began to suffer.

Nonetheless, it was the embattled *Lion* that scored the first telling blow of the action. At 9:45 one of her 13.5-inch armor-piercing shells plunged through the after deck of the *Seydlitz,* with appalling results. The scene was later described by Admiral Scheer:

> The first shell that hit her had a terrible effect. It pierced right through the upper deck in the ship's stern and through the barbette armour of the near turret, where it exploded. . . . In the reloading chamber, where the shell penetrated, part of the charge in readiness for loading was set on fire. The flames rose high up into the turret and down into the munition chamber, and thence through a connecting door usually kept shut, through which the men from the munition chamber tried to escape into

the fore turret. The flames thus made their way through to the other munition chamber, and thence again up to the second turret, and from this cause the entire gun crews of both turrets perished almost instantly. The flames rose as high as a house above the turrets.

According to some observers, the flames rose two hundred feet above the stern of the *Seydlitz*. No less than 159 men came to a dreadful end in the holocaust. Filson Young, who had a good view from the *Lion*'s foretop, wrote, "Well do I remember seeing those flames and wondering what kind of horrors they signified."

The raging fire caused by six tons of burning propellant threatened to reach the stricken ship's magazines. If it had not been for the courageous action of an executive officer and two men who worked their way through the intense heat and choking fumes to open the flooding valves to the magazines, there is no doubt that the *Seydlitz* would have blown up. Although she was down by the stern because of the hundreds of tons of water she had taken on, she had not developed a list and her engines and boilers were unaffected. It is a tribute to the sturdy construction of German warships that she was able to keep her place at the head of the line. Half of her main armament was out of action, but she soon showed she was still a force to be reckoned with.

As Hipper stood on the bridge of his battered flagship weighing the situation, he seemed outwardly impassive. To his staff, the only sign of stress was his chain smoking. He decided that his best chance of saving his squadron was to hurl everything he had at the British flagship. The *Lion* was the nearest target, and if he could disable her, it might throw the enemy line into confusion and allow him to escape. The *Derfflinger*, which had been engaging the *Tiger* and *Princess Royal*, was now ordered to switch to the *Lion*. The three German battle cruisers began a rapid and accurate fire on Beatty's flagship, their guns belching a fresh salvo every forty-five seconds.

Meanwhile, British shells were falling all round the *Blücher*, and Hipper was becoming very concerned about the plight of his weakest unit. She had been hit again, and he knew that her armor was not designed to stand up to the 1,250-pound projectiles being aimed at her. He wirelessed Ingenohl to tell him of his predicament—with one ship battered and another in mortal danger, he was still a hundred miles from the safety of Heligoland. Ingenohl was finally convinced of the urgency of the situation and ordered his battleships to sail in thirty minutes. He sent out a W/T signal in plain language, for the benefit of the enemy: "Main fleet and flotillas coming out." But he added in code, for Hipper's information: "As soon as possible." It was going to take until 2:30 P.M. before the High

Seas Fleet could clear the channels at the mouth of the Jade. By the time they arrived on the scene, they would be far too late to help Hipper.

The British were confident they were on the way to a decisive victory. The *Blücher* was being cut off and attacked by the *New Zealand* and and *Princess Royal.* The latter had also inflicted an apparently crippling blow on the *Derfflinger.* Flames and smoke were seen coming from this hit, and the British were convinced that the *Derfflinger* was as badly wounded as the *Seydlitz.* In fact, she had suffered no vital damage, and all her guns were still in action.

The Germans were given a temporary respite when some of Hipper's torpedo boats began to fall behind his battle cruisers. Beatty suspected they were planning to drop mines in his path. He had recently been warned about this possibility by the Admiralty, and he briefly turned away 45 degrees to starboard. When he judged the danger had passed, he resumed his southeasterly pursuit of the enemy battle cruisers.

It was not long before Hipper's tactics paid off. Outnumbered and outgunned, the *Lion* began to suffer heavy damage. The German battle cruisers inflicted four direct hits on her in a short space of time, the most serious of these coming at 10:01. An 11-inch shell from the *Moltke,* which was still unfired upon, penetrated the *Lion's* side armor at the waterline. Although the shell failed to explode, it caused extensive flooding, which short-circuited two of the ship's three dynamos. The *Lion* began to list to port, but her speed was unaffected and she was able to keep her station at the head of the line.

Hipper now decided to attack with his torpedo boats, but Beatty easily countered this by turning 45 degrees to starboard and ordering Tyrwhitt to drive off the attackers with his destroyers. Beatty's turn caused the range to open up, and he increased speed to twenty-seven knots on a course of east-southeast to bring the enemy within range again. At the same time, Hipper had turned east-northeast to confuse the British gunners. As a result of these maneuvers, and the poor visibility resulting from the dense smoke surrounding each ship, the two sides temporarily lost sight of each other.

By 10:18, Beatty had regained contact, and Hipper was forced to resume his previous southeasterly course to avoid being cut off. The *Lion* found the range again and began straddling the *Seydlitz* from a distance of 17,500 yards, yet she only achieved one direct hit on the German flagship, which caused little damage. But the complexion of the battle was suddenly altered when two 12-inch shells from the *Derfflinger* struck the *Lion* simultaneously and exploded. The impact was so tremendous that according to Filson Young, "We thought she had been torpedoed, and the mast, to which the fore-top was secured, rocked and waved like a tree in a storm, and the ship seemed to be shaking herself to bits. We looked at one another and prepared to alight . . . into whatever part of the sea destiny might send us; but nothing happened, and the old *Lion* seemed to pick herself up and go on again."

One of the shells penetrated the *Lion's* 6-inch armor belt at the waterline before exploding. Apart from the extensive flooding caused by the hole in the ship's side, the explosion severed pipes to one of the condensers and allowed seawater to enter the boilers. This meant that in a few hours contamination from the salt water would stop the port engine. The other shell also penetrated the side armor below the waterline and flooded several coal bunkers. The *Lion's* list increased.

The enemy fire became so accurate that Beatty was forced to zigzag to try to throw off their aim. He was also worried about the course the action was taking. After an hour and a half, his ships had not struck a decisive blow against the German battle cruisers. The damage to the *Seydlitz* had not slowed her down, and he knew that every minute the high-speed chase continued to the southeast increased Hipper's chances of reaching safety. In spite of his advantage in speed, he had not been able to bring the range down to much below seventeen thousand yards. He was determined to close the enemy, regardless of the danger from Hipper's torpedo boats, and at 10:27 he signaled his squadron: "Form on a compass line bearing NNW and proceed at your utmost speed."

Beatty thought that changing his line of bearing toward the enemy would force Hipper to alter course to a more northerly direction and improve his own tactical position. He also hoped that he might be able to drive Hipper toward Jellicoe's battle squadrons. Unfortunately, Jellicoe was still about 140 miles away at the time.

With the ships heading into the wind at twenty-five knots or better, the flags were streaming dead astern, and the *Lion's* signal was very difficult to read from the ships following. The visual signaling system was breaking down. Beatty had realized this when he ordered his ships to form on a line of bearing, hoping it would improve the situation. It didn't, partly because of the black funnel smoke, as well as the cordite fumes from repeated salvos swirling around each ship. The two nearest ships, the *Tiger* and *Princess Royal*, managed to take in the message and repeat it correctly, but Moore's 2d Battle Cruiser Squadron didn't understand it. The *Indomitable* couldn't even see the last part of the signal. Admiral Moore and his flag captain, Halsey, were thoroughly perplexed. They couldn't imagine that Beatty actually wanted them to steer northnorthwest, and they concluded something was wrong. When the flags came down, making the order executive, they decided to ignore it. They were relieved to see the leading ships stay on a southeasterly course and only change their line of bearing, and they finally realized what Beatty had intended. Luckily, this particular signaling confusion had no serious consequence.

At 10:35 Beatty signaled again: "Turn together 1 degree to port." This would bring his ships dangerously close to the enemy torpedo boat screen, but he was determined to press in on Hipper's battle cruisers and force a decision. Beatty's move brought the range down to about 16,300 yards, or just over nine miles. This was the critical point of the battle.

In the meantime, the *Blücher* had already been hit several times and was dropping farther and farther behind the German battle cruisers. She had been heavily engaged in turn by the *Tiger, Princess Royal,* and *New Zealand* and was losing speed. After she was hit again, she sheered out of line toward the north.

A few minutes later, the *Princess Royal* scored two devastating hits on the ill-fated *Blücher.* The 13.5-inch shells easily penetrated the 3-inch armor plate of her main deck and plunged through two more decks before exploding in the ship's vitals. One of them caused a disastrous ammunition fire which killed all the men inside two of the gun turrets, and the other disabled two of the ship's engines. Her steering gear was jammed and she swung sharply to port, out of control. As she turned, two more shells hit her, starting another fire. Her captain signaled Hipper: "All engines out of action." The *Blücher* was obviously doomed. Hipper was faced with the agonizing choice of turning back to try to protect her from further battering or abandoning her to her fate.

Beatty was confident that he now had the upper hand, and it was only a matter of cleaning up. He ordered the *Indomitable,* which had not yet opened fire, to engage "the enemy breaking away to the north." This was sufficient force to finish off the crippled *Blücher,* while his other four ships dealt with the rest of Hipper's squadron. He signaled for another turn together of one point to port, then a few minutes later: "Close the enemy as rapidly as possible consistent with keeping all guns bearing." He was determined to move in for the kill. Unfortunately, in the light of later events, Beatty's intentions did not get through to Admiral Moore or the other commanders. The *Tiger* received only part of the signal— "Close the enemy"—while the rest didn't see it at all.

But Beatty had not reckoned on the effect of Hipper's tactics and the accuracy of his gunners. The three German battle cruisers had the range on the *Lion* and hit her time after time with 11- and 12-inch shells. She received no less than ten more hits in the space of twenty minutes, suffering heavy damage. A turret fire led to flooding of one of her magazines, and her list was increasing. The *Lion* was also losing speed, and Beatty was beginning to lose control of the battle.

Around 11:00 A.M. the tide of battle swung in the Germans' favor. The *Lion* received her last hit of the action. It had a catastrophic effect. The shell exploded and drove in the side armor plate by two feet. This caused more flooding, which shorted out the remaining dynamo. Seawater entered the feed tanks, and the port engine had to be shut down, reducing the *Lion*'s speed to fifteen knots. She had taken on three thousand tons of water and her list had increased to 11 degrees. By now the *Lion* was in a sorry state. Altogether, she had received sixteen punishing hits from heavy shells. With one turret out of action, her main fire-control knocked out, one engine stopped, and no light or power, she was virtually disabled and unable to keep her station at the head of the line. Hipper had succeeded in his aim of putting Beatty's flagship out of action.

Soon after this, the *Tiger* raced past the limping and battered *Lion*. She became a fresh target for Hipper's battle cruisers, because the *Lion* had now dropped out of range. The *Tiger* was hit four times in rapid succession. One of the hits started a spectacular fire. The Germans thought they had put her out of action as well, and later claimed to have sunk her, but it was only the gasoline stored on deck for the ship's motor launches that had ignited, and the blaze was quickly extinguished. Another hit knocked out the *Tiger*'s fire-control system. She was the only one of Beatty's ships equipped with central director control, but her shooting so far had shown little evidence of this.

To make matters even worse, a lookout on the British flagship now sighted an imaginary submarine. In his report after the battle Beatty wrote, "Submarines were reported on the starboard bow and I personally observed the wash of a periscope, 2 points on our starboard bow (1059). I immediately (1102) signaled 'Turn 8 points to port together.'" It was later shown that there were no submarines within fifty miles, and what had probably been seen was the wash of a spent torpedo from one of Hipper's torpedo boats. Beatty didn't know this, of course, but by now all the other battle cruisers had passed the *Lion* and were well ahead of her. They could not have been threatened by a submarine that was several miles astern of them.

Beatty's signal caused bewilderment on the bridge of each of the battle cruisers, even the *Lion*. A turn of 90 degrees to port would bring them onto a course that was almost due north, practically at right angles to the direction the enemy was taking. Reginald Plunkett, Beatty's flag commander, exclaimed, "Good heavens, Sir, surely you're not going to break off the engagement?" None of the other captains could imagine that Beatty meant to abandon the chase. According to the historian James Goldrick, Beatty had acquired an "image of near infallibility" as "the man who was always right." Moore was perplexed by the order to turn, but decided that Beatty must know what he was doing. The other commanders were just as mystified by the signal since no reason had been given for the turn. The *Lion* had not hoisted the submarine warning flag, apparently because all but two of her halliards had been shot away, but this should have been done before making the signal to turn. Neither Beatty nor Seymour had foreseen the confusion that would result from the failure to do this.

Beatty quickly realized that the turn he had ordered was too sharp and would carry his ships across the tracks of the German torpedo boats, which might drop mines in their path. Also the new course meant they would lose too much ground on the fleeing enemy. A few minutes later he tried to correct the situation by hoisting the signal "Course North-East," intending to limit the turn to 45 degrees and keep his ships converging on the enemy. Unfortunately, Seymour made another disastrous signaling error. Impatient to prevent Hipper from getting too far ahead, Beatty now told Seymour to signal "Attack the rear of the enemy." This meant hoisting the flags "AF." But the compass pennant and letter flag "B"—by themselves meaning "course NE"—were still flying from the other halliard. When the compass "B" and "AF" flags were hauled down at the same time, making the signal executive, they were correctly read together as "Attack the rear of the enemy bearing NE." Without exception, the other battle cruisers all logged the signal in this way.

As Goldrick wrote, "The accumulation of missed signals, scares and snap decisions now brought disaster upon the British." By an unfortunate coincidence, the *Blücher*'s bearing at the time was almost exactly northeast of the British squadron. Moore concluded that since his flagship was disabled, Beatty had decided to abandon the pursuit of Hipper's battle cruisers and make sure of at least cutting off and sinking the *Blücher*. From his position at the rear of the line, Moore wasn't aware that she was already so badly damaged that she couldn't escape. The captains of the *Tiger* and *Indomitable* drew the same conclusion, and they too headed for the *Blücher*. Only Captain Brock of the *Princess Royal* realized that something was wrong and meant to ignore the signal and keep on after Hipper, but he was forced to turn with the others or be run down by the *Tiger*. The result was that a relieved Hipper escaped to the southeast while four British battle cruisers went to attack an already crippled armored cruiser. Beatty had completely lost control of the battle.

Hipper was baffled by what he had just seen. He had earlier considered turning back to support the *Blücher,* but his staff officers had talked him out of it. They pointed out that it would probably be futile, and Captain Egidy told him that the *Seydlitz* was running low on ammunition.

Hipper decided instead to turn in a wide arc to starboard to try to draw the enemy away from the *Blücher*, and then launch an attack on them with his torpedo boats. But when he saw the four British ships heading off to the northeast, he canceled the attack and returned to a southeasterly course toward Heligoland, leaving the *Blücher* to her fate.

Meanwhile, Beatty was both amazed and appalled to see that his battle cruisers were abandoning the chase. He tried to correct the situation by telling Seymour to hoist Nelson's famous signal at Trafalgar: "Engage the enemy more closely." Seymour discovered this was no longer in the signal book, and the best alternative he could come up with was the less decisive: "Keep nearer the enemy." Beatty told him to go ahead and hoist it. In the event, it didn't make any difference, because by now the other battle cruisers were too far away to see the *Lion*'s flags. Without electricity, Beatty was unable to signal them by searchlight or wireless.

Surrounded by four British battle cruisers, the *Blücher* had no chance whatever, but she fought courageously to the bitter end, just as Graf Spee's ships had done at the Falkands. Hammered relentlessly from close range by 12- and 13.5-inch guns, she kept spitting back defiantly with her inferior 8.2-inch armament. According to one of the survivors,

> The shells came thick and fast with a terrible droning hum. . . . When the range shortened . . . their trajectory flattened and they tore holes in the ship's sides and raked her decks. . . . The terrific air pressure resulting from explosion in a confined space left a deep impression on the minds of the men of the *Blücher*. The air, it would seem, roars through every opening and tears its way through every weak spot. . . . As one poor wretch was passing through a trap door a shell burst near him. He was exactly half way through. The trap door closed with a terrific snap. . . . Men were picked up by that terrible *luftdruck* . . . and tossed to a horrible death amidst the machinery.

Even after suffering an estimated seventy hits from heavy shells, she still would not strike her colors. After the *Arethusa* put two torpedoes into her, she developed such a heavy list that her remaining guns fell silent, unable to bear on her tormentors, and the British ceased fire. As the *Arethusa* approached to try to rescue the *Blücher*'s survivors, Tyrwhitt recalled, "she was in a pitiable condition, her upper works wrecked, and fires could be seen raging through the enormous shot holes in her sides."

Several hundred men on her deck raised a cheer as the British cruiser came near, but the *Blücher* suddenly rolled over on her beam ends. The surviving crew members could be seen scrambling down her sides into the water to try to avoid being sucked down when she took her final plunge. After capsizing and floating upside down for a few minutes, she sank at 12:15 P.M. The *Arethusa* and several of her destroyers lowered their boats and managed to pick up 234 survivors, out of a complement of 1,026. More would have been saved but for a seaplane from the German base at Borkum that callously dropped hand bombs on survivors and rescuers alike, thinking it was a British ship that had been sunk. This attack caused Tyrwhitt to recall his boats and abandon further rescue attempts. The Zeppelin L4 also watched the end of the *Blücher* from a distance. She was helpless to intervene, because every time she approached she was driven off by gunfire from British light cruisers.

Corbett later paid tribute to the crew of the *Blücher:* "As an example of discipline, courage and fighting spirit her last hours have seldom been surpassed."

By this time, Beatty was in a towering rage. He transferred from the crippled *Lion* to the nearby destroyer *Attack,* which took about twenty minutes, then raced after the other battle cruisers, arriving just in time to see the end of the *Blücher.* He boarded the *Princess Royal* and resumed command of the squadron at 12:27. He immediately gave the order for the battle cruisers to turn southeast and carry on with the chase, but it was too late. The German ships were now so far ahead—an estimated thirty thousand yards—that it would take at least two hours to catch up with them again. By this time they would be so close to Heligoland that Beatty wouldn't have time to force a decision before he came under the guns of the fortress. There was also an unconfirmed report that the German battle fleet was coming out. At 12:45, Beatty reluctantly gave up the pursuit. The battle was over. As Seymour put it, to go on would have been "like trying to win the Derby after a bad fall at Tattenham Corner."

A bitterly disappointed Beatty ordered all his forces to return to base at 12:45. There was nothing left to do now but make sure the crippled *Lion* got back safely. It was vital that the sinking of the *Blücher* not be offset by the loss of the *Lion.* Both her engines finally had to be shut down, and she was taken in tow by the *Indomitable.* The two ships were screened from enemy torpedo boat attack by all of Tyrwhitt's cruisers and destroyers as they made their slow and difficult way back to Rosyth. Room 40 had intercepted a German signal that they were planning a night attack on the *Lion,* and Jellicoe dispatched two of his destroyer flotillas (DFs) to the scene to help form an impenetrable screen around the two battle cruisers. In the event, the German plans came to nothing, because Hipper's torpedo boats were too low on fuel and it was too late to send out fresh ones. It was an uncomfortable and eerie voyage for those on board the *Lion*—there was no light or heat, and instead of the throb of the engines the only sounds to be heard were from the wind and waves.

The *Lion* reached the Scottish coast safely at 6:35 the next morning. Her battle damage was obvious to the onlookers on shore, and they cheered her as she was towed up the Firth of Forth toward Rosyth. After temporary repairs, she went to the Tyne dockyard for six weeks. Thus the Dogger Bank action had a silver lining for the *Lion*'s crew. As one of them remarked, "And so we had a nice spot of leave, the first since war broke out."

In Britain, the Battle of the Dogger Bank was hailed by the press and public as a great triumph for the Royal Navy. As the *Pall Mall Gazette* put it, "After yesterday's action, it will not be easy for the loud-mouthed boasters of Berlin to keep up the pretence that the British Fleet is hiding in terror."

Millions of readers of the *London Illustrated News* and *Daily Mail* were struck by the photographs of the end of the *Blücher*. These were some of the most dramatic pictures to come out of the war, showing the stricken ship floating on her side like a great iron whale, with antlike figures clinging desperately to her barnacle-encrusted carcass.

But the press and public heard only part of the story—they knew nothing about the advanced warning, the rendezvous and plans to intercept the German squadron, the signal mixups, or the actual damage to the enemy ships. It was enough for them that the enemy had run away and the *Blücher* had been sunk—enough to call it a great victory. "It will be some time before they go baby-killing again," crowed the *Globe* newspaper. To the press and public, Beatty was a hero. If his ship had not been disabled, he would have sunk the lot.

In terms of actual results, the Battle of the Dogger Bank was undoubtedly a British victory. The enemy had been put to flight, lost one of his big ships, and suffered heavy casualties. This was the third naval action of the war in which the German navy had lost over a thousand men. By contrast, the Royal Navy had not lost any ships, and its casualties were remarkably light in view of the battering the *Lion* had received, with only eleven killed and thirty-one wounded.

Beatty did not share the popular view. He wrote, "The disappointment of that day is more than I can bear to think of. Everybody thinks it was a great success, when in reality it was a terrible failure. I had made up my mind that we were going to get four, the lot, and four we ought to have got."

He was convinced that if Moore had kept up the chase on his own initiative, the other three German battle cruisers would have been caught and sunk. In his view, "Moore had a chance most fellows would have given the eyes in the head for, and did nothing. . . . It is inconceivable that anybody should have thought it necessary for 4 BCs 3 of them untouched to have turned on the *Blücher* which was obviously a defeated ship and couldn't steam while three others also badly hammered should have been allowed to escape."

This is arguable. British estimates of damage to Hipper's surviving ships were greatly exaggerated. Apart from the one serious hit on the *Seydlitz*, they had inflicted no significant damage. The *Derfflinger* was only slightly damaged, and the *Moltke* was completely unscathed. With the advantage of hindsight it is quite possible that Hipper's three ships would have proved a match for Moore's four. Apart from the *Princess Royal*, the others were not that formidable opponents, especially in view of the *Tiger's* inexperienced gunners and the older guns of the *New Zealand* and *Indomitable*. One thing that would have tipped the balance in favor of the British: If the Admiralty had allowed Jellicoe to get steam up in the afternoon of the twenty-third instead of the evening, he would have been on the scene with his battle squadrons to crush Hipper's force.

It was disturbing that for the second time in just over a month a British fleet, forewarned of enemy plans and with superior numbers, armament, and speed had failed to catch and destroy a German raiding force. There were several reasons for the failure: too rigid compliance with senior officers' orders and signaling errors and confusion. There is also no doubt that Hipper's tactics and handling of his squadron were superior to Beatty's.

But the main reason for Hipper's escape was the poor gunnery of the British battle cruisers. They had failed to slow down or cripple any of Hipper's ships, except for the slow and vulnerable *Blücher*. The three leading ships, *Lion, Tiger,* and *Princess Royal,* had fired a total of 869 13.5-inch shells between them yet managed to achieve only six hits on the German battle cruisers. This meant they had to expend 145 shells for every direct hit. The *New Zealand* and *Indomitable* had only scored hits on the *Blücher,* mostly at short range in the final stages. By contrast, the German battle cruisers had scored twenty-two hits on the *Lion* and *Tiger* from 976 shells, or 44 shells per direct hit. The *Moltke,* unfired on throughout the battle, had the best performance with eight hits from 276 shells.

Jellicoe concluded that the German gunners' performance was clearly superior— "thus confirming my suspicion that the gunnery of our Battlecruiser Squadron was in great need of improvement, a fact which I very frequently urged upon Sir David Beatty." Fisher went further, describing the *Tiger's* gunnery as "villainously bad." She had fired 355 shells and achieved just two hits. In mitigation, it was pointed out that she had only been in commission since 3 October, and that there were many recovered deserters among her crew. Captain Pelly had done his best to whip the crew into shape since he had joined Beatty's squadron on 6 November, but had been given little opportunity for gunnery practice, and then only at a fixed target. Why this newest and most formidable battle cruiser had been given such a motley crew was puzzling, as was Beatty's decision to place a ship that was not fully operational in such a crucial position as second in line of battle.

In explanation of the scarcity of direct hits achieved by both sides, considering that more than two thousand shells had been fired, it must be remembered that this was the first naval battle ever to be fought with ships maneuvering at thirty miles an hour or better, and firing at each other from distances of nine miles or more. Everything was new and untried under real battle conditions—spray from near-misses obscuring the range-finder lenses, smoke interfering with the spotters, and changes in position of the target ship by as much as several hundred yards during the time of flight of the shells. Judgments should not be too severe, because this was the first time that range and deflection plotting calculations had been used in action. It remained to be seen whether the gunners on both sides would profit from their experience at the Dogger Bank and improve their performance by the time the Battle of Jutland was fought.

After the results of the engagement were fully analyzed, there were serious repercussions in both fleets, neither of which could be satisfied with the outcome. Moore was made the principal scapegoat on the British side. He was castigated by Fisher, who said he "ought to have gone on, had he the slightest Nelsonic temperament in him, regardless of signals. . . . In war the first principle is to disobey orders. *Any fool can obey orders.*" It is interesting to speculate what Fisher's reaction would have been if someone had disobeyed *his* orders.

Beatty was hesitant to condemn Moore in his official report, perhaps aware that his own signaling errors had contributed to Moore's indecision, but he did tell Jellicoe that Moore was not suited to be a battle cruiser admiral. Churchill, however, recognized that Moore "took command of the squadron in circumstances of extreme difficulty," and in his words, "fortune presented herself to him in mocking and dubious guise." But in the end the Admiralty decided that Moore had to go. He was relieved of command of the 2d Battle Cruiser Squadron and shunted off to the Canary Islands to command the 9th Cruiser Squadron.

Fisher also wanted to replace Pelly, whom he called a "poltroon," but Beatty saved him. He was well known for his loyalty to his immediate subordinates and considered that Pelly had done his best with a green crew in the short time he had been given. To relieve him of his command would be bad for the squadron's morale. Amazingly, Beatty also retained Seymour as his signal officer, in spite of his repeated errors and obvious incompetence. He had a warm, personal regard for Seymour, describing him as his "jolly, round little signal officer." Beatty would live to regret this decision. Another scapegoat, who Beatty could not save, was the gunnery officer of the *Tiger,* Lt.-Cdr. Evan Bruce-Gardyne. Fisher said it was no time for sentiment and insisted that he be replaced.

Beatty himself came through unscathed by any serious criticism, in spite of the fact that with Seymour's help he had made a hash of a straightforward stern chase of an inferior and slower enemy force by his confusing and unnecessary turns and signals. Remarkably, his reputation was strongly enhanced by his performance, because Churchill and Fisher continued to believe in the exaggerated claims of battle damage to Hipper's battle cruisers. Fisher wrote Beatty several fulsome letters of praise, calling his conduct "glorious" and referring to him as "Beatty *beatus.*" Admiral Pakenham went even further, and when Churchill later paid a visit to the *Lion,* took him aside and said, "First Lord, I wish to speak to you in private." Pakenham then, "with intense conviction in his voice," told Churchill, "Nelson has come again."

Nonetheless, Fisher was not satisfied with the overall performance of the battle cruiser squadron, and he requested a full-scale inquiry. This would have served a useful purpose in light of later events at Jutland, but Churchill would have none of it. He had no wish to take the shine off a popular victory, or jeopardize his own administration at the Admiralty by giving his detractors ammunition that might come out of an inquiry. As he put it, "The future and the present claim all our attention."

In Germany, the loss of the *Blücher* and so many men had a serious effect on the morale of the High Seas Fleet. Ingenohl was made the scapegoat for the defeat. Hipper's staff officers and the captains of the three battle cruisers, Egidy, Levetzow, and Zenker, all wrote to the Admiralstab criticizing Ingenohl, and they intrigued against him at court. They placed the blame for the defeat squarely on Ingenohl's leadership. He was guilty of half measures and should have brought out his battle squadrons in support of Hipper. It had been folly to send the *Blücher,* and the operation should have been postponed until the *Von der Tann* was available. They also blamed him for breaking off action with Warrender on 16 December, when he had him in a trap. In the end, Ingenohl became a figure of public derision when a ditty about the inactivity of the High Seas Fleet was widely circulated:

Lieb Vaterland magst ruhig sein,
  die Flotte schlaft im Hafen ein.

Loosely translated, this means "Dear Fatherland fear nought, the fleet's asleep in port."

The kaiser, furious at the loss of one of his precious big ships, agreed with the critics, and in a painful interview, dismissed Ingenohl as commander in chief. He replaced him with the compliant Adm. Hugo von Pohl, the chief of the Imperial Naval Staff. Pohl was an experienced flag officer, but he turned out to be even more cautious than Ingenohl about risking the fleet and incurring the wrath of the All-Highest. As well, Pohl was in poor health, and within months would prove to be suffering from terminal cancer.

On the other hand Hipper's performance was fully approved by both Ingenohl and the Admiralstab. His reputation as a clever tactician was strengthened, even though he had abandoned the *Blücher.* Ironically, it was the presence of the *Blücher* that had probably saved his squadron. But his performance was not flawless. When he made his 180-degree turn after contacting Beatty's advanced forces, it would have been better to order his ships to turn together instead of in succession, so as to put the vulnerable *Blücher* at the head of his line, on his disengaged side. In this sheltered position, the armored cruiser might have stood a chance. Also, he made no use of the Zeppelin L4 to spot for him and give him the strength and position of the enemy force. In fact, the only contribution made by German aircraft was to drive off the rescuers of the *Blücher*'s survivors.

There were important lessons to be learned from the Dogger Bank action. The side armor of the British battle cruisers was strengthened after the results of the hits on the *Lion.* But the deck armor was not, leaving them still vulnerable to long-range plunging fire. The *Lion* had also suffered a serious fire in the handing room of one of her turrets, which had led to flooding of the magazine. The ship's chief engineer made improvements in her flash protection to prevent possible magazine explosions. Unfortunately, the information was not passed on to the other battle cruisers, and nothing was done to minimize the danger from burning cordite. The lesson would not be learned by the British until Jutland, at a terrible price.

The Germans learned a vitally important lesson from the turret fire on board the *Seydlitz.* They realized how close the flagship had come to total destruction and immediately took steps to increase the armor protection over the magazines, as well as measures to prevent flash from traveling from turret to turret and thence to the magazines. Once again they learned that British AP shells and fuses were ineffective. The shells tended to break up on oblique contact, or else failed to penetrate the armor before they exploded. This explains why so little serious damage was done by the direct hits on the German ships.

Jellicoe studied reports of the battle very carefully and made some important changes to the signal book and to the Grand Fleet Battle Orders (GFBOs) to try to avoid a repetition of the errors made at the Dogger Bank. He also continued to urge Beatty to take steps to improve the gunnery of the battle cruiser squadron. As a priority Jellicoe had central director control equipment installed in all of Beatty's ships as well as in his own battleships. Whether all the deficiencies revealed by the Dogger Bank action were suitably addressed would not be revealed until the Battle of Jutland was fought.

The Long Vigil

CHAPTER 6

*We have the game in our hands if we sit tight, but this Churchill cannot
see. He must see something tangible and can't understand that naval
warfare acts in a wholly different way from war on shore. The Fleet
in the North dominates the position. It's no business of ours to go
trying to pluck occasional small, indifferent fruits in the south.*

—Capt. Herbert Richmond

The twelve months following the Dogger Bank action saw many
changes but very little naval activity, at least in the North Sea. Jellicoe and Beatty were still trying to solve the problem of how to
entice the High Seas Fleet out of its safe haven in the Jade and meet
them in the decisive battle that everyone in Britain longed for. This
would be an even more difficult task with Pohl at the helm than it
had been with Ingenohl. Still, as the *National Review* pointed out,
the Royal Navy had succeeded in driving "the second navy in the
world to the mudbanks of the Elbe." It was "as supreme an exhi-
bition of superior sea-power as the world has witnessed."

Under Pohl's leadership the German navy made a drastic change
in strategy. Henceforth, its surface ships were to be restricted to the
protected waters of the Heligoland Bight. There would be no more
daring forays across the North Sea by Hipper's battle cruisers. The
misnamed *Riskflotte* wasn't to be risked at all. In future the Germans
intended to concentrate on undersea warfare, using mines and, especially, submarines.

By the beginning of February 1915, the Admiralstab was making
plans for a new U-boat offensive. On the sixteenth the Germans announced to the world that they had declared the waters around the
British Isles a war zone. So far, their attacks on merchant ships had
been conducted in a more or less gentlemanly fashion. U-boat commanders were officially restricted to a stop-and-search procedure,

in accordance with international law. If they discovered contraband, the crew was allowed to get off the ship safely before the U-boat sank it, usually by gunfire. Such tactics hadn't brought them great success to date: in the first three months of the war, German U-boats had only sunk 105,000 tons of merchant shipping. This led Churchill to assert, "The failure of the German submarine campaign was patent to the whole world." Those days were over.

On 18 February 1915 the Germans launched their first unrestricted U-boat campaign. Henceforth any ship entering the war zone, whether Allied or neutral, was liable to be torpedoed without warning. The Germans had some justification for adopting such ruthless tactics. The British had already begun defensively arming their merchant ships, so that any U-boat commander who surfaced in order to search a ship put himself in serious jeopardy. A single hit from a merchant ship on his fragile hull could mean that he would be unable to submerge and would be at the mercy of British naval patrols.

Even more dangerous were the Q-ships, which the British had begun using in late 1914. These were cleverly disguised tramp steamers manned by Royal Navy crews and carrying concealed armaments of up to 4-inch guns. By various ruses they would try to lure a surfaced U-boat close enough to sink it before the Germans realized the danger. After their experiences with armed merchant ships, U-boat commanders had understandably become wary of surfacing for stop-and-search procedures, and they increasingly resorted to torpedoing ships from periscope depth without warning.

The German goverment was naturally concerned about the effect the declaration of unrestricted submarine warfare would have on neutrals, above all the United States, but they felt they had to do something to offset the effect of the British blockade. Apart from the Baltic, their own merchant ships were confined to port, while the enemy's were free to transport food and vital war materials to Britain from all parts of the world. The blockade had also severed communication with the extensive German empire. The Germans were unable to reinforce their troops fighting in Africa or receive any support from their colonies, whereas thousands of Allied troops and their equipment were ferried to Europe from the dominions and colonies with little hindrance. The Germans hoped an all-out U-boat campaign would help redress the balance by acting as a kind of counterblockade.

The British also made changes after the Dogger Bank, but of a less dramatic nature. Jellicoe recognized that previous failures to trap the enemy had been at least partly due to signal confusion, and he made several important additions to the signal book. Nelson's famous "Engage the enemy more closely" was reinstated. New signals such as "Admiral unable to make signals by W/T," "Flag officer making signal is disabled," and "C-in-C transfers command" were added to make it easier for a commander in chief to explain his situation and transfer command if necessary. Priority was given to the installation of auxiliary W/T sets in the battle cruisers to avert the problem Beatty had faced when his electrical power was knocked out. Jellicoe also rewrote sections of the Grand Fleet Battle Orders to ensure better distribution of fire and prevent errors such as Pelly had made at the Dogger Bank.

Fire-control equipment was installed in all the battle cruisers. The lack of fire control was held to be largely responsible for their poor gunnery performance against Hipper. Although these ships were also given some extra armor protection, not enough attention was paid to flash protection of their magazines. Another important area which received attention was ammunition. It was strongly suspected that British armor-piercing shells were less than adequate, as Jellicoe had tried to point out before the war. New types of shell were ordered but unfortunately they would not be ready in time for Jutland.

One area that did not receive enough attention was the battle cruisers' gunnery. Jellicoe knew that the Germans were highly proficient at gunnery, in spite of their lack of automatic fire-control devices. This was partly due to their superior range finders, which enabled them to get on target quickly. But it was also due to the repeated gunnery drills they carried out in the Baltic under realistic battle conditions, with ships maneuvering at high speed in a variety of weather conditions. Jellicoe wanted to ensure that the gunnery of the Grand Fleet was just as good, before he met the High Seas Fleet in action, so he had his battle squadrons carry out frequent gunnery drills and practice firings at Scapa Flow. It now had excellent facilities for target practice inside the flow, protected from the threat of submarines.

But this was not the case for the 1st and 2d Battle Cruiser Squadrons. Excuses were made for their lack of gunnery practice. It was true that the Rosyth area was unsuitable for practice firings because of frequent fog and heavy sea traffic. There was also the danger of submarines and mines off the mouth of the Forth. Jellicoe tried to persuade Beatty to send his ships, one or two at a time, to Scapa Flow for gunnery practice, but Beatty objected. His main reason was that he was reluctant to weaken his forces, even temporarily, in case Hipper made another raid on the east coast. Some of Beatty's officers made the arrogant claim that they did their practice in action against the enemy, not on the firing range. There was a feeling in the battle cruiser squadrons that everything would be all right on the day.

The most important outcome of the Dogger Bank action was that the Battle Cruiser Force was reconstituted as a separate fleet. Three squadrons—seven ships in all, and nine by the time of Jutland—plus two light cruiser squadrons, were to be based on Rosyth. This became known as the Battle Cruiser Fleet. Although still officially part of the Grand Fleet under Jellicoe's overall command, he allowed Beatty a fairly free rein. In reply the Germans could muster only five battle cruisers, even with addition of the recently commissioned *Lützow*. The new and powerful *Hindenburg* would not be ready in time for Jutland. Hipper was going to be at a distinct disadvantage the next time he met Beatty, at least in terms of numbers.

Churchill and Fisher proposed that the battle cruisers' base be moved south to the Humber, and that Jellicoe's battle squadrons come down from Scapa to Rosyth. The antisubmarine defenses were now complete at both places, and these moves would put the Grand Fleet much closer to Wilhelmshaven, making it easier for Beatty to intercept enemy sorties and providing Jellicoe a better chance of getting to the scene of action in time to support him. These southern shifts would cut about eight hours off Beatty's steaming time and four hours off Jellicoe's, at a typical cruising speed of eighteen knots. Fisher expressed his opinion to Jellicoe with his usual vigor: "The *fundamental fact* is that you can never be in time as long as you are at Scapa Flow and therefore there will NEVER be a battle with the German High Seas Fleet unless von Pohl goes north especially to fight you *and that he never will.*"

But both Jellicoe and Beatty were strongly opposed to these shifts. They could not see that the advantages outweighed the disadvantages. To them, the Humber was too vulnerable to mines and submarines; Rosyth was unsuitable as a fleet anchorage because there were frequently thick fogs off the Forth, and its entrance was so narrow that it would take too much time to get the whole fleet out to sea. There were also fears that the fleet could be mined in, or trapped above the Forth Bridge by the tide or even the destruction of the bridge by Zeppelins or sabotage. In the face of the united opposition of their two leading admirals, Churchill and Fisher backed down. In the end the only results of their proposals were the moves of Vice-Adm. Sir Thomas Jerram's 2d Battle Squadron from Scapa to Cromarty, and Vice-Adm. Sir Edward Bradford's 3d Battle Squadron of predreadnoughts from Rosyth to the Thames.

Beatty suggested that Rear-Adm. Sir Hugh Evan-Thomas's 5th Battle Squadron of five fast superdreadnoughts be transferred from Scapa to Rosyth to reinforce him, but Jellicoe vetoed this idea. "The stronger I make Beatty," Jellicoe noted, "the greater is the temptation for him to get involved in an independent action." Jellicoe was well aware that the Germans would welcome an opportunity to catch Beatty without the Grand Fleet in support.

During the first half of 1915, the Admiralty under Churchill's dynamic leadership was preoccupied with the search for decisive action. Although the First Lord had stated that "the British Navy and the sea power which it exerts will increasingly dominate the general situation," he was not content with that situation. He grew impatient and restless. However dominant and effective British control of the sea might be, it was not in Churchill's nature to accept a passive, defensive role. He wanted more offensive action from the navy, and less of the "silent, relentless pressure." Both he and Fisher were afraid that Jellicoe's cautious defensive stance would lead to a stalemate at sea as well as on land, where the armies were bogged down in Flanders.

They devised daring plans for the occupation of Borkum in the Friesian Islands, the capture of Heligoland, and the landing of troops on the Baltic coast as a threat to the German right flank. The idea behind these proposals was to exert close pressure on the High Seas Fleet and provoke it into coming out to fight a fleet action. Such schemes had been proposed before and had already been rejected as impractical and dangerous by the cabinet and, particularly, the Army General Staff, which was not keen on the idea of depositing its troops far away on the enemy coast with no secure lines of communication. Churchill's proposals were rejected again. As Richmond, the brilliant assistant director of Naval Operations, pointed out, "We have the game in our hands if we sit tight, but this Churchill cannot see. He must see something tangible and can't understand that naval warfare acts in a wholly different way from war on shore. The Fleet in the North dominates the position. It's no business of ours to go trying to pluck occasional, small indifferent fruits in the south."

No one understood this better than Jellicoe. He was not going to throw away his advantage on reckless attempts to force a fleet action close to an enemy coastline protected by minefields, submarine bases, and shore batteries. To risk his superiority was to risk losing the war. He was content to wait patiently for the Germans to come out and meet him in the northern part of the North Sea, confident they would have to come out sooner or later. He would fight them on his terms or not at all. In the meantime he concentrated on making sure the Grand Fleet was well trained and battle-ready when that day came.

In contrast to the fire-breathing notions of the First Lord and his First Sea Lord, both Jellicoe and Beatty favored less risky methods. In addition to continuing their periodic sweeps of the North Sea, they planned sorties as far as the Skagerrak and the coast of Jutland and seaplane raids on the Zeppelin sheds in Schleswig-Holstein. They meant to carry out these raids using their light forces, backed up by Beatty's battle cruisers, with the Grand Fleet cruising behind him, out of sight and poised to strike. Jellicoe hoped to provoke the Germans into coming out in retaliation and catch them in a trap between Beatty's battle cruisers and his own battle squadrons. He didn't realize that these tactics were unlikely to bear fruit as long as Pohl remained in command of the High Seas Fleet.

At the end of March, Jellicoe wrote these perceptive lines to Beatty, giving his view of probable German tactics:

> I imagine the Germans will try to entrap you by risking their battle-cruisers as a decoy. They know the odds are that you will be 100 miles away from me, and can draw you down to the Heligoland Bight without my being in effective support. This is all right if you keep your speed, but if some of your ships have their speed badly reduced in a fight with their battlecruisers, or by submarines, their loss seems inevitable if you are drawn onto the High Seas Fleet with me too far off to extricate them before dark. The Germans know you very well and will try to take advantage of that quality of "not letting go when you have once got hold," which you possess thank God. But one must concern oneself with the result to the country of a serious decrease in relative strength. If the game looks worth the candle the risks can be taken. If not, one's duty is to be cautious. I believe you will see which is the proper course, and pursue it victoriously.

This letter was remarkably prophetic in terms of what was to happen at Jutland.

Churchill had not given up on the idea of more offensive naval operations after his first proposals were rebuffed. The armies were deadlocked on the western front, and a long, expensive war of attrition seemed inevitable if something was not done. He asked, "Are there not other alternatives than sending our armies to chew barbed wire in Flanders?" In February he came up with a brand-new scheme—to force a passage through the Dardanelles with a squadron of battleships and reach Constantinople. In his enthusiastic view this would "cut the Turkish empire in two, paralyse its capital, unite the Balkan states against our enemies, rescue Serbia, help the Grand Duke [C-in-C of the Russian armies] in the main operation of the War and, by shortening its duration, save countless lives."

Fisher had serious misgivings but went along with Churchill—at first. He was concerned about the diversion of naval strength to the Mediterranean and the risk of jeopardizing Jellicoe's superiority in the North Sea. He warned Churchill at the outset: "The Empire ceases if our Grand Fleet ceases. No risks can be taken." But Churchill was both determined and persuasive. He overrode all objections and minimized or simply ignored the practical difficulties inherent in the scheme. Churchill was able to convince a cabinet grown weary of the stalemate in France that the scheme offered the chance of a major breakthrough which would shorten the war.

The first part of the naval assault on the Dardanelles was a bombardment of the outer forts at the entrance to the straits. The attacking force initially consisted of a squadron of older predreadnoughts—five British and four French. These ships were considered expendable. Then the squadron was strengthened by the addition of seven more predreadnoughts, the valuable battle cruiser *Inflexible,* and the latest 15-inch superdreadnought *Queen Elizabeth.* These ships made their stately way into the straits to tackle the inner forts. After the loss of three battleships to Turkish mines and gunfire, and three more badly damaged ships, including the valuable *Inflexible,* the British withdrew before the squadron suffered any more losses.

The naval assault was a total failure, and the Dardanelles operation was canceled a few days later. It had been a complete fiasco from start to finish. Jellicoe later called it an "unforgivable error." Admiral Bacon went further, describing it as "an act of sheer lunacy." As Nelson had said over a hundred years earlier, "Any sailor who attacked a fort was a fool."

It had certainly been folly to try to force the Dardanelles by warships alone. It was then decided to make an amphibious assault on the Gallipoli peninsula. This was planned for April. It came too late. The Turks, forewarned by the naval bombardment, had plenty of time to strengthen their defenses using German military expertise and a large supply of Austrian guns. Sadly, an earlier combined operation might have succeeded, when the Turkish forces were much weaker. By the beginning of May the Allied invasion was hopelessly bogged down.

In the end, the Gallipoli campaign turned out be an even bigger disaster than the naval attack on the Dardanelles. Three more old battleships were lost. But the naval losses, though heavy, were insignificant beside those of the military. By the time the campaign was called off in December 1916 it had cost the Allies 250,000 casualties, the majority due to disease. Turkish casualties were also very heavy—an estimated 250,000, and probably more.

By the beginning of May Churchill and Fisher were at loggerheads, not only over the conduct of the Gallipoli campaign, which Fisher had increasingly opposed, especially when Churchill kept demanding more ships, but because of serious disagreements about the whole administration of the Admiralty. Churchill had usurped the authority and functions of all the sea lords, not just Fisher's. With his boundless enegy and incredible capacity for work, he tried to run the Admiralty as a one-man show. Jellicoe and Beatty were disturbed by the friction developing between the First Lord and the First Sea Lord, aware that there inevitably would be serious discord before long. At the time, Beatty wrote to his wife, "Two very strong and clever men, one old, wily, and of vast experience, one young, self-assertive, with a great self-satisfaction but unstable. They cannot both run the show."

By 14 May Fisher had had enough. Churchill was again demanding that more ships be sent to Gallipoli. In a rage, Fisher resigned as First Sea Lord and literally walked out of the Admiralty, vowing never to set foot in the building again. After an official inquiry into the Dardanelles operation, Churchill ended up taking most of the blame for the failure of the naval attack on the forts. To be fair to him, he had initially proposed an amphibious assault but had been blocked by Kitchener, who claimed that no troops were available. In the political crisis that followed Fisher's resignation, the ruling Liberals came under a storm of criticism from the press and Balfour's Conservative opposition. To save his government, Prime Minister Asquith agreed to form a coalition with the Conservatives. They made one condition: Churchill must go. Asquith replaced him with Balfour as First Lord, and Admiral of the Fleet Sir Henry Jackson took over from Fisher as First Sea Lord.

Meanwhile, the unrestricted U-boat campaign had been going on for nearly three months, with increasingly serious losses of merchant shipping. Its most dramatic result was the torpedoing of the British liner *Lusitania* off the southern tip of Ireland on 7 May 1915. *Korvetten-Kapitän* Schweiger of the U-20 had been unable to resist putting a torpedo into this huge and inviting target, even though she was clearly a passenger liner. The torpedo struck the *Lusitania* amidships and she went down twenty minutes later with the loss of 1,198 passengers and crew. The world was shocked by this callous act, which the Germans tried to excuse by claiming the ship had been carrying munitions. As the noted historian Corbett wrote, "Never had there been such a war loss on the sea; never one which so violently outraged the laws of war and dictates of humanity."

Among the passengers lost when the *Lusitania* went down were 128 Americans. The United States was outraged and made strong diplomatic protests, as well as claims for indemnity. Although the Germans were worried about the possibility of drawing the United States into the war, they brushed off American protests by stating that they had clearly warned all shipping entering the War Zone of the danger from submarines. The commotion died down somewhat, and the unrestricted campaign continued for another three months.

Then on 19 August the British liner *Arabic* was torpedoed and sunk without warning by the U-24, also off southern Ireland. Again there was heavy loss of life, including three Americans. This brought matters to a head. This time the American protests were so sharp that the Germans were afraid the United States might break off diplomatic relations, and they instructed their U-boat captains not to attack any more liners without warning and to give time for passengers to disembark safely if they did make an attack. Finally, under intense political pressure from German chancellor Bethmann-Hollweg and the Foreign Office, which feared that one more serious incident might cause the United States to enter the war, the Admiralstab was forced to call a halt to its first unrestricted U-boat campaign on 30 August. It had cost the Allies nine hundred thousand tons of shipping, mainly British vessels. This ended the German attempt at a counterblockade—for the moment.

By this time the Germans were feeling the effects of blockade themselves. Except for the Baltic, the German merchant marine had disappeared from the oceans of the world. Most of its vessels were tied up in the ports they had been in when war broke out. The German economy was beginning to suffer serious damage from the loss of its foreign trade. Sweden was now its only significant trading partner, and there were shortages of vital war materials apart from what they could import from Sweden. Food was in such short supply that rationing was imposed in Germany, where the brunt of the blockade was borne by the civilian population. Gen. Erich Ludendorff was to write, "If the war lasted our defeat seemed inevitable. Economically we were in a highly unfavourable position for a war of exhaustion. . . . The supply of foodstuffs caused great anxiety."

The British tightened and extended the definitions of contraband to include almost anything a merchant ship might carry. Any foreign ship that was intercepted, whatever its nationality, was escorted to the contraband-control base at Kirkwall in the Orkneys, where its cargo was inspected. If the inspectors discovered contraband, the cargo was either confiscated or purchased by the United Kingdom for its own use. This stop-and-search procedure thoroughly annoyed the neutrals, especially the United States. The ill feeling it generated caused a loss of American sympathy for the British cause.

Blockade duty was an arduous task for the men and ships of the Royal Navy. They had to cover two stretches of stormy, inhospitable sea—one between northern Scotland and Iceland, and the even more inhospitable gap between Iceland and Greenland, a total distance of more than six hundred miles. They couldn't plug the narrower gap between Scotland and Norway, because blockade runners were able to hug the Norwegian coast inside territorial waters during daylight, and then head for the open sea under cover of darkness.

Whatever the success of the Northern Patrol, the admirals looked on it merely as a way of pressuring the German fleet to come out to try to raise the blockade by fighting a fleet action. Economic strangulation was too slow a process for the admirals. They didn't realize that, as Marion Siney concluded after the war based on her detailed study of the effects of the blockade, "although economic pressure is of necessity rather slow in showing definite results, it was here that the Central Powers [Germany and Austria-Hungary] first revealed signs of collapse."

The lack of naval action in 1915 affected morale on both sides of the North Sea. The lives of the men of the Grand Fleet revolved around "patrol and coal." Jellicoe took his ships out frequently for maneuvers and gunnery exercises to keep up their fighting efficiency, but for long stretches the fleet lay at anchor inside the Flow. All there was on shore were the bleak, treeless surroundings which offered no amenities such as pubs, cinemas, or dance halls. Jellicoe tried to compensate for the boredom and monotony of the men's existence, and to keep up their spirits as well as their physical fitness. He had sports grounds built and instituted a regular program of games and races. He also encouraged amateur theatricals on board ship, which as just about the only form of entertainment available, became very popular.

There was a wardroom song at the time that reflected the mood of the officers at Scapa Flow, and probably that of the lower deck as well:

> We hate this bloody war,
>   It gives us all the blight,
> We cannot go ashore,
>   And yet we cannot fight.

The long inactivity of 1915 had a more serious effect on the morale of the High Seas Fleet. When food rations were reduced for sailors as well as for civilians, there was widespread discontent. Every day the deteriorating food situation served as a bitter reminder of the British blockade, and the sea power that sustained it and kept their fleet impotently at anchor. Unlike the Royal Navy crews, the German officers and men spent most of their time in port living ashore in separate barracks. There wasn't the same degree of contact or shared experience, which even though arduous and unpleasant at times, fostered a spirit of comradeship between the officers and men of the Royal Navy—or at least a feeling of common cause. There were no organized recreational programs such as Jellicoe had set up.

As time went by, the discontent manifested itself in a steady trickle of the best officers and men to the U-boats. Tired of the inactivity, they asked for transfer to the submarine branch, where they could be sure of action, however dangerous. The decline in morale under Pohl continued, until by late 1915 feelings of gloom and despondency had spread throughout the German fleet. Seaman Richard Strumpf, serving in the battleship *Helgoland,* wrote in his diary, "A year ago we had sailed over there and our cruisers subjected three of the coastal towns to a thorough bombardment. But it was all different then; we were still idealistic. Our enthusiasm was such that each one of us would have been willing to lay down his life in battle. But now the very thought of a battle frightens us."

There was also dissension and strife in the High Command over the policy that restricted the fleet's movements to occasional sallies into the Heligoland Bight. Senior officers made frequent demands for some form of offensive action. Pohl's response was not helpful. He in effect told them to mind their own business. They went over his head to the chief of the Admiralstab, and even to the kaiser, with persistent criticisms of his leadership. The officer corps had no confidence in the timid, ineffectual Pohl and had been pressing for his removal for some time. Pohl had only carried out five ineffective sorties in the whole of 1915, none of them proceeding more than 150 miles from the mouth of the Jade. The British were unaware of it, but a slow process of decay of the High Seas Fleet had begun.

The situation came to a head in December, when Gen. Erich von Falkenhayn, C-in-C of the army, called for an urgent conference with the Naval Staff. The Army General Staff asked the Imperial Navy to adopt a more offensive strategy and try to break the blockade that was slowly sapping Germany's military strength. The generals also urged the admirals to resume an all-out submarine campaign, timed to coincide with their planned assault on Verdun. The army saw the navy as a weapon to help them break the deadlock on the western front. This meeting between the heads of the army and navy led to the most significant event of 1915 from a naval standpoint: The Admiralstab decided to replace Pohl. By now he was mortally ill with a brain tumor, and he resigned on 18 January. Vice Adm. Reinhard Scheer was appointed in his place.

•••

Scheer actually took over as commander in chief of the High Seas Fleet on 24 January 1916, one year to the day after the Battle of the Dogger Bank. He immediately sought and obtained the kaiser's approval to adopt a more aggressive policy. Wilhelm gave him permission to take the whole of the fleet to sea if he thought it necessary to lay a trap for a weaker enemy force.

Scheer, who had been chief of staff before the war, was an able, experienced torpedo specialist and squadron commander. He had commanded the 2d and 3d Battle Squadrons, where he gained a reputation as a clever tactician. He had a determined, thrusting personality, somewhat lacking in humor, warmth, and imagination. His tactics involved nothing very different from those used previously by Ingenohl, but he meant to pursue them much more vigorously. Like his predecessors, he ruled out a head-on clash with the Grand Fleet. He believed that "systematic and constant pressure" would provoke the British into giving up their patient vigil and send out part of the fleet in response. This would offer "favourable opportunities for attack." The pressure was to take various forms: increased submarine and mine warfare against commerce, attacks on Britain's Scandinavian trade by surface ships, intensified night bombing raids on British cities by the Zeppelins of the Imperial Navy, and more active sorties by the fleet, including raids on the British coast by Hipper's battle cruisers. Scheer would prove to be just as tough a foe for Jellicoe as Hipper had been for Beatty.

Scheer wasted no time getting started. On 10 February he sent a force of light cruisers and torpedo boats to attack the British minesweeping flotilla off the Dogger Bank. The raid scattered the minesweepers and their escorts, and the sloop *Arabis* was sunk. The Admiralty had been warned of the raid by Room 40 and sent out the Harwich force to intercept the Germans, but by the time Tyrwhitt got there the Germans had turned for home. Next there came a combined raid on the British coast by Zeppelins and Hipper's battle cruisers, planned for the beginning of March. The intended targets were Rosyth and the Humber. But the raid was aborted because of bad weather, and the raiders were forced to return to base after having dropped only two bombs on Hull. Although the operation came to nothing, it was a sign that further raids on the coast were to be expected.

The next German battle cruiser raid took place on 24–25 April, timed to coincide with the expected uprising by Irish nationalists in Dublin on Easter Monday, perhaps as a show of German support for the rebels or to achieve maximum nuisance value. Hipper was ill at the time and the raid was led by Rear Adm. Friedrich Boedicker in the *Seydlitz*. It didn't start off well. The *Seydlitz* struck a mine coming through the Friesian

Islands and Boedicker had to transfer his flag to the newly commissioned *Lützow.* The targets this time were Lowestoft and Yarmouth, which had already been shelled in November 1914.

The Admiralty had learned of both the timing and target of the raid from Room 40 and sent Tyrwhitt out to meet them with his cruisers and destroyers. Beatty was already on his way with the battle cruisers, but he was too far north to have much chance of intercepting Boedicker. After the Germans had bombarded Lowestoft, Tyrwhitt sighted them and engaged Boedicker's light cruiser screen, hoping to draw the raiders away from their next target, Great Yarmouth. At first the Germans refused to be deflected by their puny opponents. When Tyrwhitt came within range of the German battle cruisers it was a case of David versus Goliath, and he was forced to withdraw. But with his usual tenaciousness and courage, he continued to harass the raiders until his flagship, the light cruiser *Conquest,* was heavily damaged by a salvo of 12-inch shells.

He had managed to save Great Yarmouth from serious damage though, because Boedicker, who was certainly no Hipper, decided to cut short the raid and head for base after this brush with British light forces. He was fearful that they might be the forerunners of the enemy battle fleet, although he had no evidence that it was anywhere near. At the time Boedicker withdrew, Beatty was still three hours' steaming distance away, and Jellicoe was even farther back. The bombardment of the two towns caused the destruction of about two hundred houses, mostly in Lowestoft, but fortunately there were few civilian casualties. The operation had achieved nothing of military significance, at the cost of two submarines sunk and a valuable battle cruiser put out of action for several weeks.

The most important outcome of the Lowestoft raid was the strengthening of the Battle Cruiser Fleet by the dispatch of the five *Queen Elizabeth*–class superdreadnoughts to Rosyth—as previously requested by Beatty and vetoed by Jellicoe. He had planned to use these ships as a fast maneuverable wing of his battle fleet, but after the Lowestoft raid he agreed to transfer them to Beatty. The move allowed Beatty to send a few of his battle cruisers at a time to Scapa for badly needed gunnery practice. He sent the 3d Battle Cruiser Squadron first, perhaps because he regarded these older *Invincible*-class ships as not really fit to stand in his line of battle. Regrettably, there was not enough time for his other more modern and powerful ships to practice at Scapa before they went into action at Jutland.

Jellicoe retaliated against Scheer's sorties by mounting raids on German Zeppelin bases on the coast of Schleswig-Holstein and mine-laying operations in the German-swept channels. The first raid was on Hoyer on 24 March, and the second on Tondern on 4 May. The raids were carried out by the seaplane tender *Vindex,* escorted by Tyrwhitt's light cruisers. The raiders were backed up by the whole of the Grand Fleet in the hope that Scheer would come out in retaliation. He did so on both occasions, but he was forced to turn back—first by heavy fog during the Hoyer raid, then by rough seas during the Tondern raid—before Jellicoe could make contact. Neither raid was very successful in terms of concrete results. Scheer didn't discover that the Grand Fleet was out in force until after Jellicoe had been obliged to turn for home to refuel his ships.

It was Scheer's next, more ambitious sortie that led to the only full-scale naval battle that would ever be fought between two fleets of dreadnoughts.

THE BATTLE

PART 2

The Fleets Sail

CHAPTER 7

Germans intend operations commencing tomorrow.
You should concentrate to eastwards of Long Forties
and be ready for eventualities.

—Admiralty telegram to C-in-C,
Grand Fleet, 30 May 1916

In the weeks following the Lowestoft raid, Scheer was planning a daring three-pronged operation designed to trap and destroy Beatty's Battle Cruiser Force. It involved the use of submarines, airships, and the
whole of the High Seas Fleet. In the first stage, Scheer sent out every
available U-boat to lay mines off Rosyth, Cromarty, and Scapa. Seven
of the eighteen U-boats were ordered to lie in wait off the Firth of
Forth, ready to ambush Beatty's ships when they left Rosyth. The next
step was for the Zeppelins to reconnoiter the area south of Scapa Flow
to make sure Jellicoe's battle squadrons were not out on a sweep at
the time the main operation—another raid on a vulnerable coastal
town—began. Once again the raid was to be carried out by Hipper's
battle cruisers, but this time Hipper would be closely backed up by
Scheer's battle fleet, lying just out of sight of land.

The target was Sunderland, barely a hundred miles from Rosyth.
The raid on Lowestoft had taken place too far south of Rosyth to
allow Beatty to get there in time to intercept the raiders. The choice
of Sunderland would give him plenty of time. Scheer knew that reports of the bombardment would immediately draw Beatty out.
Those of Beatty's ships that managed to get through the mine and
U-boat trap would be led into another trap by Hipper, where they
would be fallen on and annihilated by Scheer's battle fleet.

The operation was scheduled for 17 May, but unfortunately for
Scheer, things didn't go according to plan. The U-boats reached their
stations, but the weather was so bad that high winds prevented the
Zeppelins from taking off. Scheer was not going to chance it without

knowing where Jellicoe was, and he postponed the operation until 23 May. Then he learned that the *Seydlitz* would not be repaired in time for Hipper's raid, and when several of his battleships developed boiler-room problems, he decided to postpone the operation again, this time until 29 May, when the weather in the North Sea was forecast to be clear enough for the Zeppelins.

By now his U-boats had been at sea for nearly two weeks, and they were in no shape to carry out an efficient operation. One of them had been sunk by an armed trawler; another had sprung a leak and been forced to return to base; several more had been scattered by rough weather. There were only four of the eighteen U-boats still at their assigned positions. In any case, they were all running low on fuel and would soon have to return to base. Reluctantly, Scheer called off the operation altogether. But he hadn't given up on his plans to trap Beatty, and he decided on a less ambitious and risky scheme.

Scheer's alternative plan was to take the High Seas Fleet north from Wilhelmshaven at about midnight on 30 May, staying well off the Danish coast, and arrive next afternoon off the entrance to the Skagerrak. There he would launch an attack with Hipper's battle cruisers on British merchant ships and cruiser escorts that German intelligence had told him to expect in the area. Then, Hipper was to head north and advertise his location by steaming very close to the Norwegian coast in broad daylight, while Scheer cruised fifty miles behind him, out of sight of the shore. The Germans knew that the Norwegians would waste no time broadcasting the news of Hipper's appearance. Scheer was confident that as soon as the Admiralty learned that Hipper had gone so far north, they would send Beatty on another high-speed dash across the North Sea to cut him off from his base. When Beatty arrived the following morning, Scheer planned to crush him between Hipper's battle cruisers and his own battle squadrons. But the Germans had not reckoned with the British direction-finding stations and the code-breakers of Room 40.

For the previous two weeks the cryptographers of Room 40 had been receiving so many wireless intercepts from the direction-finders that they were aware the Germans were up to something. They knew that a large number of U-boats had been sent out on 17 May, yet there had been no sign of them along the Atlantic shipping lanes. This indicated the Germans were planning some major operation in the North Sea. Room 40 wasn't able to decipher all the intercepted signals completely, because of frequent changes to the German naval codes, but they were still able to piece together a pretty clear picture of what Scheer had in mind. They knew he had ordered the High Seas Fleet to be in a state of readiness on 28 May. Significantly, all U-boat commanders had been warned to expect German warships at sea on 30–31 May, to avoid them accidentally torpedoing one of their own ships.

It was evident that the operation was going to involve the whole fleet.

Then on the morning of 30 May, Room 40 deciphered an order for the High Seas Fleet to assemble in the outer Jade roadstead that evening. The Admiralty immediately informed Jellicoe and Beatty that the Germans were probably coming out. The same afternoon, Room 40 intercepted a cryptic message from Scheer to all his commanders. When it was decoded, all it said was, "31 GG 2490." The cryptographers could not be certain of its meaning, but based on previous experience, they concluded that it was a Most Secret (*Grösst Geheim*) signal to begin some operation designated number 2490 on 31 May.

Ninety minutes later another signal was intercepted and deciphered. This one contained instructions that the 3d Battle Squadron was to pass the Jade lightship by 3:30 A.M. on the thirty-first, to be followed by the 1st and 2d Battle Squadrons. It was now certain that the High Seas Fleet was coming out, but where was it going? From the increased minesweeping activity reported off the Schleswig coast, the best guess was that the fleet was going to take the northern route out of the Heligoland Bight and head up the coast of Jutland toward the Skagerrak.

By late afternoon on the thirtieth the atmosphere in the War Room at the Admiralty was electric. Jellicoe and Beatty were ordered to put to sea at 10:30 P.M. that evening. The two admirals were told, "Germans intend operations commencing tomorrow. You should concentrate to eastwards of Long Forties [an area roughly a hundred miles off the Scottish coast] and be ready for eventualities."

Everyone in the fleet hoped that *Der Tag* had finally arrived, although many were not convinced—they thought it was going to be "just another bloody useless sweep."

By an odd coincidence, Jellicoe had been planning a sortie himself in the Skagerrak area. He had scheduled it to begin on 1 June. His object had been to try to entice Scheer into bringing his fleet north. Here was Scheer doing just that, one day earlier than planned. It looked as if Jellicoe's hopes would be fulfilled.

He ordered Beatty to take his battle cruiser fleet to a rendezvous about ninety miles west of the entrance to the Skagerrak, and to arrive there at 2:00 P.M. on the thirty-first. Jellicoe was going to make for a rendezvous about seventy miles north of this point. If Beatty had not sighted any enemy forces by 2:00, he was instructed to search no more than twenty miles farther east before turning north to join up with Jellicoe's battle squadrons. Then the combined fleet would sweep toward the Horns Reef on the coast of Jutland and cut the High Seas Fleet off from its base.

The rendezvous chosen by Scheer to begin his operation was due south of the tip of Norway at Lindesnes. This meant that if the two enemy fleets stayed on course, they would both arrive in the area west

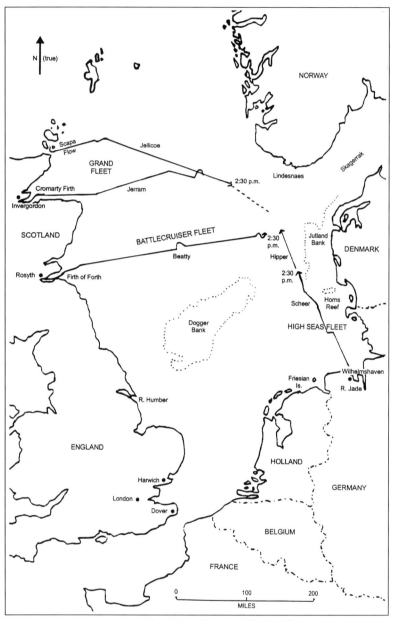

Approach of the fleets to Jutland

of the entrance to the Skagerrak during the early afternoon of 31 May, unless fate intervened.

At 10:30 P.M. on 30 May, Jellicoe's flagship *Iron Duke* steamed out of Scapa Flow, followed by the 4th Battle Squadron, then the 1st Battle Squadron. Once clear of the anchorage, the sixteen dreadnoughts took up their cruising formation of four parallel divisions, four cables apart. Rear-Adm. the Hon. Horace Hood in the *Invincible* took station ahead of them with his 3d Battle Cruiser Squadron, accompanied by the 2d Cruiser Squadron. The van and both sides of the battle fleet were protected by a screen of eleven light cruisers and forty-two destroyers. Jellicoe set the fleet on an easterly course at a cruising speed of eighteen knots, giving him plenty of time to reach the rendezvous on schedule.

Thirty minutes after the main body of the Grand Fleet left harbor, Vice-Admiral Jerram set out from Invergordon in the Cromarty Firth, about ninety miles south of Scapa. His flagship *King George V* led the 2d Battle Squadron—eight more dreadnoughts—in company with the 1st Cruiser Squadron and a screen of eleven destroyers. Jerram set a northeasterly course, converging on Jellicoe's. He expected to join up with the C-in-C at about noon on the thirty-first.

At the time Jerram left Cromarty, Beatty steamed out of the Firth of Forth in the *Lion,* at the head of the 1st and 2d Battle Cruiser Squadrons. He was followed by Evan-Thomas in the *Barham* with his 5th Battle Squadron of *Queen Elizabeth*–class superdreadnoughts. Beatty also had a protective screen of smaller ships—three light cruiser squadrons and two destroyer flotillas (DFs)—and the seaplane carrier *Engadine.* His course was east-northeast, which would take him directly to a point seventy miles south of the main rendezvous.

Thus all three sections of the Grand Fleet were at sea, heading toward the Jutland peninsula, *two hours before* any of the High Seas Fleet left the Jade estuary. The submarine trap that Scheer had set on 17 May failed to have much impact on Beatty's ships as they steamed away from the Scottish coast through the brief darkness of the summer night. Farther out to sea they were spotted by two of Scheer's U-boats, but the U-32 was the only one close enough to mount an attack. She fired two torpedoes at one of Beatty's screen, the cruiser *Galatea,* but they both missed. There was another outbreak of "periscopeitis," which resulted in no fewer than thirteen reported sightings of imaginary submarines.

Scheer's mine trap also failed to have any effect. None of Beatty's or Jellicoe's ships hit a mine, but a week later one of the mines laid by the U-75 sank the cruiser *Hampshire* off the Orkneys. She went down with all hands, including the national hero, Field-Marshal Lord Kitchener, who was headed to Russia to persuade the Russian generals to keep on fighting.

At 1:00 A.M. on the thirty-first, the ships of the High Seas Fleet began to raise anchor and move out of the roadstead toward the Jade lightship. First to leave was Hipper's flagship, the brand new *Lützow,* leading the five battle cruisers of the 1st Scouting Group. She was followed by the light cruisers of the 2d Scouting Group and thirty torpedo boats. As Hipper headed north toward the swept channel through the minefields of the Heligoland Bight, Scheer's battle squadrons were preparing to set sail.

One hour later, Scheer put to sea in his flagship *Friedrich der Grosse,* along with the rest of the High Seas Fleet; leading the way was the 3d Battle Squadron of eight *König*-class dreadnoughts, commanded by Rear Adm. Paul Behncke in the name ship, then the 1st squadron of eight *Nassaus* led by Vice Adm. Erhard Schmidt in the *Ostfriesland.* Bringing up the rear was Rear Adm. Franz Mauve in the *Deutschland,* with the six predreadnoughts of the 2d Battle Squadron. These older ships carried less than half the armament of Scheer's dreadnoughts, and they were known in the fleet as "the five minute ships"—this being the estimated time they would survive against modern battleships. Scheer had been talked into taking the 2d Battle Squadron with him by his friend Mauve, who had begged the C-in-C not to leave him behind. Scheer had a soft spot for the squadron he had once commanded. The twenty-two battleships of Scheer's battle fleet were screened by a force of six light cruisers and thirty-one torpedo boats.

In the early hours of 31 May 1916, these two great armadas were steaming inexorably toward a climactic meeting off the coast of Jutland, a meeting that only one of the two commanders in chief had sought, and that only one of them anticipated. Scheer had no idea when he started out that morning that a fleet action was likely within a matter of hours. He expected to encounter only Beatty's battle cruisers without Jellicoe in support, and not until the following day. He was so confident of this that he wasn't concerned whether or not his Zeppelins would able to make a reconnaissance such as he had planned for the earlier sortie. He reasoned that with the Danish coast on one flank and the whole of his light forces on the other, he would receive ample warning if Jellicoe did put to sea in an attempt to extricate Beatty from the trap. If this happened, Scheer could easily make a dash through the Skagerrak for the safety of the Baltic, where he knew Jellicoe would not follow him. If he had discovered that the whole of the Grand Fleet was already at sea and heading in his direction, there is little doubt that he would have turned back and canceled the operation. Thanks to British intelligence, Jellicoe had gained the element of surprise.

Scheer was outnumbered in every class of warship. His battle fleet had twenty-two battleships to Jellicoe's twenty-four—not much of a margin, perhaps, but only sixteen of Scheer's ships were true dreadnoughts. The margin against him in battle cruisers was much greater; he had only five to match the Grand Fleet's nine. In smaller ships, Scheer had only eleven light cruisers to Jellicoe's eight armored cruisers and twenty-six light cruisers. However, the British armored cruisers were obsolescent ships that were too slow and clumsy to play a proper scouting role with the battle fleet. Also, despite their heavy armament, they were too vulnerable to be much use in a fleet action. They were Jellicoe's "five-minute ships." Finally, the High Seas Fleet had sixty-one torpedo boats to counter the Grand Fleet's total of seventy-three destroyers. This was a bigger disadvantage than it looked because German torpedo boats were smaller and more lightly armed than British destroyers.

Altogether Jellicoe's fleet numbered 151 ships, while Scheer had only 99. But simple numerical comparisons do not give the whole picture. The British battle squadrons mounted 264 big guns to the Germans' 200. Yet even this comparison is deceptive, because half of the British battleships carried 13.5- and 15-inch weapons as their main armament, while their German counterparts mounted nothing more powerful than 11- or 12-inch guns. The weight of a 15-inch shell was more than twice that of a 12-inch shell. The same was true for a 13.5-inch shell compared with an 11-inch. The British battle fleet was capable of firing a total broadside of 286,000 pounds, the German 144,000 pounds, a ratio of two to one in Jellicoe's favor.

Beatty's advantage over Hipper in terms of firepower was even greater. The Battle Cruiser Fleet had six battle cruisers plus the four fast battleships temporarily attached to Beatty's force. Between them they carried eighty big guns to the forty-four of Hipper's five battle cruisers. In terms of total broadsides, Beatty could fire a weight of shell of 118,000 pounds compared with Hipper's 33,000 pounds; a ratio approaching four to one in Beatty's favor.

Considering these figures, it was no wonder that since the war began the High Seas Fleet had never sought a head-on clash with the Grand Fleet but tried to trap only part of it. But Scheer had several important advantages in matériel that tended to compensate for Jellicoe's clear superiority in firepower. Some of these were well known, or at least suspected, before the battle. Others were not realized until afterward.

German capital ships had been given more armor protection than their British counterparts. The Royal Navy, with Fisher at the helm, had made a conscious decision to sacrifice armor for greater speed. The Germans had made the opposite choice. The main belt and turret armor on German battleships was anywhere from ten to fourteen inches thick, while that of their British counterparts was in the nine- to twelve-inch range. This was not a big difference, but for the battle cruisers it was a different story. Scheer's battle cruisers were as well protected as British battleships, with nine to twelve inches of armor plate. Beatty's ships had only six to nine inches over the belt and turrets, and even thinner deck armor, making them vulnerable to long-range plunging fire.

British armor-piercing shells were also less than satisfactory. Their nose caps were too brittle and their delayed-action fuses were faulty. All too often, British shells broke up on impact, especially at the oblique angles to be expected in a long-range gunnery duel; or else the fuses detonated prematurely, causing the shells to explode before they had penetrated the enemy armor as they were meant to do before exploding, to cause maximum damage. In these cases the force of the explosion was dissipated outside the enemy armor and did little damage. The British suspected that this sometimes happened, but the Germans knew it for certain, from their experiences at the Dogger Bank and Heligoland Bight. German warships were also much more difficult to sink, whether by gunfire or underwater weapons. In fact, their builders had made them as nearly unsinkable as possible by means of many watertight compartments and double hulls. There was plenty of evidence for this. The *Scharnhorst* and *Gneisenau* had dispatched two British armored cruisers in less than an hour at Coronel, using 8.2-inch guns, yet it had taken about sixty hits from Sturdee's 12-inch guns to sink the *Scharnhorst* at the Falklands. A more striking illustration was the *Blücher*. It took two torpedoes and seventy hits from 12- and 13.5-inch shells to sink her.

Another big advantage the Germans had was the quality of their range finders. Although the British system of fire control was undoubtedly more advanced than the method used by the Germans, each depended heavily on an accurate initial estimate of the enemy's range. The Zeiss stereoscopic instruments were much better at this than the Barr and Stroud coincidence type used by the Royal Navy.

Other factors, such as the danger from cordite fires and the need for more adequate flash protection of magazines, were not fully appreciated by either side until after the battle, when some terrible and costly lessons were learned.

So, after nearly two years of war, the plans of two commanders in chief finally led to *Der Tag*—the culmination of the naval arms race that had begun in 1898 with the passage of the first German Navy Law. Where and when the climactic confrontation actually took place was to be determined as much by chance as by design.

Kaiser Wilhelm II *(Hulton Picture Library)*

Grand Adm. Alfred von Tirpitz *(Imperial War Museum)*

Adm. Sir John Fisher *(Hulton Picture Library)*

Winston Churchill inspecting sea cadets in 1912. *(Hulton Picture Library)*

HMS *Dreadnought (Imperial War Museum)*

Admiral Beatty's flagship HMS *Lion. (Imperial War Museum)*

Admiral Jellicoe climbing to the bridge of the *Iron Duke*.
(Imperial War Museum)

Vice Adm. Reinhard Scheer *(Imperial War Museum)*

Vice Adm. Franz von Hipper *(Imperial War Museum)*

King George V and Admiral Beatty in 1917
(Churchill College, Cambridge University)

Damage to houses in West Hartlepool after Rear Admiral Hipper's raid. *(Imperial War Museum)*

SMS *Blücher* capsizing at the Dogger Bank action. *(Imperial War Museum)*

SMS *Derfflinger (Imperial War Museum)*

Admiral Jellicoe's flagship *Iron Duke (Imperial War Museum)*

The hit on the *Lion's* Q turret, taken from the *Derfflinger.*
(Imperial War Museum)

Flames and smoke pouring from HMS *Indefatigable* seconds before
she blew up. *(Random House UK)*

The two halves of the *Invincible*'s hull resting on the sea bottom after she blew up. *(Imperial War Museum)*

A cloud of smoke rises from the explosion of HMS *Queen Mary*. *(Robert Hunt Picture Library)*

The effect of a 5.9-inch shell that hit above HMS *Chester*'s armor belt. *(Ullstein Bilderdienst)*

SMS *Seydlitz* down by the head and listing to port, on her way back to Wilhelmshaven after the battle. *(Random House UK)*

A hole in the *Lion's* funnel caused by a 12-inch shell. *(Random House UK)*

Shell and collision damage to HMS *Spitfire* after her encounter with
the battleship *Nassau*. *(Random House UK)*

S. M. S. „Seydlitz" nach der Skagerrak-Schlacht
schweren Treffern in der Schleuse zu Wilhelmshaven.

The heavily damaged *Seydlitz* in dock at Wilhelmshaven after she had
been pumped out. (*Imperial War Museum*)

The Run to the South

CHAPTER 8

There seems to be something wrong with our bloody ships to-day.

—Vice-Adm. Sir David Beatty

In the forenoon of 31 May, Capt. Thomas Jackson, director of the Admiralty's Operations Division, paid one of his infrequent visits to Room 40. He asked where the direction-finding stations placed the German call sign DK. According to one of those present, "He was obviously not the sort of senior officer to whom one offered gratuitous advice, and he was informed that the call sign DK was in Wilhelmshaven. Without further ado and without asking for an explanation or comment, the insufferable Jackson turned on his heel and left the room."

The staff of Room 40 knew that Scheer changed the harbor call sign of his flagship *Friedrich der Grosse* from DK to RÄ every time he went to sea to try to mislead the enemy into believing he was still in port. They had cottoned on to this ruse some time ago and could have told Jackson if he had simply asked. But because of the total lack of rapport between the "back room boys" and the operations people, Jackson didn't ask for an explanation and the men of Room 40 didn't dare offer any. They had become very sensitive about offering unsolicited comments after being rebuffed by the Naval War Staff more than once. They also were aware that Jackson had referred to their decoding reports as "damned nonsense."

At 12:30 P.M., unknown to Room 40, the Admiralty sent the following unfortunate telegram to Jellicoe and Beatty: "No definite news of enemy. They made all preparations for sailing early this morning. It was thought Fleet had sailed but Directionals place flagship in Jade at 11:10 A.M.GMT. Apparently they have been unable to carry out air reconnaissance which has delayed them."

The Admiralty's failure to make proper use of information available to it had two crucial effects on Jellicoe and Beatty. First, it removed any sense of urgency, and they wasted precious hours of daylight that might have been used to bring Scheer to action sooner. Even worse, it profoundly undermined their confidence in vital intelligence reports sent by the Admiralty during the later stages of the battle.

By the time this erroneous message was received, Beatty's battle cruiser fleet was steering a southeasterly course at eighteen knots, nearing the point it was supposed to reach before turning north to meet Jellicoe's battle fleet. Jellicoe was about sixty-five miles away, cruising toward the rendezvous at fifteen knots. Neither admiral had any reason for joining forces earlier than planned, so they maintained an economical speed to conserve their destroyers' fuel supply. If Scheer was in harbor three hundred miles away at 11:00 A.M., they knew he couldn't possibly be anywhere near the rendezvous area by 2:00 P.M. Even if he had left Wilhelmshaven immediately after the Admiralty said he was there, it would take until the next morning for his fleet to steam so far north. Jellicoe and Beatty expected to encounter nothing more than Hipper's unsupported battle cruisers that afternoon. But in fact Scheer had been at sea for nearly ten hours when the Admiralty sent the telegram, and his battle fleet was now only fifty miles astern of Hipper.

The spearhead of Beatty's main force was the 1st Battle Cruiser Squadron, three ships led by the flagship, HMS *Lion*. The 2d Squadron consisted of only two ships, the *New Zealand* and *Indefatigable* because the *Australia* was in dock. It was three miles astern on Beatty's starboard quarter. The 5th Battle Squadron, headed by Evan-Thomas in the *Barham*, was stationed five miles behind the *Lion* on her port quarter. Eight miles ahead of the flagship, the twelve ships of the 1st, 2d, and 3d Light Cruiser Squadrons were stretched out along a long lookout line that slanted across the van of the battle cruisers from west-southwest to east-northeast. It was plain from the way Beatty had deployed his advanced screen that he expected to meet Hipper's fleet coming up from a southeasterly direction. This was a reasonable assumption, but it was not clear why Beatty had decided to place his weakest division on the flank nearest to the enemy approach and his strongest division on the opposite flank.

As he approached the turning point, there had been no sign of the enemy by 2:00 P.M. Beatty kept on to the southeast for another fifteen minutes, still hoping to sight them, before signaling his ships to alter course to north by east to join up with Jellicoe.

Unknown to the two battle cruiser admirals, their flagships were only about fifty miles apart at the time Beatty's fleet began its swing to the north. Hipper's 1st Scouting Group of five battle cruisers, with the brand-new *Lützow* in the van, was heading east-northeast. The four light cruisers of the 2d Scouting Group were spread out in an arc several miles ahead of her. The outermost wings of the two cruiser screens were less than twenty miles apart, but once Beatty completed his turn to the north, the two fleets would be steaming on roughly parallel courses, just out of sight of each other. They might not have spotted the other fleet until they were much farther north, or missed each other altogether, if fate had not decided to take a hand.

The Danish tramp steamer *N. J. Fjord* happened to be midway between the two fleets, and she was sighted by the most westerly cruiser of Hipper's screen, SMS *Elbing*. Captain Madlung immediately sent two of his torpedo boats to investigate what she was doing there, in case she was a spy ship. They stopped the steamer to board her, and as she blew off steam the little group of ships was seen by the outermost cruiser on Beatty's port wing, HMS *Galatea*. She had been late receiving the order to turn north because the signal had to be relayed to her, and she was only just beginning her turn when at 2:20 P.M. the lookouts identified the torpedo boats as German ships but mistook them for light cruisers. Commodore Alexander-Sinclair headed toward them with the *Galatea* and *Phaeton* and hoisted the exciting signal: "Enemy in sight." He wirelessed Beatty: "Urgent. Two cruisers, probably hostile, in sight bearing ESE, course unknown." This chance contact was very fortunate for Hipper. If he had kept on much farther to the north before he was first spotted, he would probably have been trapped between Beatty and Jellicoe before Scheer could come to his support.

Eight minutes later, when the German ships were within his maximum range of fourteen thousand yards, the captain of the *Galatea* opened fire with his forward six-inch gun. This was the opening shot in the battle that became known to the British as Jutland, and to the Germans as Skagerrak.

As soon as the German torpedo boats came under fire, the light cruisers *Elbing, Pillau, Wiesbaden,* and *Frankfurt* came dashing to the rescue. They began firing at the *Galatea* and *Phaeton* and informed Hipper that they were engaging enemy light cruisers. There followed a running battle at a range of about seven miles. The *Elbing* scored a direct hit on the

Galatea, which caused no serious damage. Alexander-Sinclair ordered his cruiser squadron to turn northwest to try to entice the enemy toward Beatty's battle cruisers. This opened up the range and both sides ceased firing, but the Germans kept following the *Galatea* and *Phaeton.*

As soon as Beatty received the *Galatea*'s wireless message, he signaled his fleet to raise steam for full speed and prepare to alter course to south-southeast. At 2:32, when Beatty had redeployed his destroyer screen, the *Lion*'s flags were hauled down, making the signal executive. The two battle cruiser squadrons swung sharply to starboard and increased speed to twenty-two knots, hoping to cut the enemy cruisers off from their base. The exact nature of the opposition was uncertain, because no big ships had been sighted yet, but there was an atmosphere of excited anticipation on board the British battle cruisers. Beatty's men were convinced they were about to meet Hipper once more. They were confident that this time he couldn't escape and they would "bag the lot."

Ten minutes later the *Galatea*'s lookouts saw heavy smoke clouds to the northeast. Alexander-Sinclair signaled Beatty at 2:44: "Have sighted large amount of smoke bearing ENE . . . from seven vessels besides destroyers and cruisers, which have turned north." This report was not entirely accurate, but it was clear to Beatty "that the enemy was to the Northward and Eastward, and that it would be impossible for him to round the Horns Reef without being brought to action."

Unfortunately, the *Barham* had not taken in Beatty's signal to turn, which was made by flags only. She was five miles away, and although visibility was good, the *Lion*'s signal halliards were low down on foretop and notoriously difficult to read at a distance even with binoculars, particularly from astern because of funnel smoke. Although he saw the battle cruisers begin to turn, Evan-Thomas had received no definite orders to alter course, either by searchlight or W/T. He stayed on his northward course for eight precious minutes, opening up the gap between his squadron and the battle cruisers to ten miles. The confusion was partly the result of what Marder called "the lamentable failure once more of the battlecruisers' signal organization." Beatty's signal to turn should have been routinely relayed to the *Barham* by the *Tiger,* the linking ship between the two squadrons. This was not done. Seymour had erred again. As the *Lion*'s signal officer he should have realized the importance of the order to turn and made absolutely sure that his admiral's intentions were clear to all units by repeating the signal to the *Barham* by searchlight until it was repeated back as understood.

Evan-Thomas was understandably confused when he saw the battle cruisers begin their turn. Perhaps he should have followed them immediately; he had received the earlier signal to prepare for a turn, which was repeated by searchlight, but he had also been ordered to watch out for signs of Jellicoe's vanguard coming from the north. He wasn't sure whether the preparatory signal applied to him for action or was simply for information, because he never saw the *Lion's* flags being lowered to make the signal executive. For all he knew, Beatty might want him to keep on course, either to form a link with Jellicoe or to trap the enemy light cruisers between two fires if they tried to escape by going north.

In 1914 admirals were not accustomed to taking independent action, unless encouraged to do so by their commander in chief. Beatty had always advocated the use of initiative by his own squadron commanders, and his captains were well aware of this, but he had never met with Evan-Thomas to discuss tactics after the 5th Battle Squadron joined his fleet at Rosyth. Admittedly, the time available had been short, but a brief meeting between the two might have made a great deal of difference.

Evan-Thomas finally realized that something must be wrong when the battle cruisers began to disappear into the mist at high speed. He had picked up Alexander-Sinclair's first wireless message that he had made contact with enemy light cruisers to the southeast and decided to head in that direction and try to catch up with the battle cruisers before they were completely out of sight. It wouldn't be easy to close the gap, because his best speed was only twenty-four knots, and if the battle cruisers increased to full speed they would have a four-knot advantage over his battleships.

Meanwhile the German cruiser commander, Rear Admiral Boedicker, had seen several more light cruisers come up to support the *Galatea* and *Phaeton* and reported this to Hipper. Hipper wirelessed Scheer that he had made contact with enemy light forces and was engaging them. The High Seas Fleet was still fifty miles south of Hipper, steaming north at a leisurely fourteen knots. At this point neither of the German leaders had any reason to suspect he was up against anything more dangerous than a few light cruisers. Enticed by Alexander-Sinclair, Hipper pursued them to the northwest, unaware that Beatty's whole fleet was now about forty-five miles away and heading straight toward him.

Beatty needed more information about the strength and direction of the enemy force, and at 2:47 P.M. he ordered the *Engadine* to send up one of its seaplanes to reconnoiter the area. Although the crew beat their best time, it took twenty-one minutes to lower the seaplane into the water, and another thirty minutes for it to take off and spot the enemy fleet. Flight Lt. F. J. Rutland—known ever after as "Rutland of Jutland"—flew his rickety Short seaplane, reputedly "made of sticks and string," to within a mile and a half of the German fleet. The Germans opened fire on the seaplane with their 5.9-inch guns. The shells were exploding within two hundred feet of his fragile plane, but Rutland courageously stayed close enough for his observer, Asst. Paymaster G. S. Trewin, to determine the enemy strength, position, and course. He wirelessed three reports back to the *Engadine*. As Rutland described the scene, "I observed our fleet. The picture of the battlecruisers and of the Queen Elizabeth battleships, with their attendant light cruiser screen and destroyers, rushing forward to cut off the enemy can never be forgotten. At 1545 a petrol pipe broke, my engine revolutions dropped and I was forced to descend and be hoisted in."

This was the first time in history that aircraft had been used for reconnaissance during a sea battle, but regrettably, Rutland's valuable reports were wasted. The *Engadine* wasn't able to relay them to Beatty because she had fallen behind while lowering and picking up the seaplane and was too slow to catch up with the battle cruisers. She tried signaling both the *Lion* and the *Barham* by searchlight and W/T, but the messages failed to get through.

Aerial reconnaissance with Zeppelins proved to be of as equally little value to the Germans. Most were unable to take off because of high winds, and the one Zeppelin that reached the area would have had to descend so low because of cloud cover that her enormous bulk would have been an easy target for British light cruisers. Hipper was even more in the dark than Beatty was about the enemy strength and still believed he was about to catch and annihilate a single light cruiser squadron.

Although he had been unable to obtain any information from aerial reconnaissance, Beatty was still receiving continued W/T reports about Hipper's movements from the *Galatea*. Based on these, he made several turns to port, bringing him onto an easterly, then a northeasterly, course, until by 3:30 he sighted the enemy battle cruisers for himself. There were five of them, hull down on the horizon, "faintly distinguishable a very long distance away." Actually they were about fifteen miles off. Beatty increased speed to twenty-six knots and headed straight for them to try to bring them within gunnery range.

Ten minutes earlier Hipper's lookouts had sighted the dark smoke from two groups of British battle cruisers against the brighter western horizon— "six grey shapes hull down at fourteen miles." Hipper was surprised to discover that he was not merely up against a squadron of light cruisers. Georg von Hase, the chief gunnery officer of the *Derfflinger*, was equally surprised: "Suddenly my periscope revealed some big ships. Black monsters; six tall, broad beamed giants steaming in two columns."

Hipper quickly realized that he was in danger of being cut off if he kept on to the northwest. He immediately ordered his ships to turn in succession through 180 degrees to starboard and increase speed to twenty-five knots. By completely reversing course, he expected to make contact with Scheer's battle fleet in about an hour's time. When Scheer heard from Hipper that Beatty had been sighted, he also increased speed, but could only raise it to sixteen knots. This was the highest speed at which the old ships of Mauve's 2d Battle Squadron could keep their station in Scheer's line of battle.

When he turned away to the southeast, Hipper was confident that Beatty would follow suit and be led into the trap that he and Scheer had been planning for a long time.

Alexander-Sinclair saw the enemy fleet reverse course and reported this to Beatty, who immediately swung his battle cruisers around and headed east-southeast at full speed. He signaled his ships: "Assume complete readiness for action." The gun crews sprang into action at the command "Load! Load! Load!" The news spread like wildfire. There was great excitement on board the battle cruisers at the realization they were going into action against Hipper, and that he couldn't run away this time. The battle ensigns were hoisted at the yardarms of the *Princess Royal, Queen Mary, Tiger, New Zealand,* and *Indefatigable* as they followed the flagship. They were converging on the enemy, who was several miles behind on their port quarter. Because of Beatty's superior speed, Hipper had no chance of outflanking them. This was the beginning of what became known as "the Run to the South."

By now Evan-Thomas had managed to narrow the gap between his squadron and the battle cruisers by cutting corners each time Beatty altered course. He was steadily catching up, but he was still eight miles astern—too far to provide gunnery support. Beatty was going into action without his strongest units. He still had six battle cruisers against five, and with their 13.5-inch guns they clearly outgunned Hipper's ships. But if Beatty had taken steps to concentrate his forces as soon as first contact was made with the enemy, he could have brought overwhelming firepower to bear on Hipper right from the start. The presence of the four 15-inch-gunned *Queen Elizabeth*–class superdreadnoughts would have been decisive.

There had been plenty of time to do this when the *Galatea* sent her first signal more than an hour earlier. As Jellicoe concluded after reading the battle reports, "There was now an excellent opportunity to concentrate his forces. The enemy was steering towards our Battle Fleet so that the loss of two or three miles by the battlecruisers was immaterial. But the opportunity was not taken."

Beatty's failure to concentrate his forces before going into battle was contrary to accepted tactical ideas. On more than one occasion he had asked for the 5th Battle Squadron to be added to his fleet, and now that

N (true)
light breeze
3:48 p.m.
3:48 p.m.
4:10 p.m.
3:48 p.m.
Indefatigable sunk (4:05)
Hipper
Evan-Thomas
Beatty
4:30 p.m.
4:30 p.m.
4:10 p.m.
4:41 p.m.
4:48 p.m.
Queen Mary sunk (4:26)
4:48 p.m.
4:30 p.m.
Evan-Thomas
Beatty
4:48 p.m.
4:48 p.m.
Scheer
Goodenough
4:48 p.m.
0
10,000
20,000
YARDS

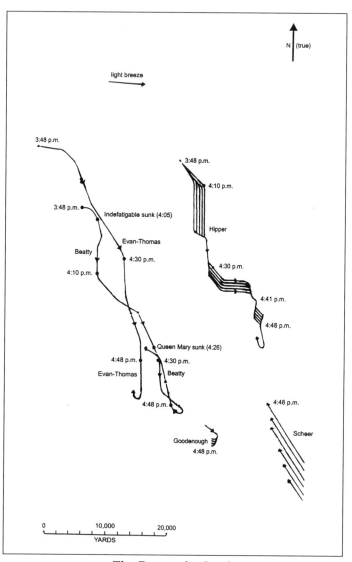

The Run to the South

he had been given its overwhelming strength, it made eminent sense to use it. The failure to do so was not due to Beatty's impetuous nature in dashing into action, as suggested by his critics, but rather to a combination of his initial deployment of the battleships on the far side of the expected enemy approach and chronic signaling problems in his squadron.

At 3:30 P.M. Beatty was steaming at full speed on an easterly course, directly toward Hipper, who was now heading southeast. The gap between the two fleets was closing rapidly, and in less than fifteen minutes they were well within gunnery range. But both sides overestimated the distance to the enemy and held their fire. Although visibility was good, the Germans had a slight advantage in firing to the west because of the light breeze which would blow the gun and funnel smoke across the range in front of Beatty's ships. To counter this, Beatty ordered his ships to form a line of battle in echelon formation, to give his gunners a clearer view with less interference from next aheads. The Germans also had a marginal advantage in terms of the position of the sun, which was high in the southwestern sky and made the western horizon somewhat brighter for their gunners.

The inadequate nine-foot range finders on the British battle cruisers could not give a proper reading of the distance to the enemy. It was estimated to be twenty thousand yards or more, which was too far for accurate shooting, and Beatty waited until the range closed before opening fire. Unfortunately, he didn't try ranging shots, as he had done successfully at the Dogger Bank.

Hipper had been very concerned that Beatty would take advantage of his larger-caliber guns and open fire at a distance beyond the maximum range of his own 11- and 12-inch guns. He was afraid the British would stay about two thousand yards out of his range and inflict serious damage on his squadron while his ships were unable to reply. But because of his headlong approach and inferior range finders, Beatty lost this advantage when he allowed the range to drop to less than seventeen thousand yards before opening fire— "to Hipper's intense relief," according to the Germans.

Finally, it was Hipper who was first to open fire at 3:48, when the range had dropped to 16,400 yards. According to Hase, "Then began an ear-splitting, stupefying din. Including the secondary armament we were firing on average one mighty salvo every seven seconds. . . . Dense masses of smoke accumulated around the muzzles of the guns, growing into clouds as high as houses, which stood for seconds like an impenetrable wall and were then driven by the wind . . . over the ship. . . . We often could see nothing of the enemy for seconds at a time."

The British could see the sharp spurts of orange-red flame ripple down the sides of the German battle cruisers. The opening salvos were well over, and even with stereoscopic range finders it took the German gunners about five minutes to correct their aim.

Beatty's flag captain, Ernle Chatfield, was on the *Lion*'s compass platform at the time with the chief gunnery officer, Gerald Longhurst. Chatfield was growing impatient. As he wrote later, "I wanted Beatty to come on the compass platform, and sent a message to Seymour, telling him to advise Beatty that the range was closing rapidly and that we ought almost at once to be opening fire. But Beatty was too busy getting a message through to Jellicoe. And every second that passed reduced the advantage of the 13.5-inch guns of the flagship and the other 'big cats.' . . . I could wait no longer and told Longhurst to open fire."

With a thunderous roar which could be heard and felt in every part of the ship, the *Lion*'s guns belched smoke and flame from one 13.5-inch gun barrel in each turret. The four huge shells, each weighing over half a ton, went hurtling toward Hipper's flagship. The range was actually just over sixteen thousand yards, but the British range finders were not giving accurate readings. The shells landed in the sea about two miles beyond the *Lützow,* endangering the German cruisers and destroyers on Hipper's disengaged side.

After the opening salvos were seen to be well over, the Germans were quicker to adjust the range. It took the *Lützow* five salvos to get on target, the *Lion* nine. But by 3:56 both sides were straddling the enemy. According to Corbett, "Tall splashes hung in the air for a few seconds before crashing down in clouds of spray." The spray drenched anyone who was standing on an open bridge. It must have been nerve-racking for an observer to see the muzzle flashes when the enemy guns fired then wait helplessly to discover whether he would feel merely the spray from a near-miss or the sickening impact as the shell struck his ship. As one of the Germans recalled, "With each salvo fired by the enemy, I was able to see distinctly four or five shells coming through the air. They looked like elongated black spots. Gradually they grew bigger, and then— crash! they were here. They exploded on striking the water or the ship with a terrific roar. After a bit I could tell from watching the shells fairly accurately whether they would fall short or over."

Beatty and Hipper soon realized they had let the enemy get too close for comfort—the range was now down to 12,500 yards, and the Germans began using their secondary batteries of 5.9-inch weapons as well as their big guns, until the different-sized splashes made spotting too confusing for their gunners. This range was much shorter than was prudent against heavy guns, and the two admirals swung their ships to starboard and port, respectively. They took up roughly parallel courses, with the Germans on Beatty's port quarter. These maneuvers opened up the distance between the lines to 15,000 yards, and the two fleets settled down to a long-range gunnery duel. Beatty ordered his ships to begin rapid fire, and the Germans responded with the command "*Gut schnell Wirkung!*"

Jellicoe was fifty-three miles away when the battle cruiser action began, and as soon as he was informed, he increased speed to twenty knots. Scheer was forty-six miles away, steaming at sixteen knots. The two battle fleets were approaching each other at more than forty miles an hour. If nothing happened to cause them to change course, they would cover the hundred miles separating them and be in sight of each other in two hours. As yet, neither of the commanders in chief was aware that the other fleet had even put to sea.

With the advantage of an extra battle cruiser, Beatty ordered the *Lion* and *Princess Royal* to concentrate their fire on the leading German ship, the *Lützow*. The other ships were signaled to engage their opposite numbers in Hipper's line. Incredibly, in view of the signaling debacle at the Dogger Bank, there was another mixup in the battle cruisers' fire distribution. The signal was made by flags only, and the *Queen Mary* didn't take it in correctly. Instead of firing at the *Derfflinger*, as Beatty intended, she engaged the third ship in the enemy line, the *Seydlitz*. This left the *Derfflinger* unfired on and completely free to carry out undisturbed target practice on the *Tiger*. It took twenty-nine minutes before the mistake was discovered and the *Queen Mary* switched her target to the *Derfflinger*. The *Tiger*, which was supposed to be firing at the *Seydlitz*, also missed the signal and engaged the *Moltke*. Thus the *Moltke* was simultaneously under fire from two ships, the *Tiger* and *New Zealand*. The last and oldest ships in line, *Indefatigable* and *Von der Tann*, fought their own private duel. Hipper ordered his ships to engage their opposite numbers starting from the left, but with one fewer ship he had to leave one of the enemy unfired on. The lucky ship was the *New Zealand*.

The German gunnery was far more effective in the opening stage of the battle. Despite being engaged by two enemy ships, the *Moltke* scored two direct hits on the *Tiger* in the first five minutes. Likewise, the *Lützow* was under fire from two opponents yet hit the *Lion* twice with her fifth salvo. All told, the Germans scored fifteen direct hits in the first twelve minutes of the battle—every one of Beatty's ships was hit at least once, except for the fortunate *New Zealand*. In the same period, the British battle cruisers made only four hits in return, two on the *Lützow* by the *Lion* and two on the *Seydlitz* by the *Queen Mary*.

The most damaging hit by either side came at about four o'clock, when one of the *Lützow*'s 12-inch shells hit the edge of the *Lion*'s midships Q turret. It peeled the roof plate back as if it were a can opener and exploded inside the turret, igniting the cordite charges in the loading cages and the handing room. The explosion and fire killed all but a few of the gun crew. If it had not been for the courage and presence of mind of one of those still alive, the flames that spread quickly through the turret and shot high in the air above it would have reached the magazines and almost certainly blown up the ship. The turret officer, Maj. F. J. W. Harvey of the Royal Marines, although mortally wounded with both legs shattered, managed to drag himself to the voice pipe and pass the word to close the doors to the magazines and flood them. He was posthumously awarded the Victoria Cross.

There were only two surviving members out of Q turret's crew of a hundred. One of them, a sergeant of marines, his clothes bloodstained and charred, hair singed and face blackened, staggered in a daze onto the bridge and in a numb voice reported what had happened. Amazingly, none of those on the bridge had noticed the hit on Q turret and had been blissfully unaware of the near disaster to the *Lion*.

The Germans were elated when they saw flames and smoke rising above the *Lion*'s midship section. They thought they had put Beatty's flagship out of action again, just as they had done at the Dogger Bank. But with her speed unchecked and six of her 13.5-inch guns still firing, she remained a formidable foe.

Five minutes later the Germans struck an even more damaging blow at Beatty's fleet. A salvo of three 11-inch, armor-piercing shells fired by the *Von der Tann* plunged onto the after deck of the *Indefatigable*. They easily penetrated the flimsy one-inch deck armor and exploded deep inside the ship, blowing up the X magazine. The crippled battle cruiser reeled out of line to starboard, sinking by the stern. The next salvo from the *Von der Tann* smashed into the stricken ship near her forward A turret. Within thirty seconds there was a far more violent magazine explosion, and the seventeen-thousand-ton ship heeled over and disappeared beneath the waves. There had been no time for a Major Harvey to flood the magazines and save the *Indefatigable*, or her crew of 1,019 officers and men. Only 2 men survived the explosion. They had been spotters in the foretop, and the blast had flung them clear of the ship. They were picked up later by a German torpedo boat.

When Lieutenant Chalmers looked back from the *Lion*'s bridge along the line of ships, he saw the huge pall of smoke astern of the last ship. As he wrote, "I gazed at this in amazement, and at the same time tumbled to the fact that there were only five battlecruisers in our line. . . .

I glanced quickly towards the enemy. How many of them were still afloat? Still five." With two salvos from the *Von der Tann*, Hipper had evened the odds—but not for long.

Beatty ordered a turn of one point to starboard to open the range and give his crews a chance to put out fires. He also ordered Captain Farie of the 13th Destroyer Flotilla to mount a torpedo attack on the German line to take the pressure off his beleaguered and battered squadron, but it would take the destroyers some time to get ahead of the line of battle cruisers and begin their attack.

The Germans were jubilant at the way the battle had gone so far and sensed they were on their way to a smashing victory. They had destroyed one of Beatty's ships and severely damaged another, and they continued to inflict many more hits than they received. Apart from one turret on the *Seydlitz*, put out of action by the *Queen Mary*, the most effective gunnery ship of Beatty's squadron, Hipper's fighting strength was practically intact. But within minutes of sinking the *Indefatigable*, he came up against an unexpected and more dangerous antagonist. Evan-Thomas had been pushing his battleships' engines to the limit in an effort to catch up with Beatty, and though the *Barham* was still eight miles astern of the *Lion*, he now had the two rearmost ships of Hipper's line in his sights. At 4:08, the 5th Battle Squadron opened fire at a range of nineteen thousand yards.

Hipper had made a tactical error when his 180-degree turn placed his light cruisers to port, on his disengaged side. They were not in position to act as scouts and warn Hipper of the approach of enemy battleships. He was completely surprised by this unpleasant turn of events.

The German reaction was described by their official historian: "As many-headed as a Hydra, the British Navy thus produced four more powerful ships to take the place of the destroyed *Indefatigable*." The timely arrival of the 5th Battle Squadron almost certainly saved Beatty from a crushing defeat.

Despite the extreme range, these battleships' gunnery was amazingly accurate from the start. These new ships were equipped with fifteen-foot range finders and the latest fire-control systems, and they made it tell. At first the leading ships, the *Barham* and *Valiant*, concentrated on the *Moltke*, and the *Warspite* and *Malaya* took on the *Von der Tann*. As Corbett wrote, "The Germans saw the salvoes falling absolutely together and closely concentrated, and were full of admiration for the remarkable fire direction it revealed."

One minute after Evan-Thomas opened fire, the *Von der Tann* was hit heavily on the stern and took in six hundred tons of seawater. A few minutes later, a hit on the *Moltke* knocked out one of her turrets. As the range dropped, the *Seydlitz* became a fresh target, and she was hit forward below the waterline, which caused some flooding. As Scheer commented later, "The fire of the English battlecruisers had resulted in no serious damage to our battlecruisers, but the ships of the 'Queen Elizabeth' class created an excellent impression." The two rearmost German ships began zigzagging to try to avoid being hit by another of the devastating 15-inch shells, which weighed nearly a ton. According to the Germans, the 5th Battle Squadron was "shooting superbly."

Meanwhile the savage and destructive duel between the battle cruisers raged on. Beatty had seen the towering splashes from the 15-inch shells and realized that the 5th Battle Squadron had joined in the action and was now pressing the rearmost ships of the German line, whose fire became ragged. He turned toward the enemy to shorten the range and put pressure on Hipper's van. The action grew more fierce as its climax approached. Hipper's leading ships kept up their accurate fire on Beatty's battle cruisers, which weren't out of trouble yet, despite the arrival of Evan-Thomas's battleships.

After the loss of the *Indefatigable* and the turret fire on the *Lion*, which caused Beatty to turn away briefly until it was put out, the Germans switched targets. Both the *Seydlitz* and the *Derfflinger* began firing at the *Queen Mary*. Her gunnery had been excellent so far. She was firing full broadsides from all eight 13.5-inch guns and had scored four damaging hits on the *Seydlitz*. But under fire from two enemy ships at 14,500 yards, the *Queen Mary* soon began to suffer heavy damage herself. At 4:26 a salvo of four 12-inch shells from the *Derfflinger* struck her amidships. There was a sheet of red flame and an explosion near her forward turret, followed by a more massive explosion midships. The second explosion literally broke the ship in half, lifting her bow and stern sections clean out of the water. As the two following ships raced past, all that could be seen of the twenty-seven-thousand-ton ship through the smoke and falling debris was its stern sticking up above the water. The *Tiger* and *New Zealand* came close enough to read the name on the stern section and see that the screws were still turning slowly, before it too disappeared beneath the waves. Only 19 men survived out of the *Queen Mary*'s crew of 1,275. Two of them were later fished out of the sea by the German torpedo boat G8 and taken prisoner; the others were rescued by the destroyers *Petard* and *Laurel*.

After seeing two of his battle cruisers blown up in the space of twenty minutes, Beatty turned to Flag Captain Chatfield and calmly made his now famous remark, which has been immortalized in British naval history: "There seems to be something wrong with our bloody ships to-day."

He is supposed to have followed this astounding bit of understatement by coolly ordering his ships to alter course two points to port, toward the German line, to "engage the enemy more closely" in the Nelson tradition. This frequently quoted addition to the Beatty legend is surely apocryphal. The track charts of the battle show clearly that the battle cruisers held their course for several minutes after the *Queen Mary* blew up, and when they next changed direction at 4:30, it was by two points to starboard, away from the enemy.

Despite this stunning success, the Germans were still badly outnumbered, and the 5th Battle Squadron was drawing closer and closer to Hipper's battle cruisers. Shooting from less than seventeen thousand yards they scored three more damaging hits on the *Moltke.* Hipper knew that his squadron could not stand up for much longer against their 15-inch guns as well as Beatty's four remaining ships, and he gave the order to turn sharply to port—by nearly 90 degrees—to try to extricate himself from his alarming predicament.

At the same time he ordered Commodore Heinrich to cover his retreat by attacking the enemy with torpedoes. Heinrich took his 9th Torpedo Boat Flotilla—nine boats led by the light cruiser *Regensburg*—into the space between the two lines. He launched a torpedo attack on the enemy's giant ships to try to relieve the pressure on his admiral. But by now twelve of Beatty's speedy destroyers, led by the light cruiser *Champion,* had worked their way to the head of the line, and they cut across in front of the *Lion* at thirty-four knots and raced to meet the new enemy threat. The more heavily armed British destroyers easily beat off the torpedo boat attack, and sank the V27 and V29. The Germans were forced to fire their torpedoes from fairly long range before turning away, and Beatty's ships avoided them without too much trouble.

The British destroyers, led by Cdr. Barrie Bingham in the *Nestor,* made two gallant torpedo attacks on the German battle cruisers from close range, but without great success. Out of twenty torpedoes, only one fired by the *Petard* from about six thousand yards managed to hit the target. It struck the *Seydlitz* and tore a huge hole in the battle cruiser's side, but in spite of some flooding which caused a slight list, she was able to keep her place in line. The frail destroyers paid a heavy price for their dauntless action. The *Nomad* and *Nestor* were crippled by the battle cruisers' secondary armament of 5.9-inch guns, firing at them almost point blank from three thousand yards. Lying stationary and helpless between the two fleets, the two little ships were later finished off by Scheer's battleships. Bingham was awarded the Victoria Cross for the fearless way he had pressed home the attack on the German battle cruisers.

The destroyer action was vividly described by Corbett:

It was a wild scene of groups of long low forms vomiting heavy trails of smoke and dashing hither and thither at thirty knots or more through the smother and splashes, and all in a rain of shell from the German battlecruisers, as well as from the *Regensburg* and the destroyers, with the heavy shell of the contending squadrons screaming overhead. Gradually a pall of gun and funnel smoke almost hid the shell-tormented sea, and beyond the fact that the German torpedo attack was crushed, little could be told of what was happening.

While all this was taking place, the four ships of the 2d Light Cruiser Squadron had also worked their way past the vanguard of the battle cruisers. Commodore William "Barge" Goodenough sensibly resisted the temptation to join in the melee and support the destroyers, because he knew his most important duty was to carry out his scouting role and keep his admiral informed. By 4:30 his flagship, HMS *Southampton*, was about two and a half miles ahead of the *Lion*. A few minutes later, Goodenough saw something that no British naval officer had seen since war broke out, and which many had despaired of ever seeing.

In the distance off the *Southampton*'s port bow there appeared huge clouds of dark funnel smoke which shortly resolved themselves into the head of a seemingly endless line of German battleships. One of the officers on the bridge told Goodenough, "Look sir, this is the day of a light cruiser's lifetime. The whole High Seas Fleet is before you." Goodenough courageously kept on course for another five minutes to obtain more details before signaling Beatty. His lookouts counted twenty-two battleships, with a destroyer screen on each bow. They were in full battle formation, steaming in single line ahead. The range was closing rapidly, and another of Goodenough's officers, worried that they were getting dangerously close to the enemy battleships, remarked, "If you're going to make that signal, you'd better do it now, sir. You may never make another."

At 4:38 Goodenough sent the electrifying news to Beatty and Jellicoe: "Have sighted enemy battle fleet bearing SE, course N."

Goodenough's squadron was now in an extremely hazardous situation, only twelve thousand yards from the nearest German battleships. The eight *König*-class dreadnoughts of the 3d Battle Squadron, led by Rear Adm. Behncke in the *König* itself, had the British ships within easy range of at least fifty 12-inch guns. They didn't open fire right away because the newcomers were approaching head on, and the Germans couldn't be sure whether they were enemy ships or Hipper's light cruisers. Once Goodenough had finished his work, he gave the order to put the helms hard over to starboard. As the four cruisers turned away sharply, they heeled over until their decks were practically awash. When the

Germans saw that they each carried four funnels, this removed all doubt about their identity, and Behncke's battleships opened fire.

The *Southampton, Birmingham, Nottingham,* and *Dublin* were soon steaming through a forest of tall splashes as German 12-inch shells landed all round them, some as close as seventy-five yards away. If any one of them had struck home, it could have crippled a light cruiser; a full salvo would probably have sunk it. Goodenough's ships were zigzagging skillfully at twenty-five knots, and they didn't make easy targets. Their captains deliberately steered toward each salvo that was over, knowing the Germans would probably correct their aim and fire short of that point. Miraculously, none of Goodenough's ships was damaged, apart from the *Southampton,* which received a glancing blow on her stern that caused no serious damage. The cruisers escaped out of gunnery range to the northeast but remained in visual contact with the enemy battle fleet, so they could keep sending scouting reports.

Beatty's initial reaction to Goodenough's signal was one of disbelief. He turned to a more easterly course to see for himself. In a few minutes he sighted Scheer's battle fleet and realized that he had been led unsuspecting into a trap. As he commented later, "What am I to think of O.D. [Operations Division] when I get that telegram and in three hours' time meet the whole of the German Fleet well out at sea?"

Scheer had arrived in the nick of time to save Hipper, just as Evan-Thomas had saved Beatty earlier. Beatty had no choice but to beat a hasty retreat from an overwhelmingly superior enemy force. At 4:40 he made a general signal for the fleet to turn north through 180 degrees and recalled his destroyers. His job now was to get his ships out of danger without suffering too much damage, and to draw Scheer toward the approaching Grand Fleet. He had a six-to-ten-knot advantage over the lumbering German battleships, and he knew that Hipper would not allow his faster ships to get too far ahead of them, in order to maintain contact with Scheer. It was now Beatty's turn to take the initiative by leading Scheer into Jellicoe's arms. He was confident that the Germans didn't suspect that the Grand Fleet was at sea and so close.

The appearance of the German battle fleet ended the Run to the South. Hipper had done very well in this first phase of Jutland. He had led Beatty into a trap, sunk two of his ships, and inflicted heavy damage on two more, the *Lion* and *Tiger.* He had suffered no serious damage himself until Evan-Thomas showed up. His squadron had clearly outfought the British battle cruisers. Even if the *Queen Mary* and *Indefatigable* had not suffered such unexpected and devastating magazine explosions, they would still have been crippled ships.

According to Campbell's exhaustive analysis of the gunnery at Jutland, the Germans scored a total of forty-four direct hits by heavy shells in the first hour of the action to only seventeen by the enemy. Six of the British hits were made by the 5th Battle Squadron, so that Hipper's battle cruisers had outhit Beatty's by a margin of four to one. The Germans' best gunnery ship, the *Moltke,* although simultaneously engaged by two opponents during much of the action, scored thirteen hits—more than all the British battle cruisers put together. As Jellicoe commented later after analyzing the first phase of the battle, the results "cannot be other than unpalatable."

When Jellicoe received Goodenough's exhilarating message he knew that the long-awaited meeting between his Grand Fleet and Scheer's High Seas Fleet was almost inevitable. He wirelessed the Admiralty at 4:50 with the fateful news they had been waiting to hear for the past two years: "Fleet action is imminent."

The Run to the North

CHAPTER 9

I wish someone would tell me who is firing and what they are firing at.

—Adm. Sir John Jellicoe

Beatty's battle cruisers completed their 180-degree turn and headed north without coming under any real threat from Scheer's battleships. The nearest of them were still about twenty-four thousand yards away, and the rear of Beatty's line was well outside their range. But the 5th Battle Squadron stayed on course to the southeast. The *Barham* was still about seven miles astern of the *New Zealand,* the last ship in Beatty's line, and she didn't take in the *Lion's* signal to turn. Once more this was made by flags only and was not repeated by searchlight or W/T. The *Lion's* main W/T had been knocked out during the fighting, and Beatty was using a short-range auxiliary set to pass important messages to the *Princess Royal,* which was supposed to relay them to other ships. This was not done, although it was surely vital to warn Evan-Thomas that he was heading straight for the whole of the enemy battle fleet. The battle cruisers' signaling staff had proved unreliable once again by not making certain that Beatty's orders were clearly received and acknowledged by all units.

When Evan-Thomas saw the battle cruisers reverse course, he was perplexed. Beatty had not informed him that Scheer's battleships had been sighted, and the 5th Battle Squadron had not picked up Goodenough's earlier W/T message that he had seen the High Seas Fleet coming up from the south. Evan-Thomas couldn't fathom why Beatty was turning northward, and since he was heavily engaging Hipper's battle cruisers, which were still heading south, he stayed on course waiting for instructions. Flag officers did not make major course changes, particularly if it meant breaking off action with the enemy, unless their fleet commander ordered them to do so.

Beatty's two main divisions were now steaming in opposite directions, and as they approached each other at nearly a mile a minute, Evan-Thomas asked which side of the battle cruisers he should take when he passed by them. He was signaled to pass on Beatty's port side. When the *Barham* came abeam of the *Lion* at about two thousand yards distance, Beatty repeated his earlier flag signal to turn north. This was hoisted at 4:46, but for some reason a further seven minutes went by before the flags were hauled down to make the signal executive.

Critics have argued that Evan-Thomas should not have waited for the executive but turned immediately on his own initiative. But as Marder wrote, "Flag officers, like Evan-Thomas, with a long background of maneuvering fleets by precise signals, did not do such things in those days." By the time his ships began their turn, they had completely passed by the tail of the battle cruisers, and they could see the enemy battle fleet for themselves. It was only now that Evan-Thomas discovered why Beatty had reversed course.

The *Lion*'s flag signal had told him to turn his ships 180 degrees to starboard, in succession. Beatty should have left it to Evan-Thomas to decide how best to reverse his course, because the 5th Battle Squadron was getting into a dangerous situation with Scheer's leading ships about twenty-five thousand yards off the *Barham*'s port bow. A turn in succession took longer to execute than a turn together, and before it had been completed the 5th Battle Squadron would be within range of Scheer's leading battleships. As each of his ships wheeled about a single point it would give the enemy gunners a focus where they could concentrate their fire. A turn to port together would also have made it easier for Evan-Thomas to stay in close touch with the battle cruisers. Beatty's tactical and signaling errors had needlessly placed Evan-Thomas in a very hazardous situation.

As each one of the *Queen Elizabeth*–class superdreadnoughts passed through the pivot point it came under a hail of shells from Hipper's battle cruisers. Hipper had also altered course to northwest, almost simultaneously with Evan-Thomas, to allow him to take his station at the head of the German battle fleet. Scheer's leading battleships had already opened fire at the rear of Beatty's line, but their shells fell far short. Scheer quickly gave orders for his battleships to switch targets and join Hipper's onslaught on the ships of the 5th Battle Squadron as they went through their turn. Fortunately, the range was still fairly long—roughly twenty thousand yards—and Scheer's gunners were not as accurate as Hipper's.

It was one of Hipper's ships that had the first success. The *Derfflinger* scored a damaging hit on the *Barham,* but the next two ships, the *Valiant* and *Warspite,* went through the turning point completely unscathed. It was the last ship in Evan-Thomas's line which came under the most concentrated fire when she reached the "hot corner." By now the range had dropped to less than nineteen thousand yards, and with seven or eight ships aiming at her there were half a dozen salvos a minute falling all round the *Malaya.* She miraculously managed to avoid being hit for about twenty minutes. All credit must go to Capt. Algernon Boyle, who turned his ship early and altered course frequently to throw off the Germans' aim.

Scheer had hoped to damage Evan-Thomas's ships enough to slow them down so they could be mopped up by the rest of his fleet, but he failed completely due to a combination of good luck and skillful maneuvering by the battleships' captains. They had narrowly averted a disaster to the 5th Battle Squadron.

This was the beginning of the second phase of Jutland, the so-called Run to the North.

Scheer ordered a general chase, and as the action developed, Beatty was heading almost due north with his ships steaming in line ahead. Hipper's battle cruisers were pursuing them in echelon formation on Beatty's starboard quarter. The two lines were about 19,000 yards apart and converging. Evan-Thomas, who by now had fallen about four miles astern of Beatty, was also steaming in line ahead. His squadron was roughly level with Hipper's ships at 17,500 yards distance, and about twelve miles ahead of Scheer's flagship *Friedrich der Grosse.* The German battle fleet was spread out in six divisions in echelon, bearing toward the northwest, which meant that the two starboard divisions of the 3d Battle Squadron were the farthest ahead and closest to Evan-Thomas. Behncke's leading ships were only about 19,000 yards from the *Malaya,* and he ordered "Utmost speed," trying desperately to close the range.

Beatty opened fire on Hipper's battle cruisers just before 5 o'clock, and once again the Germans were quicker to get on target. Inside of three minutes, the *Lützow* scored three direct hits on the *Lion,* and the *Seydlitz* hit the *Tiger* once. The British battle cruisers made no hits in return. Visibility conditions were not good for the British initially, because of mist, but they started to improve after 5 o'clock. As the sun gradually dipped lower and lower in the western sky it began to hamper the German gunners' vision.

Beatty increased speed to twenty-six knots, and as he began to pull away from Hipper, he altered course gradually to the northwest, toward

Jellicoe's position. He planned to get well ahead of the Germans so that he could turn to starboard across their line of advance and force the head of their line steadily eastward. He intended to use his squadron to conceal Jellicoe's approach from the Germans' view. Beatty hoped to turn the tables on the Germans and lead them unsuspecting into a trap, just as Hipper had done to him earlier. But this time the difference was that if he could delay their sighting of Jellicoe until the last moment, it would be impossible for the Germans to avoid action with the whole of the Grand Fleet.

By 5:10 Beatty had drawn out of Hipper's range and briefly lost sight of the German battle cruisers. Hipper was unable to narrow the gap and let him go. He reduced speed, because some of his ships were having trouble keeping up. In any case he was not anxious to pursue Beatty very closely, lest he get too far ahead of Scheer. If he became separated from the battle fleet, he would have to face Evan-Thomas's battleships on his own. Hipper had already seen what their 15-inch guns could do during the Run to the South.

With Beatty out of range, it meant that for the next half hour, Evan-Thomas was left to engage both Hipper and Scheer by himself. The 5th Battle Squadron was outnumbered two to one, because it was within range of Hipper's battle cruisers and anywhere from four to eight of Behncke's battleships at a time. Nonetheless, the four *Queen Elizabeth*–class ships acquitted themselves very well and certainly gave as good as they got.

Evan-Thomas distributed his fire so that the *Barham* and *Valiant* took on Hipper, while the *Warspite* and *Malaya* engaged Scheer's vanguard. Over the next thirty minutes the *Barham* and *Valiant* hit Hipper's leading ships very hard, firing at ranges of sixteen to eighteen thousand yards. Their 1,800-pound shells struck the *Lützow* four times, and the *Derfflinger* three times, but it was the *Seydlitz* that received the worst battering. She suffered no fewer than six direct hits from these huge shells. At times the Germans were outranged and their gunners had difficulty sighting the enemy with the sun in their eyes. All they could do was try to throw off the battleships' accurate and devastating aim. To Hase of the *Derfflinger*, it was "highly depressing, nerve-wracking and exasperating. Our only means of defence was to leave the line for a short time, when we saw the enemy had our range." They nonetheless managed to hit the *Barham* four times during this period, but the *Valiant* was untouched.

The *Warspite* and *Malaya* were firing at Behncke's leading ships at longer range, but were able to score hits on the *König, Grosser Kurfürst*, and *Markgraf.* Scheer's gunners were less effective than Hipper's at such long range and they failed to hit the *Warspite* at all, although the *Seydlitz* hit her twice. But the trailing ship *Malaya* was a better target, and she was under fire from at least four battleships. Between 5:20 and 5:35 she was hit seven times, but apart from a slight list she showed no outward signs of damage. By 5:35 both Hipper and Scheer were falling behind, and firing became intermittent for a while. This was the first real break in an action that had been going on since Hipper first opened fire almost two hours earlier.

While this fierce duel between Evan-Thomas and Scheer was taking place, Beatty had worked his way well ahead of Hipper, and he began to swing eastward across his line of advance. By 5:41 he had closed the range to about sixteen thousand yards and opened fire on Hipper's van. The *Princess Royal* scored a direct hit on the nearly crippled flagship *Lützow*, and Hipper turned due east to relieve the pressure on his beleaguered squadron from the two-pronged assault by Evan-Thomas and Beatty.

Evan-Thomas was now concentrating his fire on the leading German battle cruisers, because Scheer's slower battleships had dropped so far behind that they were out of range. His ships scored several more hits on the already battered *Lützow*, *Derfflinger*, and *Seydlitz*. Of Hipper's five ships, only the *Moltke* was in good fighting trim. The *Von der Tann*, although not badly damaged, had none of her big guns left in action due to an earlier hit by the *Tiger* and a succession of jammed turrets. Captain Zenker could only fire back with his secondary armament of 5.9-inch weapons, which were ineffective against a battleship's armor. Nonetheless he staunchly kept his position in the line to attract his share of the enemy fire.

Beatty succeeded brilliantly in bending Hipper's line back, away from the direction of Jellicoe's approach. His ships were obstructing Hipper's view to the northwest, where the visibility was deteriorating, so that he was unable to warn Scheer of the danger that lay ahead.

Jellicoe was now only about twenty-three miles away and steaming southeast at high speed. The Battle Fleet was in its cruising formation of six divisions of four battleships each. In line abreast, the divisions stretched for about five miles, to form an impenetrable barrier across Scheer's path if he maintained his present course.

Soon after 5:30 there was a fresh development. Hipper faced a new threat from a totally unexpected quarter. For the past two hours he had been in almost continuous action with enemy ships that were all firing at him from the west. Hipper was shocked to discover that he had a third enemy coming at him from the direction of the Danish coast—to the east! Approaching from the northeast about twelve miles away were the three *Invincible*-class ships of Adm. Horace Hood's 3d Battle Cruiser Squadron. Jellicoe had detached Hood's squadron from his fleet with orders to find and support Beatty. The British Hydra had sprouted another head.

During a brief lull in the main action, Hood was heading south-southeast searching for Beatty, whom he had expected to contact by now. But due to errors in dead reckoning, Beatty's battle cruisers were actually about twenty miles to Hood's southwest. Such discrepancies were not unusual when dead-reckoning calculations were employed, because these were based on a ship's last known position and estimates of its subsequent speed and course. Hood had wirelessed Beatty asking for his present course and position but had not yet received any reply.

The *Invincible, Inflexible,* and *Indomitable* were steaming in line ahead, screened by four destroyers of the 4th DF. The light cruiser *Chester* was about four to five miles off on their starboard beam, and the *Canterbury* was five or six miles ahead on their port bow. When the captain of the *Chester* heard the sound of guns and saw the muzzle flashes to the south-west, he reported this to Hood and raced off to investigate. The visibility to the west had worsened, but his lookouts were soon able to make out a three-funneled light cruiser and a destroyer through the haze to starboard. Captain Lawson turned toward them, and in a few minutes he could see three more light cruisers dimly in the distance. He wasn't sure at first whether they were enemy ships or part of Beatty's advanced screen, but all doubt was quickly removed when at 5:38 the four light cruisers of Hipper's 2d Scouting Group opened fire on the *Chester* from seven thousand yards.

Captain Lawson knew he was in serious trouble and immediately turned away. His ship presented a more visible target to the Germans, who were firing from the west, and the *Frankfurt, Elbing, Pillau,* and *Wiesbaden* hit her seventeen times with 5.9-inch shells in the space of fifteen minutes. With four of her guns disabled and gaping holes in her side, she had suffered heavy casualties. Seventy-eight out of her complement of 450 had been killed or wounded. Luckily her engines were undamaged, and the *Chester* made off at full speed toward the safety of Hood's battle cruisers, hotly pursued by Boedicker's light cruisers and destroyers.

Hood heard the sound of gunfire coming from the *Chester's* direction and headed toward the gun flashes. When he sighted the *Chester* being pursued by the 2d Scouting Group, he swung around to the northwest, broadside on, and at 5:55 he opened fire at ten thousand yards. Boedicker suddenly found himself into a more dangerous spot than Lawson had been in earlier. As he turned away, the *Indomitable* and *Invincible* both hit the *Wiesbaden* with 12-inch shells. The second hit disabled the cruiser, and she lay dead in the water with both engines stopped. The *Pillau* suffered a direct hit from the *Inflexible,* which put six of her ten boilers out of action, but remarkably she was still able to steam at twenty-four knots. In desperation Boedicker ordered an attack by his torpedo boats to cover his retreat. This was led by Heinrich in the light cruiser *Regensburg.* They fired twelve torpedoes, which didn't hit anything, but the attack forced Hood's battle cruisers to turn away briefly to avoid the clearly visible tracks. This allowed the *Elbing, Pillau,* and *Frankfurt* to escape destruction under cover of a smoke screen.

Boedicker wirelessed Hipper that he had run into what he thought were enemy battleships. His torpedo boats compounded the error by signaling Hipper that there was a fleet of "many battleships" to the northeast. These reports caused Hipper to turn south and fall back on Scheer, whose lumbering battleships had fallen several miles behind during the Run to the North. Hipper swung his ships completely around and took his place at the head of the German fleet. Hood's timely arrival had prevented the German scouting groups from giving Scheer early warning of Jellicoe's approach. Hood's role in delaying the German realization that the Grand Fleet was out in force was crucial, but it has never received sufficient recognition.

He resumed his course toward Beatty, who by now had wirelessed his position. Hood ordered his destroyers to counterattack a second wave of Boedicker's torpedo boats. In the poor visibility their torpedoes all missed—their tracks were not even spotted by the battle cruisers. The German torpedo boats were again distracted from their scouting role by the fierce action that developed between them and the four destroyers attached to Hood's squadron. The counterattack was led by Cdr. Loftus Jones in the *Shark.* Despite being outnumbered and outgunned by the *Regensburg* and the 2d Torpedo Boat Flotilla, he made such a spirited and fearless attack that the Germans were forced to turn away. Loftus Jones was mortally wounded, and his engines were disabled. The *Shark* lay helpless in the water, the target of half a dozen German ships, including the *Regensburg.* The destroyer *Acasta* came alongside to shield her from enemy fire. The *Acasta's* captain, Lieutenant-Commander Barron, asked if he could give any assistance. The dying Loftus Jones replied, "No. Tell him to look after himself."

Heavily outnumbered and crippled, the *Shark* was given the coup de grâce by a torpedo from the S54. Loftus Jones's body was washed up several weeks later on the Swedish coast. He was buried like a modern-day Viking in a nearby village churchyard and later awarded the Victoria Cross for his heroic attack, which had forced the Germans to turn away and prevented them from reporting Jellicoe's approach.

There was another posthumous winner of the Victoria Cross during this part of the action. Boy Seaman 1st Class John Cornwell of the *Chester* was the only one of his gun crew left alive after a direct hit from one of the German light cruisers. Though mortally wounded himself, he stayed quietly at his post, awaiting further orders. His shining example and his youth—he was sixteen years old at the time—inspired Beatty to write an eloquent and moving tribute. His recommendation helped immortalize Cornwell as the youngest ever winner of the Victoria Cross.

During this second phase of Jutland the tide of battle had definitely swung in favor of the British. Beatty had seized the initiative from Hipper and was skillfully luring the Germans into an ambush. The amazing thing was that Hipper and Scheer never realized this until it was too late. If Beatty had merely been trying to escape from the jaws of Scheer's battle fleet to save his own force from annihilation, he would surely not have headed north after he sighted them. His most direct route back to safety would have been due west, toward Rosyth.

Then when Beatty began to swing northeast across Hipper's path, it should have been crystal clear that he was not simply running away from a vastly superior enemy. It may have seemed to the Germans that Beatty was trying to cross Hipper's "T" to gain a tactical advantage, but this could only have brought him temporary respite with the whole of the German battle fleet coming up behind Hipper. Hipper began to suspect that something was amiss when he received the reports from the 2d Scouting Group that they had seen "many battleships" to the northeast, and heavy shells coming from that direction started landing among his ships. Scheer too began to have doubts, and in the poor visibility ahead caused by the mist and the haze from the gun and funnel smoke, he remarked to his flag captain, "Something lurks in that soup." Still he kept on to the north. He must have believed that Beatty was unsupported by Jellicoe, because it was not part of Scheer's plan to take on the Grand Fleet.

The gunnery situation had also improved for the British during the Run to the North. They had been badly outhit by the Germans in the first phase of the battle, but things had undoubtedly changed for the better during the second phase because of the accurate fire of Evan-Thomas's gunners. The *Barham* and *Valiant* had hit Hipper's battle cruisers thirteen times, and the more hotly engaged *Warspite* and *Malaya* had made five more hits on Scheer's leading battleships—a total of eighteen punishing hits by 15-inch shells. Hipper's ships were now in much worse shape than Beatty's surviving battle cruisers. In reply, Hipper had made six hits on Beatty's squadron and five on Evan-Thomas's, while the eight ships of Behncke's 3d Battle Squadron had only made seven direct hits, all of them on the *Malaya*. Thus in spite being badly outnumbered, the 5th Battle Squadron had scored as many heavy-shell hits as the German battle cruisers and battleships put together. Although Evan-Thomas had not sunk any enemy ships, his accurate gunners had inflicted far more damage than they had received.

The performance of the British battle cruisers had not improved, though, with just the one hit by the *Princess Royal* on the *Lützow* in thirty minutes of action. Taking into account the first two phases of the battle, the 1st and 2d Battle Cruiser Squadrons had been in action for about the same amount of time as the 5th Battle Squadron, firing at similar or shorter ranges and subject to the same weather conditions. So far Evan-Thomas's ships had scored twice as many hits.

Comparing the damage suffered by both sides up to this point, there is no doubt that Beatty's remaining ships were more battleworthy than Hipper's. This was largely due to the devastating effects of the 15-inch broadsides from the ships of the *Queen Elizabeth* class. All five of Hipper's battle cruisers had been holed at or below the waterline, resulting in extensive flooding. Although the holes were temporarily plugged, several of the ships were still taking on seawater because of persistent leaks. The *Lützow* was down by the head, and her flooding grew more serious as the day wore on. The *Derfflinger* had taken on fourteen hundred tons of seawater and was listing to port. The *Seydlitz* had been hit several times along the waterline, and she was badly down by the bows and listing to starboard. Her floodwater situation was becoming increasingly serious, especially at high speed, when seawater poured in through gaping holes in her bow. The *Moltke* had also taken on one thousand tons of seawater and developed a slight list. The least damaged of Hipper's squadron was the *Von der Tann,* but none of her 11-inch turrets were operating properly, although one would be back in action later on. Despite this damage, all five of these sturdy ships were able to maintain speed and keep their position in line.

By contrast, none of Beatty's surviving battle cruisers had suffered any vital damage, apart from the earlier hit on the *Lion's* Q turret. The *Princess Royal* and the *Tiger* also had one turret out of action, but they had suffered no other serious damage. The fortunate *New Zealand* was practically unscathed. The battle cruisers' engines were unaffected, and the ships' fighting efficiency was not greatly reduced by the battle damage they had received.

As far as the battleships were concerned, none of them, British or German, had suffered any vital damage so far, although both the *Barham* and *Malaya* had come close to blowing up because of cordite fires in their 6-inch loading chambers, but the magazines had been flooded in time. Both the *Malaya* and *Markgraf* had been hit on the waterline, but the flooding was not serious.

As the Run to the North drew to a close toward 6:00 P.M., the two battle fleets were just over the horizon from each other. One of the two commanders in chief knew that the enemy fleet was there—somewhere—but his opposite number was completely in the dark. Jellicoe hadn't received any detailed reports about the enemy course and position for more than an hour, and he was becoming extremely frustrated at the lack of information he was getting from his scouting forces. None of them had told him what was going on subsequent to Goodenough's report at 4:38 that he had sighted Scheer's fleet coming north. Jellicoe had heard nothing from Beatty since he had wired the Admiralty that a fleet action was imminent.

The reliable Goodenough continued reporting, even though he was heavily engaged with Scheer's battleships. He had turned a blind eye to Beatty's signal and delayed his turn north so as to stay in close contact with Scheer, and had been impudently harassing the German battle fleet with his puny 6-inch guns until he was forced to withdraw when the *König*'s 12-inch guns began straddling his fragile cruisers. He was still doggedly keeping in visual contact and reported that Scheer was now heading due north, but because of errors in dead reckoning he was unable to provide Jellicoe with the vital information he needed—the enemy's bearing.

Jellicoe could hear gunfire in the distance on both his port and starboard bow. This was coming from Hood's and Beatty's squadrons as they attacked Hipper's battle cruisers, but Jellicoe didn't know this. The exasperated admiral remarked to those on the bridge of the *Iron Duke*, "I wish someone would tell me who is firing and what they are firing at."

Then HMS *Marlborough*, the leading ship of Jellicoe's westernmost column, sighted Beatty's battle cruisers and reported this to Jellicoe. A minute later he was able to make out the dim shapes of Beatty's ships on his starboard bow, firing at some invisible enemy. He signaled Beatty by searchlight: "Where is enemy battle fleet?"

Beatty couldn't tell him because he had lost sight of Scheer an hour earlier, although his primary role as battle cruiser commander was to maintain contact with the enemy battle fleet and keep his commander in chief informed of its bearing, course, and speed. Beatty knew that Scheer was somewhere to the south, but all he could do was send back the unsatisfactory reply: "Enemy battlecruisers bearing SE."

This was not what Jellicoe needed to know. He had to know whether Scheer's battleships were approaching him from dead ahead or on one of his flanks, and how close they were, so that he could decide on the best way to deploy his ships before meeting the enemy. To change a fleet of twenty-four battleships from divisions in line abreast to battle formation in single line ahead was no simple matter, and it took time and skill to complete properly. The sooner he knew how to carry out the deployment to give himself the greatest tactical advantage the better.

When Beatty's officers saw the leading ships of Jellicoe's fleet in the distance, they were elated. The fire-breathing Walter Cowan, captain of the *Princess Royal,* recalled this exciting moment: "With the Grand Fleet in sight and within striking distance, we felt like throwing our caps into the air. It looked a certainty we had them."

The Battle Fleets Collide

CHAPTER 10

The entire arc stretching from north to east was a sea of fire.
The muzzle flashes were clearly seen through the mist
and smoke on the horizon, though there was
still no sign of the ships themselves.

—Adm. Reinhard Scheer

Shortly after 6:00 P.M. on 31 May, Jellicoe was faced with the most crucial decision of the war at sea, perhaps of the entire war. In Churchill's widely quoted view, Jellicoe was the only man on either side who could lose the war in an afternoon. It is hard to take serious issue with this dramatic and sweeping assertion. If Jellicoe were to make the wrong decision, and in so doing suffer a crushing defeat at the hands of the High Seas Fleet, British naval supremacy would be lost—and in all likelihood so would the war.

His twenty-four dreadnoughts were steaming majestically in cruising formation, headed in a southeasterly direction at eighteen knots. Somewhere to Jellicoe's south an unsuspecting Scheer was leading his sixteen dreadnoughts and six predreadnoughts northward at about the same speed. His ships were already in line ahead. The two mighty armadas were set on a collision course. Within a matter of minutes, a violent confrontation was inevitable. But exactly how the fleets would meet was less certain.

Jellicoe's six columns of battleships were still in line abreast, the divisions separated from each other by gaps of only five hundred yards. He had taken up a more compact formation so that he could deploy his ships into a single line ahead as quickly as possible, but this stately array was a mile and a half wide and it was no trivial matter to change it into a single line nearly seven miles long. In the normal course of events, Jellicoe would have had plenty of time to deploy his fleet into battle formation before sighting the enemy. But his scouting forces had so far failed to provide him with accurate information about the enemy bearing, distance, and course which he needed to make the correct deployment. The signals he had received from Beatty, Napier, and even Goodenough had been ambiguous or incomplete.

Jellicoe had three options—to deploy on the starboard or port wing or on one of the center columns—and little time to choose the best one. Whichever he chose, the maneuver would take at least fifteen minutes to complete. If he were caught in the middle of deployment the outcome would be disastrous. Scheer would be able to concentrate his fire on the leading British ships before their line of battle was fully formed, when many of Jellicoe's guns were being masked by his own ships as they executed their turns. Scheer would be in an ideal position to deliver a devastating blow while the enemy fleet was in disarray and then withdraw quickly before Jellicoe's superior firepower could be brought to bear.

Jellicoe was puzzled when he saw Beatty's ships appear to starboard because he had expected to sight Beatty around six o'clock about thirteen miles straight ahead of him. It was obvious that the dead-reckoning calculations were greatly in error because here was Beatty only about six miles away, and off Jellicoe's starboard bow. If Beatty was still in action with the enemy battle cruisers it seemed likely that Scheer's battle fleet would come into view about twenty minutes sooner than Jellicoe had anticipated.

The two fleets were closing rapidly, at well over half a mile a minute, and every minute counted. Jellicoe could wait no longer, and at 6:10 he impatiently repeated his earlier signal to Beatty: "Where is enemy battle fleet?"

There was no reply for several agonizing minutes. Beatty had briefly lost sight of the enemy battle cruisers when Hipper turned back to join Scheer, but at 6:14 he sighted the German fleet dimly through a break in the mist. He signaled Jellicoe by searchlight: "Have sighted enemy's battle fleet bearing SSW." This didn't give Jellicoe the vital information he needed—the enemy course and distance—but it was all he had to go on. He knew he probably had no more than a minute or two to reach a decision and start the deployment.

Deployment on the starboard wing would require his columns to make two successive 90-degree turns to fall in line behind his most westerly column, led by Admiral Burney in the *Marlborough*, who would become the fleet guide. This would allow Jellicoe to open fire sooner and at shorter range, because Scheer was coming up on the starboard side. But it might also allow Scheer to cross his T or launch a massed torpedo attack from close range before he had fully completed the deployment, because his columns would have to slow down to allow Burney's division to forge ahead. Deployment on a center column would also place him nearer the enemy, but it was a more awkward maneuver, taking much longer to complete. It would also result in serious bunching up at the rear of the fleet because the two outermost columns would have to slow down or even stop while they waited their turn to fall in line. Deployment on the port wing would place Jellicoe farther away from the enemy at the outset, and possibly waste ten valuable minutes before he brought them within range, but it would give him the better visibility firing to the west and place his fleet across Scheer's escape routes, either through the Skagerrak or back to Wilhelmshaven.

It was a moment of tremendous tension on the bridge of the *Iron Duke* as Jellicoe weighed the merits of each option. There was no time for consultation. Everything rested on the shoulders of the commander in chief—a short, unimposing figure in his old blue raincoat and shabby admiral's cap with its tarnished gold braid, and his neck muffled against the cold with a white scarf. Jellicoe's flag captain, Frederic Dreyer, recalled the moment:

> I heard the signalman calling each word of Beatty's reply to Jellicoe's repeated demand. . . . I then heard at once the sharp distinctive step of the Commander-in-Chief approaching. . . . He stepped quickly onto the platform round the compasses and looked at the magnetic compass card for about twenty seconds. I watched his keen, brown, weather-beaten face with tremendous interest, wondering what he would do. . . . I realised as I watched him that he was as cool and unmoved as ever. Then he looked up and broke the silence in his crisp, clear-cut voice to Commander A. R. Woods, the Fleet Signal Officer,. . . "Hoist equal-speed pendant SE."
>
> Woods said: "Would you make it a point to port, Sir, so that they will know it is on the port wing column?" Jellicoe replied at once: "Very well. Hoist equal-speed pendant SE. by E." Woods then called over the bridge rail to the signal boatswain: "Hoist equal-speed Charlie London." The signal was made by wireless at the same time.

Jellicoe told Dreyer to begin the deployment, even though the signal flags had not been hauled down. Dreyer ordered the flagship's helm to be put hard over to port. The leaders of the other columns had been watching the *Iron Duke* intently and followed suit, except for Admiral Jerram on the port wing in the *King George V*. He altered course slightly, to southeast by east, and led his division straight on. The other five leaders then made a second turn, this time to starboard, and in succession they fell in behind Jerram to form a single line of twenty-four battleships.

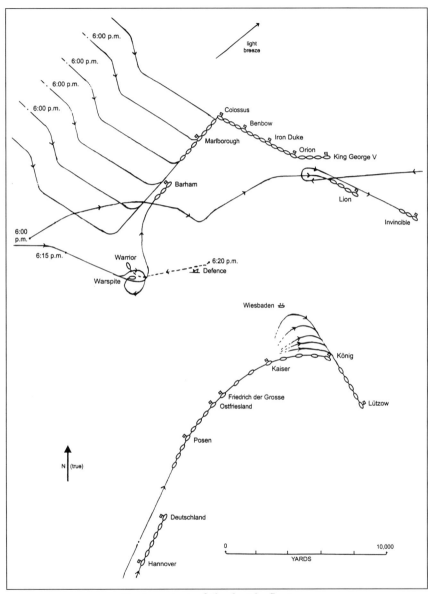

First contact of the battle fleets

Jellicoe's flagship was roughly in the middle of the line, a position from which he could keep control of his entire battle fleet.

As Dreyer wrote, "The signal was actually hauled down at 6:15 P.M. *We still had not sighted a German ship, but they were obviously very close.*"

While this stately maneuver was under way, several fierce side actions were taking place as the advanced forces clashed in the mist-shrouded no-man's-land between the two battle fleets.

The elderly armored cruisers *Defence* and *Warrior* were patrolling the starboard wing of Jellicoe's advanced screen when their lookouts caught a brief sight of enemy light cruisers about fourteen thousand yards off. It was Boedicker's 2d Scouting Group, which had just escaped from the jaws of Hood's battle cruiser squadron. The *Defence* was the flagship of Rear-Adm. Sir Robert Arbuthnot, a pugnacious individual who was itching to get into action. He had missed one splendid opportunity to come to grips with the enemy when his ship had been too late to join Sturdee at the Falkands in 1914, and he was determined not to miss another. He turned broadside on and opened fire on the *Frankfurt* and her consorts, but his shots fell short. Boedicker immediately headed for refuge in the mist.

Arbuthnot didn't hesitate for a moment. He had made up his mind beforehand and had told his friends that he would not turn in a "dull performance" that day if he got the chance for action. He swung his ships around and went after the Germans hell-for-leather. Beatty's battle cruisers were nearby, racing across the front of the fleet to take up their station in the vanguard, and Arbuthnot's headlong pursuit took him so close to the *Lion's* bows that Beatty had to swerve to avoid a collision with the *Defence*.

The German cruisers disappeared into the mist, but Arbuthnot soon found a fresh target. It was the crippled *Wiesbaden,* lying dead in the water about five thousand yards away. Arbuthnot decided to finish her off to prevent her from firing torpedoes at Beatty's ships. As the *Defence* and *Warrior* passed by, they slowed down and poured several salvos into the luckless light cruiser, leaving her ablaze and listing heavily—but she stubbornly refused to sink.

Suddenly, looming out of the mist, there appeared the massive shapes of six German dreadnoughts. They were about eight thousand yards off and couldn't miss at this range. Hopelessly outgunned, the two armored cruisers didn't stand a chance. They were immediately surrounded by a forest of tall shell splashes. Within minutes the hail of shells from the 12-inch guns of the *Lützow, Derfflinger, Markgraf, Kaiser, Kronprinz,* and *Grosser Kurfürst* had reduced Arbuthnot's fifteen-thousand-ton ships to shattered, blazing hulks. Then at 6:20 a salvo from the *Lützow* struck the *Defence* aft, and according to a shocked eyewitness on board the *Warrior,* she "suddenly disappeared completely in an immense column of smoke and flame, hundreds of feet high. It appeared to be an absolutely instantaneous destruction, the ship seeming to be dismembered at once."

The explosion of her magazines left no survivors from a crew of nine hundred, who mercifully must have perished in a fraction of a second. Arbuthnot's reckless pursuit had cost him his flagship, his life, and the lives of his shipmates. But the dauntless admiral certainly hadn't turned in a dull performance.

The *Warrior* was saved from a similar appalling fate by the seawater that came rushing through the shell holes in her side and flooded her magazines and engine rooms. She had suffered at least fifteen direct hits and more than a hundred casualties. Her decks were a scene of devastation, and she was listing heavily. Without steam or guns, she was helpless and defenseless, but she was spared further agony by the appearance of a new and more attractive target, which drew the Germans' fire. The crippled *Warrior* was taken in tow later by the *Engadine,* and she might have been saved except for the heavy seas that came up during the night. She foundered at 7:00 A.M. the following day, only 160 miles from Aberdeen.

It was the *Warspite* that had inadvertently saved the *Warrior* from annihilation. When Evan-Thomas sighted the *Marlborough,* he thought at first she was the leading ship of the battle fleet, but when he saw her division begin to deploy to port he realized his error. The proper station of the 5th Battle Squadron was in the van with Beatty's battle cruisers, acting as a fast battleship wing, but Evan-Thomas had fallen far astern of Beatty during the Run to the North. He didn't have enough speed to get to the head of the battle fleet without masking Jellicoe's fire and sensibly decided to take station at the rear. As she turned sharply to follow the *Marlborough*'s division, the *Warspite*'s steering gear jammed, and the ship began to swing helplessly toward the German ships that had been battering the *Warrior.*

The *Warspite* began turning in circles, bringing her to within ten thousand yards of the leading German battleships. One after the other, the *König, Ostfriesland, Friedrich der Grosse, Thüringen,* and *Helgoland* turned their guns on the new target. They scored thirteen heavy-shell hits on the *Warspite* before her steering was brought back under control fifteen minutes later. Fortunately, the *Queen Elizabeth*s were sturdier ships than Beatty's battle cruisers; the *Warspite*'s armor protected her from any vital damage. She was able to keep up her speed, and escaped into the mist, following Evan-Thomas. But when her steering gave trouble again a half an hour later, the admiral decided it was too risky to keep her with him. He ordered her captain to return to Rosyth.

Up to this point Scheer was under the illusion that he was only engaged with a few isolated detachments of enemy cruisers, battle cruisers, and battleships. He was confident that he would soon round them up and destroy them. Beatty had succeeded brilliantly in shielding Jellicoe's ships from the Germans' view until it was too late. Jellicoe's deployment had been perfect. He was crossing the enemy T and his almost fully deployed line lay in a vast crescent across Scheer's path. After two years of waiting for this moment, he had the High Seas Fleet exactly where he wanted it. When Jellicoe opened fire shortly before 6:30, it came as a tremendous shock to the German commander in chief to discover that the Grand Fleet was out in full force. Scheer wrote, "It was now quite obvious that we were confronted by a large portion of the English Fleet, and a few minutes later, their presence was indicated on the horizon directly ahead of us by firing of heavy calibre guns. The entire arc stretching from north to east was a sea of fire. The muzzle flashes were clearly seen through the mist and smoke on the horizon, though there was still no sign of the ships themselves."

One after the other, the *Revenge, Agincourt, Hercules, Benbow, Iron Duke, Conqueror, Orion,* and *Monarch* opened fire on the ships at the head of Scheer's line at a range of about twelve thousand yards. Although the German ships were outlined against the setting sun, no organized fire distribution was possible because of the smoke pouring from the guns and funnels of dozens of destroyers, cruisers, and battle cruisers that had been maneuvering in the space between the two battle fleets. The German line stretched back for nine miles because Scheer had kept his ships three and a half cables apart, and Jellicoe's battleships had only the ships of Admiral Behncke's 5th and 6th Divisions within their range. None of the British ships could make out more than three or four of the enemy at a time, and they simply fired at the nearest target before it disappeared into the haze. As Jellicoe put it, "Ships fired at what they could see, while they could see it."

Scheer's gunners were much worse off and were unable to make any effective reply. They fired back, but all they had to aim at were the brief muzzle flashes of the British broadsides. They failed to make a single hit on any of the British battle fleet.

The leading German battleships, the *König, Grosser Kurfürst, Kronprinz,* and *Markgraf,* came under the heaviest bombardment. The *König* in particular was subjected to accurate fire from Jellicoe's flagship *Iron Duke,* which hit her time after time with 13.5-inch shells and set her ablaze from stem to stern. Scheer could see that the head of his line was being crumpled under the British onslaught, and he ordered Behncke to turn away eastward. He realized that his whole battle fleet would be in grave danger of annihilation unless he did something quickly to extricate his ships from the perilous situation they were facing.

At the time Scheer's T was being crossed, Hipper's battle cruisers had taken station ahead of the battle fleet and found themselves in nearly as hazardous a predicament. Hipper had immediately turned southeast when he first sighted Jellicoe's battle fleet, and he was now fighting a separate action with Beatty's ships, which were following him on a parallel course. Hipper's battered force was outnumbered again, because by now Hood had maneuvered his 3d Battle Cruiser Squadron ahead of the *Lion*. He opened an accurate fire on the *Lützow, Seydlitz,* and *Derfflinger* at a range of about ten thousand yards. It must have been extremely disheartening for Hipper. He had already sunk two of Beatty's ships and reversed the initial odds against him, only to find that three more enemy battle cruisers had taken their place. Of his own ships, only the *Moltke* was in good fighting trim. The other three were either down by the head from the water they had taken on earlier or, like the *Von der Tann*, had no heavy guns left in action.

Hood's three *Invincible*s were fresh from gunnery practice at Scapa and they made it tell. The German ships were clearly outlined by the sun, and the *Invincible* and *Inflexible* scored hit after hit on the *Lützow* while the *Indomitable* made several hits on the *Seydlitz* and *Derfflinger.* Beatty's ships were two thousand yards behind Hood's squadron and were also under fire from some of Scheer's battleships, but the *Lion* managed to make two additional hits on the *Lützow.* By now Hipper's flagship was in serious danger of sinking. Her draft had increased so much that her forward deck was awash as far back as the gun turrets.

Beatty looked on with great satisfaction as his leading ships hammered away at the enemy. One of his officers remembered, "Hood pressed home his attack, and it was an inspiring sight to see this squadron of battlecruisers dashing toward the enemy with every gun in action. On the *Lion*'s bridge we felt like cheering them on, for it seemed that the decisive moment of the battle had come."

Everything seemed to be going Hood's way. He could see the enemy ships clearly outlined against the setting sun, while his own were shrouded from view by the swirling mist and haze. Using the voice pipe, he called to his gunnery officer, Lieutenant-Commander Dannreuther, who was high in the foretop, "Your fire is very good. Keep at it as quickly as you can. Every shot is telling."

Heavily damaged though they were, the Germans were far from impotent. As the *Derfflinger's* gunnery officer wrote, "It was clear that the enemy could now see us much better than we could see him. But at 1829 the veil of mist divided. Sharply silhouetted against the horizon we saw the *Invincible.*"

For a few minutes they had a clear view of Hood's flagship at about eight thousand yards distance. Hipper's men had been well trained to take advantage of such brief opportunities, and the *Derfflinger* and *Lützow* opened a rapid fire on the *Invincible* with all the 12-inch guns they had left in action. In the space of two or at most three minutes they hit her five times. The last of these shells, believed to be from the *Derfflinger,* penetrated the midships Q turret and ignited the cordite charges stored there. The flash spread almost instantaneously to the magazines, and in Corbett's vivid account, "flames shot up from the gallant flagship, and there came again the awful spectacle of a fiery burst, followed by a huge column of dark smoke which, mottled with blackened debris, swelled up hundreds of feet in the air, and the mother of all battlecruisers had gone to join the other two that were no more."

The devastating explosion of Hood's flagship took place in full view of Jellicoe's leading ships, but the commander in chief was not aware that this was the third such catastrophe that day. Beatty had not yet informed him of the loss of the *Indefatigable* and *Queen Mary,* and in fact didn't do so until the following morning. The explosion broke the seventeen-thousand-ton vessel cleanly in half. The two sections came to rest on the shallow sea bottom, their ends pointing skyward. The men on some of the British ships that passed by later actually cheered at the sight, believing it to be the wreck of a German ship.

The *Invincible's* survivors bravely cheered back as they clung to floating wreckage. There were only 6 men left out of a crew of 1,032, all of them from the foretop. The gallant Hood was not among them. One of the lucky ones was Dannreuther, who had been flung clear by the blast. He recalled later, "I just waited for the water to come up and meet me, then I stepped out and began swimming. The water was quite warm and there was no shortage of wreckage to hold on to." Dannreuther and the other survivors were soon picked up by the destroyer *Badger.*

In spite of this dazzling success, Hipper's ships were now in far worse shape than the British battle cruisers, which still outnumbered them six to four. A few minutes after the sinking of the *Invincible,* Hipper decided to to transfer his flag to another ship, before his own flagship sank beneath him. He boarded the torpedo boat G39 and told Captain Harder of the *Lützow* to withdraw his ship from the line of battle. After suffering yet more damage during the next phase of the action, Harder was ordered

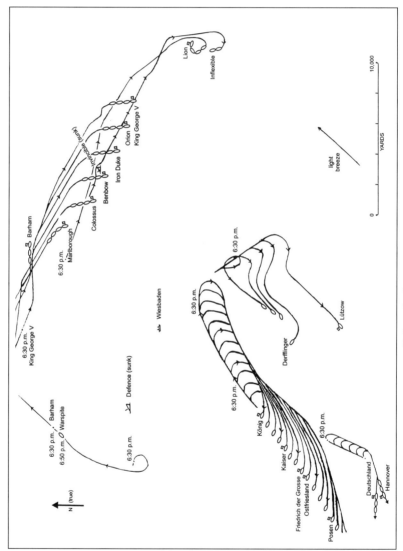

Scheer's first turnaway

to leave the battle area entirely and try to make it back to Wilhelmshaven if the pumps could manage to keep her afloat. The whole of the crippled ship's foredeck was awash, and she could only steam very slowly to avoid taking on too much water through the shell holes in her bow. She eventually had to be abandoned and sunk by her own escorts when it became clear she would never make it to port.

Hipper's problem was, Which of his remaining ships could he board to resume command of the squadron? He discovered that the *Derfflinger* and *Seydlitz* weren't in much better shape than the *Lützow,* and the *Von der Tann* was still without any heavy guns in action. This left him with the *Moltke* as the only real option, but it was several hours before he was able to board her and resume control of the battle cruisers. In the meantime, Captain Hartog of the *Derfflinger* took over command of the 1st Scouting Group.

Meanwhile, Scheer had reached a decision—one which was just as crucial to his battle fleet as Jellicoe's had been earlier. The head of his line was being bent back under the weight of the British bombardment, and if he didn't do something soon, his whole line would be thrown into disorder and destroyed piecemeal. It was absolutely out of the question to keep veering eastward, as this would gradually put his line onto a course parallel to the enemy and lead to a toe-to-toe slugging match that he was bound to lose; his fleet would be smashed by the greater weight of Jellicoe's broadsides. Nor could he turn his ships away together because his line now formed an arc, and such a maneuver would inevitably lead to collisions. There was one maneuver that the Germans had devised to get out of trouble if their T was crossed: the *Gefechtskehrtwendung,* or "battle about-turn."

This was a risky procedure, fraught with the danger of collisions or total confusion if not executed properly. The maneuver had been practiced repeatedly in peacetime but had never been performed under battle conditions. Scheer really had no alternative. At 6:35 he gave the order: *"Gefechtskehrtwendung an Steuerbord."* His twenty-two battleships wheeled through 180 degrees, one after the other, starting with the rearmost ship. Each captain waited until he saw the next ship astern begin to turn before putting his helm over to starboard. In this fashion the long line of ships reversed its course, with Mauve's predreadnoughts now in the van and Behncke's battered squadron bringing up the rear. The whole maneuver was executed without mishap in four minutes, a tribute to the seamanship of the German captains.

166

By 6:45 Scheer's battle fleet had disappeared into the mist—and the smoke being laid down by his torpedo boats. Firing died away as the British battleships were left with no targets to aim at. Jellicoe was mystified at first. One minute he had the enemy where he wanted them, steaming head on into the jaws of his battle fleet, the next minute they had vanished. Several ships at the rear of the British line, which had not yet completed their deployment, saw what was happening but didn't see fit to tell their commander in chief, assuming that he had also seen the German maneuver. When Jellicoe realized what must have happened, he refused to pursue Scheer into the murk. He had foreseen such an eventuality, and had made it plain to the Lords of the Admiralty that he would "decline to be so drawn." His reasons were clear and his tactics had been fully approved by his masters. There was too much risk involved in chasing a fleeing enemy into the unknown, with the likelihood of being led over mines dropped by the retreating ships or suddenly being faced with a massed torpedo boat attack coming at him at high speed out of the mist.

Jellicoe altered course to the southeast by divisions, intending to keep his fleet firmly between the enemy and his possible lines of retreat back to base. Although he had lost contact, he was not displeased that Scheer was heading southwest. Any westward movement meant that the enemy fleet was drawing farther and farther away from the safety of its bases. He felt confident that he would intercept Scheer later that day, or surely by the following morning.

The first clash of the battle fleets had resulted in a confused and fierce action that lasted barely forty-five minutes. Despite the loss of the *Invincible*, the British had good reason to be satisfied with this phase of the battle. They had not smashed the enemy fleet as they had hoped, but they had forced it to retreat ingloriously, and they had inflicted much more damage than they had received.

Due to Jellicoe's skillful maneuvering, the British ships had gained both the advantage of better position, lying athwart the enemy line of advance, and clearer visibility in firing to the west. Although the visibility, which never exceeded fourteen thousand yards because of the mist and smoke, had been less than ideal for the gunners on both sides, it had been far worse for the Germans, particularly for Scheer's battleships, whose gunners could scarcely make out any targets at all. It was only Scheer's skillful handling of his battle fleet that saved him from disaster.

During this brief encounter, the British scored twenty-three heavy-shell hits on the enemy's leading ships. The *König* was hit eight times by 13.5-inch shells from the *Iron Duke* and *Monarch* and suffered severe damage. The *Markgraf* received only two hits, but one of these was a near-miss by the *Orion* that bent a propeller shaft and put one of her engines out of action. The *Lützow* was hit no less than ten more times, due mostly to the superb gunnery of Hood's battle cruisers. It was one devastating hit by either the *Invincible* or *Inflexible* that led to her eventual loss. The already battered *Derfflinger* and *Seydlitz* also received more damage, mainly from the *Indomitable.*

In return, Scheer's battleships had been unable to register a single hit on any of Jellicoe's battleships, and only two on the *Princess Royal.* Even Hipper's accurate gunners could only manage five hits, all of them on the *Invincible* during those brief and devastating moments of clear visibility.

The German battle fleet had made a large number of hits on other ships, but these were all at short range and only came about as a result of an enemy steering malfunction and a foolhardy move by one of its senior officers. The Germans had wrought most of their damage at the so-called Windy Corner, near the rear of the British fleet. They had concentrated "all available fire" on the area of the *Marlborough*'s turning point in the deployment, near where the *Defence, Warrior,* and *Warspite* were, as well as on several light cruisers. According to an eyewitness on one of the cruisers, "The whole ocean was torn up by shell splashes, and the noise was terrific."

In terms of ships sunk, the *Defence* and *Warrior* were obsolescent vessels, and apart from the tragic deaths of so many men, their loss had a negligible effect on the strength of the Grand Fleet. These two ships should never have been at Jutland—they were too slow to act as scouts, a role best left to speedy light cruisers, and too lightly protected to be exposed to the gunfire of capital ships, as both the Falklands and the Dogger Bank had already shown. The sinking of the *Invincible* was a more serious blow, but as it was the oldest and weakest of Beatty's battle cruiser force, it was a sustainable loss. The loss of the *Lützow* was a much more serious blow to the Germans. She was the newest and most powerful of Hipper's battle cruisers, one which he could hardly afford to lose in view of his inferior numbers.

Mention must be made here of the gallant *Wiesbaden.* Even though crippled by Hood's battle cruisers at the end of the Run to the North, she nonetheless played a very useful role in this phase of the battle. She certainly lured Arbuthnot's ships to their destruction. More important, her presence between the battle lines proved to be a great distraction to several of Jellicoe's battleships, whose gunners fired at her as they passed by rather than concentrating their aim on more valuable targets. The *Wiesbaden* even managed to torpedo the *Marlborough.* (This was the only torpedo hit on a British capital ship during the entire battle.) The

Marlborough was not seriously damaged, and although her speed was reduced to seventeen knots, she kept her place in line.

After the *Wiesbaden* had taken uncounted direct hits from both heavy and secondary weapons, and a torpedo from the destroyer *Onslow,* the amazingly rugged little cruiser finally rolled over and sank several hours later. She took all but a handful of her heroic crew of 589 men with her to the bottom. There was only one survivor, Stoker Hugo Zenne, who was picked up from a raft by a Norwegian steamer thirty-six hours after the battle; the rest of his comrades on the raft had succumbed to their wounds or exhaustion.

As this phase of the battle ended around 7:00 P.M., Jellicoe's chief concern was to regain contact with the German fleet as quickly as possible, while there was still enough daylight left to force the battle to a finish. The sun was due to set at 8:17 P.M., which meant that even with the long northern twilight he would have only about two and a half hours of reasonable light in which to achieve victory.

Amazingly, Scheer would soon give him a second chance.

Contact Regained

As the ship surged in the swell the water swept unpleasantly from one side of the mess deck to the other. The electric light was out, and only the candle fighting lights illuminated a rather grim scene. The dead still lay here and there, and some fifty men, many seriously wounded or burnt, were awaiting treatment.

—Capt. Ernle Chatfield

During the lull in the fighting that followed Scheer's *Gefechts-kehrtwendung,* the two commanders in chief were involved in a game of blindman's buff. Jellicoe knew only that the Germans had made some course change toward the west, and at first he thought their disappearance might be due to either an increase in the mist or a smoke screen laid down by the enemy torpedo boats. Ten minutes later, when he realized that Scheer must have made a large alteration in course, he changed his own course by divisions to southeast. He also reduced speed to seventeen knots to allow the *Marlborough* to maintain her place in line. Jellicoe was determined to keep his fleet between the enemy and his bases, and just as determined not to pursue Scheer into the unknown, especially because of the threat of torpedo attacks coming at him out of the haze—an anxiety reinforced by the torpedoing of the *Marlborough.*

At the time, Beatty's battle cruisers were in the van, about three miles off the port bow of the leading battleship, *King George V.* Beatty swung his ships to starboard to mark time and help close the gap, but due to a gyro compass failure the *Lion* kept turning and made an inadvertent 360-degree turn before she returned to her original course. This movement was followed by the rest of the squadron. After the battle, Beatty for some reason refused to admit that the incident had taken place, insisting that the record be altered to show an S turn instead.

Ship after ship of the Grand Fleet, from destroyers to battleships, failed to keep their commander in chief informed of what they had seen of the German fleet movements since Scheer's about-turn—especially the light cruisers, which were supposed to be "the eyes of the fleet." There was one outstanding exception. Goodenough had courageously followed the retreating Germans with the 2d Light Cruiser Squadron, and by 7:04 he was in a position to signal Jellicoe that Scheer had reversed course for a second time and was now steaming due east—almost at right angles to Jellicoe's direction. This was welcome news indeed, and Jellicoe ordered his ships back into line ahead as he altered course to due south at 7:09.

Scheer was equally in the dark about the enemy's movements after he had headed west into the mist. The German advanced forces, especially the light cruisers, had let their admiral down as badly as Jellicoe's had. At 6:45 a report from the *Moltke* gave the enemy's bearing as nearly due east and his course as southerly, but it did not give his position. Scheer thought that Jellicoe was probably heading southward, hoping to cut him off. Confusion was caused by a scouting report that wrongly identified several of Beatty's battle cruisers as battleships of the 5th Squadron, which were actually in the rear of the fleet. This error, coupled with the assumption that Jellicoe was still steaming at his earlier speed, led Scheer to believe that the enemy battle fleet was much farther south than it actually was.

He realized he couldn't continue steaming west because it was taking him too far from his base, but he also knew that if he were to head southward he would play into Jellicoe's hands and be brought to action with at least two hours of daylight left. Scheer decided to make another *Kehrtwendung* and head due east! The only rational explanation for this curious decision is that he hoped to pass astern of the enemy fleet without being detected and reach the safety of the Skagerrak or the swept channels off the Danish coast.

Ten minutes after the *Moltke's* report, Scheer gave the order for his battleships to make a second sixteen-point turn, taking him straight for the middle of Jellicoe's line. He ordered Hipper's battered and leaking battle cruisers, which had been near the rear after the first *Kehrtwendung,* to resume their station at the head of the fleet. In effect Scheer was unwittingly inviting the enemy fleet to cross his T for a second time— and within a matter of minutes, because the two flagships were only about twenty-five thousand yards apart when Scheer made his fateful decision to turn east.

Whatever Scheer's real intentions were in making this seemingly sui-cidal maneuver, in his official report after the battle he told the kaiser:

> The enemy was in a position to do with us what he pleased before nightfall, taking the initiative from us, barring our retreat to the Ger-man Bight. There was only one way to forestall this; to strike a sec-ond blow at the enemy with a second ruthless onslaught, and to bring the torpedo boats against him with full force. This would surprise the enemy, throwing his plans into confusion for the rest of the day, and, if the blow fell heavy enough, would make easier disengagement for the night. It also offered the possibility of a final attempt to bring assistance to the hard-pressed *Wiesbaden,* and to rescue her crew.

This explanation has echoes of Nelson's intentions at Trafalgar, but as a plan of attack at 1916 speeds and gunnery ranges, it is scarcely credible in any respect. First, Scheer had not yet made a first "ruthless onslaught" on the enemy but had found himself in a trap and extricated himself as quickly as he could. Second, if he did intend to strike a blow at the enemy battle fleet, why place his most lightly armored and heavily damaged ships in the van? Third, how would allowing Jellicoe to cross his T make "disengagement for the night" any easier? The final comment about the *Wiesbaden* defies common sense. No German admiral would think of jeopardizing his whole fleet to come to the aid of a single light cruiser. At the Dogger Bank Hipper had refused to risk even a squadron to res-cue a ship much more valuable than the *Wiesbaden.*

It is simply incomprehensible that Scheer would have deliberately led his fleet back into the same snare he had so desperately escaped barely half an hour earlier. It is perhaps best to leave the last word on this controversial subject to Scheer himself. He later admitted jocularly to his chief of staff, Capt. Adolf Von Trotha, that if he had performed a similar maneuver during peacetime exercises, he would have been promptly ordered to haul down his flag.

Scheer's turn to the east brought him out of the mist at 7:10, in full view of the Grand Fleet, well within Jellicoe's gunnery range. Once more his leading ships experienced the unnerving sight of an apparently endless column of British battleships stretched directly across their line of advance. Jellicoe was crossing the German T for the second time in just over an hour. When the British opened fire, their fleet "presented a marvellously impressive spectacle as salvo after salvo rolled out along the line."

Instead of cutting across the rear of the enemy fleet toward safety, Scheer was heading for destruction at the hands of a greatly superior foe who had caught him in the worst possible tactical position. According to Corbett, "For the second time he found himself enveloped in a flaming arc of gun-flashes, and now they were so near that his predicament was more critical than ever."

As before, the poorer visibility to the west did not allow the Germans a clear view of their targets, while most of Jellicoe's fleet could at least see the leading enemy ships without difficulty. This time they were no longer in middeployment as they had been at first contact. Within five minutes, no less than seventeen of Jellicoe's battleships and four of Beatty's battle cruisers had opened rapid fire on the enemy van at ranges from nine to fourteen thousand yards. To make things worse for the Germans, there were now several 15-inch-gunned superdreadnoughts of the *Royal Sovereign* class in action to add to Evan-Thomas's *Queen Elizabeths*.

As before, no systematic fire distribution was possible, and the British gunners aimed either at Scheer's battleships or at Hipper's battle cruisers as the opportunity presented itself. They scored hit after hit, mainly on the *Grosser Kurfürst, Kaiser, Derfflinger,* and *Seydlitz,* while the unsighted Germans were unable to make any effective reply. To illustrate the difference in visibility conditions for the two sides, fifteen of the British battleships managed to score at least one hit on an enemy ship, while none of Scheer's battle fleet made a single hit.

Scheer was facing annihilation again, and in desperation he ordered his battle cruisers to make a reckless all-out assault on the British battleships to try to relieve the pressure on the head of his line, which was being forced to starboard by the enemy onslaught. The signal to Captain Hartog read "*Schlachtkreuzer ran an den Feind! Voll einsetzen!*" (Battle cruisers, at the enemy! Give it all you've got!)

The captain of the *Derfflinger* didn't hesitate; he unflinchingly led his battered ships, the *Seydlitz, Moltke,* and *Von der Tann,* through a storm of shellfire to within eight thousand yards of the enemy in an attempt to draw their fire away from Scheer's battle fleet. This became known as the "death ride of the battle cruisers." A sacrificial role had been envisaged for these ships if the situation demanded it, and such a role was enshrined in German fleet tactics. But three minutes later, when Scheer saw they were getting too close to the British battleships and were being pounded from all sides, he rescinded the order and told Hartog to turn to starboard and engage the battle cruisers at the head of the British line at a less dangerous range. At the same time, he signaled Commodore Heinrich to send the twenty torpedo boats of the 6th and 9th Flotillas in an all-out torpedo attack on the British battle fleet and to lay smoke to cover a second *Gefechtskehrtwendung.*

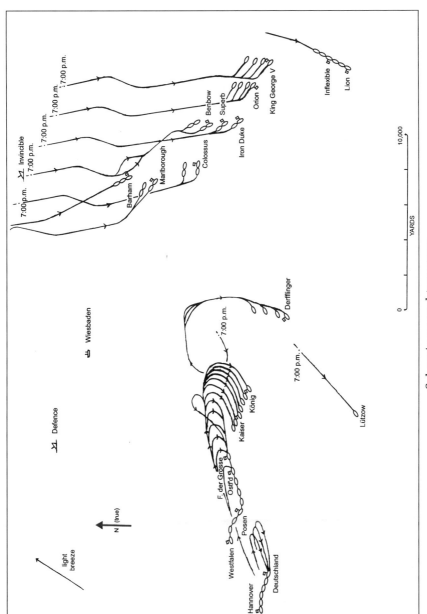

Scheer's second turnaway

Scheer's signal for the battle fleet to prepare to turn about was hoisted at 7:12, but the flags were not hauled down until 7:18. This time the maneuver was carried out in a much less orderly fashion because Scheer's battleships had already slowed down and started to bunch up under the intense bombardment of their van. Scheer's second in command, Vice Admiral Schmidt in the *Ostfriesland,* started the maneuver early on his own initiative in order to speed things up, and there were several near-collisions and a tendency to panic as some ships swung to starboard and others to port. The German fleet was in full retreat and its formation in near chaos, but by 7:30 it had completely disappeared into the mist again, and British firing died away. Ten minutes later, Scheer had straightened out his line and was heading west at his best speed.

Faced with the massed torpedo boat attack, Jellicoe ordered his battleships to turn away to port, first by two points, then by two more—45 degrees in all. At the same time he sent Commodore LeMesurier with his 4th Light Cruiser Squadron and Hawksley's 11th Destroyer Flotilla to counterattack and drive the German torpedo boats off. The battleships joined in the counterattack, mainly with their secondary armament. Despite losing two torpedo boats, with four more heavily damaged, the plucky Germans managed to fire thirty-one torpedoes at the battleships.

The standard tactical response in both fleets when faced with a massed torpedo boat attack was to turn away, so that the torpedoes could be more easily avoided as they slowed down. Their tracks were clearly visible and they were "combed" by the battleships without too much difficulty in most cases. Nevertheless, the *Collingwood, Colossus, Hercules, Iron Duke, Thunderer, Marlborough, Revenge,* and *Agincourt* all narrowly escaped being hit, some of them only by putting the helm hard over and swerving out of line. Several of the torpedoes came within thirty yards of their targets, and one of three heading for the *Marlborough* actually passed underneath the ship without exploding! It was only the alertness of the lookouts and the skill of the helmsmen that saved the British fleet from serious losses.

Jellicoe was heavily criticized later for this turnaway, especially for having turned his whole battle fleet, when it was mainly the rear of his line that was being threatened. But it had been estimated from peacetime exercises that a hit rate of about 30 percent would result if immediate and effective countermeasures were not taken against a massed torpedo attack on a line of battleships. The effect of nine torpedo hits at this stage would have been devastating. British capital ships were far from invulnerable to underwater damage, as the mining of the *Auda-*

cious had shown. A turn toward the enemy would have been a possible alternative, and kept Jellicoe nearer to the enemy, but this would have been more dangerous because the combined speeds of ship and torpedo would have given the helmsmen less time to take avoiding action. Jellicoe would probably have lost sight of the German fleet in any event because of Scheer's *Gefechtskehrtwendung* into the mist and smoke.

Thus contact between the battle fleets was lost again after an engagement even briefer than the first. This one lasted only twenty minutes. Scheer was clearly and understandably determined to avoid a head-on fight with a superior force, and there was not much Jellicoe could do about it without chasing after him into the mist and risking his superiority in battleships. Why take such a risk? There was too much to lose and not enough to gain. A glorious Trafalgar-like victory would not give Jellicoe command of the seas—he already had that—but serious losses from torpedoes and mines could easily take it away.

Although this phase of the battle was very brief, the German van, particularly the battle cruisers, had received a severe mauling. Jellicoe's battle fleet and Evan-Thomas's 5th Battle Squadron had scored an estimated thirty-seven direct hits on Scheer's battleships and Hipper's battle cruisers, the majority with 13.5- and 15-inch shells. Beatty's ships had fired at the German battle cruisers in the latter part of the action, but without any result. The most successful gunnery ships during the brief opportunity presented to Jellicoe's fleet were the *Revenge, Royal Oak, Colossus, Barham,* and *Valiant,* which registered over half of the thirty-seven hits between them. The only German ship to register any hits during this phase was the *Seydlitz.*

By now the German battle cruisers were truly a sorry sight. The *Derfflinger* had been hit no fewer than fourteen times during the "death ride," suffering altogether an incredible twenty heavy-shell hits without sinking. Most of her guns were out of action, and she had taken on thousands of tons of seawater due to shell holes and the deliberate flooding of her magazines. Down by the head, with her whole foredeck awash, she struggled on. The *Seydlitz* was nearly as badly off: five more hits had brought her total to seventeen. Surprisingly, the *Moltke* and *Von der Tann* had come through the death ride practically unscathed, although they both bore the scars of earlier action.

But the worst off by far was the *Lützow.* After Hipper had transferred to a torpedo boat, she had sheered out of the line and was limping to the southwest to get away from the battle area when she was targeted by the *Monarch* and *Orion,* who hit her five times. This brought her total since the outset to a staggering twenty-four direct hits by heavy shells.

Hipper's flagship was in desperate shape. Her guns were either out of action or had to be be operated manually; several of her magazines had been flooded because of dangerous cordite fires; and she was still taking on seawater from the holes in her bow, and her decks were awash as far as the forward turrets. She was obviously a doomed ship, even though she was being escorted by six destroyers, which were laying smoke to shield her from further punishment. Her captain was still hoping to reach base.

It says a great deal for the quality of German shipbuilding, and perhaps the effectiveness of the flash-protection systems installed after the Dogger Bank, that none of Hipper's ships were sunk or blown up by the hammering they had taken. Several dangerous cordite fires had resulted from the many direct hits, but the tendency of German cordite to burn rather than explode, coupled with the antiflash doors, had allowed the magazines to be flooded before the kind of disasters that had befallen Beatty's ships could occur.

But it is also a scathing indictment of British munitions makers that scarcely any of the shells that struck the German ships completely penetrated the armor before exploding inside, as they were meant to do. With better shells and fuses, there is little doubt that the British gunners would have been rewarded by sinking at least three of Hipper's battle cruisers, instead of just the *Lützow,* which in the end had to be abandoned and sunk by her own escorts.

The German battleships had also suffered damage, especially Behncke's 5th Division. The *König, Grosser Kurfürst, Markgraf, Kaiser,* and *Helgoland* had all received direct hits during the second crossing of the German T. The most heavily damaged were the *Grosser Kurfürst,* which was hit seven times by 13.5- and 15-inch shells from the *Barham, Valiant,* and *Marlborough,* and the *König,* which was hit once by the *Iron Duke,* to go with the nine punishing hits she had suffered earlier. Hipper's battle cruisers had undoubtedly saved these ships from more severe damage by drawing much of the enemy fire.

Total casualties were very heavy on board some of the German ships, notably the proportion of killed to wounded—the *Lützow* with 165 casualties, of which 115 were killed; the *Derfflinger,* 183, with 157 killed; the *Seydlitz,* 153, with 98 killed; and the *König,* 72, with 45 killed. Many of the dead had been immolated in raging turret fires; others had been trapped and drowned when the order was given to flood a magazine.

By contrast, the German gunners, because of poor visibility to the east, were able to register only two direct hits on British ships, both on the *Colossus,* which was hit by two 12-inch shells from the same salvo fired by the *Seydlitz*. These caused little damage and only nine casualties, none of them fatal.

Scheer's second disappearance into the mist gave the crews on both sides a timely respite. By now some of them had been in almost continuous action for five hours, and they badly needed a break to have some rest, grab something to eat, or simply to relax with their shipmates and talk over their experiences. For most of them, it was their first chance to learn what had been going on during the battle. Many of them were stationed below decks, especially the engine-room staff, and had little idea what had been happening above their heads.

The break gave the damage control parties time to put out fires and make temporary repairs to guns and other vital equipment damaged by enemy shells. A period of calm was also sorely needed by the sick-bay staff—the hard-pressed surgeons and their assistants—to allow them to take proper care of the wounded, many of them terribly mutilated or burned, and to comfort the dying or relieve their final agony with morphine. Captain Chatfield dispassionately described the scene in the *Lion*'s sick bay, which must have been fairly typical of all the heavily damaged ships:

> Passing down the gangway to the lower deck I found the gallant Fleet Surgeon, MacLean, and his only remaining surgeon, Horace Stevens, a highly skilled officer standing up to their ankles in water, dressing the wounded who were lying on mess tables. The mess-deck was flooded by the fire-mains being damaged by shellfire. . . . As the ship surged in the swell the water swept unpleasantly from one side of the mess deck to the other. The electric light was out, and only the candle fighting lights illuminated a rather grim scene. The dead still lay here and there, and some fifty men, many seriously wounded or burnt, were awaiting treatment.

There were several ships much more severely damaged than the *Lion*, and conditions on board the *Wiesbaden* and *Lützow* must have been indescribably grim.

After breaking off the action, Scheer gradually veered from west to southwest, then to south by east. His battle fleet was in line ahead, with Rear Admiral Engelhardt's 2d Division in the van. Because of the fleet's 180-degree turnabout, the *Westfalen* was now the leading ship and the *König* was bringing up the rear. Scheer had placed Mauve's old and vulnerable predreadnoughts, led by Rear Adm. von Dalwigk zu Lichtenfels in the *Hannover*, about twenty-five hundred yards off his starboard bow to shield them from the expected direction of the enemy approach. But the battered ships of the 1st Scouting Group, minus the *Lützow,* had taken station on Scheer's port bow, where they would be about three miles nearer the enemy if Jellicoe managed to regain contact. Surprisingly, Scheer did not order Hartog to take up a less vulnerable position, because his remaining battle cruisers were in no condition to accept further action. Perhaps he envisaged another "death ride" for them if it became necessary to save his battleships. Hipper still had not been able to resume command of his squadron, though Hartog had done remarkably well in his stead.

Jellicoe's turnaway to avoid torpedoes had brought his line onto a southeasterly course, and when he judged that the danger had passed, he altered course to due south, gradually veering around to south-southwest. He intended to keep his fleet firmly between the enemy and his route back to Wilhelmshaven. The battle cruisers were scouting four miles dead ahead of the battleships, and Beatty kept on to the southwest, hoping to spot the Germans and cut them off.

At this point, the two battle fleets were about eighteen miles apart, heading down the sides of a narrow V. If they stayed on their present heading, their courses would intersect around sunset. The sun was due to set at 8:17, which meant that even if Jellicoe succeeded in making contact again, he would have no more than an hour of sufficient light left for his guns to inflict further damage on Scheer's fleet.

The Fading Light

CHAPTER 12

*Urgent. Submit van of battleships follow battlecruisers.
We can then cut off the whole of enemy's battle fleet.*

—Vice-Adm. Sir David Beatty

A quarter of an hour after Scheer's second "battle turnaway," Admiral Beatty, who was about six miles ahead of Jellicoe, caught a brief glimpse of what he thought were enemy battleships, just before they disappeared into the mist. He signaled Jellicoe: "Enemy bears from me N.W. by W., distant 10 to 11 miles. My position Lat. 56° 56'N., Long. 6° 16'E. Course S.W. Speed 18 knots." What Beatty had probably seen were the battle cruisers of the 1st Scouting Group, which were about three miles off Scheer's port bow. Although this signal originated at 7:40, it had to be sent to the *Minotaur* first, because the *Lion*'s long-range W/T was out of action, and then relayed to the *Iron Duke*. It was 7:59 before it had been received in the flagship, decoded, and placed in Jellicoe's hands.

The enemy's bearing and course were still unknown to Jellicoe, because Beatty's reported position was clearly out by several miles. In addition, Jellicoe had just received an urgent and confusing signal from Goodenough about an unknown number of detached enemy ships steering northwest. The only thing he could be sure of was that Scheer was somewhere to westward, and a minute later he responded to Beatty's signal and ordered the battle fleet to turn west by divisions and proceed at seventeen knots. He informed Beatty that he was doing so. With his fleet heading west in six columns arranged in echelon over a five-mile-wide front, Jellicoe hoped to increase his chances of regaining contact with the enemy.

Even if he didn't, he was at least confident that his fleet was firmly placed between Scheer and his route back to Wilhelmshaven.

In fact, Jellicoe's turn by divisions was taking him unwittingly straight for the middle of the German battle fleet, because in the meantime Scheer had decided he was getting too far west for safety and had altered course to due south. Jellicoe was in no real danger of having his own T crossed, because his divisions were approaching the enemy fleet at an oblique angle and he could easily swing his ships back to line ahead if the enemy came in sight. This would put him broadside on to Scheer's line, which was what he wanted.

The general picture was just as obscure to Scheer. He didn't realize that his turn south was taking him closer to the enemy, or that his flagship *Friedrich der Grosse* was now only about fifteen miles from the *Iron Duke.* But Scheer had already made up his mind what he must do. As he wrote later, "Should we succeed in checking the enemy's enveloping movement and reaching the Horn Reefs before them, we should retain the initiative for next morning. To this end, all flotillas had to attack during the night, at the risk of doing without them in new engagements at dawn. The German Battle Fleet had to make for the Horn Reefs by the shortest route, maintaining this course against all attacks by the enemy."

Shortly before 8:00 P.M. there occurred one of the most controversial incidents of the entire battle. In a signal originating at 7:47, Beatty sent Jellicoe the now famous message, "Urgent. Submit van of battleships follow battlecruisers. We can then cut off the whole of enemy's battle fleet."

Because of delays in transmission the signal was not taken in by the *Iron Duke* until 7:54. A further delay in deciphering meant that it did not reach Jellicoe on the bridge until about 8:00.

It has never been clear on what basis Beatty made this dramatic proposal. The track charts of the battle show unmistakably that at the time it was sent, he was at least thirteen miles from the nearest enemy battle cruiser and more than seventeen miles from any of Scheer's battleships— much too far away to be in visual contact with the German battle fleet. He could not possibly have known Scheer's current position or course— he had probably not seen any German battleships for more than an hour. Nevertheless, he was convinced that the German battle fleet was somewhere to the northwest, and that his own southwesterly course would cut them off.

Jellicoe was puzzled by the signal. He knew that Beatty was most unlikely to be in visual contact with the enemy battle fleet because his battle cruisers were well to the south of Jerram's division in the van, and Jellicoe couldn't even see the enemy himself from his position in the center. After pondering the situation for several minutes, he signaled Jerram by searchlight at 8:07 to follow the battle cruisers as Beatty had requested. In fact, Jerram's heading at the time was four points nearer the enemy than Beatty's, and if he had obeyed Jellicoe's signal, he would have had to turn his division 45 degrees away from the enemy.

Jerram couldn't obey the order anyway, because he wasn't sure where the battle cruisers were. Beatty had not given his latest position in the "follow me" signal, and none of his battle cruisers were in sight from Jerram's flagship, *King George V.* So Jerram decided to stay on his present course until the situation became clearer. In addition, Beatty's ships were five knots faster than Jerram's, and he probably couldn't have closed Beatty in time to give him support in any case.

No opportunity was lost by not following Beatty's proposal, because Jellicoe's battleships were already heading in a direction that would cut Scheer off. Although the famous signal had no effect on the outcome of the battle, it generated an unpleasant controversy afterward. Beatty's supporters claimed that Jellicoe's failure to follow Beatty had let slip a glorious opportunity to trap and smash the German fleet, while Jellicoe's camp dismissed the signal as a meaningless piece of typical Beatty bravado. As Admiral Ramsay pointed out after the war, "The Battle Fleet was doing what Admiral Beatty had asked for, in fact doing rather more."

Shortly after eight o'clock, Beatty was still heading southwest, determined to make contact with the enemy. He ordered his light cruisers to sweep west, to try to locate the head of German fleet before sunset. The 3d Light Cruiser Squadron led by Rear-Admiral Napier in the *Falmouth* soon spotted five German cruisers bearing northwest and reported this to both Beatty and Jellicoe. Unfortunately, this wasn't much help to Jellicoe, because Napier's reported position was clearly wrong. The British cruisers headed straight for the enemy, and by 8:18 they were in action with Boedicker's light cruiser squadron, which was scouting ahead of the *Westfalen,* now the leading ship of Scheer's battle fleet. The enemy were only nine thousand yards off, but the light was too poor to enable either side to score any hits before Boedicker's ships turned away to starboard. Napier's cruisers lost sight of them in the mist.

At about the same time, Commodore Hawksley's 11th Destroyer Flotilla, supported by the 4th Light Cruiser Squadron led by LeMesurier in the *Calliope,* was farther to the north and scouting ahead of the *King George V.* They sighted a flotilla of torpedo boats led by the light cruiser *Rostock* and pursued them. This brought them within range of Reuter's 4th Scouting Group, and they opened fire. After scoring two direct hits on one of Reuter's cruisers, the *München,* the British light cruisers found themselves within range of Behncke's 3d Battle Squadron, which was bringing up the rear of Scheer's fleet. The *Markgraf* hit the *Calliope* five times with her secondary battery of 5.9-inch guns, forcing LeMesurier to turn away. The British destroyers fired torpedoes at the German battleships, without success, then zigzagged away to get out of danger.

These brief skirmishes and sightings of enemy ships were all reported to Scheer and Jellicoe, but the positions given by the signaling ships were obviously in error by miles. The two admirals still did not have a clear idea of just where the enemy battle fleet was. They knew the two fleets must be very close, because they could hear the sound of gunfire in the distance, but until they had more reliable information they stayed on their present headings—Scheer due south and Jellicoe southwest.

Then, as the sun was setting, Beatty altered course to west-southwest. He was still optimistic that he would locate the head of Scheer's fleet before nightfall. He soon sighted enemy battle cruisers about five miles to the west and caught occasional glimpses of battleships several miles farther west of them. The *Princess Royal* opened fire first, at 8:19, followed a few minutes later by the *Lion, Tiger, New Zealand,* and *Indomitable.* The enemy battleships were too far away for them to have much chance of hitting them in the fading light, so Beatty's ships turned their guns on the leading battle cruisers, firing at ranges of nine to ten thousand yards.

The Germans were surprised to find Beatty so far south. Hipper had just ordered his battle cruisers to stop engines so that he could transfer from the G39 to the *Moltke* when the *Princess Royal* opened up with her 13.5-inch guns. It was too dangerous for the *Moltke's* captain to pick Hipper up while he was under intense fire from Beatty's squadron, and the admiral was again frustrated in his attempts to resume command of his squadron.

The four surviving German battle cruisers were not the same foes Beatty had faced earlier in the day. Except for the *Moltke,* more than half of their big guns were out of action, or being operated inefficiently by hand, and the Germans had to resort to using their secondary batteries of 5.9-inch weapons as well. Indeed, it was amazing that the *Seydlitz* and *Derfflinger* were still afloat, let alone capable of going into action again, after the punishment they had taken.

Although the sun had set and the light was not good, Beatty's ships were easily able to detect the outlines of their targets in the afterglow to the west. The *Princess Royal* quickly scored two hits on the *Seydlitz,* and the *Lion* hit the *Derfflinger* once, reporting that she then turned away, on fire and listing heavily. The *Tiger's* gunnery had not improved and she made no hits, nor did the *Indomitable* from her position at the rear. The

New Zealand had the best results. She hit the *Seydlitz* three times, and the crippled ship sheered out of the line, ablaze from the fresh fires started by the *New Zealand*'s shells.

The Germans were unable to make any effective response in the fading light to the east. The only visible signs of the enemy ships were smoke clouds or muzzle flashes, and spotting their fall of shot was impossible. Hartog's battered ships were no longer a fighting unit, and he had no choice but to break off action at 8:35. He headed southwest into the mist, cutting across the head of the battle fleet to take refuge on its disengaged side. Scheer ordered the battle cruisers to take station at the rear to spare them from further punishment. He also signaled the rest of the fleet to turn southwest to get himself out of danger. He knew Jellicoe could not be far astern of Beatty, and with several of his dreadnoughts badly damaged he wanted to avoid further action before nightfall.

This left only Mauve's 2d Battle Squadron to cover the battle cruisers' retreat. Mauve gallantly held on to the south with his six predreadnoughts, and these obsolescent vessels now became the vanguard of the proud High Seas Fleet. Scheer was willing to see them sacrificed if necessary, to save his more valuable ships. These old "five-minute ships" had inadequate armor and main armaments of outdated 11-inch guns and were not meant to slug it out with modern dreadnoughts.

Beatty's battle cruisers turned their guns on these fresh targets and hit the *Schleswig-Holstein, Pommern,* and *Hessen* in quick succession. Only the *Posen* managed to strike back, making a direct hit on the *Princess Royal.* The uneven contest ended after about five minutes, when Mauve turned away sharply and headed into the mist. Mauve knew it would be suicidal to expose his old ships to Beatty's 13.5-inch salvos any longer, but his squadron had served its purpose by drawing fire away from Hartog's crippled squadron and allowing it to escape. Mauve's courageous intervention had repaid Scheer handsomely for allowing the predreadnoughts to put to sea with the High Seas Fleet against his better judgment.

Beatty did not follow Mauve's squadron. He decided it would be unwise to chase after it into the mist, possibly into the arms of Scheer's battle fleet, while he was unsupported by Jellicoe's battle squadrons. Beatty had, however, succeeded in driving Scheer farther to the west, away from his intended route to Horns Reef. Scheer was aware of his predicament and soon altered course to south by east.

While Beatty was engaging the enemy predreadnoughts, Jellicoe had turned southwest at 8:30 to follow Jerram, who was heading for the sound of the guns, although he was still unable to see any of Beatty's ships. The commander in chief was having great difficulty in getting reliable information about the exact location of the enemy battle fleet. He had signaled the *Comus,* one of LeMesurier's cruisers, when he heard gunfire and actually saw one of the German shells hit the cruiser. He asked, "Who are you firing at?" Back came the less than precise reply: "Enemy's B.F. bearing West." Jellicoe was pretty sure of this already, but it confirmed that his present course was the right one. He was confident he would soon converge on Scheer's battle fleet.

It was not until about 9:00 that scouting reports from the *Lion, Southampton,* and *Falmouth* gave the correct enemy bearing in response to Jellicoe's queries, thus making the situation reasonably clear. Scheer was now somewhere to the north of the speedy battle cruisers and steering southwest or west-southwest. Jellicoe ordered his battleships to alter course to due south in succession and maintain their formation in divisions. But as darkness began to descend on the scene, the two fleets were no longer converging down the sides of a narrow V. They had been doing so until 9.00, but Scheer's undetected turn to the south meant that Jerram was now leading the fleet on a parallel course to the Germans, and somewhat ahead of them. Beatty was so far to the southwest of Jerram that he was unknowingly in danger of taking up a station in the German van!

There were two more chances to come to grips with the enemy fleet before complete darkness blanketed the battle area. The *Caroline* and *Royalist* of the 4th Light Cruiser Squadron were on the *King George V's* starboard bow. Just before 9:00 they sighted three ships five miles westnorthwest on their starboard quarter. They were initially identified as German predreadnoughts, but in the poor light the lookouts couldn't be certain. The *Caroline* signaled Jerram to warn him of a possible enemy torpedo attack but the message was not taken in by the *King George V.* But the *Comus* and the 11th Destroyer Flotilla picked up the signal and headed toward the *Caroline.*

The ships were actually the *Westfalen* and two of the leading German dreadnoughts, screened by torpedo boats and a light cruiser. Because of the uncertainty bred by the twilight conditions the British felt it necessary to challenge them by searchlight to identify themselves before attacking. When there was no reply to the challenge, Captain Crooke of the *Royalist* gave the signal to attack. The *Caroline* and *Royalist* launched several torpedoes, two of which narrowly missed the second ship, *Nassau.* The *Nassau* then fired a star shell to light up the scene, an action which identified them as enemy ships because no British were equipped with star shell.

The Germans opened fire on the British cruisers at eight thousand yards, but after firing a few shells, they ceased fire because they couldn't make out their attackers in the twilight. The *Comus* and the 11th Destroyer Flotilla failed to press home an attack with torpedoes, for the curious reason that they expected Jerram's battle squadron to open fire at any minute. The *Westfalen* and *Nassau* turned away to avoid torpedo attacks, and the Germans were lost to sight. An excellent opportunity to inflict serious damage on the enemy battle fleet had been wasted.

Then the *Castor*'s lookouts sighted what they took to be enemy battle cruisers to the west. They were apparently approaching the British fleet. The *Caroline* reported this to Jerram, and Captain Crooke signaled his ships to attack, but his order was countermanded by Jerram. The *King George V* had also spotted these ships, and Jerram reported to Jellicoe that they were British battle cruisers. There were some who disagreed with Jerram. The *Orion*'s flag lieutenant was convinced they were enemy ships and urged Rear-Admiral Leveson to lead his division toward them and attack. He told Leveson that doing so would make his name "as famous as Nelson's." But Leveson had been taught to follow his admiral's movements, and replied, "We must follow our next ahead." Jerram's negative signal was also intercepted by the 11th Flotilla, who once again did not attack with torpedoes. Another golden opportunity to inflict some damage on the enemy fleet before dark had been thrown away. Jerram was still unaware that he was leading the fleet on a parallel course to the enemy. This was the last daylight contact between the two fleets.

At 9:27 Jellicoe signaled the battle fleet to take up its night-cruising order before it went completely dark—three columns of battleships in line ahead, with the columns one mile apart. He also ordered the destroyer flotillas to take station five miles astern of the battle fleet to act as rear guard in case the Germans attacked the tail end of his fleet or tried to pass astern of it during the night. The Grand Fleet continued to steam due south at seventeen knots.

Jellicoe had no intention of fighting a night action because he knew the Germans were well trained for night fighting. Their searchlights were vastly superior to the those of the British, and their ships were equipped with star shell. According to Campbell, "The British night-fighting technique was very inferior to the German, and indeed virtually non-existent." In any case, Jellicoe regarded night action as a lottery. His ships would never be sure whether they were firing at friend or enemy, and with so many ships maneuvering at high speed in darkness there was the ever present danger of collisions. To make things worse, there was no moon at all on the night of 31 May–1 June.

Jellicoe felt he was still in control of the situation, in spite of the losses inflicted earlier by the Germans. He didn't know about Beatty's losses yet. His own battle squadrons were virtually unscathed while Scheer's were not, and his fleet was stretched out in a line ten miles long between Scheer and his base. There was always tomorrow. Jellicoe was confident that if he kept to his present course, action would be resumed early next day. Sunrise was due at 2:51 A.M., and with eighteen hours of daylight ahead of him, there would be plenty of time to achieve another "Glorious First of June."

Scheer had other ideas. He knew what he was in for if he could not skirt around or break through the British line during the night and gain the safety of his minefields before dawn. His already battered fleet was in no condition to face the might of the Grand Fleet in a second, prolonged day action, no matter what he said later about retaining "the initiative for next morning" in the "new engagements at dawn." His one overriding object was to reach base.

At 9:14 he signaled the fleet to set a course of south-southeast and proceed at sixteen knots, taking him directly toward the Horns Reef. He added the message "*Durchhalten*": his ships were to hold this course at all costs.

Confusion in the Night

*Please give me challenge and reply now in force
as they have been lost.*

—Signal from HMS *Lion* to HMS *Princess Royal*

CHAPTER 13

The fighting during the brief northern night of 31 May–1 June was completely different from that which had taken place the day before. There were no more long-range gunnery contests or intricate maneuvers. The night actions were short, fierce, and confused. They were mainly ship-to-ship engagements that arose through chance contacts in the overcast moonless night, with little in the way of organized tactics. Uppermost in everyone's mind was the difficulty of correctly identifying the dim shapes that suddenly loomed out of the dark before deciding whether to open fire. In spite of this, there were remarkably few instances of ships attacking their own side. Several German battleships and cruisers did fire at their own torpedo boats, mistaking them for enemy destroyers, but luckily they didn't hit any of them. Several British destroyers failed to respond to enemy attacks, believing them to be British ships making a dreadful blunder.

Most of the fighting took place at nearly point-blank range; generally a thousand yards or two separated the combatants as they blazed away with their guns or launched torpedoes. The battle scene was lit only fitfully by searchlights, star shell, or flashes from the guns, and occasionally by flames from a burning vessel or a dazzling explosion as a ship was torn apart when its magazines blew up. Inevitably, there were some violent collisions—some involving confederates, others adversaries—as ships maneuvered at high speed in the gloom. The worst collisions occurred when lumbering battleships ran down hapless smaller ships that had strayed into their path.

At least seven more or less distinct engagements took place between the onset of darkness and daybreak on 1 June, but nobody on either side had much idea of what was going on outside their own immediate area—probably least of all the two commanders in chief. Communications between the ships in action and their admirals were either faulty or non-existent.

As it would be difficult to give a comprehensive account of all the night actions without it becoming somewhat indigestible, only the most significant events will be described in any detail.

As the fleets steamed southward in the darkness, neither admiral realized how close they were to each other. At 10:00 P.M. their flagships *Iron Duke* and *Friedrich der Grosse* were only thirteen miles apart, and only eight miles separated some of the opposing battleships.

Each admiral decided what he must do. Scheer's plan was simple—to stay on course for the Horns Reef and the swept channels through the minefields, where he knew Jellicoe would not dare follow him, then to head down the Danish coast to the mouth of the Jade. He was aware from intercepted British signals sent to him from Neumünster—Germany's answer to Room 40—that Jellicoe had stationed his destroyer flotillas five miles to the rear of his fleet. If Scheer ran into them, he was confident he could bludgeon his way through any light forces that barred his way, taking his chances on whatever damage they might be able to inflict in the darkness. He was resolved to get his main fleet to safety before daylight, come what may.

Jellicoe was faced with a less straightforward decision. He was determined to avoid a major night action, but he had to keep his fleet between the enemy and his possible routes back to base, so that he could renew the battle at daybreak before the Germans reached the protection of their shore defenses. His dilemma was that he had to decide which route Scheer was most likely to take. There were several options to consider. First, Scheer could turn northeast and escape into the Baltic via the Skagerrak. Jellicoe dismissed this as being too long a voyage for a fleet with several heavily damaged ships. He also thought it unlikely that Scheer would head for the Horns Reef. Twice already Scheer, by turning eastward, had run head on into the Grand Fleet and been forced to retreat. Jellicoe didn't think he would try it again. If he did, however, Jellicoe was satisfied that his destroyers and light cruisers would use their torpedoes to repulse any attempt to outflank him to the north and warn him if Scheer was headed in this direction. As insurance, he detached

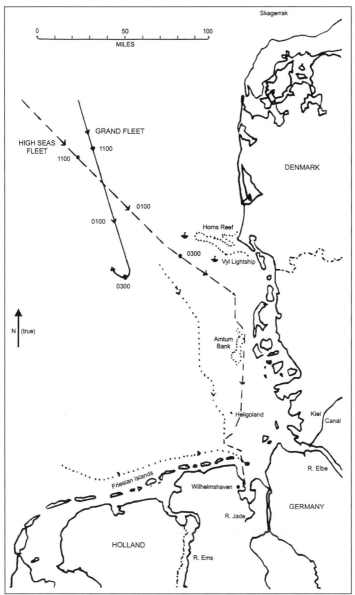

Scheer's possible routes to Wilhelmshaven

the minelayer *Abdiel* to lay more mines off the Horns Reef lightship at the mouth of the German swept channel, adding to those it had already laid on 3 May. Jellicoe also had three submarines stationed near the Vyl lightship to waylay any of Scheer's ships that managed to break through.

Jellicoe remained convinced from earlier scouting reports that the German fleet was to his northwest, and he therefore concluded that Scheer's safest and most likely routes home were to the southwest; either via the swept channels through the British minefields in the Heligoland Bight or by skirting around them to the west, then heading south to the Friesian Islands and along the Dutch coast to the mouth of the Ems. To prevent any attempt to outflank the British fleet to the south and reach the Danish coast, Beatty's battle cruisers were stationed thirteen miles southwest of the battle squadrons. Jellicoe knew the German battleships didn't have enough speed to cut across the Grand Fleet ahead of Beatty without being detected.

The first night contacts between the enemy fleets took place shortly before 10:00 P.M., but these only resulted in ineffectual brushes of their light forces. At 9:40 Schuur's 2d Torpedo Boat Flotilla and some boats of the 6th and 7th Flotillas sighted Wintour's 4th Destroyer Flotilla in the waning light. The Germans fired torpedoes without success, although one narrowly missed the *Garland*. The 4th DF opened fire, but the Germans were quickly driven off when Goodenough's light cruisers and Hawksley's 11th DF showed up. Shortly after this there was another ineffectual German attack as the cruisers *Frankfurt* and *Pillau* fired torpedoes at the 11th DF. The tracks were not seen by the British, and contact was lost again, because Hawksley's destroyers were turning to take their station astern of the battle fleet.

The Germans were not only better trained and equipped for night fighting, but they gained a valuable advantage through another incredibly inept signaling performance by Beatty's squadron. At 9:32, as the battle cruisers were heading south to take up their position at the head of the fleet, the *Lion* signaled the *Princess Royal* by flash lamp, asking, "Please give me challenge and reply now in force as they have been lost." This secret information was passed back as requested, also using a flash lamp. These messages were sent back and forth in Morse, but otherwise in plain English. The interchange was seen by the *Elbing* and *Frankfurt* in the darkness, and they intercepted part of the *Princess Royal's* reply.

The two cruisers silently withdrew before their presence was detected and soon passed this vital information on to the rest of Scheer's ships. The Germans had only picked up enough of the *Princess Royal's* signal to learn that the reply to a British challenge should begin with the letters "UA." They hoped that if they garbled the rest of the reply when they were challenged, it would be accepted for long enough to allow them to get close to the enemy without being fired on. Then they could train their guns and searchlights on the target and open fire before the British ship realized the danger. It didn't take the Germans long to make use of their newly acquired knowledge.

Shortly after ten o'clock, Boedicker's 2d Scouting Group, accompanied by the *Hamburg* and *Rostock,* sighted the 11th DF again. This time they approached Hawksley's flagship, HMS *Castor,* and when challenged gave the British reply, which was accepted at first. This allowed the *Elbing, Hamburg,* and *Rostock* to get within a mile of the *Castor* before they turned on their searchlights and opened rapid fire on the British light cruiser. They hit the *Castor* ten times, causing extensive damage and casualties. Fortunately, the cruiser's three-inch side armor saved her from any critical damage, because only the *Elbing* mounted any 5.9-inch guns, while the other German cruisers had only 4.1-inch guns. The *Castor* was quick to strike back, and she scored three 6-inch hits on the *Hamburg.* Hawksley's destroyers didn't open fire on the Germans because they were dazzled and confused by the glare of the searchlights and the flashes of the guns. Most of them believed they were being attacked in error by British ships and didn't fire their torpedoes either. But the *Magic* and the *Castor* did, and although none of them hit, one passed directly under the *Elbing* without exploding. The Germans turned away from the torpedoes and were lost to sight in the gloom.

The first serious action of the night took place about twenty minutes later, when Goodenough's 2d Light Cruiser Squadron clashed with Reuter's 4th Scouting Group. In addition to his own four ships, Reuter also had with him the *Rostock, Hamburg,* and *Elbing,* so that Goodenough was badly outnumbered. To make matters worse, his two rearmost ships, the *Birmingham* and *Nottingham,* were too far astern to take part in the action, which was short and savage. Two squadrons approached each other at a sharp angle, and both quickly decided that the other was the enemy. The Germans turned on their searchlights and smothered the two leading British ships with rapid fire. Firing at ranges of one to two thousand yards, they hit the *Southampton* twenty times with 4.1- and 5.9-inch shells during the first five minutes. The *Dublin* was hit thirteen times and sheered out of line under the onslaught. Although heavily outgunned, the two battered light cruisers fought back gamely. The *Southampton* used her searchlights to target the enemy ships, while the *Dublin* aimed at the German searchlights. Between them they managed to score nine hits with their 6-inch guns, damaging four of Reuter's ships, particularly the *Stettin* and *München.*

By this time the two British cruisers were ablaze from the fires started by the many hits they had taken, but the most serious fires were controlled before they could reach the magazines. Once again the cruisers' three-inch side armor saved them from any vital damage. But the gun crews on board these ships were poorly protected, and suffered heavy casualties from flying shrapnel. The *Southampton*'s decks were strewn with so many dead and wounded that most of her guns were no longer firing.

The most important result of the action came at 10:40, when the *Southampton* caught the *Frauenlob* in her searchlights. She was about a thousand yards away. Lieutenant King-Hall immediately launched a torpedo set for high speed, which the German cruiser probably never saw. It struck the midships section of the *Frauenlob* with a tremendous impact that made her heel over. A few minutes later she capsized and sank, taking all but 9 of her crew of 325 with her to the bottom.

Still badly outnumbered, with two of his squadron heavily damaged and most of their guns silent, Goodenough turned away to port and led his ships into the darkness. It had been a highly confused action, with many ships altering course at high speed, the din of exploding shells, the dazzling glare of searchlights, and the muzzle flashes from the guns. Unfortunately, Goodenough's main W/T had been put out of action, and it was not until later that he was able to tell Jellicoe about the contact with German cruisers, using the *Nottingham* and *Birmingham* as linking ships.

Between 10:30 and 11:20 the *Moltke* ran into the van of the British battle fleet no less than three times yet managed to escape without further damage. Hipper, now trying to make his way independently to Horns Reef, had finally managed to board his new flagship but had lost touch with the rest of his battle cruisers. The *Moltke* was sighted by the rearmost ship of Jerram's squadron at 10:30, but the captain of the *Thunderer* did not open fire because he thought it was "inadvisable to show up our battle fleet"; nor did he see fit to inform Jerram or Jellicoe of what he had seen. At about the same time the light cruiser *Boadicea* sighted several large German ships and reported them to the *Thunderer* on two separate occasions. Ironically, the *Boadicea*'s squadron had been temporarily attached to Jellicoe's fleet to act as signal-repeating ships between the battle squadrons, but once again the *Thunderer*'s captain failed to make sure this vital information was passed on to the commander in chief.

The *Moltke* turned away briefly before heading east again. She saw Jerram's battleships on two more occasions, but turned away each time before she was identified. Finally Hipper told Captain von Karpf to steer due south, which he did for about an hour, and the *Moltke* was able to pass undetected in front of Jerram's squadron and head safely for the Horns Reef. Jellicoe received no word of any of these sightings of large German vessels, which would have told him that Scheer's fleet was much nearer than he thought.

Scheer had seen and heard the destroyer and light cruiser actions for himself and received reports from some of the ships engaged. He realized that he must be headed across Jellicoe's wake, because he knew that the British destroyer flotillas were stationed five miles astern of the battle fleet. Although he had signaled his fleet to turn to southeast by east at 9:14, it took him until 10:30 to get his battleships steering on this new heading in night-cruising order—single line ahead. He repeated the signal "Durchhalten" each time a British destroyer attack deflected his ships from their main course. He also radioed for an early morning Zeppelin reconnaissance of the Horns Reef area—a message not received at the Zeppelin base but intercepted and deciphered by Room 40. It pointed unmistakably to the Germans' route back to base, but this crucial information never reached Jellicoe.

Like Scheer, Jellicoe had also seen the flashes and heard the sounds of distant gunfire. They were all coming from his north, and he concluded that it was only his destroyers skirmishing with enemy light forces that were threatening the rear of the battle fleet. Room 40 had intercepted Scheer's instructions to Commodore Michelsen, and the Admiralty had informed Jellicoe in a signal timed at 9:55 that "three destroyer flotillas have been ordered to attack you during the night." This fitted in with Jellicoe's appreciation of what was happening astern. He had received no wireless reports from his ships to suggest otherwise.

In the hardest fought action of the night, a dozen British destroyers took on the vanguard of the enemy battle fleet. For almost an hour these puny ships, none of them over sixteen hundred tons, fought a one-sided battle with Scheer's 1st Squadron of nineteen-thousand-ton *Nassau*-class and twenty-two-thousand-ton *Helgoland*-class battleships. They briefly diverted the Germans from their course toward the Horns Reef, but at terrible cost to themselves.

Captain Wintour of the *Tipperary* was leading the twelve ships of the 4th Destroyer Flotilla on the westernmost flank of the British rearguard when, shortly before 11:30, he sighted several dim shapes on his starboard quarter which he took to be three enemy light cruisers. When he flashed them the challenge signal, the only reply was a blaze of searchlights followed by a devastating barrage of shells as the cruisers *Elbing*, *Rostock*, and *Hamburg*, and the battleships *Westfalen* and *Nassau*, all opened fire on his ship at point-blank range. Most of the shooting was done by the *Westfalen,* which fired 150 5.9-inch shells from seven hundred yards in four minutes. The luckless flotilla leader was quickly turned into a shattered hulk. She was dead in the water without steam and ablaze from stem to stern. Above and below decks there was terrible carnage. All but 12 of her crew of 197 had been killed, including Captain Wintour.

The destroyers next astern swerved to avoid the wreck of the *Tipperary,* and the *Spitfire, Sparrowhawk,* and *Broke* turned toward the enemy and fired torpedoes at the light cruisers that were screening the battleships. According to the captain of the *Broke,* Commander Allen, "Much to our joy one was seen to get the second enemy ship . . . and she seemed to stop firing, heel over and all her lights went out."

It is not certain whether any of the torpedoes actually hit the *Elbing,* but it didn't matter. Captain Madlung turned away in a desperate attempt to avoid the torpedo tracks and tried to take his ships to safety through gaps in the line of battleships. Two of them made it, but the forty-four-hundred-ton *Elbing* was rammed by the nineteen-thousand-ton *Posen.* The battleship's prow sliced deep into the stern section of the light cruiser, and as the *Posen's* momentum forced the two ships apart, the *Elbing's* engine rooms were flooded and the cruiser developed a heavy list to port. She was taken in tow by the torpedo boat S35 but had to be scuttled several hours later, after her surviving crew members were taken off.

By this time the *Spitfire* had used up all her torpedoes, and her captain, Lt.-Cdr. Trelawney, went to see if he could offer any assistance to the *Tipperary.* But before he could reach his stricken flotilla leader he was sighted by the *Nassau,* which turned and rammed him at full speed. One of the destroyer's officers later described the collision: "The two ships met bow to bow in a fearful crash that rolled the *Spitfire* over to starboard as no sea had ever made her roll. The German battleship also opened fire with her 12-inch [*sic*] guns, whose blast cleared everything before it."

Fortunately the German guns couldn't be depressed enough to blow the tiny destroyer out of the water, but as the same eyewitness recorded, "Our foremast came tumbling down, and the foremost funnel was blown back like the hinged funnel of a river steamboat. The enemy surged down our port side clearing everything before her; but none of her shells hit us. When the *Nassau* disappeared, we were still afloat, but about 60 feet from our port side had been torn away, and the enemy had left 20 feet of her upper deck inside our messdeck."

Commander Allen of the *Broke* was now senior officer, and he decided to collect the rest of the flotilla and try to resume station on the battle fleet. But before he could do so he was spotted by the *Westfalen* and *Rostock* shortly after midnight. The battleship hit her minuscule opponent nine times with her secondary 5.9-inch battery, causing heavy damage and killing or wounding half the destroyer's crew. Then the *Broke*'s helm was jammed by a shell from the *Rostock*, and she collided with the *Sparrowhawk*, disabling her. The *Broke*'s bows were shattered by the collision and her speed was reduced to seven knots, but she was able to limp safely back to port.

Most of the ships following her managed to avoid the two crippled members of their flotilla, but the *Contest* didn't see them in the gloom until it was too late, and she collided with the hapless *Sparrowhawk*, slicing off her stern and badly damaging her own stem in the process. In spite of two collisions with her own ships and several hits from German shells, the *Sparrowhawk* stayed afloat for several hours, although completely disabled. She was taken in tow by the *Marksman*, but she finally had to be scuttled when the tow line parted. Most of her crew were taken off by the *Marksman*. Amazingly there were only six casualties on board the battered *Sparrowhawk*.

Commander Hutchinson of the *Achates*, who had assumed command of the remnants of the 4th Flotilla after the *Broke* was crippled, struck back at the Germans by leading a courageous torpedo attack with the six destroyers that were still fit for action. Just before midnight a torpedo fired by the *Ambuscade* or the *Contest* struck one of their tormentors, the *Rostock*. The German cruiser took on a thousand tons of seawater, which salted her boilers, and she was listing heavily and down by the head. Without electrical power or steam she had to be taken in tow by the S54. Several hours later the *Dublin* sighted her and threatened the crippled ship with destruction, but before the *Dublin* could positively identify her as an enemy ship, the S54 rescued the *Rostock*'s crew and scuttled her.

Hutchinson's gallant attackers paid a heavy price. Under fire from the battleships *Westfalen*, *Rheinland*, *Posen*, *Oldenburg*, and *Helgoland*, the *Fortune* and *Ardent* were both sunk and the *Porpoise* was badly damaged. The huge German battleships were firing at close range—fifteen hundred to two thousand yards—using an array of 12-, 11-, and 5.9-inch guns against their frail opponents. The British destroyers fought back as best they could with their puny 4-inch guns. They aimed at their opponents' towering upperworks, causing extensive minor damage and many casualties, including the captain of the *Oldenburg*. But the German heavy guns wreaked terrible havoc among the crews of the *Ardent* and *Fortune*. As many as 148 of them perished, many of them drowning or succumbing to their wounds or exposure during the night. Only 3 survivors from the two ships were picked up later by British ships.

Finally, Commander Hutchinson broke off the lopsided conflict and led what remained of his battered flotilla out of range. There were only four of them left; the other eight had been sunk or disabled. It was amazing that any of the little ships of the 4th Destroyer Flotilla came through intact after their heroic combat with enemy battleships. It was equally surprising that not one of them reported any of this to Jellicoe. The captains of the surviving destroyers must have realized that the German battle fleet was cutting across Jellicoe's wake, yet they told him nothing of what they had seen. The failure to report was excusable in view of their circumstances after the battle, with several ships badly damaged and some without W/T. Other things must have been uppermost in their minds: the damage to repair, the many dead and dying on board, and the wounded men to care for. Even those who were not injured were near to collapse from fatigue and the stress of continuous action. Their main concern was survival.

The destroyer captains were not the only ones who failed to inform their C-in-C about the presence of dreadnoughts to his rear. Betweeen 9:30 and 11:30 several other ships sighted enemy battleships and battle cruisers but did not report them to Jellicoe. The destroyers' omission may have been understandable, but these other ships were not even in action, and for them there was no excuse. There would be equally serious lapses in communication by the Admiralty's Operations Department.

It is an astonishing fact that from the onset of darkness at 9:30, Jellicoe heard nothing from his fleet for the next two hours concerning the position of Scheer's battle fleet. It was not as if no signals were being sent back and forth during the night. The official record shows that no less than eighty-six signals were sent by British ships between 9:30 and 11:30— many of them trivial, none mentioning large German ships. The last word Jellicoe had received about the position of the enemy battle fleet was Beatty's signal at 9:38, giving its bearing as north by west of him. Because Beatty's squadron was fifteen miles to the southwest of the main fleet, this signal placed Scheer well to Jellicoe's west.

The first definite news of Scheer's position since that time was reported, not surprisingly, by Goodenough. He sent two signals, timed at 11:30 and 11:38. The *Southampton's* main W/T was still out of action, and Goodenough relayed the signals via the *Birmingham* and *Nottingham.* The *Birmingham's* report was sent first: "Urgent. Priority. Battlecruisers, unknown number, probably hostile, in sight, NE. course S. My position Lat. 56° 26'N., Long. 5° 42'E."

This model scouting report was exactly what Jellicoe needed, but regrettably the message did not get through to the flagship. It would have informed Jellicoe beyond any doubt that Scheer was heading across the rear of the British fleet for the Horns Reef. Unfortunately, only the second and less important message was received on board the *Iron Duke*. This was the signal from the *Nottingham* about Goodenough's earlier clash with the enemy cruisers, which gave their bearing as west-southwest. Although the signal didn't mention any battleships, it was a fair assumption that the cruisers that had attacked Goodenough were part of Scheer's advanced screen. Unfortunately, the *Nottingham*'s signal only served to confirm Jellicoe's opinion that Scheer was somewhere to his west, and that the Grand Fleet was still between the Germans and their base.

At 11:30 the Admiralty sent Jellicoe a W/T message based on several Room 40 intercepts: "German battle fleet ordered home at 2114. Battlecruisers in rear. Course SSE3/4E. Speed 16 knots." Most of this information fitted in with what Jellicoe knew already, except for the course. If Scheer had really been steaming south-southeast for the past two hours or more, the German fleet would now be to Jellicoe's rear—due north of him. But Goodenough's last signal had placed it to the southwest. Jellicoe, having developed a deep distrust of the reliability of Admiralty reports ever since they had put Scheer's fleet in the Jade several hours after it had left harbor, decided to rely on the report of his man on the spot—Goodenough—and reject the enemy course given by the Admiralty, which sadly was quite accurate this time. Jellicoe decided to keep to his present course and try to get some rest during the few hours left before daybreak.

The Admiralty had information in its possession at the time which would have removed all doubt about where the Germans were heading: Scheer's request for an early morning reconnaissance of the Horns Reef area by Zeppelins. It was absolutely convincing evidence of Scheer's intentions, which Jellicoe could not have rejected—if it had been sent to him.

The usual procedure in the Admiralty for dealing with Room 40 intercepts was that these were sent to the chief of staff, Admiral Oliver, or in his absence to his deputy, Capt. Thomas Jackson, or in Jackson's absence to one of the duty captains. It is not absolutely clear what happened to the crucial signal after it was deciphered and sent down by Room 40, or who later saw or discussed it. Oliver was taking a well-earned rest because he had been on duty since the start of the battle. Apparently Jackson was also temporarily away from the Operations Department, and the duty officer was Capt. Allan Everett, a man who had little experience in interpreting the significance of German operational signals. It seems hard to credit that Everett would not at least have mentioned the signal to Jackson on his return to the office, but because of Jackson's arrogance and well-known contempt for the work of Room 40, discussion may have stopped there. The only thing that is certain is that the signal was put on file, where it stayed until until after the battle was over. It was never passed on to Jellicoe.

This was not the only instance of the Admiralty's failure to make proper use of Room 40's precious intelligence reports. Between 11:30 and 1:48 they intercepted several other invaluable pieces of information—particularly that Scheer had ordered all his torpedo boat flotillas to assemble at the Horns Reef at 4:00 A.M. Other intercepts gave updates on Scheer's position and course. All of this vital information made it plain where Scheer was going, yet incredibly none of it was passed on to the commander in chief by the Operations Department. The tragic result of this lamentable performance—criminal neglect is not too strong a term—was that Jellicoe was left completely in the dark, when he might have turned north to intercept Scheer at daybreak and inscribed another Glorious First of June in the annals of the Royal Navy.

The Admiralty were not the only culprits. At 11:40 the *Malaya* sighted the destroyers of the 4th DF engaged with "some enemy ships steering the same way as ours. Leading ship had two masts and a conspicuous crane—apparently 'Westfalen' class." The ships were in fact the *Westfalen* and the rest of Scheer's leading battle squadron. The *Malaya*'s gunnery officer trained his turrets on the *Westfalen* and asked his captain for permission to open fire. Captain Boyle refused and told him that the *Barham* must have seen the enemy ships as well, and that he must wait until Evan-Thomas gave the order to fire. But neither the *Barham* nor the *Valiant* had seen the German battleships, nor had the *Marlborough*'s division, which had dropped back to join Evan-Thomas at the rear of the fleet. All they had seen were destroyers attacking unidentified ships, and they did not investigate further. Incomprehensibly, Boyle made no report of his sighting of several *Westfalen*-class ships, and so the head of the German battle fleet was allowed to proceed on its way, unmolested by Evan-Thomas's three powerful *Queen Elizabeth*–class superdreadnoughts and four of Burney's battleships. This deplorable lapse in communication kept Jellicoe in complete ignorance of the fact that Scheer's fleet was now cutting across his wake, a mere three miles astern of his line of battleships.

This was not the only wasted opportunity to strike a blow at Scheer's big ships. Around midnight, the *Seydlitz* was spotted by British battleships on three separate occasions, but they did nothing to hinder her progress. Because she was badly down by the head due to the thousands of tons of water that had entered her hull through shell-holes, the *Seydlitz* had been unable to keep up with Scheer, who ordered Captain von Egidy to make his own way to the Horns Reef at his best speed. The

Marlborough was the first to sight the *Seydlitz*, but because she was not positively identified as an enemy ship, Burney did nothing. Then the *Revenge* saw the *Seydlitz* and challenged her to identify herself. The Germans gave the garbled reply they had learned from the *Princess Royal*, which was accepted. Finally, the *Agincourt* saw her, but her captain "did not challenge her so as not to give our division away."

The *Seydlitz* was also sighted by the light cruisers *Boadicea* and *Fearless*, but they didn't attack her either, because it was "too late to fire a torpedo when she could be identified." Thus five British warships allowed a crippled battle cruiser to slip safely through gaps in the tail end of the fleet, when any one of them could easily have sunk her with a few well-directed salvos or a couple of torpedoes. The *Seydlitz*'s escape was even more remarkable than that of her sister ship. The *Moltke* had at least been steaming at twenty-four knots, with all her guns in action, but she too would have been destroyed if the British had taken advantage of their brief opportunities.

By 12:30 the head of the German battle fleet had passed to the east of the Grand Fleet. The gallant destroyer actions had only served as a momentary check to Scheer's relentless drive toward Horns Reef. There were few British ships left to challenge him—three scattered groups of destroyers from the 9th, 12th, and 13th Flotillas and an old armored cruiser—and they were on his flank, not directly in his path.

Only one large British ship took any part in the night fighting, and it was involved in the saddest episode of the whole battle. After Arbuthnot's disastrous charge, the *Black Prince* had lost contact with the other surviving member of the ill-fated 1st Cruiser Squadron, the *Duke of Edinburgh*. During the night she had been wandering around like a lost sheep, trying to find her flock in the dark. Tragically, she stumbled across the wrong flock. Her captain had already opened fire on the German ships, and succeeded in scoring two hits on the *Rheinland*, but he allowed his ship to get too close to the enemy battleships.

Around 1:00 A.M. the *Thüringen* caught sight of the *Black Prince* about a thousand yards away. The Germans, much quicker than the British to take advantage of the brief opportunities offered to them during the night, turned on the *Thüringen*'s powerful searchlights and opened fire with her 12-inch battery at point-blank range. The *Black Prince* tried to get away, but it took only a few salvos to turn the fourteen-thousand-ton armored cruiser into a raging inferno. Less than a minute later there were two massive explosions as her magazines blew up. After the smoke cleared there was no sign of the ship or her 857 crew members. It was the fifth such calamity to befall a British ship that day, but in this case the *Black Prince* was such a mass of flames that no amount of magazine protection could have saved her crew from their dreadful fate.

The most effective destroyer action of the night took place between 1:45 and 2:10 A.M. Captain Stirling of the *Faulknor* led an attack against the rear of the German line with two divisions of the 12th Flotilla. One division was beaten back by heavy and accurate enemy gunfire, but the *Faulknor*'s six ships got to within two thousand yards of the German line and fired seventeen torpedoes, mainly at Mauve's predreadnoughts. The Germans avoided most of them by turning away almost at right angles, but one torpedo fired by the *Onslaught* struck home with devastating effect: "A dull red ball appeared midships in the *Pommern* which spread fore and aft and flared up the masts in red tongues of flame. Then the ends of the ship came up, as though her back was broken, before the mist shut her from our view."

The torpedo had apparently ignited stored ammunition and charges, and the flames spread rapidly to the magazines. The fourteen-thousand-ton ship disintegrated, and her entire crew of 844 perished in yet another appalling holocaust.

Stirling sent three urgent W/T signals to Jellicoe between 1:56 and 2:13 to report the enemy fleet's course, giving its position as ten miles astern of the battle fleet, but none of these signals were logged by the *Iron Duke*. It is not known if the failure of this crucial information to get through was due to the *Faulknor*'s damaged aerial, or whether her wireless transmissions were jammed by the Germans, who were very proficient at this. Thus all but one of Scheer's battleships passed safely astern of the Grand Fleet. If Stirling's reports had made it through, Jellicoe could have turned north and arrived off Horns Reef in plenty of time to intercept Scheer's fleet at daybreak. If he had, he would almost certainly have sunk several German ships, particularly the rest of Mauve's five-minute ships and the crippled *Seydlitz* and *Derfflinger*.

The final encounters of the night took place from 2:30 onward, as the first glimmer of daylight began to appear. But these were ineffectual brushes with the torpedo boats and predreadnoughts bringing up the rear of the High Seas Fleet. Captain Farie in the light cruiser *Champion*, accompanied by four destroyers of the 12th and 13th Flotillas, sighted the dim shapes of Mauve's last four ships about four thousand yards to his southeast. He decided not to press home an attack and did not report the sighting to Jellicoe. This was the last contact with any German big ships. One more chance to locate Scheer's battle fleet had been wasted.

An hour later the *Champion* and her destroyers sighted several German torpedo boats. It was now daylight, and again Farie decided not to attack. But the *Moresby* and *Odurate* did, torpedoing the V4. The German boats were loaded down with more than a thousand survivors from the *Lützow*, in no position to continue the action, and they made off at high speed. Fortunately there was time for the other boats to take off the *Lützow*'s men before the V4 sank.

By the time the sun had risen on the first of June, Scheer had succeeded in brushing aside the last of the British destroyers and now had a clear path ahead of him with no enemy battleships in sight. Shortly after 3:00 A.M. he was able to make out the Horns Reef lightship through the morning mist. With skill and determination, he had thrust his way through the enemy light forces at the acceptable price of one old battleship, four light cruisers, and a torpedo boat sunk, and several more cruisers and torpedo boats badly damaged.

Nonetheless, he was in no position to contemplate renewing action with the Grand Fleet, no matter what he was to write later on the subject. He had practically no torpedo boats left to screen his battle fleet. Most of his sixty-one torpedo boats had been sunk, damaged, or scattered. Captain Schuur had lost contact with the fleet and taken twenty of Scheer's best boats through the Skaggerak to seek refuge in the Baltic. Scheer had only three light cruisers still fit for action, and his battle cruisers were a spent force. As he reported to the kaiser in summing up his situation on the morning of 1 June, "There was, therefore, no certain prospect of defeating the enemy; so I abandoned further operations and ordered a return to port."

This was a disingenuous explanation of his decision to end the battle. There was no prospect whatever of defeating Jellicoe, and Scheer knew it. He had retreated in disarray twice when faced with the might of the Grand Fleet, and after he had come through the night actions relatively unscathed, he must have felt tremendously relieved that he had escaped annihilation, a feeling probably shared by his officers.

Although it had suffered some grievous losses, Jellicoe's fleet was still far too powerful an adversary for the High Seas Fleet. Its officers and men were ready, willing, and able to meet the Germans again, confident that with a whole day ahead of them a crushing victory was within their grasp. Sadly for them, Scheer was barely an hour's steaming from the safe channels inside the Amrum Bank, while Jellicoe was thirty miles to the northwest. Beatty was even farther away—more than forty miles to the west. Although they didn't as yet realize it, neither of them had much hope of intercepting any of Scheer's fleet and bringing them to action.

The Empty Sea

For the burial, the Admiral, the Flag Captain, and all available officers and men were on the quarterdeck. There were two parties of bearers, and planks port and starboard, on which the bodies were placed in turn under the Union Flag, to be slid off into the sea. . . . The band played hymns and the Dead March during the half hour the ceremony lasted.

—Capt. Ernle Chatfield

At daybreak on 1 June there was no sign of the enemy fleet, which Jellicoe had expected to find somewhere to his west. All that his ships could see in any direction was the empty, mist-shrouded sea. Visibility was limited, but he still hoped to catch the Germans and renew the fleet action before Scheer could reach safety. Jellicoe's concern for the moment was to gather his light forces, which had become somewhat scattered during the night, then resume the search for Scheer. His crews were confident and ready to continue the battle. Expectations ran high. One of the *Iron Duke's* midshipmen wrote of "the promise of a better day. We had plenty of ammunition left and felt that, given the chance, we would make short work of what remained of the enemy. The guns had been loaded and we were ready to start again."

Scheer's request for an early morning reconnaissance never got through to the Zeppelin base, but Captain Strasser had sent up six airships on his own initiative with orders to locate the British fleet. Because of the overcast conditions, the only one to have any success was the L11, but this was enough. As she flew over the fleet she was sighted by a dozen British ships. Several opened fire on her, and she was driven off, but the damage had been done. Her commander wirelessed his base to give the position and course of the British fleet, and Strasser wasted no time in passing this on to the Admiralstab.

Between 3:15 and 3:45 A.M. at least nine British ships reported the presence of Zeppelins overhead, and Jellicoe knew that Scheer must be aware of the whereabouts of the Grand Fleet. He realized sadly that his chances of bringing the Germans to action were now vanishingly small, and that the battle was as good as over. He decided to search the battlefield for enemy stragglers. He was intent on mopping up any crippled ships—especially the *Lützow,* unaware that she had already been scuttled. But all his ships found were oil slicks, floating debris and life jackets, dead fish and many dead bodies—some in British, others in German uniforms. They managed to pick up a few survivors, but some of them had been in the frigid water so long that they later succumbed to their wounds or exposure.

Then at 3:29 A.M. the Admiralty sent Jellicoe a dramatic telegram: "Urgent. At 2:30 German Main Fleet in Lat. 55° 33'N. Long. 6° 50'E., course SE. by S., 16 knots."

This meant that by the time the message was decoded and in Jellicoe's hands at 4:10, Scheer must have passed by Horns Reef and was now probably less than forty miles from the entrance to the minefields. As the dejected British admiral concluded, "This signal made it evident that by no possibility could I catch the enemy before he reached port, even if I disregarded the danger of following him through the minefields."

It was absolutely out of the question to follow Scheer. The Germans knew where the safe channels were because they had swept them. Jellicoe didn't.

The telegram only confirmed what Jellicoe had suspected after the Zeppelin sightings: the inescapable fact that the battle was over. As one officer wrote, there "came the gradual realization, the mounting disappointment, that we should not see the High Seas Fleet that day; there was to be no completion of yesterday's work." Scheer had eluded them, and the opportunity that Jellicoe had waited for and planned for so long had slipped through his fingers.

There was little he could do now but arrange his fleet in day-cruising order and continue the search for stragglers. For some reason Jellicoe did not pass the disheartening news on to Beatty immediately, perhaps believing that Beatty had picked up the Admiralty signal himself.

Beatty, who was still miles to the southwest of the battle squadrons, had not been involved in the night actions at all and knew even less than Jellicoe did about the enemy's movements during the hours of darkness. He had not intercepted the Admiralty signal and was still optimistic about finding the Germans. He sent a wireless to Jellicoe at 4:04 A.M.: "When last seen Enemy was to the W., steering S.W., and proceeding slowly. Zeppelin has passed astern of me steering west. Submit I may sweep S.W. to locate Enemy." There was no immediate response to this proposal.

Beatty, ever optimistic, signaled his battle cruisers at 4:30: "Damage yesterday was heavy on both sides, we hope today to cut off and annihilate the whole German Fleet. Every man must do his utmost. Lutzow is sinking and another German Battlecruiser expected to have sunk." It is hard to understand on what basis Beatty made this stirring Nelsonian signal, because he had no idea where the German fleet was. His last contact with the enemy had been seven hours earlier.

Ten minutes later Jellicoe responded to Beatty's earlier signal, giving him the crushing news: "Enemy has returned to harbour. Try to locate Lutzow." Beatty was forced to swallow this bitter pill and abandon his search for the enemy fleet. According to Lieutenant Chalmers, he entered the Lion's chart house and, "tired and depressed, he sat down on the settee and settling himself in a corner he closed his eyes. Unable to hide his disappointment at the result of the battle, he repeated in a weary voice, 'There is something wrong with our ships . . . and something wrong with our system.'" Finally, at 7:16 A.M., an equally disappointed Jellicoe gave up the fruitless search for stragglers and ordered the fleet to turn northward. He signaled the Admiralty that he was returning to port. By 11:00 A.M. the Grand Fleet had cleared the battle area. Most ships were heading directly for Scapa or Rosyth, with a few that required immediate repairs making for Immingham or Cromarty.

Thus the Battle of Jutland fizzled out, sixteen hours after it had been touched off accidentally by the N.J. Fjord. It was perhaps inevitable that it ended in anticlimax, after opportunities of such great promise had not been fully grasped by either side. The battle had started too late in the day for either admiral to achieve what he had hoped, and both had been severely hampered by poor visibility. Jellicoe had not succeeded in smashing the High Seas Fleet, and Scheer had not been able to weaken the Grand Fleet to any significant extent and achieve a Kräfteausgleich (equalization of forces or strength).

So many errors were made at Jutland, so many chances missed. But it must be remembered that this was the first fleet action in history to involve the powerful, complex, and untried dreadnoughts. Neither commander knew how the new ships would perform under real battle conditions. Communications had not kept pace with advances in weaponry; archaic methods using flags and semaphore had not yet been replaced by reliable long-range, shipborne wireless sets. The tremendous difficulties of controlling and maneuvering large formations of ships moving at high speeds in poor visibility had not been sufficiently appreciated, and peacetime exercises were scant preparation for the real thing. Additionally, technological progress had far outstripped the development of tactical thought. The single line of battle was firmly entrenched, and crossing the enemy's T was still the zenith of naval tactics.

Now that the battle was over, Jellicoe had time to check on the condition of his damaged ships, and he learned that of the battleships, only the *Marlborough, Warspite, Malaya,* and perhaps the *Barham* would require docking immediately on arrival in harbor. None of Beatty's battle cruisers required immediate docking. Jellicoe knew about the explosion of the *Pommern* and had seen the *Invincible* blow up for himself, but it wasn't until around noon that he learned the *Queen Mary* and *Indefatigable* had met a similar awful fate. This could hardly have raised his spirits.

The firing may have ended but the danger hadn't. The British ships were three hundred miles from Rosyth and four hundred from Scapa, facing the prospect of a long, dreary, and perilous voyage home through mine- and submarine-infested waters. But the expected attacks by U-boats and torpedo boats didn't materialize. Because of a signaling error by the Admiralstab, the U-boats were not ordered to stay out for another twenty-four hours after the battle. Also, there were too few undamaged torpedo boats, ready and loaded with fuel and torpedoes, to send them out against the British. Some submarine sightings—both real and imaginary—were reported to Jellicoe, but the attacks actually made by the few U-boats still patrolling off the Scottish coast were unsuccessful. None of Beatty's or Jellicoe's ships were picked off.

Throughout the day funeral services were carried out for the men killed in action. On board the *Lion,* Captain Chatfield had to conduct the service because the chaplain was among those killed. "For the burial, the Admiral, Flag Captain, and all available officers and men were on the quarterdeck," Chatfield wrote. "There were two parties of bearers, and planks, port and starboard, on which the bodies were placed in turn under the Union Flag, to be slid off on to the sea. There were 95 mutilated forms in their hammocks, shotted at the feet, including those of six officers. The band played hymns and the Dead March during the half hour the ceremony lasted."

There were many other ships where such somber and moving rituals were carried out that day.

It took until the morning of 2 June to cover the distance to Rosyth and Scapa. Beatty's ships sighted May Island off the mouth of the Firth of Forth at 6:00 A.M., but Jellicoe's battle squadrons did not arrive at

Scapa Flow until shortly before noon. Some of the heavily damaged smaller ships—*Chester, Acasta, Onslow, Broke*—had to struggle against a rising sea in near-gale conditions and didn't reach port until two days later.

Jellicoe was deeply disappointed that he had not been able to achieve a decisive victory, but he was able to report to the Admiralty at 9:45 that evening that the Grand Fleet was ready to sail at four hours' notice with twenty-five dreadnought battleships, six battle cruisers, twenty-six cruisers, and more than sixty destroyers ready for action. This was a far greater force than Scheer would be able to muster the same evening. He had only a dozen battleships, two battle cruisers, three cruisers, and a mere handful of torpedo boats still fit for battle.

By contrast, the German fleet had a short, relatively safe passage home. Once they had passed Horns Reef, they were less than a hundred miles from the mouth of the Jade. The voyage was not uneventful, though. There were frequent submarine scares, as many ships sighted torpedo tracks and periscopes and opened fire. Their targets were all phantoms. The only British submarines in the vicinity were the three that Jellicoe had stationed near the Vyl lightship on 30 May, and their orders were stay submerged until 2 June—Jellicoe had not expected the battle to end as early as it did. As the High Seas Fleet steamed overhead the three submarines were resting harmlessly on the sea bottom to save their batteries. They were unaware that a battle had taken place until they returned to port a few days later.

Then at 5:20 A.M., Admiral Schmidt's flagship *Ostfriesland* struck a mine—one of those laid by the *Abdiel* on 4 May—and sheered out of line, causing momentary panic and more wild firing at imaginary submarines. The battle fleet's progress was disrupted until mine fragments were identified on the deck of the *Ostfriesland*. Scheer ordered a general cease-fire and told his ships to resume their course. The wounded battleship was not seriously damaged and was able to stay on route for Wilhelmshaven at reduced speed.

When the German ships reached Amrum Bank, the *Seydlitz* ran aground. The crippled battle cruiser had taken on so much water that her forward draft had increased to forty-six feet, compared with her normal thirty feet. The *König* was so deep in the water that her captain had to wait three hours for a rising tide before he could make it across the sandbank. The *Markgraf* was also leaking badly and fell astern of the fleet, waiting for a pumping steamer to help reduce her draft. The *Seydlitz* floated off with the tide, but after scraping the bottom several times she finally became unmanageable and had to be taken in tow. But the tow line parted under the strain and the *Seydlitz* ran firmly aground. It took two days work by tugboats and pumping steamers to get her off. She had now taken on more than five thousand tons of water and was near to sinking. Her draft had increased so much that her whole foredeck was submerged and her propellers were out of the water. She looked like a half-submerged whale. In the end she had to be towed into harbor stern first to prevent any more water coming in through the holes in her bow, but she made it safely on 6 June. If she had been forced to brave several hundred miles of rough water, as the British ships did, she would certainly not have made it.

In spite of these misadventures, the majority of Scheer's ships were anchored in the Jade roadstead by 6:30 A.M. on 1 June, twenty-four hours before Beatty reached the Firth of Forth. But the battered High Seas Fleet would not be ready to sail again for several months.

There was widespread disappointment among the crews of Jellicoe's and Beatty's ships that they had not been able to achieve more on 31 May, and frustration that the Germans had escaped them the following day. It was a different story aboard the *Friedrich der Grosse,* where there were mixed feelings of relief and jubilation. Scheer invited his officers to the bridge to celebrate with a bottle of champagne. The crews of the other ships lined the decks to cheer the flagship as they steamed by. They had met the mighty fleet of the Royal Navy in deadly combat, and they had sunk ships that bore such proud names as *Invincible* and *Indefatigable.* They also had survived to tell the tale, with fewer losses to themselves.

Scheer wired a preliminary report of the battle to the Admiralstab, and the press office of the Reichsmarineamt wasted no time in issuing a communiqué listing the British losses—somewhat inaccurately—as one battleship, the *Warspite;* three battle cruisers; two armored cruisers; two light cruisers; and thirteen destroyers. The sinking of the *Pommern* and *Wiesbaden* were admitted, but the other German losses were suppressed. The exaggeration of enemy losses and concealment of their own would backfire on the Germans later when the full details of the battle were revealed to the world.

The German press seized on the official communiqué, which left them in no doubt about the battle's outcome. In an orgy of self-congratulation they trumpeted that it had been a smashing German victory. The headlines of the *Frankfurter Zeitung* on 2 June blared, "Great sea battle in the North Sea. Many British battleships destroyed and damaged. *Pommern, Wiesbaden* sunk; *Frauenlob* and some torpedoboats missing." Other papers followed suit. The *Berliner Tageblatt* wrote of the "great sea victory over the British." Nothing was said about the sinking of the *Lützow,* the *Seyd-*

litz aground on a sandbank, the scarcely recognizable wreck of the *Derfflinger,* or the damage to Behncke's battleships. Later on, when reality set in, there was a cartoon showing some civilians at the dockyard gates, asking the guard, "Can we see our victorious ships?" The resounding answer: "No!"

The Germans took full advantage of their twenty-four-hour head start while the British fleet was still at sea to achieve a propaganda triumph. Reuters in Amsterdam picked up the official communiqué from Berlin and wired it to their London bureau on the morning of 2 June. The news came as an absolute bombshell to the British public, who were not even aware that a sea battle had taken place.

The same afternoon Arthur Balfour, the First Lord of the Admiralty, hurriedly wrote the first official communiqué issued by the British. The statement was based on Jellicoe's brief preliminary report, made when he entered harbor. If Balfour's response was meant to offset the impact of the German communiqué and quell the spreading rumors of a British defeat, it was an utter failure. The communiqué was released to the public on the morning of 3 June. It was a factual, unvarnished account of known British losses, without any mention of specific German losses or damage, which were described using such vague terms as "severe," "serious," "must have been large," and "probably sunk." The communiqué gave few details of how the battle had been fought, and there was no attempt to present the outcome in a palatable fashion, let alone in a favorable light. It read more like an apology for a serious defeat.

As an exercise in public relations, the Admiralty's first communiqué was an absolute disaster. It would have been far better if Balfour had written nothing at all on 2 June until he had read the lengthy official dispatches sent to him by Jellicoe and Beatty late that evening.

The British people were shocked and deeply depressed by the news coming from both London and Berlin. They had expected that when the two fleets eventually clashed, the German ships would naturally end up on the bottom of the sea and their own ships would be celebrating another Trafalgar. Most British newspapers on 3 June were inclined to share the opinion of the *Manchester Guardian* that the battle "was a considerable strategic success for Germany." The *Daily News* concluded that "defeat in the Jutland engagement must be admitted." Only a few papers took a more cautious and balanced view of the outcome, until more information became available. But from the brevity of Balfour's statement, the majority of the press suspected a cover-up. There must be something discreditable to hide, they reasoned. The inevitable press search for scapegoats began. What had gone wrong, and who was to blame?

The men of the Royal Navy were perplexed and upset by what they read and heard. After a shaky start they had given the Germans a hammering, forcing them to turn away twice and in the end flee ignominiously for the shelter of their harbors. They may not have have sunk as many of the enemy as they had hoped, but they thought they had done pretty well on the whole. But because of the boastful German claims and the feeble Admiralty response, the cheers that had greeted Beatty's ships as they steamed under the Forth Bridge had turned into boos and jeers by the time they docked at Rosyth.

Meanwhile, the victory celebrations in Germany continued unabated. Flags were flown for several days, and children were given a school holiday. The Germans always referred to the battle as the *Skagerrakschlacht,* and to Scheer as the victor of the Skagerrak. This name was chosen to give the impression that the High Seas Fleet had lived up to its title and had not been afraid to steam far from its harbors to meet the British. Strictly speaking, most of the fighting had not taken place within a hundred miles of the Skagerrak, however, and Jellicoe gave it the more appropriate name, the Battle of Jutland Bank. This was later abbreviated to the Battle of Jutland, as it is generally known everywhere but in Germany.

The kaiser took the train to Wilhelmshaven to welcome his victorious fleet and shower congratulations and decorations on his sailors. In an outburst of emotion, he embraced Scheer and the captain of the *Friedrich der Grosse* and kissed them on both cheeks. Then he visited the other battleships in turn, embracing their captains. He lavished Iron Crosses and lesser medals on officers and men and decorated Scheer and Hipper with the Ordre pour le Mérite, Germany's equivalent of the Victoria Cross. Hipper was knighted by the king of Bavaria and became *Ritter von Hipper,* but Scheer declined a knighthood and was never the "von Scheer" of many accounts of the battle.

Barely able to restrain his feelings, Wilhem II addressed the crews lined up in ranks on the dock alongside the flagship. His voice quivering with emotion, he told them, "The journey I have made today means very much to me. I would like to thank you all. Whilst our army has been fighting our enemies, bringing home many victories, our fleet had to wait until they eventually came. A brave leader led our fleet and commanded the courageous sailors. The superior English armada eventually appeared and our fleet was ready for battle." He concluded extravagantly, "What happened? The English were beaten. You have started a new chapter in world history. I stand before you as your Highest Commander to thank you with all my heart."

• • •

In Britain, Prime Minister Asquith was incensed by Balfour's communiqué and appalled at its effect on press and public. Jellicoe was also irritated and wired the Admiralty to complain about its tendency to magnify British losses and minimize the enemy's, and that it gave a false impression of how the action had taken place. He asked that future communications to the press be amended to agree with his reports of the battle. Beatty wrote a letter of protest deploring the effect of the communiqué on the nation's morale, noting that he hoped the Admiralty would "be able to make a more favourable pronouncement soon."

A second communiqué was prepared late on 3 June. Balfour, although unrepentant about his first communiqué, had obviously learned his lesson, and he asked Churchill to draft this one. It was published in the newspapers the following day and went some way toward repairing the damage caused by the first communiqué. Based on the admirals' dispatches from Scapa and Rosyth, it was a fair and balanced account of the action, written in Churchill's incomparable prose. It helped restore public confidence in the navy, so badly shaken in the past few days. The gloom that had settled over Britain was beginning to lift.

King George V, who had twelve years' naval service behind him, read the copy of Jellicoe's dispatch sent to him by the Admiralty and helped put the situation in perspective by means of a telegram to the commander in chief:

> I am deeply touched by the message which you have sent me on behalf of the Grand Fleet. It reaches me on the morrow of a great battle which has once more displayed the splendid gallantry of the Officers and men under your command. I mourn the loss of brave men, many of them personal friends of my own, who have fallen in their country's cause. Yet even more do I regret that the German High Seas Fleet, in spite of its heavy losses, was enabled by the misty weather to evade the full consequences of an encounter they have always professed to desire, but for which when the opportunity arrived they showed no inclination.

He went on to note that he regretted that the enemy's speedy retirement had robbed the fleet of the opportunity of gaining a decisive victory, and he expressed his complete confidence in the navy and in Jellicoe's command.

The Admiralty issued a third statement to the press on the evening of 4 June. This one appeared in the newspapers the next day and claimed a British victory, stating that Jellicoe, "having driven the enemy into port, returned to the main scene and scoured the sea in search of disabled vessels." By the fifth public opinion had undergone a complete turnaround. The national mood was reflected in a poem titled "The Paradox," by J. Saxon Mills, published in the *Pall Mall Gazette*:

The Germans cry aloud, "We've won!"
But surely 'tis a curious view
That those are conquerors who run
And those the vanquished who pursue.

The *Globe* newspaper roared, "Will the shouting, flag-wagging [German] people get any more of the copper, rubber, and cotton their Government sorely needs? Not by a pound. Will meat and butter be cheaper in Berlin? Not by a pfennig. There is one test, and only one, of victory. Who held the field of battle at the end of the fight?"

The situation was further improved when the Germans admitted on 6 July that the *Lützow, Rostock,* and *Elbing* had been sunk and the *Frauenlob* had not returned. The evidence that their earlier reports had been less than truthful raised scepticism about the German claim of victory. The same day, the full text of Jellicoe's dispatch was published in the *London Gazette,* erasing the last traces of doubt, in Britain at any rate, that Jutland had been a British victory. The naval correspondent of the *Daily Express* wrote scathingly, "If there is anyone left in this country who still has doubts about the character of the British victory . . . he is a fit subject for a mental specialist."

As far as neutral opinion was concerned, this can be encapsulated in the now famous epigram of a New York journalist: "The German Fleet has assaulted its jailor, but it is still in jail."

THE AFTERMATH

PART 3

Who Really Won?

CHAPTER 15

Our Fleet losses were, despite the luck that smiled on us, severe,
and on June 1, 1916 it was clear to every knowledgeable person
that this battle must, and would be, the only one.
Authoritative quarters said so openly!

—Capt. Lothar Persius

Ever since the first official communiqués were issued, the question that has been endlessly debated is, Who really won the battle of Jutland? Or did nobody win?

Simply in terms of the numbers of ships sunk, the Germans clearly came out on top, as the following list shows:

TYPE OF SHIP SUNK	BRITISH	GERMAN
Battleships		*Pommern*
Battle cruisers	*Indefatigable*	*Lützow*
	Invincible	
	Queen Mary	
Armored cruisers	*Black Prince*	
	Defence	
	Warrior	
Light cruisers		*Elbing*
		Frauenlob
		Rostock
		Wiesbaden
Destroyers and Torpedo boats	*Ardent*	S35
	Fortune	V4
	Nestor	V27
	Nomad	V29
	Shark	V48
	Sparrowhawk	
	Tipperary	
	Turbulent	

Thus the Germans sank fourteen British warships of a total displacement of 113,000 tons, while losing only eleven of their own, for a total of 61,000 tons.

The military value of these ships varied considerably. Of the big ships, the *Queen Mary* and *Lützow* were both modern, first-line units. The German battle cruiser had only been completed in March 1916 and was probably the most valuable unit lost by either side. The *Invincible* and *Indefatigable* were older ships, with smaller-caliber guns than Beatty's "splendid cats." They were still first-line ships, but less valuable fighting units. The three British armored cruisers and the predreadnought battleship *Pommern* were all over ten years old and had become obsolescent with the arrival of the dreadnoughts. Aside from the tragic deaths of so many trained officers and men, they were no great loss to either Jellicoe or Scheer.

Of the smaller ships that sank, the *Frauenlob* was obsolescent, but the other German light cruisers were all brand new. Their loss meant a serious depletion of Scheer's already inadequate cruiser strength. The destroyers and torpedo boats were all modern vessels, launched within five years of Jutland. Both admirals would feel the loss of these valuable little ships.

The casualty lists showed a similar margin in favor of the Germans. The British suffered 6,945 casualties, of whom the vast majority—6,094—were either killed in action or died from their wounds. The German casualty figures were, at 3,058, less than half this number, though again, the great majority were those killed—2,551.

Jutland was a brutal and bloody conflict, with casualty lists unparalleled for a naval action between ironclads. The ten thousand men killed, wounded, or taken prisoner at Jutland meant that one in ten of those engaged in the fighting became a casualty. Senior officers were not spared. Among the dead and wounded were three admirals and eighteen ships' captains. By contrast, generals and colonels were rarely numbered among the fallen in a land battle of the Great War.

There was no doubt that the smaller German fleet had taken on a much superior enemy force and inflicted more severe losses than it had suffered itself. The Germans made great play with the numbers of men and ships lost by each side, the sole basis of their claim to victory. There could be no other. But battles are not decided simply on the basis of such balance sheets.

A closer examination of the results reveals that German claims of superiority were much less meaningful than these bald figures suggest. Although fewer German ships actually sank, the High Seas Fleet had received a more severe mauling than the Grand Fleet, as shown by the following dates when repairs to battleships and battle cruisers were completed:

GERMAN SHIPS	DATE REPAIRS COMPLETED	BRITISH SHIPS	DATE REPAIRS COMPLETED
Rheinland	10 June	Malaya	24 June
Helgoland	16 June	Tiger	1 July
Westfalen	17 June	Barham	4 July
Nassau	10 July	Princess Royal	10 July
Grosser Kurfürst	16 July	Warspite	20 July
Markgraf	20 July	Lion	20 July
König	21 July	Marlborough	2 August
Ostfriesland	26 July		
Von der Tann	2 August		
Derfflinger	15 October		
Moltke	30 July		
Seydlitz	16 September		

The damage reports for the *Kaiser, Oldenburg, Schlesien,* and *Schleswig-Holstein* have not survived, so their repair times are not included. This means that the damaged German ships must have spent at least 644 days in dry dock, compared with the 297 days taken to repair the British ships. In total, sixteen major units of the German battle fleet spent more than twice as much time in dockyard hands as their seven British counterparts, before they were returned to active service.

The larger part of Scheer's battle fleet was not ready for action until mid-August, and even then it would be without the services of its two most powerful battle cruisers, the *Seydlitz* and *Derfflinger.* Jellicoe on the other hand was ready to sail the day after the battle with most of his pre-Jutland force intact.

The casualty totals also give a misleading impression of German superiority. The British figures, appalling though they were, arose in large measure from defects in matériel rather than as a direct result of enemy gunfire. The five large ships that blew up accounted for 5,080 out of the total of 6,945 British casualties. The devastating magazine explosions of the three battle cruisers were caused by an unfortunate combination of thin armor, inadequate flash protection, and unsafe cordite. In each case the ship blew up after it had received only a few hits. Other British battle cruisers survived much greater numbers of hits from heavy shells, and it was probably only good fortune that spared more of them from coming to a similar dreadful end.

Likewise, the two armored cruisers that blew up suffered from inadequate protection. They were old, weakly armored ships and had not been designed to stand up to modern weapons, especially at close range. The *Pommern* shared their fate for similar reasons.

If the numbers of men killed in these awful explosions are separated out, the remaining casualties suffered by each side are comparable: 1,865 British and 2,214 German. If these six ships had not blown up, and reasonable estimates are made of their probable casualties resulting from gunfire alone, the two totals would have been practically the same.

The Germans tried to bolster their claim to victory by declaring that the gunnery of their battle fleet had been more accurate than that of the Grand Fleet. This claim was based on the gross figures published after the war in Germany's official history of the battle, *Der Krieg in der Nordsee.* These showed that German battleships and battle cruisers had fired a total of 3,597 heavy shells (11 inch and greater) and obtained 120 hits for a success rate of 3.33 percent. The corresponding totals for the British capital ships were 4,598 and 100, giving a success rate of only 2.17 percent. This led the official history to conclude that "the superiority of German gunnery is clearly evident."

These figures were not only inaccurate but misleading. The Germans omitted heavy-shell hits on some of their ships entirely and attributed other hits incorrectly to minor shells, which deflated the British success rate. They also failed to point out that a large fraction of their own heavy-shell hits had been made at close range on ships unable to make any effective reply, thus inflating their apparent margin of superiority.

The most reliable and accurate account of the gunnery of both sides is Campbell's book, *The Fighting at Jutland,* which was based on an amazingly exhaustive, detailed, and meticulous analysis of all available ships' records, British and German, and is remarkable for the author's even-handed evaluation of the gunnery of the two battle fleets. A close scrutiny of Campbell's figures leads to a quite different conclusion from that presented in the German official history.

Campbell's figures show that British capital ships fired 4,480 rounds of heavy shell and obtained 123 hits, for a success rate of 2.75 percent, while the Germans used 3,597 shells and scored 122 hits, for a rate of 3.39 percent. Although the difference is smaller than that given in *Der Krieg zur See,* it still appears to support the German claim of superior gunnery. But what the German figures did not take into account was the fact that 49 of their 122 hits were made at close range on practically defenseless armored cruisers, or on the *Warspite* as she circled helplessly toward the German fleet. These hits were hardly indicative of superior gunnery, whereas all but 19 of the British hits were made at typical battle ranges of eight to eighteen thousand yards.

In assessing the gunnery of the two battle fleets it would be fairer to compare the hits made by capital ships on enemy capital ships. Even including the 15 hits on the *Warspite,* the British outhit the Germans by 104 to 85. It is impossible to calculate precise rates of success with any certainty, because it is not known how many heavy shells were fired from close range at lesser targets such as the *Wiesbaden* and *Black Prince.* But if conservative estimates are made, and these shells are deducted from total number fired, it becomes clear that the gunnery of the two fleets was similar.

The figures for the numbers of heavy shells fired at all targets, and hits obtained at all ranges, are known, and these lead to an overall success rate of about 3 percent. This may seem to indicate that very poor accuracy was achieved by the gunners on both sides, compared with the results of peacetime gunnery practice. In the Royal Navy, upwards of 50 percent hits had been obtained firing at a range of eight thousand yards at targets moving at eight knots on a fixed parallel course.

But an estimate made before the war indicated that at best only about 5 percent hits could be expected at modern battle ranges of ten to twenty thousand yards with ships maneuvering at high speed. This figure was based on the difficulty of obtaining accurate values of such quantities as the range, speed, and deflection of the enemy ship, all of which could change significantly during the time of flight of the shells. There was also the problem the gunnery officers faced in making aiming corrections by spotting the fall of their own salvos amid a cluster of different shell splashes. In view of the mist and smoke that blanketed the battlefield for most of the day action, and the lack of visibility during the night fighting, a success rate of 3 percent was probably as good as could have been expected. In other words, it took on average something on the order of thirty rounds of shell to obtain each direct hit.

Examining the performance of the various squadrons highlights some striking departures from this average. The best shooting on the British side was that of Hood's 3d BCS, which achieved 4.3 percent hits, or only twenty-three shells per hit. For the Germans the best gunnery performance was obtained by Hipper's 1st Scouting Group, which scored 3.9 percent, or twenty-six shells per hit. These were both excellent results, and not far off the estimated optimum. Most other squadrons achieved acceptable results and were fairly close to the overall average of 3 percent. But there was one glaring exception: the gunnery of the 1st and 2d

Battle Cruiser Squadrons. Beatty's six battle cruisers were involved in several phases of the action and fired 1,469 rounds of heavy shell, scoring a mere twenty-one hits between them. Their success rate of 1.4 percent meant that it had taken 70 rounds for every hit they obtained. This was at least twice as bad a performance as the average achieved at Jutland and can only be described as poor shooting.

In most cases it is impossible to assess the gunnery performance of individual ships because it was not always possible to assign hits with certainty. These sometimes had to be credited to pairs of ships. As far as the data go, the best gunnery ships in the British fleet were the *Invincible* and *Inflexible,* the *Barham* and *Valiant,* and the *Iron Duke.* For the Germans, the most effective were the *Lützow, Derfflinger,* and *Moltke.* The *Von der Tann's* gunnery was also excellent until most of her main battery was put out of action. The least effective gunnery ships by far on either side were undoubtedly the *Tiger* and *New Zealand.* These two fired 723 rounds altogether yet managed a paltry total of six hits between them; in other words, more than 99 out of every 100 shells fired by these two ships landed harmlessly in the sea. This was an atrocious performance—in Fisher's terminology, "villainously bad."

It was somewhat surprising that the German gunnery was as good as the British, because it was generally accepted that the Royal Navy's system of fire control was technically more advanced. The British ships were also equipped with fire-control tables and range clocks—forerunners of the modern computer—which gave the director a plot of the course, deflection, and range of the enemy ship. The rate of change of these quantities was determined mechanically using spotting corrections, but the accuracy of the calculated range plots was dependent on the initial estimates of the enemy range. This is where the Germans had the advantage, because their stereoscopic range finders were superior to the coincidence type used by the British.

The Germans also used the "ladder" system for finding the target. They fired three salvos in rapid succession, using ranges that differed by several hundred yards, without waiting for the first salvo to land. Spotting corrections, up or down, allowed them to get on target more quickly than the British, who used the "bracket" system. The British fired one salvo, then waited for the shells to land before shifting the range up or down, depending on whether the salvo was over or short of the target. The range was then altered by four hundred yards at a time until the target was straddled. Although the British were slower to get on target, they were better at holding onto it once they had straddled. German accuracy tended to fall off, especially under fire, because the operators of the stereoscopic range finders required intense concentration as well as perfect eyesight. The continual noise, vibration, and strain caused by their own guns as well as enemy shells unavoidably led to decreasing accuracy.

One factor that has not received sufficient emphasis in comparing British and German gunnery is the importance of practice. For years the Germans made regular visits to the sheltered waters of the Baltic, where they were able to carry out battle practice using realistic ranges and different target speeds, under a variety of weather and sea conditions. Their gun crews were drilled repeatedly until loading, training, and firing the guns became almost automatic.

Prewar battle practice in the Royal Navy had been limited by the parsimony of an Admiralty concerned over the expense of shells and proved less than satisfactory. Once the war began, the Grand Fleet was largely restricted to gunnery practice inside Scapa Flow for security reasons. There was an excellent gunnery range at Scapa, and Jellicoe did everything he could to raise the level of gunnery of his battleships, but it was not possible to carry out fleet gunnery exercises under realistic battle conditions. In spite of this the training at Scapa under Jellicoe's watchful eye paid off, and the gunners of the battleships generally performed very well at Jutland, notably the flagship *Iron Duke*.

Unfortunately, there were no adequate facilities in the Firth of Forth, and the battle cruisers had not carried out a full-caliber practice shoot since 1914. Jellicoe was well aware that the gunnery of the battle cruisers was not up to standard. He rated their performance at Jutland as very poor, "as I had believed would be the case from my experience of their results at Gunnery Practice throughout the war." He had urged Beatty more than once to do something about this. But Beatty was reluctant to send even one or two of his ships at a time to Scapa for gunnery practice, because he didn't want to weaken his forces at Rosyth. But in wartime there was no excuse for not doing more than he did to improve the gunnery of his battle cruisers. There was not much point in keeping all his forces poised at Rosyth ready to strike at Hipper if his ships seldom hit the target when they did catch up with him, as the poor results at the Dogger Bank had already demonstrated.

The consequences of the lack of gunnery practice by the 1st and 2d Battle Cruiser Squadrons are starkly illustrated by a comparison of their performance at Jutland with those of Evan-Thomas's 5th Battle Squadron and Hood's 3d Battle Cruiser Squadron. Each of these squadrons had recently spent time at Scapa Flow in gunnery practice, and it showed. Hood's squadron was only in action briefly at Jutland and fired a quarter of the number of shells that Beatty's ships had expended, yet these three ships scored sixteen hits to the twenty-one made by Beatty's six.

Evan-Thomas's four ships also fired fewer shells during the battle—about three quarters of Beatty's total—but outshot the battle cruisers with twenty-nine direct hits.

Since the overall accuracy of the gunners on both sides was about the same, and the British had outhit the Germans by 104 to 85, and with mostly larger-caliber shells, a nagging question remained: Why had they not sunk more capital ships than the enemy? There were two main reasons. First was the remarkable ability of German warships to stand up to heavy punishment—their well-known *Widerstandsfähigkeit*. German naval architects had designed their ships to be nearly unsinkable floating gun platforms. British naval officers were amazed that it had taken twenty-four hits, mostly by 13.5- and 15-inch shells, to smash the *Lützow*, and that the *Seydlitz* and *Derfflinger* had suffered almost as many hits from these huge shells without sinking.

The second and probably more significant reason was the poor quality of British armor-piercing shells. These rarely penetrated German armor plate before exploding, as they were supposed to do. Too often their time-delayed fuses proved to be too sensitive and detonated the shell on impact, wasting its explosive power without doing any vital damage inside the enemy ship. In other cases the brittle nose cone of the shell resulted in it breaking up on contact, especially at oblique angles of impact. The problems could be traced to the incredibly slipshod system of testing or "proving" British shells. It was shown after the war that statistically, anywhere from 30 to 70 percent of projectiles that had passed the "proof" stage were probably duds.

If the British ships had been supplied with better shells there is no doubt they would have done far more damage than they did. The leading gunnery expert, Frederic Dreyer, estimated that with effective AP shells, six if not more German battleships and battle cruisers would have been sunk at Jutland. This may be an exaggeration, but certainly the *Seydlitz* and *Derfflinger* would have been sent to the bottom along with the *Lützow*.

Another obvious factor which led to greater British losses was the tragic vulnerability of their battle cruisers. But it must be stated that the British battleships stood up to punishment at least as well as their German counterparts. The *Barham, Malaya,* and *Warspite* were all hit heavily yet managed to stay in line. It was only the *Warspite's* erratic rudder which eventually caused her to withdraw from the battle. The *Grosser Kurfürst, König,* and *Markgraf* suffered fewer hits yet spent more time in dry dock before they were fit for action again.

All of these numbers and comparisons lead to balance-sheet types of argument. But victories are not decided on this basis. The comparisons may be interesting and instructive, but they don't really address the question of who won the battle.

Jutland was obviously not decisive in the sense that Trafalgar had been, or that the more recent one-sided battles between fleets of ironclads at the Yalu, Manila Bay, Santiago, and Tsushima had been. However, in these latter cases the defeated admirals had either chosen to stand and fight it out or couldn't avoid it. These battles also involved opposing fleets and admirals of vastly different capabilities, and thus they are not at all comparable with the situation on 31 May 1916.

At Jutland, Hipper scored an initial success against Beatty and believed he was facing an inferior enemy force. But after Beatty had skillfully led the Germans into a trap, and Scheer realized he was up against the whole of the Grand Fleet, he did his best to avoid further action. Jellicoe crossed his T twice and forced him to retreat precipitously, the second time with his battle fleet in disarray. Although Scheer cleverly managed to extricate himself from both of these dangerous predicaments, he did not seek battle again but chose to make a determined dash for safety under the cover of darkness.

After his initial misjudgments had got him into trouble, there is no doubt that Scheer's maneuvers were ably executed, but these were not the actions of a victor. Jellicoe, on the other hand, had driven his opponent from the battlefield to lick his wounds in port, relieved that he had escaped annihilation. Numerical comparisons can not alter this. Jellicoe had won a partial victory, the typical outcome of most sea battles. Smashing victories such as Trafalgar and Tsushima are the exception, not the rule. Jutland was a flawed victory, but a victory nonetheless.

Regrettably, from the British point of view, serious defects had robbed them of their chances of a clear-cut victory: inferior shells, vulnerable ships, poor communications, and lack of initiative on the part of subordinate commanders. Perhaps the most serious flaw was the stifling influence of the overlong and inflexible Grand Fleet Battle Orders, which attempted to anticipate every conceivable situation and lay down precisely what action to take. This killed off personal initiative and all too often led to fatal inaction while subordinates "waited for orders." The ghost of Admiral Tryon had not been completely laid to rest by 1916.

Jutland was certainly no Trafalgar, although it might have been, with more flexible and aggressive tactics. But tactics should always be governed by strategy. Jellicoe's responsibilities were on a different scale from those of the other admirals. He knew he was the only man on either side who could lose the war in an afternoon, and he was determined not to let this happen. As Cyril Falls put it, Jellicoe fought in such a way as to make a British defeat impossible, rather than to make a British victory certain. It may be that Jellicoe knew his commanders' strengths and weaknesses too well and believed that allowing them more freedom of action might lead to chaos and serious losses beyond his control. His main concern was that squadrons operating independently might run into the whole of the enemy battle fleet and be overwhelmed before he could go to their support.

It is wrong to conclude that Jutland was an indecisive battle, although it is frequently characterized as such. The word indecisive implies that it did not change anything. In fact, it resulted in a complete shift in German naval strategy. After the battle, Scheer was convinced that his attempts to achieve an equalization of strength with the Royal Navy, to be followed by a fight to the finish, were hopeless. He realized that on the surface of the sea, the British fleet was simply unconquerable. Other tactics were needed. As the well-known German naval correspondent Capt. Lothar Persius was to write later, "Our Fleet losses were, despite the luck that smiled on us, severe, and on 1 June 1916 it was clear to every knowledgeable person that this battle must, and would be, the only one. Authoritative quarters said so openly!"

These "authoritative quarters" meant Scheer and, above all, the kaiser. On 4 July, Scheer wrote a confidential report to the kaiser in which he said that the fleet would be ready for further action by mid-August, and that he hoped to make further damaging forays against the enemy. "Nevertheless," he continued, "there can be no doubt that even the most successful outcome of a Fleet action in this war will not *force* England to make peace." He concluded that "a victorious end to the war within a reasonable time can only be achieved through the defeat of British economic life—that is, by using the U-boats against British trade."

Scheer urged the kaiser not to adopt half measures, no matter what effect an intensified U-boat campaign might have on neutral countries. The kaiser agreed to step up submarine attacks on shipping, but it was not until February 1917 that the Germans resumed the all-out, unrestricted U-boat warfare that they had abandoned in 1915 in the wake of the torpedoing of the *Lusitania*.

In the future, the German battle fleet would play only a passive supporting role. As Scheer ruefully remarked, "The High Seas Fleet was reduced to the hilt of the weapon whose sharp blade was the U-boat."

The Germans really had no choice but to change their strategy. Jutland had clearly demonstrated both Britain's naval supremacy and its absolute control of sea communications. Its own troops and supplies would continue to pass unhindered, while the tight blockade of Germany would be maintained everywhere but in the Baltic. The blockade was slowly and relentlessly strangling the German war machine by starving it of essential raw materials and capital. The loss of seaborne trade was very damaging to the German economy. There were also increasing shortages of foodstuffs, which eventually led to food riots in the streets of German cities and sapped the people's morale and will to continue the war. The Germans could not hope to lift the blockade, but they could strike back hard with their U-boats in a kind of counterblockade.

It is probably because of this dramatic change in the Germans' conduct of the war at sea, and its far-reaching effects on the entire war, that the distinguished historian John Keegan saw fit to include Jutland in his list of the ten most decisive sea battles of all time. Author Correlli Barnett, a persistent critic of British naval and military leaders, went further and called it one of the critical battles of history.

The Admirals

CHAPTER 16

*Jellicoe has been most unfairly blamed for
not doing miracles at Jutland.*

*Scheer may have been a great tactician. But if so,
he had a very bad off-day at Jutland.*

—Professor Arthur Marder

During the prolonged action that took place off Jutland Bank on
31 May and 1 June 1916, the men on both sides—seamen, stokers,
and gunners—played their parts very well, showing tremendous
courage and stamina. Their officers acquitted themselves reasonably well, with a few glaring exceptions, and certainly showed great
courage. But what of the four principal actors in this great drama?
How well did Jellicoe, Beatty, Scheer, and Hipper perform in the
roles that fate had assigned them?

Of the four, Sir John Jellicoe's performance is the most difficult
to evaluate. He was a consummate professional and superb tech-
nician, with a thorough knowledge of ships, guns, torpedoes, and
mines, which he had acquired throughout his long career in the
navy. But his main strength lay in his organizational abilities; he
was very good at spotting imperfections and remedying them. In
his two years at Scapa, he had brought the Grand Fleet to a high
level of training in both maneuvers and gunnery. He had forged
and sharpened this mighty sword to the best of his ability, but did
he have the tactical skill to wield this formidable but cumbersome
weapon effectively?

Like the other British admirals and senior commanders, he had
received no formal instruction in strategy or tactics. There was
none available in the Royal Navy. It had no staff college, not even
a proper naval staff, in spite of Churchill's efforts when he became
First Lord of the Admiralty in 1911.

Jellicoe's greatest shortcoming was his inflexibility. He had drawn up the Grand Fleet Battle Orders—seventy closely spaced pages of orders and many more pages of detailed instructions—a document written from a decidedly defensive angle, especially when it came to the use of underwater weapons. The GFBOs lacked emphasis on offensive tactics, except for the big-gun, line-of-battle approach. Apparently, Jellicoe did not ask himself why Scheer should fall in with his ideas of how to fight a fleet action. There was very little in the GFBOs about what to do if the enemy refused to conform to his tactics, or how to force battle on an unwilling foe.

Jellicoe, like all the senior fleet admirals except Sturdee and Beatty, was wedded to the single-line-of-battle idea. As a former gunnery officer, he relied almost entirely on the big gun as his offensive weapon, and engagement of the enemy at long range on parallel lines. He was also a firm believer in centralized control of the fleet by its commander in chief. The GFBOs left little room for squadron commanders to seize the initiative if favorable opportunities arose. Jellicoe did not hold with divided tactics in a fleet action, using flexible, coordinated attacks with all kinds of weapons. He considered such tactics too risky, because they could lead to disorganized action where anything might happen, despite his overall superiority in firepower. His cautious, methodical mind wanted to leave nothing to chance. He knew his commanders, their strengths and weaknesses. These men varied from intelligent and highly trained professionals to some rather incompetent officers, who were probably unfit for command and definitely unfit to exercise independent action.

Jellicoe was a perfectionist, and as such had an inability to delegate and often became immersed in detail best left to his subordinates. He was also temperamentally unable or unwilling to relax his grip on the fleet and had already expressed concern about Beatty getting into difficulties if he was given too free a rein. He was afraid that Beatty's great courage and offensive spirit might lead him to take on more than he could handle without the close support of the battle fleet.

He was a captive of the system—it was not one he had devised himself. His ideas were generally accepted by all the senior officers except Sturdee and, to some extent, Beatty. He had no firsthand experience of modern battle to guide him, or to lead him to reject prevailing tactical ideas. Once he had carefully worked out a set of tactics, he was singleminded in his determination to follow them through to the end. With the line of battle idea so firmly entrenched, he in effect put all his tactical eggs in one basket.

Jellicoe had a cool analytical mind, and was soberly realistic about his officers' capabilities and matériel. He was under no illusions about the results of Fisher's modernization of the navy and had developed a "profound and detailed awareness of the Grand Fleet's strength; but also of its hidden and serious weaknesses." Nor did he have any illusions about the strengths of the German fleet—particularly the quality of its ship construction and the caliber of its gunnery.

In Correlli Barnett's opinion, "In view of the performance of Beatty's and his own cruiser squadrons—except for Goodenough—limp, bewildered and ineffective—and of Evan-Thomas's and Beatty's misunderstandings over simple and obvious manoeuvres, it is difficult to believe that Jellicoe was wrong to centralise his battle fleet and its tactics. The truth was that the Grand Fleet was only capable of rigid text-book manoeuvres; and Jellicoe was cool-headed enough to realise it." A harsh judgment perhaps, but a difficult one to dismiss in view of the inadequacies revealed at Jutland.

With the aid of Room 40's priceless intercepts, Jellicoe brought the two main arms of the Grand Fleet—the Battle Fleet and the Battle Cruiser Fleet—into position to fall on and crush an unsuspecting High Seas Fleet. His deployment to port, which allowed him to cross Scheer's T, was brilliant. It involved a complex maneuver, which the fleet had not practiced before. The massive deployment of the twenty-four battleships was carried out in masterly fashion—a tribute to Jellicoe's training. With little information from his scouting forces, Jellicoe had been forced to make a quick decision, which turned out to be the best one he could possibly have made, in spite of the critics.

Even the Germans agreed later that it was the best choice; they would have been delighted if the British had deployed to starboard and had to face German broadsides while they were still deploying. Churchill's widely publicized preference for deployment on a center column was based on a study of charts after the war, using information not available to Jellicoe at the time. This deployment might well have led to chaos and almost as bad a tactical position as deployment to starboard, even if it could have been carried out smoothly, which was doubtful.

Jellicoe was also criticized for failing to follow Scheer after he made his first *Kehrtwendung*. He had told the Lords of the Admiralty exactly what he would do in such an eventuality, and they had fully approved. It is therefore unfair to criticize him for not pursuing Scheer into the haze. He had stated what he would do if the enemy turned away, and he did it. He was strongly influenced by his anxiety over the risks of being led over mines sown by a retreating enemy, or being drawn into a massed counterattack by torpedo boats. He had a great respect for the destructive potential of the new underwater weapons, especially torpedoes—too much as it turned out, but he wasn't to know this. This respect was shared by all the admirals at the time of Jutland, and it tended to dominate their tactical thinking.

Perhaps Jellicoe should have sent his scouting forces after Scheer, to regain contact and report back, but he didn't. He was content to turn south and stay between Scheer and his bases. His caution paid off because of Scheer's miscalculation, which gave Jellicoe another chance, and he was in good position to cross the German T for a second time.

Jellicoe was severely criticized for turning away his whole fleet after Scheer's second *Kehrtwendung,* the one covered by a torpedo boat attack. The critics pointed out that only part of the fleet was being threatened—mainly the rear, and the van not at all. After the war his critics made much of the fact that the German torpedo boats only fired a total of thirty-one torpedoes, which proved to be of little danger to the battleships. In their view the attack shouldn't have caused Jellicoe to turn away. It was all very well for the Dewar brothers to write that "the small number of torpedoes that reached the British lines indicates that no very great risk would have been involved in maintaining the course of the fleet." Their judgment was based on dazzling hindsight, using information not available to Jellicoe. For all he knew the Germans could be planning to attack in waves using all of their available torpedo boats. As Marder remarked, "Crystal balls, alas, are not standard issue in the Royal Navy."

A more reasonable criticism is that Jellicoe failed to use his scouting forces to make a determined search for Scheer after his second turn away. There were almost two hours of daylight left, and he had an opportunity to inflict further serious damage on a German battle fleet which was already in disarray. Beatty shares some of the responsibility for failing to take advantage of this window of opportunity—after all, the principal role of the battle cruisers was to locate and hold onto the enemy battle fleet until Jellicoe's battleships could come up.

As far as the night action was concerned, the lack of good searchlights, star shell, and training may have been regrettable, but it was an undeniable fact. In any case, Jellicoe was dead set against night fighting, when his advantage in firepower would count for little. Scheer was just as averse to a night action, if it meant involving the two battle fleets, even though he had better searchlights and his men were well trained in night fighting.

Jellicoe's decision with respect to Scheer's final course remains a puzzle. His reasons are still not clear, even from his own writings. His plan was to stay on a parallel course and keep his fleet between the Germans and their bases, avoiding night action at all costs. He was content to wait until daylight, confident that he would finish them off then. It was perhaps understandable that he dismissed the Horns Reef route as a possibility; Scheer had tried heading east twice and been repulsed—it seemed reasonable that he was not likely to try it a third time, even if it was his shortest route to safety.

Once Jellicoe had decided, he stuck to his choice, again reflecting his inflexibility. But it is not clear why he did not give instructions to his rear guard—not just to the flotilla commanders, but to all ships at the rear—to watch out for and report the presence of enemy big ships in case Scheer decided to try the Horns Reef route after all. Jellicoe can be faulted for his failure to do this, as well as those officers at the rear who didn't communicate what they had seen.

It was also not clear why Jellicoe didn't send some of his destroyers to scout well ahead and to the west of the fleet, if he thought the Germans were going to take one of the southern routes. These scouts would obviously have failed to make any contact during the night, and this result, coupled with the flashes and sounds of heavy gunfire to his rear, might have led Jellicoe to reconsider and reduce the speed of the fleet or even turn it northward. If he had done so, it would have prevented Scheer from slicing through his rear guard so easily.

In summary, however competent or skillful he may have been as a fleet admiral, Jellicoe lacked that spark of genius—that "admixture of madness"—which triumphant admirals like Nelson possessed. He was in effect criticized for not being another Nelson. But there were no Nelsons at Jutland, nor was it likely there could have been in view of this new and totally different style of sea warfare. The admirals were in uncharted waters, and it was unrealistic to expect any of them to display the adventurous spirit and daring initiative that Nelson had shown in his three great victories. They didn't have the same long experience of what to expect of their ships and men, or the same awareness of the risks and time to weigh them carefully before going into action—advantages based on the hard-won knowledge accumulated from a hundred similar sea battles under sail. Nelson had no unknown variables such as mines or torpedoes to worry about.

It is also important to remember that even if Nelson's fleet had been badly defeated at Trafalgar, there was an equally powerful British fleet waiting in home waters to thwart Napoleonic ambitions. But if Jellicoe had suffered a crushing defeat at Jutland, it would have been a catastrophe. He had virtually the whole of British naval strength in his hands.

Jellicoe may have lacked the "Nelson touch," but he did the best he could in difficult circumstances, with the time and the weather both working against his chances of achieving a smashing victory. Nonetheless he managed to cross the enemy T twice and gave the Germans a hammering they would not forget. It is difficult to see what he could have done very differently in order to force battle on a reluctant enemy. Jellicoe was also bedeviled—in a way he could not have predicted—by deficiencies in his matériel: vulnerable ships, defective fuses and shells, and unsafe cordite. He was also badly let down by his officers' poor communications and the incredible intelligence failures at the Admiralty. These shortcomings robbed him of a second chance at a Trafalgar-like victory on the morning of 1 June. He may have missed the first chance through his own caution and absolute determination not to jeopardize British naval supremacy, but the chances that were missed on 1 June were no fault of Jellicoe's.

In Marder's judgment, "Jellicoe has been most unfairly blamed for not doing miracles at Jutland. He was as brave and enterprising as the best of them, and he did the best that was possible."

As Barnett aptly characterized him, Jellicoe was the "Sailor with a Flawed Cutlass."

The problem in appraising Sir David Beatty's performance objectively is to take account of the widely divergent and strongly held views of his abilities and tactics. To some he was a cool-headed and farsighted tactician who had fought and maneuvered brilliantly and handed the German fleet to Jellicoe on a plate; to others he was an impetuous and reckless fighter who made frequent tactical mistakes and failed in his primary role of scouting for the battle fleet and keeping his commander in chief informed. As always, the truth lies somewhere between the two extremes. It is important to try to separate out the rhetoric and judge him dispassionately in terms of results, which in the end is all that really counts.

Beatty and Jellicoe were a study in contrasts, not just in their physical appearance and dress, but in their temperament, strengths, and weaknesses. While Jellicoe was calm, deliberate, and realistic in assessing both his own forces and those of his enemy, Beatty was highly strung, impatient for action, and supremely confident of his superiority over the enemy. He wrote to his wife about the battle cruisers, "Here I have the finest striking force in the world." Even after his experience at the Dogger Bank, when Hipper had held his own against superior numbers and knocked Beatty's flagship out of the battle, his confidence was undiminished. Two months before Jutland, he wrote, "If I meet Hipper and his battlecruisers, I can deal with them."

Beatty has been credited with many qualities: great tactical skill, a cool brain, a phenomenally quick grasp of a situation, and sureness of judgment. Some of Beatty's great qualities are beyond question—his physical courage, fighting spirit, inspiring leadership, and determination to defeat the enemy—but the evidence for the other attributes is less apparent. He certainly had the ability to inspire his officers and men, who universally admired and respected him. His captains had absolute faith in his capabilities and his unquenchable will to win.

In contrast to Jellicoe, he encouraged his subordinates to use their initiative, and he had established an excellent rapport with them and an understanding of how he meant to fight a sea action. He achieved this through frequent meetings and discussion with his sea captains and staff officers. Unfortunately, this rapport did not extend to others less close to him, such as Moore and Evan-Thomas, and this led to less than satisfactory collaboration. No matter what he thought of these two personally, he did not take the time to acquaint them with his style of leadership, with predictable results. In the brief spell of ten days that was available after the 5th Battle Squadron joined his force at Rosyth, Beatty managed to find time for social activities, but not apparently for tactical discussions with Evan-Thomas.

Beatty's judgment, tactical ability, professional depth, and experience are open to question. Unlike Jellicoe, he tended to leave too much to his subordinates, sometimes with unfortunate consequences—the chronically substandard performance by his signaling and gunnery officers, for instance. His lack of respect for the fighting qualities of the German battle cruisers also contrasts with Jellicoe's more sober and realistic appraisal. Detailed information was there in print for Beatty to read, in such well-known publications as *Brassey's Naval Annual* and *Jane's Fighting Ships*. This should have told him that Hipper's ships would prove to be formidable opponents. The continued reference to his own ships as the "splendid cats" reveals a lack of appreciation of the realities, by both Beatty and others. The *Lion*-class battle cruisers have been evaluated by an authoritative reference work: "Thanks to the adroit manipulation of the press they were regarded with affection by the public, but they must surely be ton-for-ton the least satisfactory ships built for the RN in modern times."

Beatty's performance at Jutland betrayed a lack of professional experience coupled with an inability to learn from past mistakes, or an unwillingness to accept that he had made any mistakes—his refusal to admit that the *Lion* had made an inadvertent 360-degree turn is an illustration. His rise through the ranks had been nothing less than meteoric—captain at the unheard-of age of twenty-nine and rear admiral at thirty-nine. His promotion to flag rank had required Fisher's intercession because of Beatty's lack of seagoing experience. Churchill's reasons for appointing him to command the Battle Cruiser Fleet have been described already, but it is an inescapable fact that Beatty had never commanded a major squadron before, let alone a fleet. This lack of experience was bound to show.

During the Run to the South, Beatty made several elementary but critical mistakes, partly through his impatience to get into action. First was his failure to concentrate his forces before attacking the enemy. He had been given the four most powerful battleships the navy possessed, but didn't use them properly to bring overwhelming firepower against Hipper, and he suffered grievously for his error. But Churchill argued that "Beatty's six battlecruisers were in themselves superior in numbers, speed and gunpower to the whole of the German battlecruisers. . . . Why should he wait to become stronger when by every test of paper and every memory of battle he was already strong enough?" This view disregards the memory of the Dogger Bank action, and as Barnett commented acidly, "Beatty's decision rested on the assumption that his ships were at least as good as the Germans. . . . That Beatty and Churchill were so ignorant of even the published facts is sufficient comment on their professional depth."

This may be a jaundiced verdict, but the fact remains that Beatty did not bring his maximum force to bear when he had the opportunity to do so. It is surely axiomatic that if you have the chance to overpower your enemy from the outset, you take it. Beatty's supporters have argued that if he had concentrated his forces, Hipper might well have refused action as soon as he sighted Beatty's ships. But Beatty had no way of knowing whether Hipper was being supported by other units, and in any event Beatty himself concluded that his superior speed made it impossible for Hipper to avoid action.

Beatty's second mistake was to fail to take advantage of his 13.5-inch guns, which outranged Hipper's smaller-caliber weapons by several thousand yards. He could have opened fire long before Hipper was able to reply. But he badly misjudged the initial distance to the enemy—by at least two thousand yards, which even for British range finders seems excessive. He also failed to realize how quickly the range was closing, and at one point allowed it to fall to thirteen thousand yards, where Hipper was able to open up with his secondary armament as well as his big guns. By the time Beatty had realized his error and opened the range, Hipper's accurate broadsides had already bracketed Beatty's ships with a devastating barrage. There was also the usual confusion in the British battle cruisers' fire distribution, which didn't help matters.

Then, when Scheer's battle fleet came in sight, Beatty unnecessarily put Evan-Thomas's ships at great risk by delaying the order to turn north. It would also have been better to order them to turn to port together rather than to starboard in succession, to keep them in closer support of Beatty's battered force.

As the Run to the South ended, it was undeniable that Hipper, with less ships and firepower, had outmaneuvered and outfought Beatty. Even apart from the tragic destruction of the *Indefatigable* and *Queen Mary*, which of course was no fault of his, Beatty was badly beaten in the first phase of Jutland. His tactical errors had contributed greatly to this result, which could have been even worse had it not been for the belated intervention of Evan-Thomas's *Queen Elizabeths*. As Jellicoe was to conclude later, showing remarkable restraint, the outcome "cannot be other than unpalatable."

Beatty certainly redeemed himself with his performance in the next phase, showing both courage and skill. Instead of heading straight toward Jellicoe and safety, which would have been understandable in view of what he and his remaining battle cruisers had just been through, he kept on course parallel to the Danish coast. When he had drawn far enough ahead of the pursuing Germans, he cleverly and courageously cut across their line of their advance, forcing Hipper to turn gradually eastward until he was obliged to fall back on Scheer. Although Beatty was exposing his squadron to the risk of a further hammering, he held on course and with Hood's timely arrival, managed to screen Jellicoe's approach from the unsuspecting Germans until the last possible moment, when it was too late for them to avoid the trap he had laid.

Beatty has been most unfairly blamed for screening the fire of Jellicoe's battleships for fifteen valuable minutes at the beginning of the fleet action, as he cut across the van of the battle fleet. This may have been regrettable, but it was absolutely unavoidable because of Beatty's position at the end of the Run to the North, and his duty to take up his proper station at the head of the fleet. Evan-Thomas was well astern of the battle cruisers and had little choice but to head for the rear of the fleet with his slower ships, but Beatty would have been roundly condemned if he had done the same with his fast scouting force.

Beatty's tactics during this phase have been described as brilliant, as undoubtedly they were, but it remains a mystery why neither Hipper or Scheer realized what Beatty was up to in time to avoid running head on into Jellicoe's battle fleet.

Beatty's overall performance suffered badly from his failure to acknowledge the ineffective gunnery of his battle cruisers, and he can be faulted for not making greater efforts to improve it. He had been given plenty of time to do this since taking over command in 1914. Many excuses have been made for the poor gunnery results obtained at Jutland, not all of them by obvious Beattyites. Marder, for example, lists no less than ten different reasons why the battle cruisers did not achieve greater success during the Run to the South! All but two of these involved factors beyond Beatty's control. Chief among Marder's five major reasons were the poor visibility and interference from funnel and gun smoke. Yet according to Beatty himself, at the start of the action, "the visibility was good, the sun behind us and the wind SE." Also, when the 5th Battle Squadron joined in the action, they were subject to the same visibility conditions yet managed to shoot effectively from a much longer range than Beatty's ships. It is interesting that among Marder's five lesser reasons, the last one to be mentioned was that "the Battle Cruiser Fleet gunnery (except perhaps for the *Queen Mary*) was not up to the battle-fleet standard." Nowhere is a lack of training and gunnery practice emphasized as a crucial factor. Part of the problem was that Beatty believed he could improve the gunnery results simply by increasing the battle cruisers' rate of fire.

Others have pointed out that the *Queen Elizabeth*s had more up-to-date fire-control equipment, particularly the Argo Tower and later versions of the Dreyer Fire Control Table. But a check on the various ships involved in the fighting at Jutland reveals little correlation between the type of equipment installed and the accuracy they achieved. For instance, the *Invincible* and *Inflexible* shot very well in spite of their older-model fire-control eqipment, while the *Lion* and *Princess Royal,* fitted with gyro-stabilized range finders and modern versions of the Dreyer Table, didn't.

The visibility was obviously an important factor in determining the overall success of the gunners at Jutland, but there are frequently inconsistencies in the accounts of eyewitnesses written after the battle, as well as those of writers who were not present. Although the visibility undoubtedly deteriorated as the day wore on, one gets the impression that poor visibility was too often used as an excuse for poor shooting, especially in the first few hours, before the buildup of smoke from guns and funnels had blanketed the battle area. It is clear from photographs of ships taken at distances of ten to sixteen thousand yards that the visibility at the outset was not as bad as it is sometimes made out to be.

Beatty's tactics were not helped by his lamentable signaling performance. Efficient signaling is crucial to an admiral's control over his fleet, yet mistake after mistake was made by his woefully inept staff, particularly the error-prone Ralph Seymour. This led to confusion and bewilderment in the Battle Cruiser Force. Too often important signals were made by flags only and not repeated by searchlight or W/T as Jellicoe had ordered. The difficulty of reading the *Lion*'s halliards was well known and should have been recognized. The reporting of information to Jellicoe also left a lot to be desired, and the inexcusable lapse of security in openly exchanging the British recognition signals was another example of the battle cruisers' signaling woes.

As was the case with the battle cruisers' gunnery, obvious deficiencies were not corrected or any significant improvements made, and Beatty must bear the ultimate responsibility for the lack of attention to such important organizational details. He did add Capt. Rudolph Bentinck to his staff after the mixup at the Dogger Bank, but this did not lead to any detectable improvement in signaling. It is amazing that Beatty retained Seymour as the *Lion's* signals officer. He should have replaced him after the Dogger Bank, but Seymour was still a member of Beatty's staff at the end of the war! Beatty was well-known to be fiercely loyal to his immediate subordinates, but this was surely carrying loyalty too far. As Beatty himself ruefully remarked after the war, Seymour had cost him three victories.

Many reasons have been advanced to rationalize why Beatty's elite force did not achieve greater success than it did, both before Jutland and during the battle itself. Among these were serious lapses by senior officers in other squadrons—Warrender, Goodenough, Moore, and Evan-Thomas; poor visibility due to the weather; unfavorable wind direction and position of the sun; the frailty of the battle cruisers; poor range finders; ineffective spotting rules; lack of facilities for gunnery practice; defective ammunition; and omissions from the navy's signal book. Some of these points are certainly valid, but it is hard to avoid the conclusion that Beatty was either an extremely unfortunate victim of circumstances or a not-very-skilled fleet commander.

He had been at the forefront of the action in the only three significant engagements that took place in the North Sea, and if what he achieved in terms of concrete results is judged dispassionately, the bald fact is that he accomplished very little. He had sunk one armored cruiser and two light cruisers before Jutland, and during the battle itself did not inflict any critical damage on a single enemy vessel.

It is interesting that Sturdee sank more enemy ships in one afternoon at the Falkland Islands than Beatty did in all three of his battles. Yet Sturdee was castigated by Fisher and Richmond for taking so long about it, and for using up so much ammunition. By contrast, Beatty was praised to the skies for his role at Jutland. It is noteworthy that Sturdee's battle cruisers had only the obsolescent Dreyer Mark I fire-control tables fitted in 1914, and their gunners were not under central director control. Their gunnery at the Falklands was unquestionably poor. Yet they still achieved a higher percentage of long-range hits than any of the better equipped ships of the 1st and 2d Battle Cruiser Squadrons did at Jutland.

A widely held view after the battle was that while Beatty's ships had borne the brunt of the fighting, which was certainly true, Jellicoe's battleships had scarcely been involved in the action at all and had done little damage to the German fleet. Because the battle fleet had suffered hardly any damage, the battle cruiser officers were scornful of the battleships' contribution and maintained that the battle fleet had merely "got wet" at Jutland. Sir Hedworth Meux, a retired admiral of the fleet who should have known better, typified this view in a letter to the king's private secretary in which he claimed among other things that "Jellicoe's despatch stating that his battle fleet was engaged for two hours is most disingenious [sic] and has naturally created a false impression in the country. Practically the whole of the fighting was done by our battlecruisers, and our battle fleet only fired a very few rounds—hardly any of them were touched and probably did a similar amount of damage to the enemy!"

The facts were that while Jellicoe's fleet was only in action for scarcely an hour during their two brief encounters with the enemy, his battleships fired more heavy shells than Beatty's battle cruisers did in three and a half hours of more or less nonstop action. They also scored nearly three times as many hits, and inflicted more serious damage on German ships, including Beatty's principal adversaries, the enemy battle cruisers.

In contrast to Jellicoe, who was unreasonably blamed for not being another Nelson, Beatty was applauded for his bold, aggressive action and achieved near Nelson-like stature in the eyes of a credulous public. The adulation was fostered by the popular press, in spite of the absence of any solid evidence. The press had been largely responsible for creating the myth of a dashing and victorious admiral in the first place and were not about to tear down their own idol.

Many influential people, among them Churchill and Richmond, said that if only Beatty had been in command of the Grand Fleet—especially if he had been given time to put his stamp on it—things would have been different. He would have seized the chances that eluded Jellicoe and soundly thrashed the Germans. In view of Beatty's tactical mistakes at the Dogger Bank and Jutland, and his failure to remedy obvious deficiencies in the BCF, it was just as likely that things would have turned out disastrously.

Nonetheless, the charismatic figure of Beatty became the hero of Jutland in the popular mind. Unlike Jellicoe, his image remained untarnished after the battle. After their disappointment at the results, the British needed a hero figure, and the quiet, steady, and unassuming Jellicoe did not fill the bill.

Reinhard Scheer was an experienced officer with a reputation as a brilliant and offensive-minded tactician, which he had acquired during exercises before the war in command of torpedo boat flotillas and battle squadrons. He was one of the most able and quick thinking flag officers in the Kaiserliche Marine and was well known to the British for his vigorous leadership and aggressive spirit. He shared Jellicoe's ability to make rapid decisions but was inclined to do this more by instinct born of experience and training than by analysis.

He was also a flexible C-in-C who encouraged the use of initiative by his ship captains as well as his squadron commanders. There were several striking instances of individual initiative by German officers during the battle—such as Redlich, Schmidt, and Hartog. Scheer's was a young navy, unfettered by the dead weight of tradition and protocol. His officers were less hidebound than the British in their acceptance of new ideas and tactics.

It is interesting to compare the number of signals sent back and forth by the Germans and British on 31 May. In the seven hours of daylight from the first contact until nightfall, the British ships made 732 signals! The *Iron Duke* issued 93 of these, while the *Friedrich der Grosse* sent out only 56. Scheer's officers knew what to do after a simple order or two and didn't need a lot of detailed instructions from their flagship, whereas in the British fleet the centralization and sheer mass of signals made subordinates fatally inclined to "wait for orders" before taking action.

In fairness to Jellicoe, it should be remembered that the German High Seas Fleet was of secondary importance to its nation's cause, compared with that of the British Grand Fleet. This allowed Scheer to make more imaginative and flexible use of his fleet and to take more risks than Jellicoe. The kaiser had given Scheer more leeway than he had allowed his predecessors Ingenohl and Pohl.

When Scheer took over, he didn't alter the basic German strategy of engaging only part of the British fleet at a time. His tactics were to bring a rapid and overwhelming concentration of gunfire to bear on an inferior force, followed by an equally rapid withdrawal under cover of a smoke screen and torpedo boat attack if a superior enemy force showed up. This may partially explain why he fell into Beatty's trap so readily. Scheer was not blessed with the kind of intelligence supplied by Room 40, and had no idea that Jellicoe was even at sea.

But this does not excuse Scheer's failure to understand why Beatty had headed almost due north after sighting the German battle fleet. He could not possibly have been fleeing for safety after the battering his squadron had received from Hipper, because in that case he would have headed northwest toward Rosyth. Therefore he must have had something else in mind. Then when Beatty veered eastward toward the Danish coast, he surely could not be intending to cross Hipper's T, with Scheer's battle squadrons pounding up from astern. This would have been a suicidal move even if it had succeeded, because the inevitable delay would have given Scheer time to cut off the British escape route and catch both Beatty and Evan-Thomas in a pincer movement between his battle fleet and Hipper's 1st Scouting Group.

By this point it should have been obvious that Beatty was up to something, and it could only be that he was trying to screen the Germans' view from what lay ahead in the mists to the north. What else could it have been but Jellicoe's battle fleet? But in his anxiety to capitalize on Hipper's success and demolish Beatty's fleet, Scheer rushed headlong into the trap. It seems evident from the remark "something lurks in that soup" that the Germans half suspected that the British might be out in force.

Nevertheless, Scheer proved to be skillful and resolute at getting out of serious difficulty when his tactics misfired. His first *Gefechtskehrtwendung* was executed brilliantly. Even though it had been practiced by the fleet, it was a tricky maneuver and required excellent seamanship in order to avoid collisions. It was greatly helped by Captain Redlich's initiative when he turned early with the *Westfalen's* division and took over from Mauve's slower predreadnoughts as the guide of the fleet.

Scheer's 180-degree turnabout was a difficult move for an enemy to counter effectively. Jellicoe was at first baffled by the sudden disappearance of the enemy battlefleet into the mist, and even when he realized what must have happened, he could think of no adequate response. He concluded that "nothing but ample time and superior speed can be an answer, and this means that unless the meeting of the fleets takes place early in the day, it is most difficult, if not impossible, to fight the action to a finish."

Scheer's next turnabout was a serious tactical mistake, no matter what reasons he gave later for making this move. No competent admiral would deliberately charge at the center of the enemy line and put himself in the same dangerous predicament he had just escaped barely thirty minutes earlier. Nor would he have put his least protected and most heavily damaged ships in the van if, as he claimed, he intended to surprise and confuse Jellicoe by means of a "second ruthless onslaught" on his battle fleet. Scheer's chief of staff later admitted that if the admiral had made such a move during peacetime exercises he would have promptly been ordered to haul down his flag. Scheer's order to Captain Hartog to carry out the so-called death ride was a sign of desperation, and he quickly changed it when he saw what was happening to his battle cruisers.

Rather than striking "a second heavy blow" at the enemy, Scheer was obliged to make another *Gefechtskehrtwendung* to save his fleet from disaster. This time the maneuver was executed less smoothly, with a touch of panic at the head of the line as it came under an intense barrage from Jellicoe's battle squadrons. Scheer's fleet would have been in worse disarray if it had not been for Admiral Schmidt's initiative in starting the turn early with the *Ostfriesland*'s division. But once more Scheer showed his skill at extricating his fleet from danger, this time with the aid of a smoke screen and a counterattack with his torpedo boats.

All these turns had placed Scheer's weakest division in the van of the battle fleet—Admiral Mauve's 2d Squadron of six old predreadnoughts. Scheer has been criticized for taking these slow and vulnerable ships with him, because their presence restricted the fleet to eighteen knots at best, compared with the Grand Fleet's twenty-one knots. It is said that he took the 2d Squadron to Jutland against his better judgment, after his friend Mauve pleaded not to be left behind, and because he had a soft spot for the squadron he had once commanded himself. It is possible that Scheer took them because he envisaged a sacrificial role for the predreadnoughts in the event they were needed to shield more valuable units from destruction. He didn't hesitate to use them in the final daylight stage of the battle to cover the retreat of Hipper's crippled squadron.

To Scheer's great credit, his breakthrough during the night showed imagination, nerve, and determination. This time he judged the position of the enemy fleet much more accurately than he had done on the previous occasion he had headed eastward. He also deserves much of the credit for his men being so well trained and equipped for night fighting.

As far as 1 June was concerned, Scheer had one thing in mind, in spite of what he wrote later about retaining the initiative as he waited for the battle to be renewed at daylight. The course he had set—and the repeated signal *"Durchhalten!"*—showed that he was intent on making a beeline for the Horns Reef and safety and had no thoughts of renewing the action if he could possibly avoid it. This was a sensible decision in view of the condition of his fleet and the enemy's superiority, and it was sheer hypocrisy for Scheer to claim otherwise.

In summary, Scheer's performance was less than brilliant, even though he proved to be amazingly adroit at extricating his fleet from danger each time he got himself into a potentially disastrous situation. But for an admiral to allow his T to be crossed twice in the same battle was unprecedented. As Marder concluded, "Scheer may have been a great tactician. But if so, he had a very bad off-day at Jutland."

His fleet had fought extremely well against heavy odds, but in the end Scheer had not really won anything, except an escape from annihilation.

Franz von Hipper was an officer of undoubted talent and experience, and had been commander in chief of the fleet's scouting Groups since before the war. He was a thoroughgoing professional who knew the capabilities of his men and ships inside out. He was an unusual type of senior officer for the German navy; he had never taken a course at the staff college and disliked paperwork and theoretical argument. He was a man of action, vigorous and impulsive, with the spirit of a privateer. He was admired in Germany for his daring raids on the English coast, which had badly shaken British complacency and earned him their epithet: "the baby-killer of Scarborough."

The value of his gunnery training and drill had proved itself at the Dogger Bank, when he had fought a skillful rear-guard action against a superior force. Although he lost the *Blücher,* his reputation as a dashing and clever tactician was if anything enhanced by this engagement.

At Jutland he led his battle cruisers with great skill and courage, fighting against heavy odds during most of the battle. Although designed to fight opposing battle cruisers, his fine ships stood up remarkably well to the gunfire of 13.5- and 15-inch battleships, but as Hipper admitted later, "it was nothing but the poor quality of their bursting charges that saved us from disaster."

In the Run to the South, Hipper maneuvered superbly to overcome the disadvantage of his smaller-caliber armament and led an unsuspecting Beatty into a trap. His shooting was excellent from the start, and he inflicted heavy damage on his opponent during this phase of the battle. His gunners later showed their ability to take quick advantage of their opportunities when they sank Hood's flagship.

Hipper also did an excellent job of keeping Scheer informed throughout the battle. All in all he performed very well in his dual role as spearhead and scout. It is true that he fell into Beatty's trap along with Scheer, but he really cannot be blamed for obeying the direct orders of his C-in-C to increase speed and head north after Beatty. Hipper's performance would have been flawless but for two minor lapses. First, he left his flank unprotected during the Run to the South by placing his cruiser screen on his disengaged side, then when he turned away from Evan-Thomas's onslaught in the Run to the North, he exposed his ships to danger by turning his ships in succession rather than together. Fortunately for him, neither of these lapses had any serious consequence.

After the *Lützow* was crippled, Hipper was not involved in his battle cruisers' death ride. But Hartog's immediate and heroic response to Scheer's suicidal order was a tribute to Hipper's discipline and training. By the end of the battle it was clear that Hipper's squadron had borne the brunt of the enemy attack. His flagship was sinking, two more ships were down by the head with decks awash, and another had no guns left in action. Only the *Moltke* was still fit for battle. But these stalwart ships and gallant crews had served their battle fleet superbly as both its sword and shield.

Hipper deserves the highest praise for his brilliant performance. He had kept his nerve in the most daunting circumstances and shown himself to be a masterly tactician. He was the only one of the four leaders to come out of Jutland with his reputation unblemished. Hipper is surely the greatest war admiral the German navy has ever produced.

It has often been remarked that the admirals at Jutland made little use of the two weapons that were to dominate the naval warfare of the future—the aircraft carrier and the submarine.

The Grand Fleet had two "aircraft carriers" in the form of the seaplane tenders *Engadine* and *Campania*. Beatty, who was probably the most forward-looking of the four admirals, tried to use the *Engadine* to obtain vital information about the location of the enemy forces. It was not his fault that Rutland's brave efforts came to nothing. If seaplane engines and shipborne wireless had been more reliable in those days, aerial reconnaissance could have changed the whole tide of battle. In the end, the *Engadine* was relegated to the role of tugboat. Jellicoe had the *Campania,* but faulty W/T communications and engine problems delayed her departure from Scapa Flow. Jellicoe thought so little of her value that he ordered her to return to port, and she played no part in the battle.

The Germans had no vessels of this kind, but Scheer did try to obtain aerial reconnaissance before the battle using navy Zeppelins. His efforts were thwarted by the weather; the Zeppelins were at first prevented from taking off by high winds, then when they did take off, they were unable to report anything useful because of cloud cover. They did succeed in reconnoitering the Horns Reef area, but only after the battle was as good as over.

Likewise, the submarine played no significant role at Jutland. These boats were too slow to keep up with a rapidly maneuvering battle fleet, and wireless communication with submarines was difficult if not impossible when they were submerged. There was also the danger that they might torpedo one of their own ships in the confusion of battle. Scheer did try to use his U-boats before the battle, but his submarine trap off the Scottish coast failed to reap any reward. After the battle, his U-boats were unable to harass the homeward-bound Grand Fleet because they didn't receive the signal to remain at sea. Jellicoe's only use of submarines also failed to bear fruit, because those he had stationed off the Vyl lightship weren't able to communicate with ships on the surface.

In similar vein, the torpedo and mine did not live up to their destructive potential. The admirals were greatly concerned about the vulnerability of their dreadnoughts to these deadly weapons. Yet of the approximately two hundred torpedoes fired by surface ships at Jutland, only six found their target. Two dreadnoughts were torpedoed—one British, one German—but neither of them was forced to leave the line, let alone sink. The only big ship to be sunk by a torpedo was the old battleship *Pommern*.

Jellicoe was apprehensive about the danger of mines being sown in his path by a retreating enemy, and wasn't to know that Scheer had no intention of having his ships do this after he made his turnabouts. Ironically, it was Jellicoe who achieved the only success from mine laying, when one of the *Abdiel*'s mines damaged the *Ostfriesland* as she was returning to base.

Despite the lack of success of these new weapons at Jutland, it would not be many years before technical advances in aircraft and submarines spelled the end of the dreadnought's brief reign as the mightiest warship the world had ever seen.

The Road to Scapa Flow

*The German flag will be hauled down at sunset today, Thursday,
and will not be hoisted again without permission.*

—Adm. Sir David Beatty

CHAPTER 17

The serious flaws that had been revealed so starkly at Jutland shook
up the Royal Navy as seldom before in its long history. Jellicoe told
the First Sea Lord, "There are many lessons to be learned"—and he
was determined to profit from them. He wasted no time in initiat-
ing sweeping reforms in tactics, gunnery, matériel, and communications. He set up committees of experts to inquire into such areas
as torpedoes, fire control, antiflash measures, armor protection,
wireless, intelligence operations, and, most critical of all, shell quality. The welter of activity that sprang from the committees' delib-
erations resulted in a tremendous improvement in fighting efficiency, although it took until the end of 1917 to complete all the
reforms. But by 1918 the Grand Fleet had been transformed into a
vastly more effective force than it had been at Jutland.

Jellicoe also instituted significant changes in tactics. These were
a marked improvement: more decentralized and flexible use of the
battle squadrons, especially the van squadron in keeping touch with
a retreating enemy; greater emphasis on the destroyers' attacking
role using torpedoes; an improved signal book; and a more clearly
defined scouting role for the light cruisers. But the GFBOs remained
as long and as detailed as before.

The greatest advances came in the area of matériel, especially
better AP shells, the installation of antiflash devices, and greater
armor protection. Extra armor plate was added to the decks over the
magazines to reduce the ships' vulnerability to long-range plunging

fire. Jellicoe wanted to ensure that things would turn out very differently the next time he met the High Seas Fleet in battle.

There were also increases in the Grand Fleet's strength as well as its efficiency. Within a few months of Jutland, the addition of newly commissioned ships meant that Jellicoe had forty dreadnoughts at his disposal, including three new 15-inch-gunned superdreadnoughts. This brought the total number of battleships to thirty-one. The three battle cruisers lost at Jutland had been replaced, bringing their number back to nine. In comparison, Scheer could only muster the same nineteen battleships he had at the time of Jutland, plus the brand new 15-inch *Bayern,* and a mere two battle cruisers. The *Seydlitz* and *Derfflinger* were still under repair, and the recently launched *Hindenburg* would not be ready for service until 1917. In the late summer of 1916, Jellicoe's margin in dreadnoughts was nearly two to one—larger than it had been at the start of hostilities. The High Seas Fleet's chances of defeating the Grand Fleet had never been very good in the first place—now they were much worse.

Scheer also learned some lessons from Jutland. Most important was the need for better reconnaissance ahead of the battle fleet, to make sure that he would not be as badly surprised as he had been on 31 May. He also saw a need to protect his flanks using a U-boat screen. He didn't alter his basic strategy of trying to cut off part of the enemy fleet, and planned a sortie for 18–19 August 1916. According to the German official history, its objective was "to bombard Sunderland, to force the English Fleet to come out and show the world the unbroken strength of the German Fleet." More likely Scheer's main objective was to boost the morale and confidence of his men after their traumatic experience of near-disaster at Jutland.

He revived the original pre-Jutland plan that he been forced to abandon on 30 May because of bad weather. Hipper's 1st Scouting Group was to lead the way with his two operational battle cruisers, strengthened by three battleships detached from Scheer's fleet. Hipper's dawn attack on the British coast would be backed up by Scheer, twenty miles astern with sixteen more battleships. Scheer took twenty-four U-boats as well to cover his flanks and attack any British force that showed up. Most important, the fleet was to be preceded by a reconnaissance screen of ten Zeppelins, spread across its line of advance. If the British sent out a stronger force than expected in response to the raid on Sunderland, Scheer would be alerted by his Zeppelins. He wasn't going to let Jellicoe ambush him again.

The Admiralty was warned of the impending sortie by Room 40, and it ordered the Grand Fleet out—Jellicoe with twenty-nine battleships and

Beatty with six battle cruisers. The warning came in plenty of time for the British ships to put to sea, which they did two hours before Scheer left the Jade. The British showed up "unpleasantly soon as usual," according to *Der Krieg zur See*. Beatty was stationed only thirty miles ahead of the battle fleet—another lesson of Jutland.

The scene was set for a major engagement as the two fleets steamed toward each other at a rate of forty miles an hour. It seemed very likely that they would clash in a rematch of Jutland, this time with a full day of clear visibility ahead of them. Jellicoe was so confident of meeting the Germans that he ordered all ships to be in full readiness for action. He signaled his fleet: "High Seas Fleet may be sighted at any moment. I look forward with entire confidence on the result."

It was not to be. Scheer had received a signal from the Zeppelin L13 that it had spotted a British force off the Norfolk coast consisting of about thirty ships, "including some battleships." Believing he was in a position to trap an inferior detachment of the Grand Fleet, Scheer immediately turned about and headed southeast at full speed. This took him in the opposite direction to Jellicoe's line of advance. What the Zeppelin had actually sighted was merely Tyrwhitt's Harwich force of five light cruisers and twenty destroyers.

Jellicoe, who was trying to get behind Scheer to block his line of retreat, was diverted from his southerly course by a series of explosions that wracked one of the ships of his advanced cruiser screen. At first he believed he was heading into a minefield trap and turned north. In fact, the *Nottingham* had been hit by three torpedoes from the *U-52*. It was three hours before he was back on his previous course.

These diversions resulted in the two battle fleets narrowly failing to make contact. At one stage they had come within forty miles of each other. Sometime later Scheer received a report from the *U-53* that it had spotted the Grand Fleet steaming south, giving its position as about sixty-five miles to his north. He immediately canceled the Sunderland operation and headed for Wilhelmshaven at full speed. Scheer realized that but for the erroneous report from his Zeppelin, he would have almost certainly run into the whole of the Grand Fleet. This was the last time he ventured so far out into the North Sea.

The only damage resulting from this sortie was the loss of two British light cruisers, the *Nottingham* and *Falmouth*, both sunk by U-boats, and the torpedoing of the *Westfalen* by one of Jellicoe's submarines, the *E-23*. This forced the battleship to reduce speed and limp back to base. The most important consequence of the operation was that the Admiralstab decided that while such sorties might yield further results in terms of damage to British ships, they were not likely to produce anything decisive that would bring the war any nearer to a successful conclusion. They withdrew the U-boats from service with the battle fleet to concentrate on attacking merchant shipping. The High Seas Fleet was reduced to that of backstop for the submarine offensive, and gradually faded out of the picture.

Nevertheless, Scheer did mount one more fleet operation, in October 1916. It was to be along the same lines as the previous sortie. Once again the Admiralty was forewarned by Room 40, but this time it wasn't necessary to send the Grand Fleet out, because Scheer turned back a few hours after leaving the Jade when the *München* was torpedoed by the submarine *E-38*. Fearing a submarine trap, Scheer canceled the planned raid. This half-hearted sortie was the last operation of the High Seas Fleet as a whole until April 1918, when it made an ineffectual raid on a Scandinavian convoy. Scheer did carry out one minor sortie in 1916. On 16 November he sent out a force to rescue the submarines *U-20* and *U-30*, which had run aground on the Danish coast. The *Moltke* and a division of battleships covered the operation, but it almost cost Scheer dearly when the British submarine *J1* torpedoed the *Grosser Kurfürst* and *Kronprinz*. Both ships made it back to port, but Scheer's dreadnoughts did not leave the Jade again for the next eighteen months.

The naval war in the North Sea had reached a stalemate, just as the fighting in France had done after the failure of the Somme offensive. The German fleet lapsed into a state of inertia. The propaganda-fed glow of the "Victory of the Skagerrak" had long since worn off, replaced by feelings of frustration and impotence in the face of British sea power. Inevitably the enforced stagnation caused rot to set in. The High Seas Fleet was on the road that would lead it to an inglorious end at Scapa Flow.

The U-boats were still officially restricted to a stop-and-search procedure before sinking merchant ships, but the stepped-up offensive meant that Allied losses were nonetheless serious. The U-boats sank more than two million tons of shipping in 1916, nearly double the 1915 figure. The hemhorraging of Britain's maritime lifeblood could not be allowed to go on unchecked. If the flow was not stemmed soon, the British faced the distinct possibility of starvation and defeat. There was great pressure on the Admiralty to do something to reduce shipping losses. The First Lord, Arthur Balfour, offered the post of First Sea Lord to Jellicoe and asked him to take charge of antisubmarine warfare. Although reluctant to leave the Grand Fleet, Jellicoe accepted on 22 November. There was a moving scene on board the *Iron Duke* as he left Scapa for Whitehall, with the crew cheering and the band playing "Auld Lang Syne."

Jellicoe's departure raised the question of who was to succeed him as commander in chief. As commander of the Battle Cruiser Force, Beatty was an obvious possibility, but there were eight men on the vice admirals list who were senior to him, three of them in command of battle squadrons—Burney, Jerram, and Sturdee. None of them was really acceptable. Burney was not considered to have the necessary physical or mental capacity for such a demanding position. Sturdee had an excellent war record and a reputation as a skillful tactician, but his abrasive personality and radical ideas ruled him out. Jerram had ruled himself out by his feeble performance at Jutland.

Jellicoe recommended his chief of staff, Vice-Admiral Madden, as a more suitable successor than Beatty, of whom he wrote privately, "[He] had not experience enough and made many mistakes." Others, including Prime Minister Asquith, also had reservations about Beatty's lack of fleet experience, but since the conservative Lords of the Admiralty were not inclined to appoint anyone from the rear admirals list, the position was offered to Beatty *faute de mieux*. He accepted without hesitation and took over as C-in-C, Grand Fleet on 27 November. There was some discontent within the navy, but the choice was a popular one with the public and the press—to them he was the hero of Jutland and the natural successor to Jellicoe.

Beatty confounded his critics by staying with Jellicoe's cautious strategy in the North Sea, rather than the adventurous and reckless approach they had envisioned. But he wasted no time in undertaking a much more radical revision of the GFBOs than his predecessor had contemplated. Gone were the pages upon pages of detailed orders and instructions to be replaced by two pages of short, clear statements of tactical principles— flexible guidelines instead of rigid directives. Even the title was changed from "Battle Orders" to "Battle Instructions." However, Beatty's most important contribution was to keep up the spirits of his men and sustain their confidence in final victory during the monotonous, dreary, and wearisome months at Scapa Flow while the enemy fleet languished at anchor in the Jade.

After the Germans changed their naval strategy—a direct result of Jutland—the High Seas Fleet gradually sank into a state of resentful torpor. Bored and frustrated by the lack of action, more and more of its best officers and men transferred to the submarine service. With the battle fleet clearly relegated to a secondary role, it became a breeding ground for malcontents and agitators. There was widespread dissatisfaction over poor pay, short rations, the untreated grievances of ratings and underofficers, and the callous attitude of the executive officers toward their problems. The situation was inflamed by the subversive propaganda of left-wing deputies in the Reichstag, who called for peace negotiations and an end to the war. As the morale of the fleet deteriorated, there came the first stirrings of dangerous unrest. By the summer of 1917 these had flared up into incidents of mutiny. Scheer quickly suppressed these outbreaks by shooting the ringleaders, but this didn't stop the steady decay of the High Seas Fleet.

The U-boat offensive was also having an increasingly serious impact in Britain. Scheer, supported by the Army General Staff, insisted that half measures were not working quickly enough to win the war and continued to press for the removal of all restrictions on his U-boat commanders. The kaiser and the chancellor, Theobald von Bethmann-Hollweg, had always worried about the effect this would have on neutrals such as the United States, but they finally yielded. Germany officially declared unrestricted warfare on all merchant shipping on 1 February 1917—an indirect result of Jutland.

What had been a distant possibility now became a life and death struggle. Allied shipping losses leapt to a staggering 6.15 million tons in 1917, and the ratio of sinkings to ships getting through reached alarming proportions. Food reserves in Britain dwindled to a mere five weeks' supply at one stage, and the prospect of starvation and defeat loomed ever closer.

It seemed to many that the only answer was the navy's traditional convoy system. Amazingly, this had not even been tried since the beginning of the war. The idea of convoys had fallen out of favor, and its opponents, in particular Jellicoe inside the Admiralty and Admiral Sir Reginald Bacon, flag officer, Dover, stubbornly resisted the introduction of a convoy system. They argued that convoys were too complex and difficult to organize effectively, that captains of merchantmen were not trained to keep station, and that the convoy system required too many escort vessels, which in any case were better employed in hunting down U-boats. The navy had adopted an offensive rather than defensive stance toward antisubmarine warfare. It was thought better to patrol the focal points on the trade routes and sink the U-boats before they could attack shipping, or try to pen them in their bases. This approach was clearly not working.

The unrestricted U-boat campaign soon backfired on the Germans. The United States was finally pushed beyond the limits of its patience by the continued attacks on its shipping, and on 6 April 1917 President Wilson declared war on Germany. This tipped the balance in favor of the Allies, making Germany's final defeat inevitable.

The Americans sent a welcome squadron of six battleships, led by Rear Adm. Hugh Rodman in the USS *New York*, in support of the Grand Fleet. They also provided an even more welcome supply of capital: hundreds of millions of pounds in the form of loans to relieve the strain on Britain's economy caused by the war effort. By the end of the year the U.S. Navy had supplied large numbers of badly needed destroyers to help patrol the sea lanes and attack U-boats. Some of these ships were used on blockade duty and helped tighten the stranglehold on German trade. American ships also took over the laying of mine barrages at the entrance to the Channel and across the North Sea, stretching from Norway to the Orkneys. The staggering number of seventy thousand mines were laid altogether. These vast minefields made it extremely hazardous for U-boats to get to the Atlantic shipping lanes. For the rest of the war, the U.S. Navy cooperated magnificently with the Royal Navy, thanks in large measure to the capability and goodwill of Admiral Rodman and the American C-in-C in Europe, Adm. William Sims.

But the most significant naval event of 1917 was the introduction of the convoy system. Naval officers were finally able to convince Jellicoe and the other opponents in the Admiralty to give convoys a trial on some routes. Its success was so dramatic that convoys were in full operation on all routes by the autumn of 1917. By the end of the year, shipping losses had fallen so drastically that the threat of starvation receded, even though food rationing was still necessary. The U-boats nonetheless managed to sink 2.75 million tons in 1918, but the worst was over. The Allies had the situation firmly under control using new methods of attacking U-boats with mines, depth charges, and submarine chasers. Altogether, the Germans lost 178 U-boats during the war.

Jellicoe had undoubtedly been a failure as First Sea Lord, because of his inflexibility and inability to delegate and his stubborn resistance to the idea of convoys. He was worn out from the enormous strain of the past three years, depressed, and in poor physical health. The new First Lord, Sir Eric Geddes, unceremoniously removed him from office, cold-heartedly informing Jellicoe, by means of a curt letter on Christmas Eve 1917, that he was dismissed. In his letter Geddes gave no reasons for Jellicoe's dismissal, nor did he express appreciation for Jellicoe's services to the nation as C-in-C, Grand Fleet.

While food supplies to Britain improved, the tightened blockade had the opposite effect in Germany. Shortages and the imposition of strict rationing led to civil unrest. There were more food riots in German cities, and in January 1918 there was a general strike. The morale of the populace was at a very low ebb, and the war-weary Germans—civilians and soldiers alike—were losing their will to continue the conflict. But control of the situation remained in the iron grip of the Army General Staff.

Scheer was appointed as chief of the Admiralstab on 11 August 1918. Hipper was his obvious successor, and replaced him as C-in-C of the High Seas Fleet. The unfortunate Hipper had to face a rapidly deteriorating situation in the fleet. Subversion, spurred on by professional agitators, including Communists, resulted in the formation of secret Sailors Unions in every ship, with their headquarters on board the flagship *Friedrich der Grosse*. There were varying degrees of insubordination, disobedience, outright refusal obey orders, and threats of violence. The situation finally spiralled into open revolt as the fleet mutinied on 30 October 1918.

Scheer and Hipper had planned a major sortie for this date—a last heroic venture by the High Seas Fleet. An all-out assault on shipping in the Thames estuary was intended to provoke the Royal Navy into a fight to the finish. The best that could be hoped for was that the outcome might influence armistice negotiations in the Germans favor. In any event, as Scheer put it, the fleet "must be thrown into the scales: it is a matter of honour for the Navy to have done its utmost in the last battle."

The operation was disguised as a routine fleet exercise, but rumors of its true nature reached the men. They referred to it as the "the admirals' death ride." With the end of the war so near, the sailors had no intention of joining their officers on a voyage to Valhalla. The stokers on board the *Derfflinger* refused to obey orders to raise steam. Other stokers and seamen failed to return from shore leave and had to be rounded up at gunpoint and dragged back to their ships. When the fleet was ordered to sea on 29 October, the *Thüringen, Helgoland,* and *Markgraf* refused to sail. Hipper had no choice but to cancel the operation. He tried to maintain order and discipline by arresting agitators and dispersing the more rebellious ships to other ports, but the mutiny spread. By 4 November the Red Flag was flying in place of the Imperial Eagle at all German naval bases.

The Battle of Jutland had played a pivotal role in the deterioration of the German fleet, and in its eventual mutiny. The experience at Jutland had driven home the fact that the Grand Fleet was invincible, and it lit the slow fuse of discontent that finally touched off the explosive situation at Wilhelmshaven and Kiel in 1918. It is noteworthy that some of the most serious outbreaks of mutiny occurred on board ships that had been badly hit at Jutland—the *Derfflinger, Von der Tann, Markgraf, König,* and *Regensburg.*

The relentless pressure of the blockade finally led to similar chaos inside Germany as a whole. The near-starvation of the German people led to a collapse of civil order, then to insurrection, sparked by the sailors' revolt. The Central Powers, Gemany and Austria-Hungary, were going down to ruin and revolution. The kaiser was forced to abdicate on 9 November, and he fled across the border to seek sanctuary in Holland. Even the Army General Staff accepted that the war was lost, and Germany capitulated on 11 November. Armistice was signed at 5:00 A.M. in Marshal Foch's railway car in the forest of Compiégne, northeast of Paris. Hostilities ceased at 11:00 A.M.

In assessing the part played by the Royal Navy in this outcome, the distinguished historian Liddell Hart concluded, "That Navy was to win no Trafalgar, but it was to do more than any other factor towards winning the war for the Allies. For the navy was the instrument of the blockade, and as the fog of war disperses in the clearer light of these post-war years, that blockade is seen to assume larger and larger proportions, to be more clearly the decisive agency in the struggle."

Allied wrangling over peace terms left the German fleet in limbo. Its ships had not been formally surrendered to the Allies, and it was decided that until agreement was reached on what to do with them, the bulk of the fleet was to be interned at Scapa Flow. Warships remaining in German ports were to be decommissioned and disarmed.

On 21 November the core of the High Seas Fleet—nine battleships, five battle cruisers, seven light cruisers, and forty-nine torpedo boats—steamed out of the Jade for the last time. They were commanded by Rear Adm. Ludwig von Reuter, who had led the 4th Scouting Group at Jutland, and manned by skeleton crews. As they headed for a rendezvous with the British fleet off the coast of Scotland, they sailed in line ahead, led by the battle cruisers *Seydlitz, Moltke, Hindenburg, Derfflinger,* and *Von der Tann.* Beatty took out the whole of the Grand Fleet to meet them. The contributions of the empire countries were acknowledged by the presence of the *Australia, Canada, Malaya,* and *New Zealand.* Including an American battle squadron and a French cruiser, there were 270 ships in this awesome assembly of naval power, arrayed in two seemingly endless lines.

As the fleets approached the rendezvous fifty miles off the mouth of the Forth on a gray autumn morning, the German ships were directed to steam between the lines of Allied ships. The British ships had their guns at the ready, in case the Germans were planning some final gesture of defiance. The gun crews were issued with gas masks and wore their fireproof clothing. But the German ships sailed past silently and submissively, without incident.

Beatty must have had mixed feelings as he watched the German battle cruisers steam by, some of which he had claimed to have sunk at Jutland. Undefeated in battle, these were not the same foes he had faced at the Dogger Bank and Jutland—now they were filthy, bedraggled ships with sullen, mutinous crews. Curiously, those two architects of the Grand Fleet, Fisher and Jellicoe, were not there to see the spectacle. It would have been a gracious gesture to invite them as guests on board his flagship to take part in such a momentous and historic event, but Beatty was not willing to share his moment of triumph—the bloodless victory that all three had done so much to bring about.

When the leading British ships reached the end of the German line, they wheeled about and escorted them to a temporary anchorage in the Firth of Forth. This was where Beatty had been based for most of the war, and the symbolism was not lost on the Germans. When all their ships had dropped anchor in Aberlady Bay, he signaled them: "The German flag will be hauled down at sunset today, Thursday, and will not be hoisted again without permission."

This was rubbing salt in the wound, but Beatty wanted to make it crystal clear to the Germans that although they had not formally surrendered, their ships were now under British orders. At sunset he addressed his wildly cheering men on the quarterdeck of his new flagship, *Queen Elizabeth*. He congratulated his officers and men for their efforts in achieving victory and concluded by saying, "I always told you they would have to come out."

Two days later, as the German fleet was on its way to its final internment in the Orkneys, the Admiralty sent its congratulations to the Fleet by a signal which read in part, "The surrender of the German Fleet, accomplished without shock of battle, will remain for all time the example of the wonderful silence and sureness with which sea power attains its ends."

While the German warships rusted at anchor in Scapa Flow, discussions of what to do with them dragged on for six months. The Allies couldn't agree who was to take possession of which ships as part of war reparations. The Germans had different ideas. They were not going to turn their ships over to foreign navies for possible use against Germany in some future conflict.

Reuter and his officers secretly planned to scuttle the whole fleet. To ensure the plan was carried out swiftly on his command, he transferred his flag from the mutinous *Friedrich der Grosse* to the brand new cruiser *Emden*. At 10:30 A.M. on 21 June 1919, he sent a cryptic signal to trusted officers on board each ship. Their orders were to open the sea cocks and smash the valve wheels so that they could not be closed again. They had also been told to open all doors, portholes, condensers, torpedo tubes, and drains and make sure they stayed open.

It was a strange sight. All seventy-four German ships slowly began to settle in the water, as blue-green seawater gushed in through hundreds of openings. Most of them developed a list, and their towering masts began to tilt at odd angles. A few ships settled on an even keel. The crews slowly and quietly began to disembark in the ships' boats.

The 1st Battle Squadron, which had been assigned to guard the internees, had temporarily put to sea on maneuvers the day before, and at first the few British patrol vessels left in harbor didn't observe what was happening. Probably the first to notice were children from a local school who were on a day trip to Scapa to see the German fleet. When the crews of the British ships finally realized what the Germans were doing, it was too late to prevent the scuttling.

The British officers were very angry, and rightly regarded the German action as a betrayal of the terms of the Armistice and a hostile act. There were several ugly incidents as some officers ordered the German crews to go back on board their ships and stop the flooding. Others tried to prevent the Germans from going ashore. Anger at what they saw as German treachery gave rise to panicky outbreaks of rifle and machine-gun fire, resulting in nine German sailors being killed, including Captain Schumann of the *Markgraf*. Sixteen more suffered gunshot wounds. They were the last casualties of the Great War.

It took six hours before the scuttling was complete. Ship after ship capsized and sank—the *Friedrich der Grosse* was the first to go, followed by the *König Albert*. Others took much longer to sink. The *Derfflinger* rolled over but refused to sink because of air trapped inside her hull. The brand new battle cruiser *Hindenburg* settled on an even keel and rested on the shallow bottom with her masts and funnels showing. The British managed to take the equally new *Baden* in tow and beach her, but another ten battleships sank, as did the four remaining battle cruisers. The British were able to take twenty-one smaller ships in tow in sinking condition and beach them—three cruisers and eighteen torpedo boats. But when it was all over, fifty-two ships had gone to the bottom of Scapa Flow. Nearly half a million tons of valuable and complicated equipment was now only fit for salvage as scrap iron.

The world had never known anything like this astounding act of self-immolation by a whole armada. It was a melancholy and inglorious end to the career of the once proud High Seas Fleet, a fleet which had proved its toughness and courage at the Battle of Jutland. For years afterward the funnels and masts of the *Hindenburg* sticking above the water and the *Derfflinger* floating upside down like a huge whale were the only visible memorial to the tragic death of a great fleet.

The Jutland Controversy

No battle in history has spilt so much—ink.

—Basil Liddell Hart

The Battle of Jutland wasn't really over when the firing died away on 1 June 1916. It would be refought again and again in the pages of countless books, articles, and letters, some written by partisans of the major protagonists, others by avowed neutrals. As Liddell Hart expressed somewhat sardonically, "No battle in history has spilt so much—ink." It obviously continues to do so, more than eighty years later.

For more than a decade following the Armistice, a heated and often bitter controversy raged in Britain over what had actually happened at Jutland. Its genesis was the inept and demoralizing communiqué issued by the Admiralty immediately after the battle, written by Balfour when few details were available. Churchill's supplementary communiqué and the official dispatches of Jellicoe and Beatty went some way to repairing the damage done by Balfour's premature announcement, but too many questions were left unanswered. The British people had expected a second Trafalgar, and when it became clear that Jutland was no Trafalgar, everyone wanted to know what had gone wrong. Why had the Germans not been decisively defeated, and who was to blame?

There were widespread and disagreeable rumors, and uninformed and unfair criticisms in the newspapers, all fueled by disappointment at what was known about the outcome of the battle. Most of the criticism was directed at Jellicoe, who was blamed for not achieving a smashing victory. Beatty had led the German fleet into his grasp, and he had failed to annihilate it. Some of the criticism in the gutter press was virulent, accusing Jellicoe of indecisiveness and implying timidity verging on cowardliness. The serious newspapers adopted a more evenhanded and responsible approach, but even they were not satisfied with the scarcity of detailed official information about the course of the battle.

The continual sniping and mud slinging had its effect. Jellicoe was upset and deeply hurt by the harsh criticism in the newspapers but maintained a dignified silence, at least in public. One of Jellicoe's supporters went so far as to blame his dismissal from the Admiralty directly on the anti-Jellicoe campaign waged by the Northcliffe press, particularly the *Daily Mail:* "And so another great man goes down under the sea of Mud of the Gutter Press." This was not true, of course, but it illustrates the depth of feeling engendered in Jellicoe's supporters at the time.

There were also public criticisms aimed at Jellicoe by Beatty's admirers, notably by Cdr. Carlyon Bellairs, a retired naval officer and member of Parliament, who raised questions in the House about Jellicoe's conduct of the battle; and by the inventor and journalist Arthur Pollen, who wrote a book and several articles strongly critical of Jellicoe. It should be recalled that Pollen's fire-control device had been rejected by the Admiralty in favor of the inferior Dreyer system, and Jellicoe had been one of those responsible for the decision.

Like Jellicoe, Beatty was understandably reluctant to enter into a distasteful public slinging match and remained silent. It would however have been a simple matter for him to check the more outrageous personal attacks some of his supporters were making on his former chief. He could have done so with a few well-chosen remarks in a brief public statement defending Jellicoe. But he didn't do this, and his continued silence lent the critics his tacit approval.

The lack of official response to repeated questions and criticisms in the House and in the press generated a strong suspicion that the public were not being told the full story of Jutland, and that a deliberate cover-up of something unpleasant or discreditable was going on. It was in the national interest to dispel the rumors and doubts as soon as possible by publishing all the relevant facts and information in such a way that the layman could understand the essential elements of this huge and complex fleet action. The only body in a position to undertake such a task was the Admiralty, but due to an unfortunate combination of circumstances and personalities, it proved itself in the end to be both unable and unwilling to provide a complete, balanced, and readable narrative of the action at Jutland. The clouds of discontent and disappointment created by the

Balfour communiqué lingered for more than a decade after the war, and even today they have not been entirely dispelled.

Shortly after the war ended, it was generally known that the unemployed Jellicoe was using his enforced leisure to write a book about the operations of the Grand Fleet during the period he had been C-in-C. It was feared in some quarters that if he were to publish his own version of events at Jutland before anyone else, it might be to the discredit of the other participants. They need not have worried. Jellicoe was not the man to criticize anyone unjustifiably, and certainly not in a vindictive or distorted way. He was always mild in any criticisms he did make, and he didn't spare himself from blame when things had gone wrong, at the same time strongly defending the actions of subordinates. When the book, titled *The Grand Fleet, 1914–1916,* came out in 1919, it proved to be a damp squib rather than the anticipated bombshell. Although it provided some essential information about the battle for the first time, it was long-winded, dull, and self-effacing. Bellairs and other self-appointed Jellicoe critics perceived it as an apologia for what they saw as the Grand Fleet's ineffectual performance.

Nonetheless, in January 1919 the First Sea Lord, Sir Rosslyn Wemyss, was not to know that the book would have so little impact, and he was sufficiently concerned to recommend to Walter Long, then the First Lord, that it was important for the Admiralty to produce "a detailed, historically accurate record of the Battle of Jutland."

Thus it came about that in February 1919, Wemyss appointed a committee of five naval officers, chaired by Capt. John Harper, to prepare a complete, authoritative, and official account of the battle. Harper's committee was given access to all battle reports, signal logs, track charts, and engine-room records—in fact, every single official document relating to the battle. Harper was told not to accept any oral evidence or make subjective comments or judgments. As he explained, the account was to be "a Record, with plans, showing in chronological order what actually occurred at the Battle."

Harper, who was a navigational specialist and the navy's director of navigation, had not been present at Jutland and had no obvious axe to grind. He thought it vital to reconcile discrepancies in reported positions caused by inevitable errors in dead reckoning, especially the distance between the Battle Fleet and Battle Cruiser Fleet at the start of the fleet action. Working from often sketchy ships' records, the committee had great difficulty plotting the movements of some vessels. In order to obtain a fixed reference point, Harper went to the length of having a minesweeper sent out to locate the exact position of the wreck of the *Invincible.* With this information, the committee was able to check and recheck the track charts of all ships, doing their best to arrive at an accurate description of the various squadrons' movements.

The Harper Record was completed in October 1919. It was essentially a straightforward narrative of the battle, incorporating all available evidence and accompanied by charts and diagrams to help the reader follow the action. Unfortunately, Harper went against his instructions and included some personal comments, particularly involving the battle cruiser action. He found it a "disturbing" and "unpalatable" outcome that six British battle cruisers, supported by four battleships, had engaged five German battle cruisers and lost the *Indefatigable* and *Queen Mary* while sinking no enemy ships. Harper did not assign any blame for this result, which he described as a "partial defeat," and the facts were undeniable. His comments were no more than Jellicoe had already made to the Admiralty in his official dispatch after the battle. But they were to have disastrous consequences for the record. If it had been published there and then, and given the Admiralty imprimatur, it would have averted the worst excesses of the unsavory and divisive controversy that was to prove so damaging to the morale and prestige of the Royal Navy.

At the time Harper submitted the record of the Battle of Jutland to the Board of Admiralty for approval, Wemyss, the First Sea Lord and chief of Naval Staff, happened to be out of the country on vacation. The document was read by his deputy chief of staff, Rear-Admiral Brock, and on 24 October he was on the point of signing it to signify Admiralty approval when he changed his mind. He told Harper, "As Lord Beatty is assuming office as First Sea Lord in a few days it must wait for his approval." Preparation of the record had been authorized by Wemyss, and it was his board's responsibility to approve or disapprove it. It is significant that Brock had been commander of Beatty's 1st Battle Cruiser Squadron at Jutland, and following Beatty's appointment as C-in-C Grand Fleet, he had served as Beatty's Chief of Staff.

On 1 November 1919 Beatty, who had already been promoted to admiral of the fleet, was appointed First Sea Lord and chief of Naval Staff. By taking this final step in his spectacular climb to the top, he had reached the pinnacle of a naval officer's career at the unparalleled early age of forty-eight. He brought with him Chatfield, his former flag captain from the *Lion*, as his assistant chief of staff, and Cdr. Ralph Seymour, at first as his naval secretary and later as his assistant. It seemed to some that with Beatty, Brock, Chatfield, and Seymour in positions of power or influence, the battle cruiser men might try to take over at the Admiralty. Events soon proved them right.

Once in office, Beatty wasted no time in reading the Harper Record, and predictably did not like the sections dealing with the battle cruiser action. By now he was extremely sensitive to any hint of criticism of his maneuvering, tactics, signaling, or gunnery at Jutland. He became upset at suggestions that these had been less than perfect. Over the next few months, Beatty sent messages to Harper via Seymour, who at one stage, according to Harper, indiscreetly remarked that "we do not wish to advertise the fact that the Battle Fleet was in action, more than we can help." Beatty also sent for the unfortunate captain on several occasions to make objections and suggest changes to the record. Among the things he objected to principally were the famous 360-degree turn, which Beatty still insisted had never happened, and the gunnery range at which the battle cruiser action had been fought. Harper's track charts showed that this had varied from fourteen to nineteen thousand yards, and for most of the action it was about sixteen thousand yards. Beatty claimed that he had never allowed the battle cruisers' range to open to more than fourteen thousand yards. Harper pointed out that Beatty's suggested changes were not in accord with the evidence of the ships' records and track charts and bravely and doggedly resisted all Beatty's attempts to alter the record in any material way.

Several significant developments took place on 11 February 1920. Beatty summoned Harper to an interview, at which he directly ordered him—in writing—to make amendments and additions to the text and delete certain sections dealing with the battle cruisers' shooting. The same day, Jellicoe happened to be visiting the Admiralty to report on his recently completed official tour of the Dominions, and by chance ran into Harper, who told him of the problems he was having. Ever since he had arrived back in England, Jellicoe had heard disquieting rumors about the preparation of the record, and the meeting with Harper confirmed that there was trouble ahead. When Wemyss had commissioned the record, he had stipulated that neither Jellicoe nor Beatty should read it before it was ready for publication. Jellicoe had agreed to this. Beatty evidently had not.

From the moment Beatty intervened in the preparation of the record, it was inevitable that the Jutland controversy would evolve into a Beatty-Jellicoe controversy. Naval officers soon lined up into pro-Beatty and pro-Jellicoe factions, with naval correspondents and journalists "ranged behind them," as Marder put it.

The discussions in the Admiralty on 11 February coincided with the publication that same day of a book by Carlyon Bellairs titled *The Battle of Jutland: The Sowing and the Reaping*. Bellairs was a well-known admirer of Beatty and a harsh critic of Jellicoe. His book was a shrill polemic in which Beatty could do nothing wrong and Jellicoe could do nothing right.

It was a rambling account of the battle, full of sweeping and unsubstantiated statements, inaccuracies, and distorted depictions of events about which Bellairs could not have had any detailed information at the time. Chapter headings and subtitles give an idea of the tenor of the criticism of Jellicoe: "I came, I saw, I turned away"; and "Eleven Destroyers Dismiss 27 Battleships." In addition, the book libeled Harper, who considered legal action but was talked out of suing Bellairs by the First Lord, Walter Long, who pointed out that the results might not cover his legal expenses. Although Bellairs's book has since been dismissed as "unreadable and unread," it enraged Jellicoe's supporters and stoked the fires of controversy.

From February onward there is no doubt that Beatty tried to use his influential position to impose his view of the battle on Harper and the Board of Admiralty, to manipulate the record to show the Battle Cruiser Fleet in a more favorable light, and to minimize the role of the Battle Fleet. He kept insisting that Harper make changes to the record. One change in particular was the insertion of a newly discovered chart that showed the *Lion* had made two successive 180-degree turns in an S-shaped maneuver rather than the 360-degree turn that Beatty could not accept had taken place. When this chart was actually drawn is not certain. It was dated 17 July 1916, but was unsigned. To make it official it had to be signed, and this was apparently done by Beatty in 1920. At least the signature was different from that on Beatty's official 1916 documents. It is remarkable that Beatty went to these lengths to doctor the record on such an unimportant point, and is indicative of his sensitivity to criticism.

Harper, naturally perturbed by the continual pressure he was being subjected to by Beatty and Seymour, went to see the First Lord. Long was concerned about the delay in producing the record, as well as the effect it might have on Jellicoe if it were to be published with Beatty's amendments. Jellicoe was still highly respected in the Admiralty, and in the country at large, in spite of the vicious personal attacks in some sections of the press. He had not seen any drafts yet, but had stated that he would not take up his post as governor general of New Zealand unless he was satisfied that he would have an opportunity see the record and comment on it before publication.

It seems fairly clear that Long was able to convince Beatty to back down, because on 11 March, Beatty canceled his written orders to Harper to make alterations. Two days later the final draft—with only minor changes—went to the board, where it was approved. It appeared that publication of the record would now go ahead.

But when copies of the final proofs were sent to Long and Beatty on 14 May, with a note to the effect that no changes had been made to the record since the board had approved it, the trouble began all over again. As soon as he had read the proofs, Beatty summoned Harper to demand that he make changes. On 26 May he sent Harper a list of the changes he wanted. As a disconsolate Harper remarked, "We were now back where we were in February."

Beatty's next move was to propose that all the sea lords be given a copy of the record and that each be invited to give Harper his own suggestions for changes, additions, and deletions. Then the whole board would meet to consider these proposed alterations, and Harper's responses to them, before approving the final report. This was an unusual procedure because proposals were normally submitted to the sea lords, not by them. Nevertheless it was done, and the Board of Admiralty met on 21 June to consider the proposed amendments, including some submitted by Brock and Chatfield, as well as those by Beatty himself. After a lengthy discussion, with Harper present, and doggedly sticking to his guns when he believed that alterations did not square with the evidence, a number of changes were finally agreed upon. Apart from the deletion of one section dealing with the battle cruisers' gunnery, most of the amendments were not all that contentious.

Beatty was still not satisfied, and he proposed that a preface be added to the record. It was most probably drafted by Beatty and Chatfield, and its first two paragraphs read:

> The following narrative of events, amplified by detailed proceedings of each Squadron and Flotilla, shows that the enemy's advanced forces were reinforced by their main Fleet some hours before the British main Fleet was able to reach the scene of action. During this period, therefore, the British were in greatly inferior force.
>
> On learning of the approach of the British main Fleet the Germans avoided further action and returned to base.

This statement was an absolute travesty, since it implied that Beatty's forces had been greatly outnumbered by the enemy for several hours before Jellicoe showed up, when in fact this was only the case during the Run to the North, a period of just over an hour. Furthermore, the battle cruisers were not within gunnery range of the enemy battle fleet for much of this phase. The preface also omitted any mention of the first phase of the action, when Beatty was in clearly superior force, particularly after Evan-Thomas's ships had joined in. Finally, the suggestion that the Grand Fleet had not been in action at all was preposterous.

How Beatty could have imagined that such a flagrant distortion of events could be included in an official Admiralty record without causing tremendous dissension is hard to fathom.

Up until this point, Jellicoe had been very reluctant to get involved in the dispute over the preparation of the Harper Record. At first he had been quite willing to agree to Wemyss's stipulation that he not read it until it was ready for publication, but he had heard disturbing reports about what was going on in the Admiralty. By now gossip and rumors about the dispute over the record had spread to officers' messes and service clubs. Long sent him a copy, with all the proposed changes noted and the new preface included, and asked for his comments. Jellicoe objected so strongly to many of Beatty's amendments, especially the preface, that he told Long he would not sail for New Zealand until he received Long's assurance that the offending passages would be deleted. Such a refusal would have caused a scandal, because Jellicoe's appointment as governor general had already been announced.

There was another lengthy board meeting on 14 July, held to consider Jellicoe's objections. The discussion became heated as both Beatty and Harper stuck to their positions, and when the atmosphere became acrimonious the meeting broke up without any firm decision being reached. The tone of the meeting can be gauged from a remark Beatty reportedly made during a discussion of a salvo that had straddled one of Jellicoe's ships, HMS *Hercules*. The near-misses had drenched the battleship's upper deck, and Harper and Long wanted the passage to be included to show that the Grand Fleet was within the Germans' gunnery range at the time of deployment. Beatty wanted it deleted, but in the end gave in ungraciously with, "Well I suppose there is no harm in the public knowing that someone in the Battle Fleet got wet, as that is about all they had to do with Jutland."

By this time Long realized that it would be impossible to reconcile the views of the two admirals and knew that Harper's position was becoming unbearable. At one stage Harper tried to insist that if the record were to be published with Beatty's amendments, a statement be included to make it clear that he, Harper, was not responsible for any corrections to the text that were not in accord with the documentary evidence. Long knew that it would be politically out of the question to include such a disclaimer, and after Harper hinted strongly that he wanted out of his now unenviable assignment, Long relieved him of his duties.

The First Lord called a final meeting of the board on 22 September, at which he proposed that publication of the Harper Record be abandoned, and that as a way out of the impasse, the Naval Staff be asked to prepare a narrative of the battle instead of the record. All the board members agreed with this suggestion, except Beatty. He proposed that all Harper's charts, dispatches, and signals—amended as per his orders—

be published, but not the text of the record. When Harper's opinion was sought, he said this would only make things worse and raise even more questions among members of the press, who were demanding publication of the record. Harper recommended that the Admiralty "either refuse to publish anything or publish everything and hide nothing, as there was nothing to hide."

In the end, eighteen months after the Harper committee had begun its work, plans to publish an official record were suspended indefinitely as other options were explored.

While Beatty's attempts to tamper with the record had been delaying proceedings inside the Admiralty, a parallel drama had been enacted in Parliament. The government had announced as early as March 1919 that an official record was being prepared by Captain Harper, and it repeatedly stated that when it was completed, probably at the end of September, "publication will be considered." Finally, on 29 October, it promised that "a narrative of events has been completed and will be published when printed."

But a few days later, after Beatty had taken up his appointment as First Sea Lord, there began an amazing litany of official excuses, prevarications, and even some outright falsehoods as government spokesmen struggled to explain the continued nonappearance of the Harper Record. Answers to Opposition questions were often inconsistent with what had been stated previously. Excuses were made that it was necessary to check Admiralty information against Admiral Scheer's official report, although this had been available for some time; that there were technical difficulties with production that "make it improbable that publication can take place in much less than three months from now"; and that the difficulty in providing paper for the charts was causing delay!

Then on 4 August it was announced that "fresh evidence has recently come to light which must be considered before the Official Report, which had almost reached completion, can be published." This came nine months after the government had stated in Parliament that the report "has been completed." It is hard to know what this "fresh evidence" could have been, other than oral evidence based on personal recollections of events that had taken place four years earlier.

This lamentable performance went on in Parliament until 27 October 1920—a year from the time the Harper committee had actually completed the record—when the government was forced to admit, "It is not now proposed to publish an Official account. . . . Any record based on British official evidence only would inevitably present a one-sided version. . . . Moreover, Sir Julian Corbett's 'Naval History of the War' [which] includes Jutland, is likely to be published within the course of the next year. . . . All material prepared by the Admiralty will be placed at Sir Julian Corbett's disposal."

A few days later the prime minister, Lloyd George, explained that the Admiralty had gone back on its decision to publish the record because it was a "highly controversial topic"—that at least was true—and that it was possibly not "desirable that there should be a separate account," which was at best arguable. Then on 4 November he stated, "In view of the general wish expressed on Monday for the immediate publication of documents relating to the Battle of Jutland, a Parliamentary Paper will be issued at an early date containing all these documents whether reports, despatches or signals."

This certainly appeared to promise that publication of the Harper Record was imminent, as one of the documents referred to in the prime minister's announcement; and in reply to a further question in the House as to when the official record would appear, it was stated, "It is hoped that publication will be possible within a month." But it soon became clear that this was not at all what the government or the Admiralty had in mind.

After stalling in Parliament from March 1919 to December 1920, the government issued a blue book entitled *The Battle of Jutland. Official Despatches with Appendices.* As a substitute for the record it was totally inadequate. The book was a stupefying mass of undigested documents, dispatches, and ship's reports—603 pages in all—and included more than seven hundred signals, ranging from the vitally important to the mind-numbingly trivial. It gave no commentary or analysis, and there was no attempt whatever to provide a cohesive narrative linking the various engagements that took place during the battle. Nor were there any of the charts or diagrams that Harper's committee had so painstakingly prepared to help the reader follow the course of the action. Maps and diagrams were included—both accurate and inaccurate—but without explanatory notes.

As one retired admiral predicted, "The Official Despatches will be so much Greek to the general public and to most of the Members of this House, and that it is only by such a report as Captain Harper's that anything intelligible can be made out of them."

Official Despatches was unlikely to be read by anyone but a serious historian or naval analyst. As an exercise in official obfuscation, its publication was brilliant. No one could accuse the Admiralty of concealing the facts—they were all there, somewhere. But as a way out of the dilemma over the nonpublication of the Harper Record, *Official Despatches* was an absolute fiasco and did nothing to allay public or press suspicions of a cover-up.

The next step taken by the Admiralty to solve the problem posed by the dispute over the Harper Record proved even less successful. Beatty initiated the preparation of a confidential *Naval Staff Appreciation.* This was intended for limited distribution only within the Navy. Its authors were two inexperienced and unknown junior officers from the Admiralty's Historical Section, the brothers Cdr. Alfred Dewar and Capt. Kenneth Dewar, both longtime admirers of Beatty. They were selected for this task by Admiral Brock, possibly on instructions from Beatty, but certainly with his knowledge and approval. The Dewars completed their assignment in August 1921. The *Naval Staff Appreciation* was critical of just about everything and everybody at Jutland, especially Jellicoe, but not of Beatty, who was delighted with it.

The *Naval Staff Appreciation* was a grossly distorted version of events at Jutland. It strongly emphasized the role of the Battle Cruiser Fleet and downplayed or concealed the contributions of the Battle Fleet, the 5th Battle Squadron, and even Hood's 3d Battle Cruiser Squadron. Nearly everyone who read the *Staff Appreciation* agreed that the Dewar brothers had gone far beyond what was justified or reasonable in their judgments. Early in 1922 the Admiralty suppressed further printing or circulation of the document—now classified as "secret." Even Chatfield agreed that if it were published, it "would rend the service to its foundations." Years later, in 1930, after Jellicoe's former chief of staff, Admiral Madden, had succeeded Beatty as First Sea Lord, he ordered all copies of the notorious *Staff Appreciation* burned. Fortunately for naval historians, several copies escaped the holocaust and are now in the public domain in various libraries.

Then in 1923, the year after the suppression of the *Naval Staff Appreciation,* the appearance of volume 3 of the official British history of the war at sea marked a turning point in the Jutland controversy. This series, entitled *Naval Operations,* was prepared by direction of the Committee of Imperial Defence (CID) as part of its overall history of the Great War. Volume 3 covered the period from May 1915 to June 1916. Its author was Sir Julian Corbett, a well-known and highly respected historian and a leading expert on naval strategy. He had been allowed access to all official documents relating to the battle, including the Harper Record and the *Naval Staff Appreciation,* but the Admiralty would not permit Corbett to use or even refer to any information concerning secret intelligence or the cryptography of Room 40. This prohibition was nominally for security reasons, but it was just as likely due to the Admiralty's unwillingness to reveal its failures to pass on vital intelligence to the fleet both before and during the battle.

Corbett's book gave the first clear, balanced, and unbiased account of Jutland. His narrative presented an unvarnished, comprehensive description of the action and offered no overt criticisms or judgments of any of the participants. Corbett was content to let the facts speak for themselves. By providing a clear and detailed account of the situations facing the commanders, and the information available to them at the time, the book came as a revelation to the public and served as a vindication of Jellicoe's actions and decisions. The admiral derived great consolation from Corbett's book, especially after suffering the ill-informed or ignorant criticisms he had received from the press and authors such as Bellairs and Filson Young.

Predictably, Beatty's supporters didn't like the book and thought Corbett had been biased in favor of Jellicoe. Beatty himself, and especially Chatfield, were critical of Corbett's account of the battle cruiser action. Chatfield was a persistent defender of the battle cruisers' shooting. He attributed their failure to inflict any serious damage on Hipper's ships to defective British shells, ignoring the fact that other British ships were able to deal out heavy punishment using the same ammunition. Beatty's supporters used the lack of adequate fire-control equipment to excuse the poor shooting of his battle cruisers, yet other ships with similar or less adequate fire-control systems did quite well, and the Germans, with no comparable fire-control equipment at all, managed to outhit the Battle Cruiser Force by nearly four to one.

The Beatty-dominated Board of Admiralty was in a quandary. Corbett was a very distinguished author, commissioned by the powerful CID, and the board couldn't easily tamper with his finished work. The Admiralty did interfere by interrogating Corbett persistently after reading drafts of volume 3, in a manner that some thought bordered on censorship. This interference must have taken place with Beatty's acquiescence, at the very least. Churchill also read the draft, which didn't fit in with his views on Jutland or the Dardanelles, and he too tried to interfere with Corbett. As a cabinet minister, he was able to delay publication of the book.

Corbett died suddenly in 1922 shortly after completion of the final draft. Col. E. Y. Daniel, the secretary of the CID's Historical Section, bravely and adamantly resisted all attempts by the Admiralty to make alterations to the text, and his refusal to make any significant changes was supported by his publishers. In the end the Admiralty had to settle for the insertion of a strong official disclaimer on the first page. This is worth quoting in full to illustrate that the controversy was far from settled by the appearance of Corbett's book:

The Lords Commissioners of the Admiralty have given the author access to official documents in the preparation of this work, but they are in no way responsible for its production or for the accuracy of its statements.

Their Lordships find that some of the principles advocated in the book, especially the tendency to minimise the importance of seeking battle and forcing it to a conclusion, are directly in conflict with their views.

Beatty's hand in drafting this disclaimer is patently obvious from the second paragraph.

This was not the Admiralty's last word on the subject. In August 1924 it issued what was apparently intended to be a riposte to Corbett's book, entitled *Narrative of the Battle of Jutland.* It was essentially a replacement for the suppressed *Naval Staff Appreciation,* toned down and omitting its harsh judgments and criticisms. Roskill, one of Beatty's biographers, described it as a "devenomized" version of the *Staff Appreciation.* Oddly enough, the *Narrative's* authorship was not openly acknowledged, although it has been generally attributed to the Dewar brothers; nor was it indicated on the title page that it was an official Admiralty publication. Yet in an appendix, it was repeatedly referred to as "the Admiralty Narrative" or "the Official Narrative."

The *Narrative* has been described by Winton, one of Jellicoe's biographers, as "one of the least generous publications ever issued, even by the Admiralty." As a narrative, it was disjointed and poorly written, and it continued to present a distorted picture of events at Jutland. It was blatantly pro-Beatty throughout and persisted in overemphasizing the role of the 1st and 2d BCS while downplaying or glossing over the parts played by other forces, especially the battle fleet, which barely seemed to have been involved in the action at all. Also, the number of hits it claimed to have been made by Beatty's battle cruisers on Hipper's squadron was exaggerated, while the hits made by the Germans in return were comparably underestimated.

When Jellicoe was shown a copy of the *Narrative* before publication, he pointed out the many inaccuracies it contained and made numerous objections to misleading deductions and insinuations in the text, mainly in defense of subordinates such as Evan-Thomas rather than himself. The Admiralty agreed to include some, but not all, of Jellicoe's comments in the book, and showed scant respect for a former C-in-C by consigning them to Appendix G of the published version. Instead of leaving readers to judge the merits of Jellicoe's critical remarks for themselves, the Admiralty accompanied them by contentious and copious footnotes that took up almost as much space as the Admiral's original comments. The Admiralty also saw fit to preface the appendix with the following disclaimer:

> This Appendix has been added to the Admiralty Narrative, to meet the wishes of Admiral of the Fleet, Viscount Jellicoe.
>
> Where, however, the Appendix differs from the Admiralty Narrative Their Lordships are satisfied that the Narrative is more in accordance with the evidence available.
>
> Notes have been added, where necessary, mainly in amplification or elucidation of the text criticised in the Appendix.

The Admiralty's idea of "amplification" and "elucidation" seemed to consist of bland responses to Jellicoe's criticisms, such as, "Their Lordships are satisfied . . . ," "Their Lordships cannot accept . . . ," and "The facts as stated in the Narrative are correct." Some of their rebuttals were simple categorical assertions that where there was any conflict in interpretation, the Admiralty view was the correct one.

Winton concluded, "It seems that Beatty, his Board and the civil servants behind them took leave of all the normal rules of courtesy."

It seemed that each attempt by the Admiralty to damp down the fires of controversy only made things worse. Their problem lay in trying to present the results of Jutland in a light favorable to Beatty, without giving too much offense to Jellicoe. This was an impossible task. The *Narrative* only succeeded in heating up the situation, and giving offense to many naval officers, who were unable to reply to criticisms while they were still serving.

The same year the *Narrative* appeared, Admiral Bacon fanned the flames of controversy to new heights by the publication of his book, *The Jutland Scandal*. It was a fiercely partisan defense of Jellicoe, and the book's title and dedication—to "Those Two Neglected Goddesses, Justice and Truth, Now Worshipped in an Obscure Corner of the British Pantheon"—illustrate its contentious nature.

Bacon was obviously upset by what he regarded as ignorant attacks on Jellicoe in the popular press, and by the failure of the Admiralty to present a balanced account of Jutland that would answer uninformed criticisms of the actions of Jellicoe and others such as Evan-Thomas. He did not regard the *Narrative* as such an account, saying that it only added to the discredit of the Admiralty.

Bacon was particularly upset by the comments of the journalist Filson Young, who had written an article in the *Sunday Express* that was highly critical of Jellicoe's conduct of the battle. Young had already published a book in 1921 entitled *With the Battlecruisers,* which also criticized Jellicoe's leadership, mainly by innuendo. Young had been attached to Beatty's staff as a supernumerary RNVR lieutenant during the Heligoland Bight and Dogger Bank actions, and his book was a starry-eyed account of life with the battle cruisers, and a panegyric to Beatty, whom he regarded as a "brilliant tactician" who had a "steel-bright, steel-hard genius for battle."

In his book, Bacon reproduced the *Sunday Express* article and accompanied it by a scathing point-by-point refutation of Young's criticisms of Jellicoe and his commendations of Beatty. Young's immediate response was to threaten to bring a lawsuit against Bacon for infringement of copyright. This caused the book to be withdrawn temporarily, but it was reissued in 1925.

In 1926 an English translation of the official German account of Jutland came out. The original version, *Der Krieg in der Nordsee* (volume 5 of *Der Krieg zur See, 1914–1918*), written by Otto Groos, not surprisingly was not widely read in Britain, and the English version provided more details of the battle from the German side. Groos's account was much more balanced and reliable than Scheer's earlier reminiscences of the battle in his book *Die deutsche Flotte im Weltkrieg,* which Hough later evaluated as "egocentric, idiosyncratic, unreliable, and execrably translated, but should be read," in marked contrast to Groos, whose work he rated as "stately and irreplaceable."

Groos naturally continued to uphold the official view that the *Skagerrakschlacht* had been a German victory but admitted that the High Seas Fleet had suffered heavy damage. He made no criticisms of Scheer's tactics or sometimes curious decisions. Groos, who had been navigator of the *Von der Tann* at Jutland, was generally complimentary toward Jellicoe, who was repeatedly praised for his tactics, especially the deployment. But Groos took a less favorable view of Beatty's performance, particularly the poor shooting of the battle cruisers, although he was most impressed by the accurate gunnery of Evan-Thomas's 5th Battle Squadron. He was also critical of important inaccuracies he had found in the *Narrative of the Battle of Jutland,* which tended to lend credence to Jellicoe's objections in the appendix.

By 1927 the controversy was beginning to die down, when Churchill weighed in with his version of Jutland and set it ablaze again. In a lengthy account of the battle in volume 3 of *The World Crisis,* he was severely critical of Jellicoe and strongly pro-Beatty. It was hardly surprising that Churchill was an ardent Beatty supporter, since he had chosen him to lead the battle cruisers in the first place, and to find fault would have reflected on his judgment. But his harsh treatment of Jellicoe was unexpected and upset the admiral considerably. It was somewhat ironic that Churchill should condemn Jellicoe for being overcautious in a book that contained his widely quoted remark that Jellicoe was the only man who could lose the war in an afternoon. Churchill apparently forgot that it was he, while he was First Lord of the Admiralty in 1914, who had fully approved Jellicoe's cautious tactical approach.

In writing about Jutland, Churchill had clearly based his account of the battle heavily on the condemned and suppressed *Naval Staff Appreciation*. His account was prejudiced, often inaccurate, and self-serving. In the fashion of an armchair admiral, Churchill did not allow for the fact that he had information and charts to hand, and plenty of time to study them, none of which were available to Jellicoe or the other admirals during the battle.

The book provoked an immediate and angry response from Jellicoe supporters, first in letters to the newspapers and, within the year, in a book. The latter was compiled by Lord Sydenham and titled *The World Crisis by Winston Churchill: A Criticism*. The section on Jutland was written by Bacon, whose critique was biting. Churchill's version of Jutland has since been widely criticized by historians for its inaccuracies, distortion, and prejudice, but its shortcomings have been partly excused by some historians because of Churchill's magnificent literary style, although as Robin Prior remarked, "he does seem to have his knife into Admiral Jellicoe."

The same year, there were two more publications on Jutland. According to Bennett, "Taken together these two documents did much to cut rival arguments down to size; at last, a decade after the war, it seemed possible to make an objective evaluation of the battle." The first of these was a book by Harper entitled *The Truth about Jutland*. In it he described the preparation of the Harper Record and the battle itself. Although his commentary on Jutland was decidedly pro-Jellicoe, his criticisms of Beatty were remarkably restrained. Harper was much more critical of authors such as Young, Pollen, Bellairs, and Churchill, whom he castigated for misrepresentation of the facts and suppression of important details.

The day before Harper's book came out, it was announced in the House of Commons that the Harper Record was to be published "as originally compiled, without any amendment." As with previous government statements, this proved to be less than forthright. Madden, who had replaced Beatty as First Sea Lord, authorized publication, but when the *Reproduction of the Record of the Battle of Jutland* appeared, it was not exactly as "originally compiled." While there were only minor changes to the text, the document had been emasculated by removal of the maps and diagrams. These had been omitted apparently to "save expense"!

By now public interest in the controversy had waned. Apart from the protagonists and their supporters, most people had wearied of the argument, and the Harper Record made little public impact. In Winton's words, it was "greeted with a great roar of uninterest."

It was to be even longer before the so-called Harper Papers were made available to the public and revealed the full details of the preparation of the record. These documents were the notes and proofs of the original text and diagrams, along with Beatty's marginal notations and alterations, Jellicoe's objections to the proposed changes, Beatty's preface, and the Admiralty minutes concerning the dispute. They revealed in detail Beatty's attempts to manipulate the record to conceal the battle cruisers' poor gunnery in the early phases, and to magnify its part in the ensuing fleet action. Harper had entrusted these documents to the Royal United Institution under seal, but for some reason they were not released to the public until forty years after the Harper committee had completed its work! They are now in the British Library.

At first, the pro-Beatty forces appeared to have won the paper battle over what had happened at Jutland. They were more numerous, and for the most part had the press on their side. From the onset of the controversy, the pro-Jellicoe forces were put on the defensive, and most of their criticisms of Beatty sprang from what they saw as misrepresentation of the respective contributions of the battle cruiser fleet and the battle fleet, and their anger over unwarranted attacks on Jellicoe. Most of the pro-Jellicoe books and articles were written in reaction—or, rather, overreaction—to the works of authors such as Bellairs, Pollen, and Young. However intemperate or biased their treatment of Beatty and the battle cruisers, this was largely provoked by Beattyite attempts—aided by the press—to propagate what they considered to be a distorted view of the battle.

Another thing that had rankled was the inequity of the government's recognition of the two admirals after the war. Beatty was created an earl, Jellicoe merely a viscount. As an illustration of the difference, Field Marshal Haig, who had led the British forces in France, became an earl, while Allenby in what was by comparison a sideshow in the Middle East was made a viscount. Parliament also voted Beatty a gratuity of one hundred thousand pounds, while Jellicoe received only fifty thousand pounds. In the public mind these differences were taken as the official evaluation of the relative merits of the two admirals. Later, after reassessments of Jutland, the government came to appreciate Jellicoe's great contributions during the war, and they acknowledged the injustice done to him by belatedly equalizing the honors. On Jellicoe's return from New Zealand in 1925, he too was made an earl.

Following Corbett's death, the *Naval Operations* series was completed by Sir Henry Newbolt, and in 1940 he published a revised edition of volume 3. Newbolt was allowed unrestricted use of all official information on Jutland, including the secret intelligence operations of Room 40. The "new" edition revealed for the first time the consequences of crucial Admiralty signaling errors and failures to pass on vital information during the battle. This completed the story of what had happened at Jutland and why. Even after all this time—seventeen years after Corbett's first edition—the Admiralty still added a formal disclaimer, prominent on the first page, although it was toned down by omitting the second paragraph of the one that appeared in the first edition. But by 1940 everyone was much more concerned with what was happening in Europe than what had occurred in the North Sea in 1916, and Newbolt's book made little impact. The once bitter Jutland controversy was over, and the flood of books, articles, and correspondence about the battle slowed to a trickle.

The fuss over the preparation of the Harper Record and the divisiveness it produced was an inglorious episode in the long and illustrious history of the Royal Navy. The dispute arose in large measure because of one man's pride and sensitivity to criticism. The ensuing row was exacerbated and unnecessarily prolonged by the Admiralty's inept handling of the situation, coupled with its unwillingness to admit any responsibility for the disappointing outcome of the battle. But in the end its overzealous protectiveness of its reputation and authority only succeeded in lowering its esteem in the eyes of many naval officers.

Long after World War II, interest in Jutland revived, at least among naval historians. As time went by, more balanced and straightforward narratives by Bennett, Hough, Irving, Macintyre, Marder, Roskill, and Winton helped to put the battle in clearer perspective. Even so, attempts to give an impartial treatment were sometimes condemned as being either too pro-Jellicoe or too pro-Beatty by admirers of one side or the other.

The controversy may have died out, but debate still persisted. It even spawned a second-order controversy in the 1980s between Roskill and Marder over their interpretations of the battle. Marder was perceived as being pro-Jellicoe, and Roskill as pro-Beatty, although in his 1966 book Marder had claimed to be neither. As he expressed it in the preface, "There has been altogether too much passion and bias in the 'Jutland Controversy,' more particularly as regards the two British principals. Montagus and Capulets still abound. I am myself neither."

The battle was obviously still capable of generating strong feelings and abiding loyalties.

None of this changes the basic facts or results of Jutland. Nor do intangibles such as unsupported statements about the abilities or talents of one admiral or another, and justifications or rationalizations of their actions. All that matters in the end is what they actually achieved. Too much weight has also been given to the many memorable comments— made by Beatty or about him—that have been quoted endlessly, and are now immortalized in the naval literature. To the average man in the street, these are often the only things they can recall about Jutland. However irrelevant these quotes may be to a serious evaluation of the outcome of the battle, they are remarkably pervasive and influential.

Myths that were largely created by the popular press and nurtured by acolytes have also proved surprisingly durable. This can be demonstrated by citing a recent review of Gordon's book about the naval command at Jutland, titled *The Rules of the Game,* published as late as 1996. While the book itself was thoroughly researched, carefully written, and well balanced, the review was neither. The article (*Sunday Times,* 22 September 1996) was headed "Something wrong with our bloody ships"— what else?

The reviewer concluded that

> Admiral Jellicoe's Grand Fleet was barely engaged, was not struck by a single shell and suffered only two dead and five wounded from shrapnel.
>   Most of the fighting . . . was between the subordinate Battle Cruiser Fleet and elements of the High Seas Fleet.

It is nothing less than amazing that this canard is still being perpetuated eighty years after the battle. The facts remain that Jellicoe's battleships fired more heavy shells at the enemy in their two brief engagements than Beatty's battle cruisers did all day, and moreover scored nearly three times as many direct hits on the ships of the High Seas Fleet. Scheer's fleet may have only had to face the full might of Jellicoe's Grand Fleet for less than an hour altogether, but that was quite long enough for Scheer to decide never to risk it again.

Appendix 1

Details of British and German Dreadnoughts, 1914–1918

BRITISH BATTLESHIPS

Dreadnought (1906)
Displacement: 18,110 tons (21,845 full load). Dimensions: 527 x 82 x 31 feet (load). Speed: 21 knots. Armor: belt, 11–4 inches; decks, 3–1.5 inches. Armament: 10–12 inch. Complement: 695–773.

Bellerophon class (1909)
(*Bellerophon, Superb, Téméraire*)
Displacement: 18,800 tons (22,102 full load). Dimensions: 526 x 82.5 x 27 feet. Speed: 21 knots. Armor: belt, 10–5 inches; decks, 4–0.5 inches. Armament: 10–12 inch; 16–4 inch. Complement: 732.

St. Vincent class (1908–9)
(*Collingwood, St. Vincent, Vanguard*)
Displacement: 19,650 tons (23,030 full load). Dimensions: 536 x 84 x 28 feet. Speed: 21 knots. Armor: belt, 10–7 inches; decks, 3–0.75 inches. Armament: 10–12 inch; 20–4 inch. Complement: 718.

Neptune (1911)
Displacement: 19,680 tons (22,720 full load). Dimensions: 546 x 85 x 28.5 feet. Speed: 21 knots. Armor: belt, 10–2.5 inches; decks, 3–0.75 inches. Armament: 10–12 inch; 16–4 inch. Complement: 759.

Colossus class (1911)
(Colossus, Hercules)
Displacement: 20,255 tons (23,050 full load). Dimensions: 546 x 85 x 29 feet. Speed: 21 knots. Armor: belt, 11-7 inches; decks, 4-1.75 inches. Armament: 10-12 inch; 16-4 inch. Complement: 755.

Orion class (1912)
(Conqueror, Monarch, Orion, Thunderer)
Displacement: 22,200 tons (25,870 full load). Dimensions: 581 x 88.5 x 25 feet. Speed: 21 knots. Armor: belt, 12-8 inches; decks, 4-1 inches. Armament: 10-13.5 inch; 16-4 inch. Complement: 752.

King George V class (1911-12)
(King George V, Centurion, Audacious, Ajax)
Displacement: 23,000 tons (25,700 full load). Dimensions: 597.5 x 89 x 29 feet. Speed: 21 knots. Armor: belt, 12-8 inches; decks, 4-1 inches. Armament: 10-13.5 inch; 16-4 inch. Complement: 782.

Iron Duke class (1914)
(Iron Duke, Marlborough, Benbow, Emperor of India)
Displacement: 25,000 tons (29,560 full load). Dimensions: 622 x 90 x 29.5 feet. Speed: 21.25 knots. Armor: belt, 12-4 inches; decks, 2.5-1 inches. Armament: 10-13.5 inch; 12-6 inch. Complement: 995-1,022.

Queen Elizabeth class (1915-16)
(Queen Elizabeth, Warspite, Valiant, Barham, Malaya)
Displacement: 27,500 tons (31,500 full load). Dimensions: 646 x 90.5 x 29 feet. Speed: 23 knots. Armor: belt, 13-6 inches; decks, 3-1 inches. Armament: 8-15 inch; 14 or 16-6 inch. Complement: 925-991.

Royal Sovereign class (1916-17)
(Ramillies, Resolution, Revenge, Royal Oak, Royal Sovereign)
Displacement: 28,000 tons (31,000 full load). Dimensions: 624 x 88.5 x 28.5 feet. Speed: 23 knots. Armor: belt, 13-1 inches: decks, 2-1 inches. Armament: 8-15 inch; 14-6 inch. Complement: 908-977.

Erin (1914)
Displacement: 22,780 tons (25,250 full load). Dimensions: 559.5 x 92 x 28.5 feet. Speed: 21 knots. Armor: belt, 12-4 inches; decks, 3-1.5 inches. Armament: 10-13.5 inch; 16-6 inch. Complement: 1,070.

Agincourt (1914)
Displacement: 27,500 tons (30,250 full load). Dimensions: 671.5 x 89 x 27 feet. Speed: 22 knots. Armor: belt, 9-4 inches; decks, 2.5-1 inches. Armament: 14-12 inch; 20-6 inch. Complement: 1,115.

Canada (1915)
Displacement: 28,600 tons (32,120 full load). Dimensions: 661 x 92 x 29 feet. Speed: 22.75 knots. Armor: belt, 9-4 inches; decks, 4-1 inches. Armament: 10-14 inch; 16-6 inch. Complement: 1,167.

GERMAN BATTLESHIPS

Nassau class (1910)
(*Nassau, Westfalen, Rheinland, Posen*)
Displacement: 18,750 tons (21,000 full load). Dimensions: 479 x 88.5 x 26.5 feet. Speed: 19.5 knots. Armor: belt, 11-3.1 inches; decks, 3.1-1.5 inches. Armament: 12-11 inch; 12-5.9 inch. Complement: 1,008-1,139.

Helgoland class (1911-12)
(*Helgoland, Ostfriesland, Thüringen, Oldenburg*)
Displacement: 22,440 tons (25,200 full load). Dimensions: 549 x 93.5 x 27 feet. Speed: 20.3 knots. Armor: belt, 11.8-3.1 inches; decks, 3.1-1 inches. Armament: 12 12-inch; 14-5.9 inch. Complement: 1,113-1,390.

Kaiser class (1911-12)
(*Kaiser, Friedrich der Grosse, Kaiserin, König, Prinzregent Luitpold*)
Displacement: 24,330 tons (27,400 full load). Dimensions: 566 x 95 x 27 feet. Speed: 21 knots. Armor: belt, 13.8-3.1 inches; decks, 4.7-1 inches. Armament: 10-12 inch; 14-5.9 inch. Complement: 1,084-1,278.

König class (1913-14)
(*König, Grosser Kurfürst, Markgraf, Kronprinz*)
Displacement: 25,390 tons (29,200 full load), Dimensions: 575.5 x 97 x 27 feet. Speed: 21 knots. Armor: belt, 13.8-3.1 inches; decks, 4.7-1.2 inches. Armament: 10-12 inch; 14-5.9 inch. Complement: 1,136-1,315.

Bayern class (1916-17)
(*Bayern, Baden*)
Displacement: 28,074 (31,690 full load). Dimensions: 590 x 98 x 28 feet. Speed: 21 knots. Armor: belt, 13.8-4.7 inches; decks, 4.7-1.6 inches. Armament: 8-15 inch; 16-5.9 inch. Complement: 1,187-1,221.

BRITISH BATTLE CRUISERS

Invincible class (1908–9)
(*Indomitable, Inflexible, Invincible*)
Displacement: 17,373 tons (20,078 full load). Dimensions: 567 x 78.5 x 26 feet. Speed: 25.5 knots. Armor: belt, 6–4 inches; decks, 2.5–0.75 inches. Armament: 8–12 inch; 16–4 inch. Complement: 784–1,027.

Indefatigable class (1911–13)
(*Indefatigable, Australia, New Zealand*)
Displacement: 18,500 tons (22,110 full load). Dimensions: 590 x 80 x 26.5 feet. Speed: 25 knots. Armor: belt, 6–4 inches; decks, 2.5–1 inches. Armament: 8–12 inch; 16–4 inch. Complement: 800–1,019.

Lion (1912)
Displacement: 26,270 tons (29,680 full load). Dimensions: 700 x 88.5 x 28 feet. Speed: 27 knots. Armor: belt, 9–4 inches; decks, 2.5–1 inches. Armament: 8–13.5 inch; 16–4 inch. Complement: 997.

Queen Mary (1913)
Displacement: 26,770 tons (31,650 full load). Dimensions: 703.5 x 89 x 28 feet. Speed: 27.5 knots. Armor: belt, 9–4 inches; decks, 2.5–1 inches. Armament: 8–13.5 inch; 16–4 inch. Complement: 997–1,274.

Tiger (1914)
Displacement: 28,430 tons (35,710 full load). Dimensions: 704 x 90.5 x 28.5 feet. Speed: 28 knots. Armor: belt, 9–3 inches; decks, 3–1 inches. Armament: 8–13.5 inch; 12–6 inch. Complement: 1,121.

Renown class (1916)
(*Renown, Repulse*)
Displacement: 27,650 tons (30,835 full load). Dimensions: 794 x 90 x 25.6 feet. Speed: 31.5 knots. Armor: belt, 6–1.5 inches; decks, 3–0.5 inches. Complement: 999–1,016.

GERMAN BATTLE CRUISERS

Von der Tann (1911)
Displacement: 19,064 tons (21,750 full load). Dimensions: 563 x 87 x 26.5 feet. Speed: 24.75 knots. Armor: belt, 9.8–3.1 inches; decks, 3.1–1 inches. Armament: 8–11 inch; 10–5.9 inch. Complement: 923–1,174.

Moltke class (1912)
(*Moltke, Goeben*)
Displacement: 22,616 tons (25,300 full load). Dimensions: 612 x 97 x 29 feet. Speed: 25.5 knots. Armor: belt, 10.6–3.9 inches; decks, 3.1–1 inches. Armament: 10–11 inch; 12–5.9 inch. Complement: 1,053–1,355.

Seydlitz (1913)
Displacement: 24,594 tons (28,100 full load). Dimensions: 658 x 93.5 x 27 feet. Speed: 26.5 knots. Armor: belt, 11.8–3.9 inches; decks, 3.1–1.2 inches. Armament: 10–11 inch; 12–5.9 inch. Complement: 1,068–1,425.

Derfflinger class (1914–16)
(*Derfflinger, Lützow*)
Displacement: 26,180–26,318 tons (30,700 full load). Dimensions: 690 x 95 x 27 feet. Speed: 26.5 knots. Armor: belt, 11.8–3.9 inches; decks, 3.1–0.8 inches. Armament: 8–12 inch; 12–5.9 inch. Complement: 1,112–1,391.

Hindenburg (1917)
Displacement: 26,513 tons (31,000 full load). Dimensions: 698 x 95 x 27 feet. Speed: 27.5 knots. Armor: belt, 11.8–3.9 inches; decks, 3.1–0.8 inches. Armament: 8–12 inch; 14–5.9 inch. Complement: 1,182.

Notes: The dates for each class are those in which the ships were completed for service. In most cases, the vessels were launched in the preceding year and laid down the year before that. The first displacement given is the so-called normal figure. Those in parentheses are the displacements when the vessel was fully loaded with fuel, ammunition, charges, and so on. The dimensions listed are the overall (not waterline) length, the beam, and the mean draft, except where noted. The speeds listed are the designed speeds attained at maximum shaft horsepower; these were sometimes exceeded by forcing the engines.

The thickness of armor provided for the turret faces, barbettes, bulkheads, and conning tower varied considerably but was close to the range given for the belt armor. Where two figures are listed for the ship's complement, the higher one is the number of crew present at Jutland.

Appendix 2

The Organization of the Fleets at Jutland

THE BATTLE FLEET
(in order from van to rear)

2d Battle Squadron
1st Division
    King George V; Capt. F. L. Field (flagship of Vice-Adm. Sir M. Jerram)
    Ajax; Capt. G. H. Baird
    Centurion; Capt. M. Culme-Seymour
    Erin; Capt. the Hon. V. A. Stanley
2d Division
    Orion; Capt. O. Backhouse (flagship of Rear-Adm. A. C. Leveson)
    Monarch; Capt. G. H. Borrett
    Conqueror; Capt. H. H. D. Tothill
    Thunderer; Capt. J. A. Fergusson

4th Battle Squadron
3d Division
    Iron Duke; Capt. F. C. Dreyer (flagship of Adm. Sir John Jellicoe)
    Royal Oak; Capt. C. MacLachlan
    Superb; Capt. E. Hyde-Parker (flagship of Rear-Adm. A. L. Duff)
    Canada; Capt. W. C. M. Nicholson
4th Division
    Benbow; Capt. H. W. Parker (flagship of Vice-Adm. Sir Doveton Sturdee)
    Bellerophon; Capt. E. F. Bruen
    Téméraire; Capt. E. V. Underhill
    Vanguard; Capt. J. D. Dick

1st Battle Squadron
6th Division
　　Marlborough; Capt. G. P. Ross (flagship of Vice-Adm. Sir C. Burney)
　　Revenge; Capt. E. B. Kiddle
　　Hercules; Capt. L. Clinton-Baker
　　Agincourt; Capt. H. M. Doughty
5th Division
　　Colossus; Capt. A. D. P. R. Pound (flagship of Rear-Adm. E. F. A. Gaunt)
　　Collingwood; Capt. J. C. Ley
　　Neptune; Capt. V. H. G. Bernard
　　St. Vincent; Capt. W. W. Fisher

3d Battle Cruiser Squadron
Invincible; Capt. A. L. Cay (flagship of Rear-Adm. the Hon. Horace Hood)
Inflexible; Capt. E. F. H. Heaton-Ellis
Indomitable; Capt. F. W. Kennedy

1st Cruiser Squadron (armored cruisers)
Defence; Capt. S. V. Ellis (flagship of Rear-Adm. Sir Robert Arbuthnot)
Warrior; Capt. V. B. Molteno
Duke of Edinburgh; Capt. H. Blackett
Black Prince; Capt. T. P. Bonham

2d Cruiser Squadron (armored cruisers)
Minotaur; Capt. A. C. S. H d'Aeth (flagship of Rear-Adm. H. L. Heath)
Hampshire; Capt. H. J. Savill
Cochrane; Capt. E. la T. Leatham
Shannon; Capt. J. S. Dumaresq

4th Light Cruiser Squadron
Calliope; Commodore C. E. LeMesurier
Constance; Capt. C. S. Townsend
Caroline; Capt. H. R. Crooke
Royalist; Capt. the Hon. H. R. Meade
Comus; Capt. A. G. Hotham

Attached Cruisers (chiefly as signal-repeating ships)
Active; Capt. P. Withers
Bellona; Capt. A. B. S. Dutton
Blanche; Capt. J. M. Casement
Boadicea; Capt. L. C. S. Woollcombe
Canterbury; Capt. P. M. R. Royds
Chester; Capt. R. N. Lawson

Destroyers
4th Destroyer Flotilla
Flotilla leader *Tipperary* (Capt. C. J. Wintour), *Acasta, Achates, Ambuscade, Ardent, Broke, Christopher, Contest, Fortune, Garland, Hardy, Midge, Ophelia, Owl, Porpoise, Shark, Sparrowhawk, Spitfire, Unity.*
11th Destroyer Flotilla
Flotilla leader *Castor* (light cruiser) (Commodore J. R. P. Hawksley), *Kempenfelt, Magic, Mandate, Manners, Marne, Martial, Michael, Milbrook, Minion, Mons, Moon, Morning Star, Mounsey, Mystic, Ossory.*
12th Destroyer Flotilla
Flotilla leader *Faulknor* (Capt. A. J. B. Stirling), *Maenad, Marksman, Marvel, Mary Rose, Menace, Mindful, Mischief, Munster, Narwhal, Nessus, Noble, Nonsuch, Obedient, Onslaught, Opal.*

Other Attached Ships
Abdiel (minelayer)
Oak (destroyer tender to fleet flagship)

THE BATTLE CRUISER FLEET
(in order from van to rear)

Lion; Capt. A. E. Chatfield (flagship of Vice-Adm. Sir David Beatty)

1st Battle Cruiser Squadron
Princess Royal; Capt. W. H. Cowan (flagship of Rear-Adm. O. deB. Brock)
Queen Mary; Capt. C. I. Prowse
Tiger; Capt. H. B. Pelly

2d Battle Cruiser Squadron
New Zealand; Capt. J. F. E. Green (flagship of Rear-Adm. W. C. Pakenham)
Indefatigable; Capt. C. F. Sowerby

5th Battle Squadron (fast battleships)
Barham; Capt. A. W. Craig (flagship of Rear-Adm. Hugh Evan-Thomas)
Valiant; Capt. M. Woollcombe
Warspite; Capt. E. M. Philpotts
Malaya; Capt. A. D. E. H. Boyle

1st Light Cruiser Squadron
Galatea; Commodore E. S. Alexander-Sinclair
Phaeton; Capt. J. E. Cameron
Inconstant; Capt. B. S. Thesiger
Cordelia; Capt. T. P. H. Beamish

2d Light Cruiser Squadron
Southampton; Commodore W. E. Goodenough
Birmingham; Capt. A. A. M. Duff
Nottingham; Capt. C. B. Miller
Dublin; Capt. A. C. Scott

3d Light Cruiser Squadron
Falmouth; Capt. J. D. Edwards (flagship of Rear-Adm. T. D. W. Napier)
Yarmouth; Capt. T. D. Pratt
Birkenhead; Capt. E. Reeves
Gloucester; Capt. W. F. Blunt

Destroyers
1st Destroyer Flotilla
   Flotilla leader *Fearless* (light cruiser) (Capt. D. C. Roper), *Acheron, Ariel, Attack, Badger, Defender, Goshawk, Hydra, Lapwing, Lizard.*
9th and 10th Destroyer Flotilla
   Flotilla leader *Lydiard* (Cdr. M. L. Goldsmith), *Landrail, Laurel, Liberty, Moorsom, Morris, Termagant, Turbulent.*
13th Destroyer Flotilla
   Flotilla leader *Champion* (light cruiser) (Capt. J. U. Farie), *Moresby, Narborough, Nerissa, Nestor, Nicator, Nomad, Obdurate, Onslow, Pelican, Petard.*

Other Attached Ships
Engadine (seaplane carrier)

THE HIGH SEAS FLEET

THE BATTLE FLEET
(in order from van to rear)

3d Battle Squadron
5th Division
   König; Capt. Brüninghaus (flagship of Rear Adm. Paul Behncke)
   Grosser Kurfürst; Capt. E. Goette
   Kronprinz; Capt. C. Feldt
   Markgraf; Capt. Seiferling
6th Division
   Kaiser; Capt. Freiherr von Keyserlingk (flagship of Rear Adm. H. Nordmann)
   Kaiserin; Captain Sievers
   Prinzregent Luitpold; Capt. K. Heuser
   Friedrich der Grosse; Capt. T. Fuchs (flagship of Vice Adm. Reinhard Scheer)

1st Battle Squadron
1st Division
Ostfriesland; Captain von Natzmer (flagship of Vice Adm. E. Schmidt)
Thüringen; Capt. H. Küsel
Helgoland; Captain von Kameke
Oldenburg; Captain Höpfner
2d Division
Posen; Capt. R. Lange (flagship of Rear Adm. W. Engelhardt)
Rheinland; Captain Rohardt
Nassau; Capt. H. Klappenbach
Westfalen; Captain Redlich

2d Battle Squadron
3d Division
Deutschland; Capt. H. Meurer (flagship of Rear Adm. Franz Mauve)
Hessen; Capt. R. Bartels
Pommern; Captain Bölken
4th Division
Hannover; Capt. W. Heine (flagship of Rear Adm. Freiherr von Dalwigk zu Lichtenfels)
Schlesien; Capt. F. Behncke
Schleswig Holstein; Captain Barrentrapp

4th Scouting Group (light cruisers)
Stettin; Capt. F. Rebensburg (broad pendant of Commodore L. von Reuter)
München; Capt. O. Böcker
Hamburg; Captain von Gaudecker
Frauenlob; Capt. G. Hoffmann
Stuttgart; Capt. Hagedorn

Torpedo Boats
Regensburg (light cruiser); Capt. O. Feldmann (broad pendant of Commodore A. Michelsen)

1st Torpedo Boat Flotilla (half flotilla)
Flotilla leader *G39* (Cdr. C. Albrecht), *G40, G38, S32*

3d Torpedo Boat Flotilla
Flotilla leader *S53* (Cdr. Hollmann), *V71, V73, G88, S54, V48, G42.*

5th Torpedo Boat Flotilla
Flotilla leader *G11* (Cdr. Heinecke), *V2, V4, V6, V1, V3, G8, G7, V5, G9, G10.*

7th Torpedo Boat Flotilla
Flotilla leader *S24* (Commander von Koch), *S15, S17, S20, S16, S18, S19, S23, V189.*

THE BATTLE CRUISER FORCE

1st Scouting Group
Lützow; Captain Harder (flagship of Vice Adm. Franz Hipper)
Derfflinger; Captain Hartog
Seydlitz; Capt. M. von Egidy
Moltke; Captain von Karpf
Von der Tann; Capt. W. Zenker

2d Scouting Group
Light Cruisers
Frankfurt; Capt. T. von Trotha (flagship of Rear Adm. F. Boedicker)
Wiesbaden; Captain Reiss
Pillau; Capt. K. Mommsen
Elbing; Captain Madlung
Torpedo Boats
Regensburg (light cruiser); Captain Heuberer (broad pendant of Commodore P. Heinrich)

2d Torpedo Boat Flotilla
Flotilla leader *B98* (Captain Schuur), *G101, G102, B112, B97, B109, B110, B111, G103, G104.*

6th Torpedo Boat Flotilla
Flotilla leader *G41* (Cdr. M. Schultz), *V44, G87, G86, V9, V45, V46, S50, G37.*

9th Torpedo Boat Flotilla
Flotilla leader *V28* (Commander Goehle), *V27, V26, S36, S52, V30, S34, S33, V29, S35.*

Appendix 3

British Casualties at Jutland

Destroyers

SHIP	KILLED	WOUNDED	TAKEN PRISONER	TOTAL
Acasta	6	1	—	7
*Ardent**	78	1	—	79
Broke	47	36	—	83
Defender	1	2	—	3
*Fortune**	67	2	—	69
Moorsom	—	1	—	1
Nessus	7	7	—	14
*Nestor**	6	8	80	94
*Nomad**	8	4	72	84
Obdurate	1	1	—	2
Onslaught	5	3	—	8
Onslow	2	3	—	5
Petard	9	6	—	15
Porpoise	2	2	—	4
*Shark**	86	3	—	89
*Sparrowhawk**	—	6	—	6
Spitfire	6	20	—	26
*Tipperary**	185	4	8	197
*Turbulent**	96	—	13	109
Total	612	110	173	895

*Indicates a ship or boat that was sunk.

Battleships

SHIP	KILLED	WOUNDED	TAKEN PRISONER	TOTAL
Barham	26	46	—	72
Colossus	—	9	—	9
Malaya	63	68	—	131
Marlborough	2	2	—	4
Valiant	—	1	—	1
Warspite	14	32	—	46
Total	105	158	—	263

Battle cruisers

SHIP	KILLED	WOUNDED	TAKEN PRISONER	TOTAL
Indefatigable*	1,017	—	2	1,019
Invincible*	1,026	1	—	1,027
Lion	99	51	—	150
Princess Royal	22	81	—	103
Queen Mary*	1,266	6	2	1,274
Tiger	24	46	—	70
Total	3,454	185	4	3,643

Armored cruisers

SHIP	KILLED	WOUNDED	TAKEN PRISONER	TOTAL
Black Prince*	857	—	—	857
Defence*	903	—	—	903
Warrior*	71	36	—	107
Total	1,831	36	—	1,867

Light cruisers

SHIP	KILLED	WOUNDED	TAKEN PRISONER	TOTAL
Calliope	10	29	—	39
Caroline	2	—	—	2
Castor	13	26	—	39
Chester	29	49	—	78
Dublin	3	27	—	30
Southampton	29	60	—	89
Total	96	191	—	277
Totals	**6,088**	**680**	**177**	**6,945**

Appendix 4

German Casualties at Jutland

Torpedo boats

VESSEL	KILLED	WOUNDED	TOTAL
B98	2	11	13
G40	1	2	3
G41	—	5	5
G86	1	7	8
G87	1	5	6
S32	3	1	4
S35*	88	—	88
S36	—	4	4
S51	—	3	3
S52	1	1	2
V4*	18	4	22
V27*	—	1	1
V29*	33	4	37
V48*	90	—	90
Total	238	48	286

*Indicates a ship or boat that was sunk.

Battleships

VESSEL	KILLED	WOUNDED	TOTAL
Grosser Kurfürst	15	10	25
Kaiser	—	1	1
König	45	27	72
Markgraf	11	13	24
Nassau	11	16	27
Oldenburg	8	14	22
Ostfriesland	1	10	11
Pr.Luitpold	—	11	11
Pommern*	844	—	844
Rheinland	10	20	30
Schlesien	1	—	1
Schleswig Holstein	3	9	12
Westfalen	2	8	10
Total	951	139	1,090

Battle cruisers

VESSEL	KILLED	WOUNDED	TOTAL
Derfflinger	157	26	183
Lützow*	115	50	165
Moltke	17	23	40
Seydlitz	98	55	153
Von der Tann	11	35	46
Total	398	189	587

Light cruisers

VESSEL	KILLED	WOUNDED	TOTAL
Elbing*	4	12	16
Frankfurt	3	18	21
Frauenlob*	320	1	321
München	8	20	28
Pillau	4	19	23
Rostock*	14	6	20
Stettin	8	28	36
Wiesbaden*	589	—	589
Total	964	129	1,093
Totals	**2,551**	**505**	**3,056**

Appendix 5

Gunnery Results at Jutland

Heavy-Shell Hits Obtained by British Capital Ships

Target Vessel	1st and 2d BCS	3d BCS	5th BS	1st, 2d, and 4th BS	Total Hits
BATTLE CRUISERS					
Lützow	7	8	4	5	24
Derfflinger	1	3	3	14	21
Seydlitz	9	1	7	5	22
Moltke	1	—	4	—	5
Von der Tann	2	—	1	1	4
BATTLESHIPS					
König	—	—	1	9	10
Grosser Kurfürst	—	—	5	3	8
Markgraf	—	—	3	2	5
Kaiser	—	—	—	2	2
Helgoland	—	—	1	—	1
Pommern	—	1	—	—	1
Schleswig-Holstein	1	—	—	—	1
CRUISERS					
Wiesbaden	—	2	—	13	15[*]
Pillau	—	1	—	—	1
TORPEDO BOATS					
G86	—	—	—	1	1
S35	—	—	—	2	2
Total hits	21	16	29	57	123
Total hits on capital ships	21	13	29	41	104

Note: Heavy shells are defined as 12-, 13.5- and 15-inch shells. BCS = Battle Cruiser Squadron; BS = Battle Squadron.
[*] An estimate.

Summary of British Gunnery Results

Squadrons	Heavy Shells Fired	Hits	Percentage of Hits	Shells per Hit
1st and 2d BCS	1,469	21	1.43	70
3d BCS	373*	16	4.3	23
5th BS	1,099	29	2.64	38
1st, 2d, and 4th BS	1,593	57	3.58	27
All British capital ships	4,534	123	2.71	37
(excluding 1st and 2d BCS)	(3,065)	(102)	(3.33)	(30)

Note: BCS = Battle Cruiser Squadron; BS = Battle Squadron.
*An estimate.

Heavy shell hits obtained by German capital ships

Target Vessel	By 1st SG	By 1st, 2d, and 3d BS	Total Hits
BATTLE CRUISERS			
Lion	13	—	13
Princess Royal	6	3	9
Queen Mary	7*	—	7
Tiger	15	—	15
New Zealand	1	—	1
Indefatigable	5*	—	5
Invincible	5*	—	5
BATTLESHIPS			
Barham	6	—	6
Warspite	2	13	15
Malaya	—	7	7
Colossus	2	—	2
CRUISERS			
Defence	3	4	7
Warrior	—	15	15
Black Prince	—	12	12
Southampton	—	1	1
DESTROYERS			
Marvel	—	1	1
Defender	—	1	1
Total hits	65	57	122
Total hits on capital ships	62	23	85

Note: Heavy shells are defined as 11- and 12-inch shells. SG = Scouting Group; BS = Battle Squadron.
*An estimate.

Summary of German Gunnery Results

Squadrons	Heavy Shells Fired	Hits	Percentage of Hits	Shells per Hit
1st SG	1,670	65	3.89	26
1st, 2d, and 3d BS	1,927	57	2.96	34
All German capital ships	3,597	122	3.39	29
(excluding hits on *Black Prince*)	3,570*	110	3.08	32

Note: SG = Scouting Group; BS = Battle Squadron.
*An estimate.

Bibliography

Bacon, Reginald Hugh Spencer. *The Jutland Scandal.* London: Hutchinson, 1925.
———. *The Life of John Rushworth, Earl Jellicoe.* London: Cassell, 1936.
———. *The Life of Lord Fisher of Kilverstone, Admiral of the Fleet.* Vols. 1 and 2. London: Hodder and Stoughton, 1929.
———. *Modern Naval Strategy.* London: F. Muller, 1941.
Barnett, Correlli. *The Swordbearers: Studies in Supreme Command.* London: Eyre and Spottiswoode, 1963.
Bassett, Ronald. *Battlecruisers: A History, 1908–1948.* London: Macmillan, 1981.
Baynham, Henry. *Men from the Dreadnoughts.* London: Hutchinson, 1976.
Beatty, Charles. *The Beatty Papers.* Edited by B. McL. Ranft. Aldershot, England: Navy Records Society, 1989.
———. *Our Admiral: A Biography of Admiral of the Fleet, Earl Beatty.* London: W. H. Allen, 1980.
Beesly, Patrick. *Room 40: British Naval Intelligence 1914–1918.* London: Hamish Hamilton, 1988.
Bellairs, Carlyon Wilfroy. *The Battle of Jutland: The Sowing and the Reaping.* London: Hodder and Stoughton, 1920.
Bennett, Geoffrey M. *The Battle of Jutland.* London: Batsford, 1964.
———. *Naval Battles of the First World War.* London: Pan Books, 1974.
Berghahn, V. *Der Tirpitz-Plan.* Dusseldorf: Droste Verlag, 1971.
Bernadac, Christian. *La Kriegsmarine.* Paris: Éditions France-Empire, 1983.
Bingham, Barry. *Falklands, Jutland and the Bight.* London: John Murray, 1919.
Breyer, Siegfried. *Battleships and Battlecruisers.* London: Macdonald and Jane's, 1973.
———. *Battleships of the World, 1905–1970.* New York: Mayflower Books, 1980.
Breyer, Siegfried, and Gerhard Koop. *Von der "Emden" zur "Tirpitz."* Bonn: Wehr und Wissen, 1981.
Bruce, George. *Sea Battles of the Twentieth Century.* London: Hamlyn, 1975.
Burt, R. A. *British Battleships of World War One.* Annapolis, Md.: Naval Institute Press, 1986.
Busch, Fritz Otto. *Die Seeschlacht am Skagerrak.* Leipzig: Schneider, 1933.
Campbell, N. J. M. *Battlecruisers: The Design and Development of British and German Battlecruisers of the First World War Era.* Greenwich, England: Conway Maritime Press, 1978.

————. *Jutland: An Analysis of the Fighting.* London: Conway Maritime Press, 1986.

Chack, P., and J. L. Antier. *Histoire maritime de la Premiere Guerre Mondiale.* Paris: Éditions France-Empire, 1969.

Chalmers, William Scott. *The Life and Letters of David, Earl Beatty, Admiral of the Fleet.* London: Hodder and Stoughton, 1951.

Chatfield, A. E. M. *The Navy and Defence: The Autobiography of Admiral of the Fleet, Lord Chatfield.* Vols. 1 and 2. London: Heinemann, 1942.

Churchill, Winston. *The World Crisis.* Vol. 3. London: Thornton Butterworth, 1927.

Corbett, Julian. *Official History of the War: Naval Operations.* Vols. 2 and 3. London: Longmans Green, 1920–1931. Reprint, vol. 3, London: Henry Newbolt, 1940.

Costello, John, and Terry Hughes. *Jutland, 1916.* London: Weidenfeld and Nicholson, 1976.

Cruttwell, C. R. M. F. *A History of the Great War, 1914–1918.* London: Grafton, 1982.

Dewar, K. G. B. *The Navy from Within.* London: Gollancz, 1939.

Dorwart, J. M. *The Office of Naval Intelligence.* Annapolis, Md.: Naval Institute Press, 1977.

Dreyer, Frederic. *The Sea Heritage: A Study of Maritime Warfare.* London: Museum Press, 1955.

Ewing, Alfred W. *The Man of Room 40: The Life of Sir Alfred Ewing.* London: Hutchinson, 1939.

Falls, Cyril Bentham. *The First World War.* London: Longmans, 1960.

Fawcett, Harold William, and G. W. W. Hooper, eds. *The Fighting at Jutland: The Personal Experiences of Forty-Five Officers and Men.* London: Macmillan, 1921.

Fisher, John Arbuthnot. *Fear God and Dread Nought.* London: Cape, 1952.

Freiwald, Ludwig. *The Last Days of the German Fleet.* London: Constable, 1932.

Frost, Holloway Halstead. *The Battle of Jutland.* Annapolis, Md.: Naval Institute Press, 1936.

Frothingham, T. G. *The Naval History of the World War.* Vol. 1, *1914–1915.* Freeport, N.Y.: Books for Libraries Press, 1924. Vol. 2, *1916–1918.* Cambridge: Harvard University Press, 1925.

George, Sidney Charles. *Jutland to Junkyard: The Raising of the Scuttled German High Seas Fleet from Scapa Flow.* Cambridge: Stephens, 1973.

Gibson, Langhorne, and J. E. T. Harper. *The Riddle of Jutland: An Authentic History.* New York: Coward-McCann, 1934.

Gilbert, Martin. *The Challenge of War: Winston S. Churchill, 1914–1916.* London: Minerva, 1971.

Goldrick, James. *The King's Ships Were at Sea: The War in the North Sea, August 1914–February 1915.* Annapolis, Md.: Naval Institute Press, 1984.

Gordon, Andrew. *The Rules of the Game: Jutland and British Naval Command.* London: John Murray, 1996.

Gröner, Erich. *Die deutschen Kriegschiffe, 1815–1945.* Band 1. Munich: Bernard and Graefe, 1982.

————. *German Warships, 1815–1945.* Annapolis, Md.: Naval Institute Press, 1990.

Groos, Otto. *Der Krieg in der Nordsee, January–June 1916.* Vol. 5, translated by W. T. Bagot. Berlin: E. S. Mittler, 1925.

Grove, Eric. *Fleet to Fleet Encounters: Tsushima, Jutland, Phillipine Sea*. London: Arms and Armour Press, 1991.

Halpern, Paul. *A Naval History of the First World War*. Annapolis, Md.: Naval Institute Press, 1993.

Hansen, Hans Jürgen. *The Ships of the German Fleets, 1848–1945*. London: Hamlyn, 1974.

Harper, J. E. T. *Reproduction of the Record of the Battle of Jutland*. London: H.M. Stationery Office, 1927.

———. *The Royal Navy at War*. London: J. Murray, 1941.

———. *The Truth about Jutland*. London: J. Murray, 1927.

Hase, Georg Oskar Immanuel von. *Die deutsche Sieg vor dem Skagerrak*. Leipzig: K. F. Koehler, 1926.

———. *Kiel and Jutland*. London: Skeffington and Son, 1921.

Herwig, Holger Heinrich. *The German Naval Officer Corps*. Oxford: Clarendon, 1973.

———. *The Luxury Fleet: The Imperial German Navy, 1888–1914*. London: Allen and Unwin, 1980.

Heydecker, Joe Julius. *Der Grosser Krieg 1914–1918*. Frankfurt am Main: Ullstein, 1988.

Hezlet, Arthur Richard. *The Electron and Sea-power*. London: Peter Davies, 1975.

Hildebrand, Hans Jürgen. *Die deutschen Kriegsschiffe: Biographen*. Herford: Koehler, 1979.

Hildebrand, Hans Jürgen, and Ernest Henriot. *Deutschlands Admirale 1849–1945*. Osnabruck: Biblio, 1988.

Hill, J. R., ed. *The Oxford Illustrated History of the Royal Navy*. Oxford: Oxford University Press, 1995.

Hodges, Peter. *The Big Gun: Battleship Main Armament, 1860–1945*. Greenwich, England: Conway, 1981.

Horn, Daniel, ed. *The German Naval Mutinies of World War I*. New Brunswick, N.J.: Rutgers University Press, 1969.

———. *War, Mutiny and Revolution in the German Navy: The World War I Diary of Seaman Richard Strumpf*. New Brunswick, N.J.: Rutgers University Press, 1969.

Hough, Richard. *The Battle of Jutland*. London: Hamish Hamilton, 1964.

———. *Dreadnought: A History of the Modern Battleship*. Cambridge: P. Stephens, 1975.

———. *First Sea Lord: An Authorized Biography of Admiral Lord Fisher*. London: Allen and Unwin 1969.

———. *Former Naval Person: Churchill and the Wars at Sea*. London: Weidenfeld and Nicholson, 1985.

———. *The Great War at Sea, 1914–1918*. Oxford: Oxford University Press, 1983.

Hurd, Archibald. *From Heligoland to Keeling Island; One Hundred Days of Naval War*. London: Hodder, 1914.

Hurd, Archibald, and Henry Castle. *German Sea Power*. London: Murray, 1913. Reprint, Westport, Conn.: Greenwood Press, 1971.

Irving, John James Cawdell. *The Smoke Screen of Jutland*. New York: D. McKay, 1967.

James, William M. *The Eyes of the Navy: A Biographical Study of Admiral Sir Reginald Hall.* London: Methuen, 1955.

Jameson, Sir William. *The Fleet that Jack Built: Nine Men Who Made a Modern Navy.* London: Hart Davies, 1962.

Jane, Fred T. *Jane's Fighting Ships.* London: S. Low, 1906–7, 1914, 1919.

Jellicoe, Sir John. *The Grand Fleet, 1914–1916: Its Creation, Development and Work.* New York: George H. Doran and Company, 1919.

————. *The Jellicoe Papers.* Edited by A. Temple Patterson. London: Navy Records Society, 1968.

Keegan, John. *A History of Warfare.* Toronto: Vintage Books, 1994.

————. *The Price of Admiralty.* London: Hutchinson, 1988.

Kennedy, Paul M. *The Rise and Fall of British Naval Mastery.* London: Fontana Press, 1991.

Der Krieg zur See, 1914–1918. Editor in chief, Adm. E. von Mantey. 6 vols. Berlin: Mittler and Sons, 1920–1937.

Kroschel, Gunter. *Die deutsche Flotte 1848–1945.* Wilhelmshaven: Lohse-Eissing, 1963.

Legg, Stuart, ed. *Jutland: An Eyewitness Account of a Great Battle.* London: Hart-Davis, 1966.

Liddle, Peter. *The Sailor's War, 1914–1918.* Poole, England: Blandford Press, 1985.

Liddell Hart, Basil. *History of the First World War.* London: Cassell, 1970.

Livesey, Anthony. *Great Battles of World War I.* New York: Macmillan, 1989.

Macintyre, Donald G. F. W. *Jutland.* London: Evans Brothers, 1957.

Marder, Arthur. *Fear God and Dread Nought: The Correspondence of Admiral Lord Fisher.* Vols. 1 and 3. London: Jonathan Cape, 1952, 1956, 1959.

————. *From the Dreadnought to Scapa Flow: The Royal Navy in the Fisher Era, 1904–1919.* Vols. 2 and 3. Oxford: Oxford University Press, 1978.

Massie, Robert K. *Dreadnought.* New York: Random House, 1991.

McMahon, William E. *Dreadnought Battleships and Battlecruisers.* Washington, D.C.: University Press of America, 1978.

Mirow, Jürgen. *Der Seekrieg im Umrissen.* Göttingen: Musterschmidt, 1976.

Morris, James (Jan). *Fisher's Face.* New York: Random House, 1995.

————. *Pax Britannica.* London: Faber, 1968.

Morton, Frederic. *Thunder at Twilight.* New York: Scribner, 1989.

Newbolt, Henry. *A Naval History of the War: 1914–1918.* London: Hodder and Stoughton, 1921.

No primary author. *Admiralty Documents: The Battle of Jutland. Official Despatches with Appendices.* London: H.M. Stationery Office, 1920.

————. *Conway's All the World's Battleships, 1906 to the Present.* Edited by Ian Sturton. Annapolis, Md.: Naval Institute Press, 1987.

————. *Conway's All the World's Fighting Ships, 1860–1905.* Annapolis, Md.: Naval Institute Press, 1979.

————. *Conway's All the World's Fighting Ships, 1906–1921.* Annapolis, Md.: Naval Institute Press, 1986.

————. *Fighting Ships of World Wars One and Two.* London: Peerage Books, 1986.

————. *Great Britain. Admiralty. Report of Admiral of the Fleet Viscount Jellicoe of Scapa . . .* N.p., 1919. Ottawa, Canada: Kings Printer, 1920.

———. *Jane's Fighting Ships of World War I.* London: Studio Editions, 1990.

———. *Narrative of the Battle of Jutland.* London: H.M. Stationery Office, 1924.

———. *Warships and Sea Battles of World War I.* London: Phoebus, 1973.

Padfield, Peter. *Aim Straight: A Biography of Admiral Sir Percy Scott.* London: Hodder and Stoughton, 1966.

———. *The Battleship Era.* London: D. McKay, 1972.

———. *Guns at Sea.* London: Hugh Evelyn, 1973.

Pastfield, J. L. *New Light on Jutland.* London: Heinemann, 1933.

Patterson, Alfred Temple. *Jellicoe: A Biography.* London: Macmillan, 1969.

Persius, Lothar. *Der Seekrieg; die Seekämpfe der deutschen Flotte im Weltkrieg.* Charlottenburg, Germany: Verlag der Weltbühne, 1919.

Philbin, Tobias R. *Admiral von Hipper, the Inconvenient Hero.* Amsterdam: Gruner, 1982.

Pollen, Anthony. *The Great Gunnery Scandal: The Mystery of Jutland.* London: Collins, 1980.

Pollen, Arthur J. H. *The Navy in Battle.* London: Chatto and Windus, 1919.

Rasor, Eugene. *The Battle of Jutland: A Bibliography.* New York: Greenwood Press, 1992.

Roskill, Stephen Wentworth. *Admiral of the Fleet Earl Beatty: The Last Naval Hero, an Intimate Biography.* London: Collins, 1980.

———. *Churchill and the Admirals.* London: Collins, 1977.

Scheer, Reinhard. *Deutschlands Hochseeflotte im Weltkrieg.* Berlin: August Scherl, 1920.

———. *Germany's High Seas Fleet in the World War.* London: Cassell, 1920.

Schoultz, G. von. *With the British Battle Fleet; War Recollections of a Russian Naval Officer.* London: Hutchinson, 1925.

Schurman, Donald M. *Julian S. Corbett, 1854–1922.* Royal Historical Society, London, 1981.

Siney, Marion. *The Allied Blockade of Germany, 1914–1916.* Ann Arbor: University of Michigan Press, 1957.

Smith, Myron J. *Battleships and Battlecruisers, 1884–1984: A Bibliography and Chronology.* New York: Garland, 1965.

Steinberg, J. *Yesterday's Deterrent: Tirpitz and the Birth of the German Battle Fleet.* London: Macdonald, 1965.

Sumida, Jon Tetsuro. *In Defence of Naval Supremacy.* Boston: Unwin Hyman, 1989.

Tarrant, V. E. *Battlecruiser Invincible.* London: Arms and Armour Press, 1986.

———. *Jutland—The German Perspective.* London: Arms and Armour Press, 1995.

Terraine, John. *The First World War 1914–1918.* London: Macmillan, 1984.

Terry, Charles Sanford. *The Battle of Jutland Bank, May 21–June 1, 1916.* Oxford: Oxford University Press, 1916.

Tirpitz, Alfred von. *My Memoirs.* London: Hurst and Blackett, 1919.

Trotter, Wilfrid Pym. *The Royal Navy in Old Photographs.* London: Dent, 1975.

Tuchman, Barbara. *The Guns of August.* New York: Macmillan, 1962.

Van der Vat, Dan. *The Grand Scuttle.* London: Hodder and Stoughton, 1982.

Waldeyer-Hartz, Hugo von. *Admiral von Hipper.* London: Rich and Cowan, 1933.

Warner, Oliver. *Great Sea Battles.* London: Spring Books, 1968.

Wester Wemyss, Lady. *The Life and Letters of Lord Wester Wemyss, GCB, Admiral of the Fleet.* London: Eyre and Spottiswoode, 1935.

Winton, John. *Jellicoe.* London: Michael Joseph, 1981.

Wyllie, William Lionel, and M. F. Wren. *More Sea Fights of the Great War, including the Battle of Jutland.* London: Cassell, 1919.

Young, Filson. *With the Battlecruisers.* London: Cassell, 1921.

Index

About the Author

Keith Yates served in the Royal Navy from 1946 to 1948. After earning doctoral degrees at the University of British Columbia and Oxford University, he joined the Department of Chemistry at the University of Toronto in 1961 and has been professor emeritus since 1991. He also taught at the Université de Paris and Université Paul Sabatier at Toulouse, among other institutions.

Dr. Yates's other publications include *Graf Spee's Raiders: Challenge to the Royal Navy, 1914–1915,* published by the Naval Institute Press, as well as nearly two hundred journal articles, conference papers, and reviews. He is currently writing a history of Japanese seapower from Mayne Island, British Columbia, where he resides with his wife.